Falmer Library
Falmer
Brighton BN1 9PH
Telephone 01273 643571

Short Loan

Online renewal http://library.brighton.ac.uk

Please return or renew on or before the last date stamped
A fine will be charged if items are returned late

WOMEN PLAYERS IN ENGLAND,
1500–1660

Offering evidence of women's extensive contributions to the theatrical landscape, this volume sharply challenges the assumption that the stage was 'all male' in early modern England. The editors and contributors argue that the pervasiveness of female performance affected cultural production, even on the professional London stages that used men and boys for women's parts. English spectators saw women players in professional and amateur contexts, in elite and popular settings, at home and abroad. Women acted in scripted and improvised roles, performed in local festive drama, and took part in dancing, singing, and masquing. English travelers saw professional actresses on the continent and Italian and French actresses visited England.

Essays in this volume explore: the impact of women players outside London; the relationship between women's performance on the Continent and in England; working women's participation in a performative culture of commerce; the importance of the visual record; the use of theatrical techniques by queens and aristocrats for political ends; and the role of female performance on the imitation of femininity.

In short, *Women Players in England, 1500–1660* shows that women were dynamic cultural players in the early modern world.

Pamela Allen Brown is an Associate Professor of English at the University of Connecticut, Stamford, USA and author of *Better a Shrew than a Sheep: Women, Drama and the Culture of Jest in Early Modern England.*

Peter Parolin is an Associate Professor of English at the University of Wyoming, USA.

STUDIES IN PERFORMANCE AND EARLY MODERN DRAMA

General Editor: Helen Ostovich, McMaster University

This series presents original research on theatre histories and performance histories; the time period covered is from about 1500 to the early 18th century. Studies in which women's activities are a central feature of discussion are especially of interest; this may include women as financial or technical support (patrons, musicians, dancers, seamstresses, wig-makers) or house support staff (e.g., gatherers), rather than performance per se. We also welcome critiques of early modern drama that take into account the production values of the plays and rely on period records of performance.

Women Players in England, 1500–1660

1500–1660

Beyond the All-Male Stage

Edited by

PAMELA ALLEN BROWN
University of Connecticut, USA

PETER PAROLIN
University of Wyoming, USA

ASHGATE

Published by
Ashgate Publishing Limited
Gower House
Croft Road
Aldershot
Hampshire GU11 3HR
England

Ashgate Publishing Company
Suite 420
101 Cherry Street
Burlington, VT 05401-4405
USA

Ashgate website: http://www.ashgate.com

British Library Cataloguing in Publication Data
Women Players in England 1500–1660 : beyond the all-male stage. – (Studies in performance and early modern drama)
1. Actresses – England – History – 16th century 2. Actresses – England – History – 17th century 3. Actresses – England – Public opinion – History – 16th century 4. Actresses – England – Public opinion – History – 17th century 5. Public opinion – England – History – 16th century. 6. Public opinion – England – History – 17th century 7. English drama – Early modern and Elizabethan, 1500–1600 – History and criticism 8. English drama – 17th century – History and criticism 9. Women – England – Social conditions – 16th century 10. Women – England – Social conditions – 17th century
I. Brown, Pamela Allen II. Parolin, Peter
792′.028′082′0942

Library of Congress Cataloging-in-Publication Data
Women players in England, 1500–1660 : beyond the all-male stage / edited by Pamela Allen Brown and Peter Parolin.
    p. cm. – (Studies in performance and early modern drama)
Includes bibliographical references.
ISBN 0-7546-0953-7 (alk. paper)
1. Theater – England – History – 16th century. 2. Theater – England – History –17th century. 3. Actresses – England. 4. English drama – Early modern and Elizabethan, 1500–1600 – History and criticism. I. Brown, Pamela Allen. II. Parolin, Peter, 1966– III. Series.

PN2590.A36W66 2004
792′.082′094209031–dc22

2004020756

ISBN-10: 0 7546 0953 7
ISBN-13: 978-0-7546-0953-7

Reprinted 2006

Typeset by Tradespools, Frome, Somerset.
Printed and bound in Great Britain by Antony Rowe Ltd, Chippenham, Wiltshire.

Contents

v

List of Illustrations

List of Musical Transcriptions

Contributors

Pamela Allen Brown is an Associate Professor of English at the University of Connecticut, Stamford, and author of *Better a Shrew than a Sheep: Women, Drama and the Culture of Jest in Early Modern England.* Her publications address women's active roles in popular culture, focusing on the impact of Italian actresses on Shakespeare, female rogues and gossips on Jonson, and female spectators and players on early modern writing and performance. With Jean E. Howard, she is co-editing *As You Like It: Texts and Contexts.*

Julie D. Campbell is an Associate Professor of English at Eastern Illinois University. Her areas of specialization include Shakespeare, Renaissance women writers, and Renaissance literary circles. Her translation of Isabella Andreini's play *La Mirtilla* was published by Medieval and Renaissance Texts and Studies in 2002.

Julie Crawford is an Associate Professor of English and Comparative Literature at Columbia University, where she teaches early modern English literature. She has published articles on a diverse array of topics, ranging from Sidney's sapphics to Mary Wroth's cabinets. Her book *Marvelous Protestantism* will be published by Johns Hopkins University Press this year, and she is working on a second book about women's coteries and the production of literature in early modern England.

Alison Findlay is Professor of Renaissance Drama at Lancaster University. She has published work on Shakespeare and his male contemporaries, including the books *Illegitimate Power in Renaissance Drama* and *A Feminist Perspective on Renaissance Drama,* and on women's drama of the sixteenth and seventeenth centuries. She is currently writing *Playing Spaces in Early Women's Drama* for Cambridge University Press, and *Women in Shakespeare* for the Continuum Shakespeare Dictionary Series.

Melinda J. Gough is Assistant Professor of English and Women's Studies at McMaster University. She has published on the Renaissance enchantress in epic and popular drama, the Swetnam controversy and women's popular culture, and the French court ballets and English masques performed by Henrietta Maria. Her essay "'Not as Myself': The Queen's Voice in *Tempe*

Restored' (*Modern Philology* 101.1) won the Society for the Study of Early Modern Women's award for best article published in 2003. Her book in progress focuses on Henrietta Maria and women's performance in early seventeenth-century France and England.

Stephanie Hodgson-Wright is Senior Lecturer at the University of Queensfield with research interests in the field of early modern women's writing, especially drama. She has edited *The Tragedy of Mariam* (2000), a volume of plays for the Early Modern Englishwoman facsimile series (2000), and an anthology entitled *Women's Writing of the Early Modern Period 1588–1688* (2002); she also co-wrote *Women and Dramatic Production 1550–1700* with Alison Findlay and Gweno Williams (2000). She is currently preparing a second volume for the Early Modern Englishwoman series and working on a study of liberty and bondage in tragedy by women from 1660 to 1720.

Jean E. Howard, William E. Ransford Professor of English at Columbia University, is author of *Shakespeare's Art of Orchestration, the Stage and Social Struggle in Early Modern England*, and, with Phyllis Rackin, of *Engendering a Nation: A Feminist Reading of Shakespeare's English Histories*. A past president of the Shakespeare Association of America and one of the co-editors of *The Norton Shakespeare*, she is completing a new book entitled *Theater of a City*.

M. A. (Peg) Katritzky is Wilkes Research Fellow in Theatre Studies in the Department of Literature of The Open University, Milton Keynes, and a Research Associate of St Catherine's College, University of Oxford. Her researches into theater iconography, court festival, the commedia dell'arte, and quacks and mountebanks generally, focus on gendered aspects and early modern transalpine cultural exchanges.

Natasha Korda is Associate Professor of English at Wesleyan University. She is author of *Shakespeare's Domestic Economies: Gender and Property in Early Modern England* (University of Pennsylvania Press, 2002) and co-editor with Jonathan Gil Harris of *Staged Properties in Early Modern English Drama* (Cambridge University Press, 2002).

Bella Mirabella is Associate Professor of Humanities and Literature at the Gallatin School of New York University. She has written about the lives of women in the Renaissance, particularly women and performance. She is co-editor of *Left Politics and the Literary Tradition*.

Peter Parolin is an Associate Professor of English at the University of Wyoming. He has published on early modern women and performance and he has an ongoing research interest in early modern English representations of Italy. His essays have appeared in *Renaissance Drama* and *Shakespeare Studies*.

Rachel Poulsen recently completed her PhD at Loyola University, Chicago. She is at work on a book about female homoeroticism in early modern English drama, from its roots in Italian literature through the late Caroline period. Her article "The 'plentiful lady-feast' in Brome's *A Mad Couple Well Match'd*," a runner-up for the J. Douglas Canfield Award for Postgraduate Scholarship, is forthcoming in the *Journal for Early Modern Cultural Studies*.

Phyllis Rackin is Professor Emerita of English at the University of Pennsylvania, where she taught courses in Shakespeare and Renaissance drama for forty years. A former president of the Shakespeare Association of America, she is the author of numerous scholarly articles on Shakespeare and related subjects as well as three books: *Shakespeare's Tragedies*; *Stages of History: Shakespeare's English Chronicles*: and *Engendering a Nation: A Feminist Account of Shakespeare's English Histories*, which she wrote in collaboration with Professor Jean E. Howard of Columbia University. At present, she has just completed a book entitled *Shakespeare and Women*, which will be published in 2005 as part of the Oxford Shakespeare Topics series.

Bruce R. Smith is USC College Distinguished Professor of English at the University of Southern California. His books include *Homosexual Desire in Shakespeare's England* (1991), *The Acoustic World of Early Modern England* (1999), and *Shakespeare and Masculinity* (2000). He is at work on a book on passionate perception in early modern culture, focused on the color green.

James Stokes is Professor of English, University of Wisconsin-Stevens Point. He is editor of the two-volume *REED: Somerset* (1996) and *REED: Lincolnshire* (forthcoming). He has authored numerous articles on the documentary history of medieval and early modern performance and culture.

Gweno Williams is Reader in Early Modern Drama at York St John University College. Her main research interest is staging productions of plays by early modern women. In June 2004 she produced a three and a half hour DVD, *Margaret Cavendish: Plays in Performance* (details at www.margaret-cavendish.net). In 2002 she was awarded a British National Teaching Fellowship for excellence in university teaching.

General Editor's Preface

Helen Ostovich
McMaster University

Performance assumes a string of creative, analytical, and collaborative acts that, in defiance of theatrical ephemerality, live on through records, manuscripts, and printed books. The monographs and essay collections in this series offer original research which addresses theatre histories and performance histories in the context of the sixteenth and seventeenth century life. Of especial interest are studies in which women's activities are a central feature of discussion as financial or technical supporters (patrons, musicians, dancers, seamstresses, wig-makers, or 'gatherers'), if not authors or performers per se. Welcome too are critiques of early modern drama that not only take into account the production values of the plays, but also speculate on how intellectual advances or popular culture affect the theatre.

The series logo, selected by my colleague Mary V. Silcox, derives from Thomas Combe's duodecimo volume, *The Theater of Fine Devices* (London, 1592), Emblem VI, sig. B. The emblem of four masks has a verse which makes claims for the increasing complexity of early modern experience, a complexity that makes interpretation difficult. Hence the corresponding perhaps uneasy rise in sophistication:

> Masks will be more hereafter in request,
> And grow more deare than they did heretofore.

No longer simply signs of performance 'in play and jest', the mask has become the 'double face' worn 'in earnest' even by 'the best' of people, in order to manipulate or profit from the world around them. The books stamped with this design attempt to understand the complications of performance produced on stage and interpreted by the audience, whose experiences outside the theatre may reflect the emblem's argument:

> Most men do use some colour'd shift
> For to conceal their craftie drift.

Centuries after their first presentations, the possible performance choices and meanings they engender still stir the imaginations of actors, audiences, and readers of early plays. The products of scholarly creativity in this series, I hope, will also stir imaginations to new ways of thinking about performance.

Chapter 1

Introduction

Pamela Allen Brown and Peter Parolin

Scholars of early modern English drama are coming to recognize that while women were never members of professional troupes, they had long appeared as players in a variety of arenas, and at every level of society. It is no longer enough to say, along with E. K. Chambers, that women who performed were the exceptions that proved the rule. As Stephen Orgel points out, "it is no longer clear just what the rule is" (Chambers 1: 137; Orgel, 8). Queens, aristocrats, and gentlewomen danced, sang, and recited in masques, plays, and court and manor entertainments; non-elite women in village, town and city took roles in parish drama and festive pageantry; Italian prima donnas and French actresses came to England to perform for both courtiers and commoners; and poorer women worked as itinerant entertainers, ballad singers and mountebanks. Despite the opprobrium heaped on the theatrical woman, a few elite women took the female player as a model in staging their own identities. In the alternative playing areas of the street, alehouse, market square, parish green, manorhouse and court, women could be found performing; connecting these places were female spectators, patrons, and traveling entertainers.[1] The cultural knowledge about female playing that a spectator, actor, or playwright carried to the "all-male" stage was therefore enormous.

This pattern of mimetic activity in many places, by many sorts of women, constitutes what Ann Thompson calls "the relatively hidden tradition of female performance" (103) – a tradition usually ignored or downplayed in discussions that focus exclusively on courtly performances and the transition to Restoration drama. Bringing more of this half-hidden tradition into the light and arguing for its profound importance to dramatic and cultural history is the work of this volume.[2] Several conditions make this project timely: ongoing

---

1   Details in this paragraph taken from Baskervill, Cerasano and Wynne-Davies, Davidson, Findlay and Hodgson-Wright, Fox, Gossett, Hutton, Ingram, Smith, Stokes, Thompson, Wiles.

2   Thompson is among the scholars whose work on early modern women as performers blazed the way for this volume: they include Frances Barasch, Louise

work on the politics of queenly performance, especially masquing, and its relationship to public theater plays; the rapid expansion of scholarship on self-staging and theatricality in writings by women; and a lively new debate about the mimetic visibility of non-elite and working women, which has been given an enormous boost by the Records of Early English Drama project.[3] At the same time, scholars are calling for a re-examination of the English stage in light of the growing perception that theatrical forms were far more transnational and border-blind than previously presumed. The skilled foreign diva was an influential "go-between" in this process, circulating generic and dramatic innovations that changed the course of theater, despite the charge of whorishness that spectacular women inevitably aroused.[4]

"Notorious whores," unnatural bearded ladies, "lean-cheek'd Moors," "French women, or monsters rayther," "immodest and lascivious" entertainers, actresses "hissed, hooted and pippin-pelted from the stage," "unchaste, shamelesse and unnaturall" Italian acrobats, "squirting baudie comedians," "common Curtizens," "a Pantaloun, a Whore and a Zanie" – all are contemporary reactions to women players.[5] Reading such phrases in the scanty

---

George Clubb, Elizabeth Howe, Clare McManus, Stephen Orgel, James Stokes, and Sophie Tomlinson. We particularly wish to acknowledge Jim Stokes's work for REED and his foundational essay "Women and Mimesis," which stimulated our research into female playing at all social levels, paid and unpaid.

3 See, for example, McManus, Tomlinson 1992 and 1998, Findlay ("Playing"), Barroll, Sale, Stokes, Smith.

4 Clubb, Barasch, Henke. On anti-foreign actress sentiment, see Brown 2000.

5 William Prynne's phrase "women-actors – notorious whores" in *Histrio-Mastix* (1633) was taken as an attack on Henrietta Maria and her ladies. He was imprisoned, massively fined, and lost his ears (McManus, 209; Cerasano and Wynne-Davies, 222). In *Artenice* (1626) Henrietta Maria's ladies shocked some courtiers by cross-dressing as "men with beards" (Tomlinson 1992, 189). After seeing *Masque of Blackness* (1605), Sir Dudley Carleton called Queen Anna and her ladies "a Troop of lean-cheek'd Moors" whose costumes were "too light and Curtizanlike for such great ones" (Cerasano and Wynne-Davies, 169). Moll Frith, the inspiration for Middleton and Dekker's *Roaring Girl*, made a famous appearance on stage at the Fortune and was charged with making "immodest & lascivious speeches" (Mulholland, 31).

In 1629 a French troupe with actresses appeared at the Blackfriars but was "hissed, hooted, and pippin-pelted from the stage" wrote one observer – although, as Stephen Orgel points out, the same players went on to the Red Bull and Fortune, and Prynne decried "the great resort" of Londoners to see "French women, or monsters rayther" (7; also Walker, 389). In Elizabeth's reign, Italian female acrobats drew crowds in London, prompting Thomas Norton to complain about "that unnecessarie and scarslie honeste resorts to plaies ... and especiallie the assemblies to the unchaste, shamelesse and unnaturall tomblinges of the Italion Woemen" (Lea, 354).

literature on the topic, one might assume that everyone found female performers repellent. Nonetheless, such stridency spiked with xenophobia utterly failed to master the fascination of the woman who deliberately takes the stage. This volume, which grew out of a 2000 Shakespeare Association of America seminar, "Women Players In and Around Shakespeare," demonstrates that the women under attack – Queen Henrietta Maria and her ladies, Queen Anna and her ladies, roaring girl Moll Frith, French actresses, Italian acrobats, and Italian divas – were not the great and singular exceptions to the rule of the all-male stage. In fact, the evolving picture pieced together by our contributors shows the woman player was a lively presence whose impact on culture and drama was profound, and demands more attention than given the subject by studies focused on anomalies, absences, and "firsts."

Because what constitutes theater and acting is highly debatable, and because theater does not always make its way into written records, attempts to fix a single moment for the advent of the actress invite skepticism. Accounts of "the first English actress," for example, generally begin in 1660, with the entrance of the first female Desdemona, in Thomas Killigrew's production of *Othello*.[6] While the word "actress" is treated as transparent, her Englishness is held to be a crucial distinction – otherwise the visiting Frenchwomen who acted in comedies on London stages in 1629, or the Italian actresses who performed at Elizabeth's court in 1578–9, would have a claim to first prize (Orgel, 7; Chambers 2: 262). Getting paid is also assumed to be essential, or Queen Henrietta Maria and her ladies would have been first in 1626, when they performed speaking roles in Racan's *Artenice* (McManus, 209). It seems her playing must be rooted in written, not traditional, culture, else the women who entertained Elizabeth at Kenilworth in 1575 by taking roles in a mock bride-ale might also be deemed actresses.[7] An actress must operate in a secular world; if

---

Thomas Nashe boasted of his nation's histrionic manliness: "Our Players are not as the players beyond the sea, a sort of squirting baudie Comedians, that have Whores and common Curtizens to playe womens partes, and forbeare no immodest speech, or unchast action that may procure laughter, but our Sceane is more stately furnisht than ever it was in the time of Roscius, our representations honorable and full of gallant resolution, not consisting like theirs of a Pantaloun, a Whore, and a Zanie, but of Emperors, Kings and Princes, whose true tragedies ... they do vaunt" (215).

6   Killigrew's King's Company presented *Othello* at the Vere Street theater on 8 December 1660; records are unclear whether Margaret Hughes or Anne Marshall played Desdemona. Thomas Jordan's new Prologue promised audiences that "The woman plays today; mistake me not / No man in gown, or page in petticoat" (Richards, 3).

7   See Robert Laneham's *A Letter Describing the Entertainment of the Queen at Kenilworth* (Paster and Howard, 130–1). The bride-ale preceded Coventry's Hock

religious drama were admitted, then the women who played "Anne Prophetissa" and the Virgins in the Digby "Killing of the Children" would have to count, too.[8] And a real actress must speak, not sing, else the musical nuns of Barking Convent might be in the running. Directed by Abbess Katherine Sutton, the nuns personated the worthy souls trapped in hell. Waiting behind a screen on Easter morning, the women were "harrowed" out by a priest playing Christ. Bearing palms, the released souls processed to the sepulcher, singing triumphantly. This remarkable performance took place in the fourteenth century (Davidson, 102).[9]

Evidently these "musts" do not hold for the early modern period. The very concept of "the English actress" derives from the Restoration theater and its descendants, not the early modern stage, which was far more intimately connected to traditional and religious forms of pageantry and festivity and to non-elite audiences. Restoration theater exploited the sexual allure of the new actress while defining her social identity, but the all-male theater that preceded it was also alive to the pressure of the performing women who surrounded and influenced its productions of "women" (Tomlinson 1992). Early modern theater was never the exclusive property of the male professionals, who were called "players" far more often than "actors," underlining the reality that their art encompassed many mimetic forms, such as singing songs and ballads, dancing jigs, cross-dressing, miming, jesting, and masking. Nonprofessional players, both men and women, also used all these mimetic forms to draw and entertain their audiences. For these reasons, we have set our sights on the "woman player," finding that concept more historically rooted and appropriate to our subject than "actress."[10]

Tuesday play, featuring women leading captive Danes in triumph; women may have played those parts as well (Fletcher, 264). Hock Tuesday was part of hocktide, a holiday dominated by women, who raised church and parish funds by capturing men and demanding cash for their release; this mimetic tradition survived the Reformation in many places (Hutton, 120).

8 "Anne Prophetissa," the prophet Simeon's wife in the Purification segment of the drama, "overshadowed" him, speaking the final words of the play; the Virgins held candles and filed past the altar "in reenactment of the womanly rite of postpartum churching" (Gibson, 99).

9 Other instances of female theatrical singers predating 1660 include "Madame Coniack" and "Madame Shepard," who performed in Aurelian Townshend's *Tempe Restored* in 1632 (Gossett; Orgel, 6).

10 The word *actress* in the sense of "female stage player" was not in use in early modern England. The sole instance that Sophie Tomlinson was able to find dates to 1626, when "actress" appeared in a letter referring to Henrietta Maria; the *OED* does not cite a first use until 1700 (Tomlinson 1992, 189). In this volume "actress" is used primarily to refer to professional players in continental troupes.

Our approach strives to be extensive – categorically, temporally, and geographically. We include geographical locations beyond London, physical spaces beyond the public amphitheaters and the private playhouses, and social categories beyond those of the professional players and elite masquers. Our definition of performance is fittingly broad and inclusive: *a performance is any act of embodied display or representation intended for an audience.* Our essays examine singing, dancing, and role-playing in aristocratic houses and on the street; staging rituals and festive drama in parish and market contexts; taking part in jesting and holiday games; engaging in acrobatic feats; putting on entertainments for visiting elites; devising shows to sell wares; and staging identity in theatrical ways to achieve desired ends. We have set a time frame of 1500–1660 to stress the connection between late medieval and traditional modes of playing and the new arenas of the public stage, and to make the point that Jacobean and Caroline masquing and acting by queens and female aristocrats grew out of practices at the sixteenth-century courts of England and Europe. Because women performers were part of a theatrical world that did not end at the outskirts of London or even at the Channel, we have expanded the ambit of native drama to other regions, focusing attention on female performance in Lincolnshire, Lancashire, Yorkshire, and Gloucestershire; and we have enlarged our scope to include professional and royal players in Italy and France, to assess the ways in which their performances intersected with, and affected, the English scene. Methodologically, then, we seek to read different cultures and categories of female performance in relation to each other. However, we have limited our scope – we deal primarily with women players in England, Italy, and France rather than Spain, Scotland, and Ireland, to name three noteworthy omissions.[11] Comprehensive as we have tried to be, this volume begins rather than exhausts the work of synthesizing different fields of female performance.

While the critical emphasis thus far has been on royal and aristocratic woman performers and courtly politics, our volume pays special attention to non-elite woman and their workaday performances in less formal settings: ballad singers (the subject of Bruce Smith's essay), participants in parish drama (James Stokes), mountebanks (Bella Mirabella), and even clothes-brokers with a penchant for performing (Natasha Korda). Seeing common women as potential players provides a rich source of extradramatic reference, offering

---

11   For queenly performances in Scotland, see McManus. Spain is a particularly regretted omission in this volume; Spanish companies employed women starting in the 1580s, spurred by the example of touring Italian commedia troupes. Actresses were continually subjected to misogynist attacks, attempts at regulation, and temporary bans, but became a fixture of Golden Age drama (McKendrick, 49, 186, 188–9, 194–5).

insights for both historians of early modern women and scholars of drama and literature. For example, because women took part in popular dramatics ranging from shaming rituals to Maygames to festive drama to jigs and jesting, their participation surely had an as-yet unexamined impact on "the politics of mirth" (in Leah Marcus's phrase) that made such pastimes so controversial.

Being alert to female performance means revisiting familiar works which feature "women on top of the world of play," ranging from Tudor farces like *Johan the Husband* to Jacobean comedies like Fletcher's *The Woman's Prize*; or in which "boy actresses" produce and act in playlets and tricks, such as Heywood's *Wise Woman of Hogsdon* and Jonson's *The Alchemist*. As different as they are, these plays share connections to the myriad forms of jigging, disguising, and masking in which real women took part, and which so deeply marked the vocabulary of theater.[12] In Shakespeare plays, for example, the transvestite heroines Rosalind, Viola, and Portia have their counterparts in the "open-air theater" of festive play, long before the *Hic Mulier* era of cross-dressing. Women in a "holiday humour," from revelers at Horn Fair to Scottish queens, were known to steal the breeches.[13] In *Two Noble Kinsmen*, a chambermaid and a hostess play the Queen of May and Maid Marian in the morris – just as some female audience members, or their grandmothers, may have done.[14] When Mistresses Page and Ford trick and mock the horned Falstaff at the end of *Merry Wives*, Shakespeare draws on a vast panorama of street satire and shaming ritual in which women took part. And in *Twelfth Night* Maria engineers the practice used to shame Malvolio, in

---

12 Consider the example of the jig, which was not only a bawdy stage skit in song and dance performed by male clowns, but a lively dance between couples, involving much leaping and body contact (Wiles, 45). Occasionally a woman staged her own satiric skit-jig, in the style of the stage clowns (Ingram, 166–7). Noting that Will Kemp danced with women during his jig from London to Norwich, Douglas Bruster argues that all-male playhouses "shunned the gender inclusiveness of the folk tradition that Kemp reproduced in dancing with these women. ... London's professional theaters denied women the freedom to perform that they enjoyed in more rural environments" (296).

13 On female cross-dressing and other amusements at Charlton's Horn Fair, known as a women's holiday, see Brown, 91–2. In the 1560s, Mary Queen of Scots and her ladies dressed as men and brandished daggers at an after-dinner masque (McManus, 69).

14 While the morris was ruled male-only a century ago, scholars have since shown that women took part in morris dancing in the early modern period; that Robin Hood plays and the morris featured women who played the Lady of May; and that the comic Maid Marian was played by women into the Elizabethan period, when it became a transvestite role (Hutton, 263–5).

a plot that strongly resembles popular satires in which women helped caricature Puritans who attacked their plays and games.[15]

Attending to the cultural visibility of female players will also further the debate over whether spectators "took boys for women." Arguments that the boy's body vanished to consciousness, or co-existed with an acceptance of the female mask as female, weaken in the face of evidence that even the unprivileged playgoer had often seen women playing women. Having such a mental image might well increase a spectator's curiosity about the actor's body beneath his skirts; and, rather than banishing ambiguity, his or her knowledge of female performers would multiply and intensify it. The erotic frisson of the transvestite theatre likely derives in part from its very artificiality, from its artful and anomalous erasure of women from the world of traditional performance that they participated in elsewhere – a world that London audiences would have known well.

On the other hand, it is vital to recognize that not all staged echoes of female performance derive from familiar English contexts. In the 1590s, boy players in professional companies began to present radically new kinds of roles that never had been performed by Englishwomen. Many of these roles are startlingly similar to those created by the rising stars of the commedia dell'arte, such as Isabella Andreini, Vittoria Piisimi, Diana Ponti, and Angelica Martinelli, who emerged onto the international theater scene in the 1570s and 1580s, skillfully playing tragic parts and light innamorata roles in scripted and improvised pastorals, tragedies, comedies, and farces. Praised by Montaigne, Fynes Moryson, and Thomas Coryat and seen by diplomats abroad and courtiers at home, the professional actress was a startling innovation whose fame spread rapidly among the players of London, eliciting both hostility and imitation (Brown, 1999). Although scholars seeking to pinpoint the relationship between the Italian and English drama have rarely looked beyond the Capitanos and Pantalouns of the commedia troupes, a few have addressed the far-ranging influence of the foreign actress (Barasch, Clubb, Nicholson). Some have noted the fascinating congruency between the vogue for female mad scenes in late Elizabethan plays such as *Tamburlaine*, *The Spanish Tragedy*, and *Hamlet*, and the acclaimed mad scenes of actresses such as Isabella Andreini, renowned for the highly literary frenzy she displayed in several plays, most famously *La Pazzia d'Isabella*, or "The Madness of Isabella" (see Clubb, 263–4).

---

15 On shaming and horning satires see Fox, 314, Gowing, 72, Ingram, 180; on anti-Puritan satire see Ingram, 166–7. See also Stokes and Smith on the Wells shows of 1607, in which a godly citizen became the butt of his neighbors, including women, who performed roles in mocking street dramas; the victim filed suit afterward. On Maria's leading role in *Twelfth Night*'s theatrics, and her possible counterpart in the Wells scandal, see Sale.

To recognize women as performers raises important questions of agency and subjectivity. Discussing the controversy that erupted over Henrietta Maria's acting, Sophie Tomlinson attributes it to "the threat of the actress in performance," disruptive because it has "the potential for presenting femininity as a vivid and mobile force: the spectacle of the woman-actor summoning up the spectre of the female subject" (1992, 192).[16] Certainly women players could at least be imagined to have access to forms of cultural agency, and in the context of the male-dominated professional theater such a development caused consternation. Even a Caroline dramatist such as James Shirley, who courted the queen's favor and who seemed sympathetic to elite female performance, encoded critiques of women's acting in his plays (Walker; Tomlinson, 1999). In some instances, however, performance seems unlikely to have translated into agency for women or to have endowed them with the benefits of subjectivity. Early moderns also gaped at "hairy women" displayed as freaks, black women exhibited in Tudor and Stuart pageants, and women paraded to cuckstool or whipping post (Thompson, 104; Andrea, 256–7). These women cannot be seen as players in the agential sense because they were entirely subjected to the violence of representation, experiencing its coercive power without designing or controlling their own display. Although most performances offer moments in which the performer can take control, reinterpret the scenario, and mock or otherwise resist authority, we seek to track the power dynamics that women had to negotiate when they performed, even women who did wield a measure of representational autonomy.

Outside the professional theatre, the implications of women's performance are only just beginning to emerge, with some scholars probing women's impact on popular culture and providing frames for studying female performance. Both Laura Gowing, who has recently explored early modern women's self-defense against slander charges, and Pamela Brown, who has analyzed women's engagement in the public culture of jest, suggest that representing themselves publicly gave women considerable power to affect their own lives and the lives of others. Women's performance introduced contingency and unpredictability even into spaces that we think of as patriarchal. Women's wit, humor, mockery, and narrative skill could all destabilize masculinist structures of authority and put a woman in charge of any given moment by helping her win the sympathy of her audience. In the elite context of the court masque, even women's silence could speak volumes. Clare McManus has dispelled the

---

16   In the pastoral *Artenice*, performed in French, all the women spoke and some appeared as men in beards, exciting shocked comment. Tomlinson calls the performance politically and sexually transgressive: "a theatrical overturning of Salic law" and a reversal of "the order of things which placed 'woman' on the side of absence and silence" (1992, 189, 192).

notion that the court ladies who appeared in masques lacked expressive power by virtue of the fact that, unlike professional actors, they did not speak. Focusing on dance, McManus shows the complex expressiveness of the body in motion: the injunction that women remain silent could thus free the eloquent potential of their physical bodies – the tools of control become in this process women's tools of expression. McManus argues that merely by accepting or denying the invitations to dance they received during the masque, women exercised substantial control over what the audience would see (9, 18).

Moreover, the audiences to which women appealed by no means consisted exclusively of men: women performing could provoke laughter and delight in female audience members who might in turn incorporate what they saw into their own lives in unpredictable ways. If, as many scholars suggest, audiences shape performance, then any study of female performance must also account for women in audiences, who did not merely consume but also helped to produce the theatrical entertainments they watched. Indeed, Alison Findlay takes women's playgoing as her starting point in *A Feminist Perspective on Renaissance Drama*, assuming that women contributed to the meaning of what they saw on stage and also that they could apply the performative strategies they watched as audience members to situations in their own lives (1–2). In this way, women who avidly consumed performances could become players outside of the theater: not only women on stage, but also their counterparts in the audience summoned the specter of the female subject. Building on Jean Howard's argument about women's power as paying subjects, Findlay calls theatergoing a feminist act that potentially cancels gender inequality (at least temporarily) through the woman spectator's act of paying the price of admission (Findlay, 3; Howard, 79).

For our purposes, the presence of women in the audience shapes the meaning of performance in that it calls for us to imagine women's desire in addition to men's. Once we understand the many ways women performed, our analysis of the dynamics of early modern performance in England must change: we do not merely have a closed loop in which men spoke to men, or a situation in which male performers alternately flattered and berated women audience members, or an environment in which a few exceptional women pleaded for male spectators' forbearance. We do have a world in which women geared their performances for other women, in which they remembered their past performances and spoke to each other in the present.[17] This situation does not of course mean that

---

17 In her recent book, for example, McManus has found intriguing precedents for Anna's masquing in her experience of women's performances at the Danish and Scottish courts (67, 68–9, 73–4, 82–7); see also Melinda Gough's essay in this volume on Henrietta Maria, her performing female kin, and her female courtier-players.

female performance ensured a wholly progressive space of women's freedom; it does mean that female performance enabled women to make their mark on culture, both singly and in collaboration with other women.

In our first section, "Beyond London," contributors James Stokes, Alison Findlay, Stephanie Hodgson-Wright, and Gweno Williams argue that in order to chart a history of early modern female performance, we need to move beyond a narrow focus on the male-dominated professional theater. Searching through county records published in the REED volumes for Lincolnshire, Yorkshire, Lancashire, and Gloucestershire, they discover an astonishing wealth of evidence showing that women sponsored, produced, and performed in local entertainments. In "Women and Performance: Evidences of Universal Cultural Suffrage in Medieval and Early Modern Lincolnshire," Stokes tests the premise that since women held prominent positions within the guilds, they must also have participated in the plays, pageants, and other entertainments that the guilds sponsored. For Stokes, the Lincolnshire records confirm that "women were major, indeed co-equal, contributors in a variety of ways to the entertainments associated with traditional culture in Lincolnshire, a presence that can be documented at every level of society" (25). In "Payments, Permits and Punishments: Women Performers and the Politics of Place," Findlay, Hodgson-Wright, and Williams compare women's opportunities for perfor-mance across county divides, discovering that particular civic structures, the degree of proximity to the central government, and different religious affiliations all affected the nature and extent of women's playing in Yorkshire, Lancashire, and Gloucestershire. Writing about York, Williams shows that the all-encompassing civic nature of the Corpus Christi plays ensured women's involvement as producers and supporters of the cycle, and perhaps also as performers. In Lancashire, Findlay finds that women's dramatic participation often registers Catholic sympathies, while in Gloucestershire, suggests Hodgson-Wright, the relative paucity of women in the dramatic records may reflect the strong Puritan and parliamentarian affiliations that made this county increasingly hostile to all forms of female performance.

By interrogating the scholarly assumptions that have long obscured women's contributions to early modern dramatic forms, the contributors in this section typify the approach of all the authors in this book. Stokes, for example, recognizes that in Lincoln the enduring scholarly focus on the provenance of the N-Town plays has discouraged research into socio-religious guild entertainments where there is plentiful evidence of women's participation. Findlay, Hodgson-Wright, and Williams maintain that while the written evidence of women's performance is often difficult to interpret, it is abundant enough that it "allows us to redefine our perceptions of dramatic production by speculating on regional and gender differences" (46). Even – or especially – where definitive evidence of women performers is lacking, we should not assume that males played all parts. Building on this conviction, Williams makes an impressive case for considering the possibility that women took roles in the York Corpus Christi cycle; she also argues that the cycle continued to influence Catholic women in highly theatrical acts of resistance and martyrdom after religious drama was suppressed in the 1570s. Taken together, then, the first two chapters show that when research moves beyond London, it can reveal a rich world of female performance that makes the "all-male" professional stage of the metropolis look distinctly anomalous.

In the next two chapters, "Beyond Elites," Natasha Korda and Bella Mirabella move beyond the aristocratic focus that characterizes much recent work on women performers. They broaden our sense of stage history to include female pawnbrokers in the informal networks of commerce supporting the London theaters, as well as the female mountebanks who used their performance skills to hawk their trinkets and medicinal potions. In "The Case of Moll Frith: Women's Work and the 'All-Male Stage,'" Korda considers the supposed exceptional status of Moll Frith, the "roaring girl" of Middleton and Dekker's play, a minor London celebrity who played her lute and sang on the stage of the Fortune theater in 1612. Paying special attention to Frith's work as a dealer in second-hand clothes and a broker of stolen goods, Korda suggests Moll was one of many working women who contributed to theatrical production. Not only did women provide and often restitch the costumes that actors wore on the professional stages, but their success in the theater's underground economy depended upon qualities – flexibility, deceit, tenacity, and ingenuity – that were crucial to theatrical performers, too. As Korda puts it, "The 'wench that cries the kitchin stuff' and 'sings her note so merry' belongs to the same nexus of performative commerce as the 'players on the Banckeside' who 'sing [their] rhymes'; both depend upon a tactical mix of publicity, performance, and flexible commerce to earn a living" (82). Korda argues that within this theatrical-economic context, Frith's appearance on the Fortune stage can best be understood as a useful publicity stunt that helped refashion her public persona from that of a notorious cutpurse to that of a more socially respectable (and financially secure) broker of second-hand and stolen goods. In Moll's "altered case," then, Korda sees an opportunistic convergence of economic ingenuity and performance strategies that was typical, not exceptional, in the working women of early modern London.

In "'Quacking Delilahs': Female Mountebanks in Early Modern England and Italy," Bella Mirabella, too, explores the world of performative commerce, tracing the history of the female mountebanks to show how their reputation as healers combined with their theatrical skills to earn them a measure of cultural authority. Like many researchers into the history of women's performance, Mirabella contends with the paucity of the available evidence: when searching for traces of female mountebanks, "one must seek out the flicker, the brief mention of the female performer"; however, she asserts that by examining these traces, "we discover many references which reveal a rich and vibrant picture of the role of women as performers and healers" (89). Indeed, Mirabella argues that the female mountebanks who played instruments, sang, and performed skits were equal partners with their male colleagues in the business of using theatrical techniques to sell home remedies and other wares. Mirabella also discovers a world in which the critics of mountebank performances took particularly virulent aim at women, describing them as frauds and whores who deserve whipping, or worse. According to Mirabella the demonization of female mountebanks reveals the anxiety of newly professionalized men seeking to create exclusive rights for themselves both in the theater and in the field of medicine. As does Korda, Mirabella conclusively shows that women's performance was not solely an elite phenomenon; rather, performance skills were essential to many lower-class women struggling to find economic security in a world that increasingly restricted legitimate economic activity to men.

In our next section, "Beyond the Channel," our contributors assess the history of female playing on the Continent, and document its wide-ranging effects on theatrical practices and the mental horizons of playwrights, audiences, artists, and courtiers. The English professional stage was never as isolated from and impervious to Continental theater as its more jingoistic supporters claimed. The Continental connection was forged through extensive touring by English players, word of mouth by returned travelers and merchants, texts and images that circulated between Europe and England, and courtiers who were keenly attuned to the tastes of a native-born woman player, Elizabeth, and two foreign queens, Anna and Henrietta Maria, who brought traditions of female performance to the English court from abroad.

Contributors M. A. Katritzky, Julie Campbell, Rachel Poulsen, and Melinda Gough investigate the crucial contribution of the professional actress of the Italian commedia dell'arte troupes to female playing at the amateur, professional, and court levels. Artists produced a rich array of images attesting to her increasing prominence on the international theatrical and political scene. Theater historian M. A. Katritzky draws on and interprets this rich but under-explored archive of visual material, from drawings and paintings to engravings and frescoes. In "Reading the Actress in Commedia Imagery," she presents an overview of the early history of the commedia actress, then goes on to identify the salient characteristics of roles that appear most frequently in artworks, such as the *innamorata*, the courtesan, the servant, the gypsy, the exotic "Turkish" girl, and the old woman. She provides guidance about the reliability of various types of visual evidence, attending to the frequent ambiguities and uncertainties that complicate the reading of what seem at first to be straightforward depictions of a theatrical event. Many images of women "acting" depend on art-historical tropes and genres, or copy elements of other artworks; other images seem to be portraits of celebrated actresses, but may be based on unfounded attributions; still others may seem to be women on stage, but may well depict cross-dressed men during carnival, or female entertainers at a feast. The most illuminating type of commedia imagery for theater historians, she maintains, is the serial image depicting a number of scenes and characters. Katritzky also observes that over time artists began to move the female player closer and closer to the center of the visual frame, suggesting her growing importance in dramatic plots, theatrical staging, and the profession of theater itself.

The novelty of professional female players – some of them poet-playwrights like Isabella Andreini – affected the writing and reception of all kinds of drama, from masques and court entertainments, to scripted dramas and tragicomedies, to improvised farces and pastorals. Shakespeare showed he was fully aware of this development by creating expanded and greatly demanding female roles, following the model set by the Italian writers and players who had abandoned the longstanding practice of keeping women offstage or limiting their appearance to domestic interiors, glimpsed only through doors and windows. The *innamorata*, or elegant young maid in love, became the focus of the greatest expansion; at the same time a handful of women who played the *innamorata* became leaders of troupes. Most famous was Andreini, known as "La divina Isabella" (see fig. 7.1), whose writings and performances made her far more famous internationally than Shakespeare: "Like Shakespeare her contemporary," Clubb writes, "Isabella was called the wonder of her profession and her age, but unlike him she was called so in her own time by a vast international audience" (259–60). These celebrities exhibited their rhetorical prowess and high status through their educated speech and command of languages, their poetic skill, and their witty capacity to dilate on lovers' themes. Whether debating her lover in long volleys of conceits, mocking her suitors with mimicry and challenges, or lamenting in soliloquy and song, the *innamorata*-actress had to display not only beauty and grace, but the ability to speak at length on stage with poise and wit. Her appearance on Italian stages in the mid-sixteenth century drew crowds and attracted royal patrons, and playwrights all over Europe took notice.

In "'Merry, nimble, stirring spirit[s]': Academic, Salon and Commedia dell'arte Influence on the *Innamorate* in *Love's Labour's Lost*," Julie Campbell perceives an intricate layering of allusion to female performance in Shakespeare's play. While the play has long been read topically, as a thinly disguised portrayal of the pastimes of French noblewomen and their suitors, Campbell sees a far more complex encoding of female speech, rhetorical display, inter-gender debate, and embodied action that draws on Italian models, as well as French. Shakespeare's court ladies possess not only the vivacity of the *escadron volant* – Marguerite de Valois' ladies, who performed in contemporary entertainments at the French court – but the intellectual acumen of the Parisian *salonnistes* and Italian and French women who famously participated in academic debates. In addition, Campbell sees distinct traces of the Italian woman player in the figures of the Princess and her ladies, who indeed possess many of the skills that the starring *innamorate* were displaying to such acclaim at the time of Shakespeare's play. Campbell makes the case that Isabella Andreini herself shadows the play, as a leading exemplar of the kind of theatricality that Shakespeare's Frenchwomen exhibit.

Scholars of early modern sexuality usually restrict their investigations to urban or national borders, often relying on localized legal and medical discourses to explore theatrical stagings of sexuality and desire. Not enough attention is paid, however, to investigating the Italian models that Shakespeare relied on in his forays into the erotically charged world of comedy. Many of the bawdy Italian comedies that were "ransackt to furnish the Playe houses in London," in Stephen Gosson's famous phrase (qtd in Clubb, 49), were surprisingly explicit in their treatment of homoerotic desire and sexual acts between women. The lovesick lady pressing herself on a flustered cross-dressed maiden was a staple scenario of the learned comedies, many of which were performed by, or adapted by, the traveling commedia dell'arte troupes. As a result, Italian actresses who were adept at making and responding to same-sex overtures played a key role in disseminating plays such as Bibbiena's *La Calandria* to places far beyond Italy, including London. In "Women Performing Homoeratic Desire in English and Italian Comedy: *La Calandria, Gl'Ingannati* and *Twelfth Night*," Rachel Poulsen shows how Shakespeare's comedy bears a distinct imprint of this female performance tradition, creating what she calls "an actress effect" (172). Furthermore, even in a play intended for performance by men and boys, Shakespeare "muted but did not erase the overt lesbian eroticism that so deeply marks [his] Italian models" (171). In her reading *Twelfth Night* concerns itself with the sexual dynamics of service and subversive cross-class desires, making it "a comedy about claiming power through appropriation and improvisation – not only in the world of the play, but in the metatheatrical sense of the English dramatic enterprise" (171).

Continental courtiership and intellectual trends had obvious effects on royal and aristocratic performers in England, as studies of Elizabeth's theatricality and Anna's masques have shown. Essays by Melinda Gough, Peter Parolin, and Julie Crawford look at the ways in which an elite woman could use offstage and onstage performances to construct a public self and to solidify or protect her hold on power; in each case the woman in question was exposed early to female performance at court and had traveled abroad. In "Courtly *Comédiantes*: Henrietta Maria and Amateur Women's Stage Plays in France and England," Melinda Gough places Queen Henrietta Maria in a family tradition of performance at the French court, marked by contact with Italian troupes and their actresses. While commentators from Harbage onward have

dismissed the Queen's acting as mediocre or vapid, Gough presents evidence
that the Queen learned the importance of polished performance from an early
age. Under the critical eye of her mother, Marie de Medici, she and her siblings
took part in amateur plays at court; they also may have learned by watching
visiting commedia actresses perform with grace and skill. As evidence that
Henrietta Maria took performing seriously in her years at the English court,
Gough cites her hiring of Joseph Taylor, a professional actor, to train her
women players in elocution, gesture and delivery; she also points to the
Queen's decision to postpone the performance of *Shepherds' Paradise* to allow
for more time to perfect the production. Gough speculates that there was a
political motive behind Henrietta Maria's precedent-setting performance in a
speaking role in *Artenice* in 1626: at a time in which the king was attempting to
curb her privileges, "producing and acting in a French play ... might forcefully
assert the royal status she enjoyed not primarily as Charles I's queen but
independently of her married station, that is, as a member of the French royal
family" (208).

   In "The Venetian Theater of Aletheia Talbot, Countess of Arundel," Peter
Parolin describes how an English countess successfully staged herself as an
innocent wronged in a scandal played out before the Venetian authorities.
Parolin attributes her canny management of the dangerous charge of abetting a
traitor to her far-ranging experiences with female performance, both
impromptu and rehearsed, professional and amateur, courtly and intellectual.
Having danced in masques with Queen Anna at the English court, the
Countess was well aware of the important role of theatrical staging in any
strategic display of power; she could also draw on the verbal defenses and
alliance-building ordinary women used to counter slanderous challenges to
their reputations. Living in Venice, she was exposed to the celebrated
performances of the commedia actresses and their companies, as well as the
renowned rhetorical displays of the *cortigiane oneste*. Using the arts of timing,
delivery, and gesture, as well as artful planning and pressure from high-placed
friends, she managed to redirect criticism from herself to the Venetian
Ambassador, Sir Henry Wotton, whom she suspected of originating the
rumors about her role in the treason scandal. As Parolin writes, "Lady
Arundel's performance in the Venetian Collegio can thus be seen as an act of
high-stakes theater in which she exploited elements of English and Italian
theatrical experience to fashion herself into a representative of her husband and
her country even as she asserted her independent right to pursue desired social
and political goals" (220; on traces of the Countess in *Volpone*, see Parolin
1998).

   By boldly stating her opinions in writing, a woman author stood the risk of
becoming a spectacle. It is no coincidence that one of the most prolific women
writers of the period, Margaret Cavendish, Duchess of Newcastle, was self-
consciously theatrical and politically outspoken, and that she was widely

dismissed as bizarre or mad. In " 'Pleaders, Atturneys, Petitioners and the like': Margaret Cavendish and the Dramatic Petition," Julie Crawford argues for a degree of political pragmatism as motivating force behind many of Cavendish's plays and performances. Always keenly aware of the respect due to her position and bent on regaining the fortune her husband had lost in supporting Charles, Cavendish used drama and her own public display to negotiate "for noble privileges *from* royalty. ... the plays are meant to exist in dialogue with Cavendish's own political performances – those dramatically public, audience-soliciting self-presentations which she made both in country and court, and, most famously, in London" (242). Cavendish used drama as a kind of "dramatized petition" for redress and restoration of her rights and her husband's property; she also treated it as an educational tool, teaching the public and her readers about the forms of status and respect due to herself and her husband. Crawford argues that Cavendish's playwriting was often intended for "noble education and even reprimand, and her plays serve both as indictments of the improperly restored court, and as models for the ideal royalist society she sought to establish" (242).

In our final section, "Beyond the 'All-Male,' " we turn to the impact of women players and spectators on the imitation of female voices and bodies. Essays by Jean Howard and Bruce Smith consider the performance of femininity through representational codes. While both Howard and Smith predominantly discuss male impersonations of women, they also insist that all such performances depend on the citation of certain codes of femininity that necessarily evoke the bodies, voices, and postures of women in the audiences and beyond, thereby underscoring the impossibility of any all-male dramatic representation. In "Staging the Absent Woman: The Theatrical Evocation of Elizabeth Tudor in Heywood's *If You Know Not Me, You Know Nobody, Part I*," Jean Howard takes the example of the recently deceased Queen Elizabeth to explore how "a dead woman with 'no bodie' was made into a recognizable 'some bodie' on the Jacobean stage through the help of the boy actor" (277). For Howard, this process occurs through "the discursive citation of femininity (through dress, cosmetics, wigs, and verbal conventions) to evoke women" (264). In the case of Heywood's play, Elizabeth is an imperiled princess who has not yet achieved her "final social shape" (267) so Heywood must evoke her according to codes of femininity other than the familiar red wig, crown, orb, and scepter that define her as queen. Howard shows that Heywood meets this challenge by positioning Elizabeth within a Protestant martyrology that defines her according to simple clothing, patient suffering, and above all the Bible and other devotional books that she holds throughout the play. Exploring the process by which Heywood materializes Elizabeth as a gendered being, Howard rejects the argument that all such materializations necessarily travesty femininity. Instead, she suggests that the rituals and implements through which the theater cites femininity have the power to bring

women's history, materiality, and agency onto the very stages that excluded
their bodies: "To the extent that this theater was performatively successful ...
it was necessarily haunted by its own exclusions, confronted with
materializations of femininity in many ways as 'real' and as unpredictable
in their consequences as the empirical bodies of the 'women' who sat or stood
in the audience but did not perform as members of the London acting
companies" (264).

   In "Female Impersonation in Early Modern Ballads," Bruce Smith considers
ballad singing as another element in the discursive citation of femininity. Not
only was ballad singing associated with women, but it was thought to induce
physiological changes that pushed the singers into a physical and mental
condition, a "state of being-in-music," linked to femininity (298). Seeking a
phenomenology of singing, Smith attempts to "reconstruct the bodily
experience of ballads in historically specific terms" (287). To recover the place
of the human body in ballad culture, he compares oral and printed versions of
three early modern ballads, asking whether they engage and gender the body in
different ways. He finds that within the ballads, the female body in particular
"is experienced in terms of parts: hands, knee, bosom, but above all a mouth"
(296); singing the ballads, the performer calls up those same aspects of him or
herself, and in this way "the space between the dramatic object and the
experiencing subject is radically foreshortened" (301). A similar foreshortening
occurs between singer and audience as well, since ballads frequently call upon
their male and female listeners to sing along, assuming new subject positions
through the voices they impersonate. Like Jean Howard, Smith sees that the
construction of "virtual women" through discursive citation necessarily
engages a familiar world of "real" women – in this case the world of women's
voices, bodies, and gestures – thus making the site of representation an
unpredictable space indeed, where "the boundary between male and female is
liquified" (301) and men and women alike give in to the physical passions
associated with song.

   Pamela Brown concludes the volume by examining women's participation in
the risky social performance of jesting. In "Jesting Rights: Women Players in
the Manuscript Jestbook of Sir Nicholas Le Strange," Brown traces the culture
of jest at the great house of a powerful royalist family in Norfolk, arguing that
Sir Nicholas's *Merry Passages and Jeasts* is "replete with markers of female
performance" (306). Many jests recorded in the manuscript were told to Le
Strange by his female kin and friends, or concern women performing physical
or verbal tricks, or include women as internal jester figures. Given this
emphasis on women as speakers, Brown notes that to speak a jest or to tell a
joke depends upon key features of performance, such as timing, accent, and
gesture. A large proportion of these transcribed jokes are explicitly sexual and
scatological, and cry out for bawdy inflection and even movement. Since the
manuscript names Le Strange's mother, wife, and aunts as the sources of

dozens of these jests, Brown is able to build a case that early modern women –
even noblewomen like Sir Nicholas's mother Dame Alice – were intimately
involved in a culture of jesting that foregrounded their skills as performers.
Taking issue with the Freudian precept that the racy culture of joke-telling
silences women, Brown encourages us to attend to women as keen spectators,
speakers, laugh-getters, and physical performers in the world of jest. By
focusing on women as both spectators and performers, Brown reasserts the
major argument of all the contributors to this book: early modern performance
– high and low, urban and rural, domestic and foreign, public and private –
was a field on which women could and did play.

Now that scholars are piecing together a tradition of female performance, one
may ask why these women have been unnoticed for so long. Stephen Orgel
suggests that, rather than deliberately excluding women players, "culture [and]
history may have had an interest in rendering them unnoticeable" (9).[18] After
1660, the London theater industry certainly exploited the novelty of its own
practice of featuring women on the professional stage. This theater sought to
attract new audiences by perpetuating the notion of a great divide separating
an all-male theatrical past from an inclusive present with actresses as objects of
the salacious gaze. But much contemporary criticism has also failed to notice
the woman player, simply by restricting its scope of inquiry to London's
resident professional theaters and courtly performance. Again, we contend that
this restriction prevents a supple analysis of even the professional stage, let
alone the myriad other kinds of performances that took place in the city and
throughout the country, many of them rooted in traditional culture and earlier
times.

    We want to tread carefully and responsibly as we urge others to recognize
the importance of women's playing, avoiding what Dympna Callaghan has
called "the critical trend whereby some endeavours to ascribe female agency
almost deny women's oppression altogether." In her view, women's "exclusion
from the stage ... bespeaks an aspect of women's secondary social status and
is not remedied by those rare instances of female performance" (8). Outside the
narrow context of the professional London stage, as we have already noted, it
is inaccurate to say that only "rare instances of female performance" existed.
Furthermore, our volume shows that this argument also requires rethinking

---

18   For discussions of reasons for, and effects of, the absence of women from the stage,
     see also Shapiro and Callaghan. Shapiro takes issue with Orgel's stress on "male
     fears of female sexuality," and argues that economic factors and business practices
     may have delayed the introduction of actresses, including "gendered rivalries,
     concern over employment opportunities, methods of recruitment, managerial
     assessment of practicality, availability of potential actresses" (188).

within the context of the London theater, where women did have a strong presence as spectators and workers, and where the awareness of women as players affected the impact and meaning of plays performed by men and boys. A feminist project like ours must not lose sight of the ways female performance takes shape under the pressure of masculinist and misogynist dogma; but it is equally important to understand that the "recognition of women's oppression does not de facto render women abject victims of patriarchal culture, or deny them agency," as Callaghan herself points out (8). Somehow, alongside the all-male stage – *and within a culture that assigned women secondary status as a matter of course* – female performance thrived, and individual women emerged as cultural agents through their brilliant playing. This volume, then, looks at women's manifold negotiations within a schizophrenic culture that bewhored queens and exotic foreigners for daring to act, but barely noticed the women players in its own front yard.

Works Cited and Consulted

Andrea, Bernadette. "Black Skin, the Queen's Masques: Africanist Ambivalence and Feminine Author(ity) in The Masques of Blackness and Beauty." *English Literary Renaissance* 29.2 (1999): 246–81.

Barasch, Frances. "Italian Actresses in Shakespeare's World: Vittoria and Isabella." *Shakespeare Bulletin* 19.3 (Summer 2001): 5–9.

Barroll, Leeds. *Anna Queen of Denmark: A Cultural Biography*. Philadelphia: University of Pennsylvania Press, 2001.

Baskervill, Charles Read. *The Elizabethan Jig and Related Song Drama*. Chicago: University of Chicago Press, 1929.

Brown, Pamela Allen. "The Counterfeit Innamorata, or, The Diva Vanishes." *Shakespeare Yearbook* 10 (1999): 402–26.

———. *Better a Shrew than a Sheep: Women, Drama, and the Culture of Jest in Early Modern England*. Ithaca: Cornell University Press, 2003.

Bruster, Douglas. "The Jailer's Daughter and the Politics of Madwomen's Language." *Shakespeare Quarterly* 46 (Autumn 1995): 277–300.

Callaghan, Dympna. *Shakespeare Without Women*. New York: Routledge, 2000.

Cerasano, S. P. and Marion Wynne-Davies. *Renaissance Drama by Women: Texts and Documents*. New York: Routledge, 1996.

Chambers, E. K. *The Elizabethan Stage*. 4 vols. Oxford: Clarendon, 1923.

Clubb, Louise George. *Italian Drama in Shakespeare's Time*. New Haven: Yale University Press, 1989.

Comensoli, Viviana and Anne Russell, eds. *Enacting Gender on the Renaissance Stage*. Urbana: University of Illinois Press, 1999.

Davidson, Clifford. "Women and the Medieval Stage." *Women's Studies* 11 (1984): 99–113.

Findlay, Alison. *A Feminist Perspective on Renaissance Drama*. Oxford: Blackwell, 1999.

———. "Playing the 'Scene Self': Jane Cavendish and Elizabeth Brackley's *The Concealed Fancies*." In Comsensoli and Russell, 154–76.

———. and Stephanie Hodgson-Wright, with Gweno Williams. *Women and Dramatic Production 1550–1700*. Harlow, UK: Pearson, 2000.

Fletcher, Anthony. *Gender, Sex, and Subordination in England 1500–1800*. New Haven, Yale University Press, 1995.

Fox, Adam. *Oral and Literate Culture in England 1500–1700*. Oxford: Clarendon, 2000.

Gibson, Gail McMurray. *The Theater of Devotion: East Anglian Drama and Society in the Late Middle Ages*. Chicago: University of Chicago Press, 1989.

Gossett, Suzanne. "'Man-Maid, Begone!' Women in Masques." *English Literary Renaissance* 18 (1988): 96–113.

Gowing, Laura. *Domestic Dangers: Women, Words, and Sex in Early Modern London*. Oxford: Clarendon Press, 1996.

Graves, Thornton Shirley. "Women on the Pre-Restoration Stage." *Studies in Philology* 22 (1925): 184–97.

Henke, Robert. *Performance and Literature in the Commedia dell'Arte*. Cambridge: Cambridge University Press, 2002.

Howard, Jean E. *The Stage and Social Struggle in Early Modern England*. London: Routledge, 1994.

Howe, Elizabeth. *The First English Actresses: Women and Drama, 1660–1700*. Cambridge: Cambridge University Press, 1992.

Hutton, Ronald. *The Stations of the Sun: A History of the Rural Year in Britain*. Oxford: Oxford University Press, 1996.

Ingram, Martin. "Ridings, Rough Music and Mocking Rhymes in Early Modern England." *Popular Culture in Seventeenth Century England*. Ed. Barry Reay. London: Croom Helm, 1985, 166–97.

Lea, K. M. *Italian Popular Comedy: A Study in the Commedia dell'arte, 1560–1620, with Special Reference to the English Stage*. 2 vols. Oxford: Clarendon Press, 1934.

Maus, Katharine Eisaman. "'Playhouse Flesh and Blood': Sexual Ideology and the Restoration Actress." *English Literary History* 46 (1979): 595–617.

McKendrick, Malveena. *Theatre in Spain, 1490–1700*. Cambridge: Cambridge University Press, 1989.

McManus, Clare. *Women and the Renaissance Stage: Anna of Denmark and Female Masquing in the Stuart Court 1590–1619*. Manchester: Manchester University Press, 2002.

Mulholland, Paul. Ed. *The Roaring Girl*. By Thomas Middleton and Thomas Dekker. Manchester: Manchester University Press, 1987.

Nashe, Thomas. "Pierce Penilesse his supplication to the Divell." [1592]. *The Works of Thomas Nashe*, vol. I. Ed. Ronald McKerrow. Oxford: Blackwell, 1966.

Nicholson, Eric. "Romance as Role Model: Early Female Performances of *Orlando Furioso* and *Gerusalemme liberata*." *Renaissance Transactions: Ariosto and Tasso*. Ed. Valeria Finucci. Durham: Duke University Press, 1999, 246–69.

Orgel, Stephen. *Impersonations: The Performance of Gender in Shakespeare's England*. Cambridge: Cambridge University Press, 1996.

Parolin, Peter. "'A Strange Fury Entered My House': Italian Actresses and Female Performance in *Volpone*." *Renaissance Drama* n.s. 39 (1998): 107–35.

Paster, Gail Kern and Skiles Howard. *A Midsummer Night's Dream: Texts and Contexts*. Boston: Bedford, 1999.

Richards, Sandra. *The Rise of the English Actress*. New York: St. Martins Press, 1993.

Sale, Carolyn. "Slanderous Aesthetics and Women Writer: The Case of *Hole v. White*." In *From Script to Stage in Early Modern England*, ed. Peter Holland. New York: Palgrave Macmillan, 2005, 181–94.

Shapiro, Michael. "The Introduction of Actresses in England: Delay or Defensiveness?" In Comensoli and Russell, 177–200.

Smith, Bruce R. *The Acoustic World of Early Modern England: Attending to the O-Factor*. Chicago: University of Chicago Press, 1999.

Stokes, James. "The Wells Cordwainers Show: New Evidence of Guild Drama in Somerset." *Comparative Drama* 19.4 (Winter 1985–86): 322–46.

———. "Women and Mimesis in Medieval and Renaissance Somerset (and Beyond)." *Comparative Drama* 27.2 (Summer 1993): 186–96.

Thompson, Ann. "Women/'women' and the stage." *Women and Literature in Britain 1500–1700*. Ed. Helen Wilcox. Cambridge: Cambridge University Press, 1996, 100–16.

Tomlinson, Sophie. "She That Plays the King: Henrietta Maria and the Threat of the Actress in Caroline Culture." *The Politics of Tragicomedy: Shakespeare and After*. Ed. Gordon McMullen and Jonathan Hope. London: Routledge, 1992, 189–207.

———. "'My Brain the Stage': Margaret Cavendish and the Fantasy of Female Performance." *Readings in Renaissance Women's Drama*. Ed. S. P. Cerasano and Marion Wynne-Davies. New York: Routledge, 1998, 272–92.

———. "Too Theatrical? Female Subjectivity in Caroline and Interregnum Drama." *Women's Writing* 6.1 (1999): 65–79.

Walker, Kim. "'New Prison': Representing the Female Actor in Shirley's *The Bird in a Cage*." *English Literary Renaissance* 21 (1991): 385–400.

Wiles, David. *Shakespeare's Clown: Actor and Text in the Elizabethan Playhouse*. Cambridge: Cambridge University Press, 1987.

PART I
BEYOND LONDON

PART 1
BEYOND LONDON

Chapter 2

Women and Performance: Evidences of Universal Cultural Suffrage in Medieval and Early Modern Lincolnshire

James Stokes

Since 1895 when the Historical Manuscripts Commission published its calendar of the Corporation Records of Lincoln, with references to plays, processions, ceremonies and music in Lincoln, the history of early drama in Lincolnshire has received considerable attention from a succession of major scholars (Great Britain, HMC, Macray, 1–120).[1] They all tend to agree that, historically, the county had a rich culture of performance ranging from religious plays and ceremonies to civic shows to many other traditional forms, both amateur and professional, traveling and local. But curiously, in none of those studies is there reference to participation by women in drama and related entertainments; it is as if they did not exist within the rich entertainment culture of the county. Yet current research for the REED (Records of Early English Drama) Lincolnshire volume confirms that women were major, indeed co-equal, contributors in a variety of ways to the entertainments associated with traditional culture in Lincolnshire, a presence that can be documented at almost every level of society. Now that the basic research for the REED volume is complete (meaning that all relevant documents up to 1642 have been searched for their references to drama, music, custom, and ceremony), it is possible to summarize what those records help us to see about women and

---

1 See also Great Britain, HMC, Bennett, which provides a useful overview of the Lincoln Cathedral records but does not mention the many references to religious plays in those records. An early version of this article was presented at the annual meeting of the Shakespeare Association of America, April 2000, Montreal, Canada. I would like to acknowledge the University Personnel Development Committee, University of Wisconsin-Stevens Point, for research and publication fund grants which made development of this article possible.

performance in that county. Recognizing the many contributions made by women fundamentally alters our perception of that culture and requires new descriptions of performative traditions in England during the medieval and early modern periods.

Women's absence from published history is not the result of any conscious animus or purposeful effort to exclude them. Instead it appears to reflect the peculiar way in which earlier research evolved, together with the particular research obsessions of those who essentially ended up shaping our understanding of drama in Lincolnshire for the entire twentieth century.

Most of the performance entries in the Historical Manuscripts Commisson report refer to the "pageants" which the St Anne Guild and the occupations of the town "brought forth" annually, in cooperation with the cathedral chapter, on St Anne Day (Great Britain, HMC, Macray, 1, 25–9, 32, 36, 38, 41, 47–8, 56–65). Scholars – most notably A. F. Leach and E. K. Chambers – almost immediately began to assume that those entries referred to the production of craft cycle plays, as at York, Chester, or elsewhere. Leach concluded that in Lincoln "as at Beverley the play [the presumed cycle play] was a city function, and that the various craft guilds of the city acted, or were responsible for, different acts or scenes in the play" (224). E. K. Chambers, in his enormously influential *Medieval Stage*, seems to have been the first to assume a possible link between the plays in Lincoln and the N-Town plays, basing his judgment on the plays' common interest in Mary. He also wrote that the Corpus Christi play and the "sights" on St Anne Day were "identical" and that they "appear to have been cyclic and processional." The Assumption play in the cathedral, he concluded, was the "wind-up to a cycle." Yet he found such sponsorship of a presumed cycle play by a religious, not a craft, guild to be "anomalous," just as he found the N-Town unusual among cycles, which it clearly is (2: 378, 126, 65, 118).

With Chambers, the course of drama scholarship concerning Lincolnshire had been set: it would thereafter focus on the supposed cycle drama in Lincoln, and it would be driven by the belief of its two main proponents, Hardin Craig and Stanley Kahrl, that the N-Town plays, the only one of the four cycles for which no home has been established, were really the Lincoln Plays. That mindset accelerated when Craig, a great Shakespearean scholar, examined a Cordwainers' Guild book in Lincoln Central Library, and discovered in it many entries for that guild's pageant called the "Bethlehem Pageant." He made the same argument (that N-Town was from Lincoln) in a succession of articles spanning fully fifty years (the last of them appearing in 1964), never wavering from that conviction.[2] In 1965, one year after Craig's last article on the topic, Stanley Kahrl wrote the first of numerous pieces putting forth

---

2 See, for example, Craig's five articles listed in the Works Cited.

essentially the same argument as Craig, culminating with Kahrl's volume of Lincolnshire dramatic records for the Malone Society, which has been the standard source on Lincolnshire drama since 1969. His thesis, like Craig's, was simple: Lincolnshire had a cycle, now lost; the themes and content of the N-Town plays match many features of the culture in Lincoln, especially its particular interest in the Virgin Mary; therefore, that cycle was from Lincoln.[3] Though since disproved on linguistic grounds, this view persists in Lincoln itself, which periodically stages the N-Town plays, calling them "The Lincoln Mystery Cycle."[4]

More significantly, the power of the Craig–Kahrl thesis had several profound effects on subsequent research. Perhaps without even realizing that they were doing so, their thesis privileged Lincoln's religious and craft guild drama over any other forms in the county, making the question of the relationship of the N-Town plays to Lincoln the central research question; and the consequent slimness of Kahrl's Malone Society volume gave the unfortunate impression that there really weren't many dramatic records in Lincolnshire and that nothing else – certainly nothing else of interest or significance as performance – had been present in the county during the medieval and early modern periods. The effect was to eclipse many forms, many segments of the population (including women), and most attempts to place drama within a cultural context.

Current research is revealing a rich array of interrelated performance traditions in the county, of which cathedral and civic guild entertainments form but one part. One result has been to confirm substantial contributions by women within all aspects of that society. Among the most significant of these emerging contributions, for which we have evidence, involves female participation in traditional entertainments sponsored by local socio-religious guilds. These ubiquitous guilds were central to religious, social, and cultural life

---

3 See the articles by Kahrl, and those by Cameron and Kahrl listed in the Works Cited. The one exception among Lincolnshire historians, in substantively acknowledging the contributions of women in the history of the county, is Dorothy Owen, ecclesiastical historian, fellow of Wolfson College, Cambridge, and former archivist at Lincolnshire Archives and Cambridge University Library. Her article, "Lincolnshire Women in History," *The Lincolnshire Historian* 2.6 (1959): 31–45, describes notable Lincolnshire women and their contributions between 1066 and the seventeenth century, but without reference to entertainments. Her *Church and Society in Medieval Lincolnshire* offers the best available overview of parish entertainments during the Middle Ages, though with few references to contributions by women to those entertainments.

4 For the linguistic argument, compellingly made, see Eccles. For a Lincoln perspective on the N-Town plays and their modern production in the cathedral close, see Harris.

in the pre-Reformation parishes of Lincolnshire. They provided the infrastructure that supported and produced traditional parish drama, customs, and festive celebrations. They were also a visible expression of what might be called universal cultural suffrage within the context of the guilds, in that their charters equitably enfranchised everyone – man and woman alike – in the life of the guilds.

By so saying, I do not mean to deny the obvious fact that women in medieval and early modern England lived within a patriarchal environment that used theology, the law, and tradition to subjugate them in the most flagrant ways. But paradoxically, within that larger imbalanced society, the local religious guilds provided quite a different, more structurally and actually equitable, model whose balance was demonstratively reflected in the performative elements of local life that they sponsored.

The evidence from Lincolnshire parish guilds provides a more comprehensive and accurate picture than do the traditional histories of life as it was actually lived at the parish level, describing a local culture, especially before the Reformation, in which women contributed as equals, performatively and otherwise. The destruction of these local religious guilds, which began in 1545 under Henry VIII, was completed in 1547 under Edward VI. They were not restored during Mary's short reign, but many of the practices formerly supported by these guilds continued under the authority of parish oligarchies (for example, churchwardens) during Mary and the early years of Elizabeth I (Bainbridge, 151–2). Strong documentary evidence shows that parishes in Lincolnshire continued to produce plays and to support traditional mixed-gender customs that had formerly been supported by religious guilds into the 1570s and 1580s (Stokes and Wright, 76–9). But it is no exaggeration to say that the abolishment of religious guilds in 1547 began the painful death not only of parish drama but of that universal cultural suffrage that historically had been present in the guilds. Evidences of participation by women in entertainments in Lincolnshire decline with the death of the guilds, but so do references to parish-sponsored entertainments in general. The relentless official assault on traditional culture – especially its performative elements – during the sixteenth century mirrors the curious and equally relentless official assault on women as unfettered participants in that culture, which occurred in the ecclesiastical and secular courts. I would suggest that this parallel assault has not been sufficiently recognized, despite its importance in helping one to appreciate the major, but contested, contributions by early modern women to performance, especially in the provinces.

One of the more illustrative, and hitherto unnoticed, examples from Lincolnshire of co-equal participation by men and women in traditional mimetic customs and drama concerns the guilds of Gainsborough, a town in the northern part of the county. We know of it because in 1587 a special commission of inquiry of the Exchequer deposed aged, trustworthy witnesses of that town concerning a disputed piece of ground called Chapel Garth, where once had stood a chapel which, they all agreed, had been the site of traditional parish entertainments. Edward Deverling, 57, a sadler, testified that until guilds were abolished, there had been:

> ... one guilde called the trinitie guilde mentained by the younge people of the same towne of Gainesbrough who vsuallie on trinitie sondaie after dinner assembled them selues together & did ryde or go to Lea a mile distant from Gainesbrough and there were chosen a Lorde and a Ladie of the same guilde who by the space of a yeare after were called by that name, and after they were so chosen they returned to a Chappell then standinge on the said grownde called Chappell garth and there continued vntil towards nighte havinge there breade and drinck and vsing pastyme & gathering money for the same bread & drincke whereof the overplus aboue the charge of the said bread and drink was imploied toward<es the> mentenance of the same guilde and of a light called trinitie light mentained in the church of Gainesbrough and of an other light sometymes sett vpp before the Image of our Ladie called the Ladie of the chappell in the same chappell.

Further, he said,

> ... he did knowe that at the same tyme there was a brotherhood or fraternitie of the auncient people of the same towne called brothers and sisters who mett at the same chappell yearlie vppon corpus cristie daie in the afternoone and there had meat & drinck and gaue money towardes the vses aforesaid which money was deliuered to certaine persons called guild masters who were masters of both the foresaid companies

and that "the chief persons of the said guild and brotherhood were called the Lord & Ladie and guild masters" (Great Britain, PRO, Exchequer, mb 1).[5]

These descriptions contain a wealth of information. They show that traditional parish entertainments in Gainsborough were clustered in a ten-day period between Whitsun and Corpus Christi Day; that a man and a woman jointly "ruled" over the entertainments and held various titles (lord and lady, king and queen, masters); that the dual mastership of the young people's guild mirrored that of the older people's guild; that in this instance "brethren" was a term referring not to gender but to affiliation (both men and women were brethren); that the ruling couple led processions to neighboring parishes and back, including religious processions on feast days; and that they presided over fund-raising "pasttimes," which surely were entertainments (were either similar to the May Games or were in fact May Games).

---

5 In the original document the scribe occasionally abbreviates words. For readability I have silently expanded those parts of the words rather than italicizing or otherwise indicating them.

Ordinances of other Lincolnshire guilds – both religious and craft – indicate a similar shared membership by "brethren and sistern" of those guilds, so there seems every reason to assume that this kind of customary mixed-gender play was typical in Lincolnshire. Records of this kind also show the extent to which Shakespeare seems to have been evoking similar mixed-gender customs in some of his plays, notably *The Winter's Tale*, when Perdita plays the Sheep-Shearing Queen at the country May Games, and *Two Gentlemen of Verona*, when Julia says, "At Pentecost, / When all our pageants of delight were play'd / Our youth got me to play the woman's part, / And I was trimm'd in Madam Julia's gown" (4.4.158–61).

Lincolnshire guilds were no anomaly within the East Midlands. Scholars have identified 350 parish guilds in nearby Cambridgeshire (Bainbridge, 33). In guild returns that 25 counties sent to the Crown in 1389, Lincolnshire was second only to Norfolk in the number of local religious guilds that it reported (Westlake, 38). What Barbara Hanawalt says of parish guilds in general was also true of Lincolnshire, as surviving charters and other guild records make clear:

> Gilds [that is religious guilds] were integrated by sex as well as social status. All but five of the 500 returns of 1389 included women as members. In all gilds for which membership lists have been published, women made up about 50 percent after the clerical members are excluded from the count. Single women as well as wives could usually belong. (Hanawalt, 25)

By virtue of this co-equal membership in the local religious guilds, central participation by women in traditional entertainments was the cultural norm in pre-Reformation Lincolnshire. That involvement can be documented at every level from village to town to city. Once one begins to look for it, considerable corroborating evidence begins to appear throughout the county. In the fenland village of Baston, as of 1389 it was already the custom that:

> All the sisters [of the guild] come together on St. John the Baptist's Day to dance with each other on pain of a fine. The sisters attend vespers and mattins of the Vigil [of St. John the Baptist or Midsummer Eve] and carry lights as also when they dance. They may be excused on the ground of old age, sickness, and so on. (Westlake, 55)

In the parish of Great Hale in 1634, during a metropolitical visitation, the presiding official addressed "The business of the May Lady" (Great Britain, PRO, Abstract, fo. 25). The reference is obscure but confirms the presence of a traditional May Queen in that village.

In the important port and market town of Boston, one payment confirms that women participated in public performances. In 1526, the Guild of the Blessed Virgin Mary (BVM) paid 2 shillings 8 pence to one of the town worthies "Nicholao feild pro vino expendito tempore filie sue existentis Regine apud Boston [to Nicholas Field for wine used at the time that his daughter was queen at Boston]" (Lincoln, Boston Borough, Guild, fo. 28v). The Guild of the BVM sponsored the town's elaborate Corpus Christi procession and related entertainments, so it may be that Field's daughter had portrayed the Virgin Mary during Corpus Christi. But it also seems possible, maybe even more likely, that Field's daughter had instead played the role of a customary May Queen. One record shows that by 1660, Boston had a well-established, civic-sponsored, tradition commemorating May Day (though elected in March, mayors served from May Day to May Day). On 18 May 1660, for example, the town council ordered that "the succeeding Major [mayor] of this Borrough shall not suffer any Arbors to be made before the dores of their houses on Mayday as the custome hath beene" (Lincoln, Boston Borough, Minute Book III, fo. 444v). No unequivocal records survive to confirm that these May Day ceremonies existed as early as 1526, but they may well have since the entry of 1660 describes them as a custom, meaning that by 1660 they were something acknowledged to be traditional in the town. Before Boston received a civic charter in 1545, the Guild of the BVM, which was one of the largest and most important guilds in England (Lambert and Walker, 40), had managed not only secular religious life among the laity in Boston, but local governance as well. The guild's early sixteenth-century accounts include payments for both religious and civic matters in equal measure. As was true of the town's fourteen other religious guilds, the membership of the Guild of the BVM included women and men in equal measure, as the records of the guilds themselves make clear (Lambert and Walker, 50; Thompson, 1856, 115–26, 134–5). In that context, the payment to Field's daughter in 1526 may just as well be referring to a May Queen as to the Virgin Mary. The reference to her being queen for a period of time, and to the large expenditure for wine, could be seen as suggestive of a festive parish custom such as a May Game. The one certain fact is that in early sixteenth-century Boston, women participated in public performances sponsored by the town's religious and civic governors.

Women's co-equal membership and participation in Lincoln's guilds – both religious and craft – is particularly striking since, as the county's cathedral city, Lincoln was a model to every other community. The principal guild in Lincoln in the sixteenth century was the Guild of St Anne. Nominally, every citizen of Lincoln was a member. St Anne Guild was responsible for overseeing the city's processions, guild pageants, and plays, the most important of these by far being the procession and pageants mounted by the city on St Anne's Day (26 July). In Lincoln then, authority over the shows lay with this powerful religious guild, not with the craft guilds, though they supplied pageants and took part in the other events of St Anne's Day. Entries in the city's Corporation Minute Books repeatedly emphasize the joint obligation of both men and women, under penalty of fine, to be paying members of St Anne Guild, as in 1519:

Also it is Agreid yat euery man And woman with in this Citie beyng Able Schall be Broder & Syster in Scaynt Anne gyld & to pay yerly iiij d Man & Wyf at the lest. (Lincoln, Lincoln Civic Minute Book, 1511–41, fo. 97)

Further, they were required to have regalia, as in 1544 when it was ordered:

that euery alderman within this Cytye that haith not ben Mayor schall herafter prepare and haue for hymselff and his wyff Gownes of Cremysen and euery alderman that haith ben mayor schall herafter prepare and haue for hymselff and his wyff Gownes of Skarlett and & Typettes of velvyt ... [and that] thensforth they the seid aldermen & ther wyffes aforseid schall weare the seid Gownes of Cremysen & Skarlett, at & vpon all pryncypall feistes. (Lincoln, Lincoln Civic Minute Book 1541–64, fos 23, 139v, 145)[6]

This use of regalia has an obvious theatrical dimension in that they are presenting themselves not as individual citizens but as members of a ruling oligarchy, a symbolism made explicit in the uniform requirements concerning their regalia that set them apart from others both in the oligarchy and in the citizenry as a whole.

The guild book of the Cordwainers' Guild, in addition to confirming its own co-equal membership by men and women, also confirms, in the wording of the oath to be taken by the brothers and sisters of that guild in 1527, that both men and women took part in the procession on St Anne's Day:

... I shalbe redy to goo in procession with the Graceman Brether & Susters of this ffraternite ffrom the chapell of Saint thomas of ye hy brige in Lincoln vnto the cathedrall churche of Lincoln & ther to offer one ffarthyng as custom is. (Lincoln, Lincoln Central Library, fo. 1)

The procession of the Cordwainers indisputably included mimetic elements, namely a pageant of Bethlehem, for which the guild book lists properties and a place of storage (Lincoln, Lincoln Central Library, fo. 1). Every other guild also contributed (or was supposed to contribute) pageants to the procession on St Anne's Day as well. Whether the women had roles as actors (or indeed whether the pageants even involved more than silent tableaus) is unclear, but since a woman played "Regina" (either the Virgin Mary or a queen) at Boston, it seems reasonable to think that she could have done so at Lincoln as well. But in any event it is quite obvious that women were integral participants in the mimetic civic spectacle itself.

Just as at Boston the influence of the guild and its entertainments and spectacles extended into the countryside. Women from nearby communities,

---

6   The same orders are repeated on fo. 139v (1558), and fo. 145 (1559).

including the gentry and members of religious orders, saw themselves as members of the guild and contributed to its ceremonies and plays. In 1521, the acting "graceman" of St Anne Guild (the person charged with mounting the procession and arranging for the pageants on St Anne's Day) said that because

> the plage is reynyng in yis Citie wherfore he Cannot gayt Sutch garmentes and other honormentes as Schauld be in ye pagentes off ye procession off Scaynt Anne day wherfore it is agreid yat Master Alanson Schalbe Instantly desyred to bowro agowne off my lady powes ffor one of the maryes & thother mary To be a rayed in the Cremsysing gowne off veluet yat longith to the Same gyld Also it is agreid yat Master Sammes & Master halton Schalbe Instanted To Spek with the prior off Scaynt Kateryns To haue Sutch honormentes as yat we haue had afore tyme to the preparyng off the Same Gyld. (Lincoln, Civic Minute Book 1511–41, 132)[7]

As can be seen from these examples, female membership in both the religious and the craft guilds of Lincolnshire covered the social spectrum, including everyone from servants and members of religious houses to the most important women in the country. In Stamford, membership in the important St Katherine's Guild included Lady Margaret Beaufort and Cecily Lady Welles, daughter of Edward IV (Rogers, 35). The Corpus Christi Guild of Boston included Blanche, Duchess of Lancaster and Alicia, Countess of Lincoln, among other notables, but also Agnes, servant of Simon de Wode and, interestingly, "Matilda Manfleete, Mistress of the School in Boston" (Thompson, 1856, 116; Lambert and Walker, 57), a rare identification of a secular female schoolmaster in that early period.[8] The co-equal leadership by

---

7   Lady Powes appears to be Margaret Grey Powis of Burton by Lincoln, daughter of Sir Edward Sutton, knight, Lord Dudley; widow of Sir John Grey, knight, Lord Powis; and second wife of Robert Sutton, of Burton (Maddison, 939).

8   Eve Rachele Sanders has shown that during the Middle Ages women held a central theological position as educators of small children, and that "images of women learning and teaching became common features of Christian art" during that time (9). She cites commonly depicted scenes of St Anne teaching Mary to read, and of Mary (and sometimes Anne) teaching Jesus to read, a noteworthy image in Lincolnshire given the focus on Mary and St Anne in that county's drama and ceremony. As Sanders also shows, the nuns in convents commonly ran schools for girls and acted as teachers there, a contribution taken from them – to the detriment of girls' education – with the dissolution of religious houses and a "shift in iconography" during the sixteenth century that placed Christ (not Anne and Mary) at the center of culture as teachers (9). The schoolmistress in Boston is part of that pre-Reformation culture, but she is unusual in seeming to be a secular schoolmistress of either a school for girls or of a pre-Reformation school in Boston that had both a schoolmaster and a schoolmistress, and which therefore taught both boys and girls.

men and women that we see in Gainsborough seems to have been the norm in parish guilds at every level, from village to town to city.

Even in the face of such evidence, there seems a residual inclination to see the evidence from parish religious guilds and their entertainments as somehow ancillary in comparison to the evidence from craft cycle plays which apparently were, in the main, acted by men though exceptions can be found, as in Wells, Somerset (Stokes, "Wells Cordwainers," 322–46).[9] But before they were abolished, the local religious guilds were the chartered center of parish life and the principal source of local religious drama by the laity. Women were fully enfranchised participants within that world. To recognize the centrality of the religious guilds, along with the fully enfranchised participation by women within the world of those guilds, is to fundamentally alter our understanding of pre-Reformation culture and performance and the place of women within it. What seems needed is a sea change in perception that would see the evidence from the religious guilds, not just from the cycles, as the key to pre-Reformation life and traditional entertainments in most parishes, a life in which participation by women was the norm.

Numerous antiquarian sources in Lincolnshire describe later local traditions that echo the festive parish entertainments that one sees in the records of the pre-Reformation religious guilds and parish records. It is not possible to know whether they are survivals of those traditions or are eighteenth- and nineteenth-century revivals. But many documents, especially quarter sessions and other legal records, show that some of the traditional entertainments – May Games and skimmingtons, and seasonal wakes, for example – survived into the early years of the eighteenth century. Without systematically searching the records through the eighteenth and nineteenth centuries (as is done by REED for earlier periods), it is impossible to know whether a tradition described by antiquarians is a survival of an unbroken tradition, or rather a revival. But when, for example, one finds a hill called "Maypole Hill" in

---

9   Historically, the surviving mystery "cycles" (some of them are not actually cycles but collections) have been treated as the principal kind of medieval play, and the craft guilds that staged them as the principal patrons and producers of local religious drama. And since documentary records indicate that most cycle plays were acted by men, most criticism of medieval drama reflects those several assumptions. But my research (now completed) for the REED volume for Lincolnshire shows no evidence of cycle plays in that county, nor that craft guilds necessarily controlled drama there. Indeed the evidence from the East Midlands in general shows different kinds of plays – large, multi-stage, fixed-site, outdoor, non-cycle plays – to have been the norm in that region. Nor does evidence concerning the cycle plays always indicate men-only performances. For discussions of that evidence and a summary of scholarship reflecting more traditional views, see Stokes, "Wells Cordwainers" and "Women and Mimesis."

sixteenth-century records or on an eighteenth-century map, and learns that an annual May Game was being held on that same hill in the nineteenth century, then the game is either a survival or is a revival that is consciously alluding to an earlier local tradition. The British have always been keen to preserve local traditions, but official suppressions or changing political climates have periodically forced them underground. When they reappear, as they often do, they are not revivals so much as resurfacings, sometimes with a measure of their original form and purpose having been lost. The nineteenth-century examples cited below are notable for their descriptions of participation by women. One cannot, of course, declare them to be survivals of unbroken sixteenth- or seventeenth-century practices, but sixteenth-century records take women's participation as a given and so do these. So if the tradition itself has not survived unbroken, the performative assumptions within it have been preserved in these examples.

The village of South Kyme, for example, reported (in antiquarian collections) that "there used to be a Queen of the May and great festivities on May Day," meaning within the memory of residents still living in the early nineteenth century. Kyme certainly still had an annual May Game at the beginning of the seventeenth century. In a Star Chamber of 1601, contemporary witnesses describe in great detail elaborate May Games including a play held on the village green (Gutch and Peacock, 197; Great Britain, PRO, Clinton vs Dymock STAC 5/L1/29, [No. 1]). May Games were similarly reported at Somerby near Grantham in the early nineteenth century, though apparently involving children at that date (Gutch and Peacock, 196). In the parish of Winteringham in the same period, villagers would "dress the lugs of milk-kits with leaves on May-morning" and in the evening they "danced and played kiss-in-the-ring … round a May garland set up in the cattle pasture" (24). The then village of Clee (now part of a heavily populated area) had Hock Tuesday games in which "the girls were the most active" using "the custom of binding." The writer says, "It was a merry festival at which the female part of the community reigned absolute." The young men and women together "amused themselves on this day by stopping the streets round the market-place, and seizing on the passengers, kept them in durance until they purchased their emancipation with a small fine" (193). At Maytide in Messingham, the young men and women "assembled at Perestow Hills" and "danced their way to the town" preceded by a fiddler (195). Gouch and Peacock report the term "Harvest-lady" being used to mean "the second reaper, who supplies the 'lord's place in his absence'" (208).

In the nineteenth century, the port town of Grimsby had a Whitsun festival which included a green arbor in the churchyard "where maidens gathered contributions." As part of the ceremonies, according to the local historian writing about it (as quoted by Gutch and Peacock), the parish chose a "lord and lady of the feast, who dressed themselves in character." The "great tithebarn" became their court, where they presided over dancing and revels and "were attended by the proper officers, and a jester dressed in a party coloured jacket" (194–5). May Day in Grimsby, it was reported, included a Maypole and a queen of the May attended by several maidens and "a young man called the captain" and his officers, as well as a Robin Hood, a dragon, and a hobby horse, among other figures (201–2). The precedent for traditional parish entertainments of which these would have formed a part appears to be well documented in the earlier records. In 1527, for example, the Grimsby Borough Court Book includes an order that a man "prepare for the play of holy Iohn of bowre," which one takes to mean the parish play of St John parish church at the bower erected for that purpose (Grimsby, mb 2).

Another stratum of women's involvement with entertainments during the medieval and early modern periods is also recorded in some of the Diocese of Lincoln's many religious houses. The evidence suggests that some convents and priories permitted entertainments in which the nuns might engage as sponsors, audiences, or participants. In his visitation to Nun Coton Priory in 1531, Bishop John Longland charged the prioress that she: "suffre nomore hereafter eny lorde of mysrule to be within your house, nouther to suffre hereafter eny suche disgysinges as in tymes past haue bene used in your monastery in nunnes apparell ne otherwise" (Lincoln, Bishop's Register, fo. 218). This record gives the impression that the nuns were being chastised not for acting roles, but for being hosts and audience, both for festive games involving lords (whether Christmas, Harvest, Summer, or otherwise) and for other "disgysinges" in which gender roles were being parodied. Men were being welcomed into the house as actors and audience in traditional festive entertainments jointly enjoyed by men and women, in ways that clearly must have reflected the practices then current in secular society. The bishop also ordered that henceforth the prioress not allow certain noblemen and religious men "to come within the precincte of your monasterye" and that she "streight vpon sight herof [of this order] dymynishe the nombre of your seruantes aswell men as women, whiche excessyve nombre that ye kepe of them bothe is oon of the grette causes of your miserable pouertye."

The nuns of Nun Coton appear to have been greatly involved in secular society in many ways because the bishop also warned that "frome hensforth ye do nomore burden ne chardge your house with suche a nombre of your kynnesfolkes as ye haue in tymes past vsed"; and he complained that "dyuerse of your susters hath wandred a brode in the world, some vndre the pretense of pylgrymages, some to see ther frendes, and otherwise wherby hath growen many Inconuenyences, insolent behauioures, and moche slaunder." Some had even gone "att lybertie where they wold some att thornton some att Newsom [near Thornton], some at Hull some att other places att their pleasures" (fo. 218v). Similarly, at St. Michael's Priory, during a visitation in 1440, Bishop Alnwick ordered that the prioress there seek diligently to find Agnes Butler, a nun who had fled the priory in apostasy with a harper named Robert Abbot and had made her way to another city (Lincoln, Vj/1, fo. 83). In 1442 at the Priory of Catesby (Northamptonshire in the Diocese of Lincoln), one of the nuns, it was charged, "did pass the night with the Austin friars at Northampton and did dance and play the lute with them in the same place until midnight, and on the night following she passed the night with the friars preachers at Northampton, luting and dancing in like manner" (93).[10] In 1437, the monks of Peterborough Abbey were presented for dancing with women in the town and in the monastery (Lincoln, Vj/1, 1; Thompson, *Bishop Alnwick's*, 272).

But nowhere is the role of women as sponsors, hosts, and sometimes participants more vividly recorded than among the important women of the laity. Most notable among them, and perhaps the most important person and patron in the county, was Katherine, widowed Duchess of Suffolk, daughter and heir of William Willoughby, Lord of Eresby, and only sister of Edward, Second Earl of Oxford (see fig. 2.1). She lived with her second husband, Richard Bertie, at Grimsthorpe Castle in the heart of Lincolnshire. As Protestants they had been forced to flee to the Continent during the reign of Mary. When Elizabeth came to the throne, they returned to Grimsthorpe, where they lived in a convivial atmosphere. A set of household accounts from 1560–2 shows the Duchess making payments to almost every kind of performer then current in England, including: (in 1560) livery for a Christmas lord and his men (December); (in 1561) to unidentified players, gifts and furniture for the Christmas lord, and rewards to the Berties' own troupe of players (January), a hobby horse performer (February), music by the waits of Lincoln (March), a company of fencers (July), two puppeteers (August), four musicians and a hobby horse at a wedding (September), Lord Robert Dudley's players (October), and Master Rose and his daughters who played, Lord Dudley's men, Arundel's players, and the waits of London (December); (and in 1562) a lute for her own son and daughter, and a player's boy (January), assorted players (between January and April, and in July), morris dancers from another town (May), a bagpiper and a juggler together with a musician (July), and another bag piper (September) (Lincoln, ANC/7/A/2, fos 52, 52v, 53v, 54, 56, 56v, 57, 58, 58v–59, 31v, 60, 63, 64, 66).

Three striking features arise from these accounts. The first is the apparent concern, even affection, with which both professional and amateur performers approached her when she was ill, and to which she responded positively:

To master Rose and his daughters which played before [yo] herr grace in her syckynes xiij s iiij d

---

10   This translation is taken from Thompson, *Visitations*, 50.

2.1   Katherine Willoughby (1519–1580), Duchess of Suffolk and Baroness Willoughby de Eresby, of Grimsthorpe, Lincolnshire.

To a servant of my Lorde willowbies which offered to playe and sing before my
master and herr grace the xiiijth daye by Boucher xx d. (fo. 58v)

The second is her apparent liking for performances of almost any imaginable
kind, ranging from the most rustic traditional forms to professional plays to
music by the waits of London and other places. The third is her apparent
seriousness about the role of music in her household, including the purchase of
a lute for both her young daughter and her son, and the involvement of both
males and females in performances. The Master Rose of the entry above was a
musician (and perhaps an instrument maker) who must have lived in the area.
He seems to have been a music tutor to the Duchess's children Perigrine and
Susan Bertie, and in January 1562 the family bought a lute from him for the
children (Lincoln, ANC/7/A/2, fo. 31v). In that same January, the Duchess
paid Rose's boy (either his apprentice or his son) 20 pence (fo. 60). In March
1562, Rose mended the lute belonging to Perigrine, and in July 1562, the
Duchess's two children appear to have performed in a play (fo. 64v).

Clearly the daughters of Master Rose were accomplished musicians capable
of playing with their father in a consort. That both the musician Rose's
daughters and the Duchess's own daughter performed should not surprise. The
sixteenth and seventeenth centuries were a time of great and powerful women
who were not only patrons, but audiences. Performers tailored performances to
please that important audience. In Somerset, for example, the craft guilds of
Wells shaped their civic guild shows to include themes and story lines pleasing
to the monarch when she visited; and senior guildsmen made certain that their
own daughters played roles in those same shows (Stokes, "Wells Cordwainers"). In the performances by sons and daughters alike at Grimsthorpe one can
see the universal cultural suffrage that is routinely ignored in discussions of the
participation (or more usually the non-participation) by women in performance during that period.

As the highest-ranking person in Lincolnshire, the Duchess appears to have
projected her presence into the county via her own company of players – this
display being a political performance of sorts. Her players traveled to perform
at a variety of places throughout the county, where they must have been
warmly welcomed since they were always paid, never turned away. Her troupe
also performed several times in the county with the Queen's players. These
joint appearances by the players of the most important person in the nation
and the most important person in the county – both women – provide valuable
evidence of patronage as the projection of self, as the personification of power,
by women, during the first two decades of Elizabeth's reign.

We can know that, among other places, the Duchess's troupe performed at
Louth in 1539–40; at Long Sutton in 1550–1551 and 1564–5; and at Lincoln in
1561–2 and 1563–4 (Lincoln, Louth Parish, fo. 50; Lincoln, Long Sutton
Parish, fos 42v, 87; Lincoln, Cathedral Account, fo. 125v). Bertie household

accounts indicate that in 1561 the Duchess's own troupe included five players (all men) because each received an award of 15 shillings – either for a performance or as part or all of an annual wage. Another payment of 15 shillings in that account to "the players" (Lincoln, ANC/7/A/2, fo. 60) also appears to refer to her own troupe because similar payments to other troupes always identify them and their patron if they have one. When her players visited Long Sutton in 1550, the churchwardens' accounts referred to them as "My Lady Suffolk's Players" (Lincoln, Long Sutton Par 7/1, fo. 42v). When they performed at Lincoln (either in the cathedral or in the close) in 1561–2 and 1563–4, the cathedral accounts refer to them as "The Players of the Duchess of Suffolk" (Lincoln, Cathedral Bj/3/6, fo. 125v; Bj/3/8, fo. 129v). Whatever they received as an annual wage from the Duchess, they made most of their income by traveling to perform. For each of the three performances above they received 6 shillings 8 pence, which seems to have been their standard fee. In 1561–2 they were paid in an entry that also paid the Queen's players, who received 13 shillings 4 pence (also their standard fee), twice as much as the Duchess's troupe. It appears that the players of these two great female patrons may have been performing together at the cathedral or elsewhere in the close. Whether the Duchess and her husband had separate troupes is unclear, but it seems likely. In 1539–40, the churchwardens of Louth paid the Lord of Suffolk's players, described as "fabule actoribus," 20 pence (Lincoln, Louth Parish, fo. 50). The Duchess's players were not just a local troupe. Records show them being paid at Rye, Sussex in 1552–3; at Newcastle on Tyne in 1562; and at Cambridge in 1562–3.

The content of her players' performances is unknown, but the Duchess (and therefore probably her players) may also have contributed support to the staging of a major religious play late in the reign of Henry VIII in the town of Spalding, about 15 miles from Grimsthorpe. An antiquarian source describes churchwardens' accounts (now lost) as saying that among the contributors to the play (apparently "contributor" in this context means one giving financial support) were "the Lord Willoughby, the Lady Fitzwilliam, the Champion Dymocke, the Lady Kyme," and others; so several of the county's important women served as patrons for this play (Gooch, 128). Clearly the tastes found in the households of the Duchess and other great ladies would have exerted influence on drama in Lincolnshire in many ways.

So what is one to make of this variety of evidence? In collecting documentary records for an earlier article on women and performance in Somerset, I had wondered if that county were typical or atypical, in that its records contain evidences of involvement by women in performance. Lincolnshire suggests to me that what I found in Somerset may be quite typical. In fact, the evidence in Lincolnshire is even more copious than that in Somerset, and gives a more complete picture of women and performance because it includes more social

strata and shows the ways in which they overlapped, from village maids to
women of the burgess class to nuns to landed gentry to the nobility to royalty.
   For me, the most compelling part of the evidence from Lincolnshire – as it
relates to this volume – is what emerges in relation to the religious and the craft
guilds, and what the records of those guilds tell us about the participation by
women in performance, as in every other aspect of traditional culture. Until
they were abolished by Edward VI, the socio-religious guilds were the essential
expression of local religious culture by the laity, and the chief means of pious
self-governance by the laity in villages, towns and cities throughout England,
just as the parish was the religious, social, and administrative unit that unified
pre-Reformation culture and sponsored local performance. Clearly women
participated as players, sponsors, producers, and audiences in revels; in
customary mimetic games, processions, and enactments blending worship and
play; in mimetically conceived ceremonies publicly enacting the rituals of
power, authority, and life's passages. The copious evidence of dual and co-
equal presence by men and women within the life of these guilds is not merely
an expression of something within that culture, it is the principal vehicle for the
customary expression of that culture, often taking the form of performance.
The suppression, repression, pursuit and exile of women from the stage in
sixteenth-century England needs to be seen not as the norm of that culture but
as the aberrant historical moment that it was – a genuine religious and political
revolution that descended into an unspeakably vicious culture war focusing on
the most vulnerable elements of that culture. The guilds in pre-Reformation
England were very much a family affair. The records from Somerset and
Lincolnshire alike copiously illustrate participation by women in the life of the
guilds. The rich culture of the East Midlands needs to be seen whole: the
signature female presence in the traditional entertainments of the local guilds,
the female iconography in the region's religious art, and the Marian focus that
can be seen in religious drama sponsored by the towns of East Anglia and
Lincolnshire.
   A thorough, comprehensive, objective study of the socio-religious guilds in
these terms is urgently needed. It would, I believe, fundamentally alter our
perception of that culture and reveal the central place of women within it – a
point that should be painfully obvious to any objective student of the records.
It would also necessarily change our perception of the contributions by women
to entertainments within that culture, rightly moving them from the shadows
to the center of that cultural "stage."

Works Cited

Bainbridge, Virginia. *Guilds in the Medieval Countryside: Society and Religious Change
   in Cambridgeshire c. 1350–1558.* Woodbridge, Suffolk: Boydell, 1996.

Cameron, Kenneth, and Stanley J. Kahrl. "The N-Town Plays at Lincoln." *Theatre Notebook* 20.2 (1965–6): 61–9.

———. "Staging the N-Town Cycle." *Theatre Notebook* 21 (1967): 122–38, 152–65.

Chambers, E. K. *The Medieval Stage*. 2 vols. Oxford: Clarendon, 1903.

Craig, Hardin. "News for Bibliophiles." *The Nation* July–Dec. 1913: 308–9.

———. "Notes on the Home of Ludus Coventriae." *University of Minnesota Studies in Language and Literature* 1 (1914): 72–83.

———. "An Elementary Account of Miracle Plays in Lincoln." *The Lincoln Diocesan Magazine* 30 (Sept. 1914): 135–9.

———. "The Lincoln Cordwainers' Pageant." *Publications of the Modern Language Association* 32 (1917): 605–15.

———. "Mystery Plays at Lincoln – Further Research Needed." *The Lincolnshire Historian* 2.11 (1964): 37–41.

Eccles, Mark. "*Ludus* Coventriae: Lincoln or Norfolk." *Medium Aevum* 40 (1971): 135–41.

Gooch, E. H. *A History of Spalding*. Spalding: The Spalding Free Press, 1940.

Great Britain. Historical Manuscripts Commission. Ed. J. A. Bennett. "The Manuscripts of the Dean and Chapter of Lincoln," *12th Report of the Manuscripts Commission*. Part 9. London: HMSO, 1891.

———. ———. Ed. William Dunn Macray. "The Manuscripts of the Corporation of Lincoln," *14th Report of the Manuscripts Commission*. Part 8. London: HMSO, 1895.

———. ———. Ed. S. C. Lomas. *Report of the Manuscripts of the Earl of Lancaster Preserved at Grimsthorpe*. Vol. 37. Dublin: HMSO, 1907.

Great Britain. Public Record Office. Abstract of Metropolitical Visitation. PRO: SP/16/274/12, fo. 25.

———. ———. Clinton vs Dymock, 1601. PRO: STAC 5/L1/ 29, no. [1].

———. ———. Exchequer, Special Commission of Inquiry. PRO: E 178/1315, no. [3], mb 1.

Grimsby. North East Lincolnshire Archives. Mayor's Court Book, 1507–8. NELA: 1/102/2, mb 2.

Gutch, E., and M. Peacock. *Examples of Printed Folk-Lore Concerning Lincolnshire*. County Folk-Lore. Vol. 5. London, 1908.

Hanawalt, Barbara. "Keepers of the Lights: Late Medieval English Parish Gilds." *Journal of Medieval and Renaissance Studies* 14 (1984): 21–37.

Harris, John Wesley. *Medieval Plays at Lincoln*. Lincoln Cathedral Library: Honywood, 1994.

Kahrl, Stanley J. *Plays and Players in Lincolnshire, 1300–1585*. Malone Society Collections, vol 8. Oxford: Malone Society, 1974.

———. "Teaching Medieval Drama as Theatre." *The Learned and the Lewed*. Ed. Larry D. Benson. Cambridge: Harvard University Press, 1974.

Lambert, M. R., and R. Walker. *Boston Tattershall & Croyland*. Oxford: Blackwell, 1930.

Leach, A. F. "Some English Plays and Players, 1220–1548." *An English Miscellany Presented to Dr. Furnivall in Honour of His Seventy-Fifth Birthday*. Ed. W. P. Ker, A. S. Napier, and W. W. Skeat. Oxford: Clarendon, 1901.

Lincoln. Lincolnshire Archives. Bertie Household Accounts, 1560–2. LA: ANC/7/A/2.

———. ———. LA: Bishop's Register 26, 1541–7.

———. ———. LA: Boston Borough 2/A/1/3, Council Minute Book III, 1638–71.
———. ———. LA: Boston Borough 4/C/1/1, Guild of the BVM Account, 1525–6.
———. ———. Cathedral Accounts, 1552–77. LA: Bj/3/6, fo. 125v.
———. ———. Cathedral Accounts, 1524–95. LA: Bj/3/8, fo. 129v.
———. ———. Churchwardens' Accounts, 1527–59. LA: Louth Parish 7/2.
———. ———. Churchwardens' Accounts, 1542–73. LA: Long Sutton St. Mary Parish 7/1.
———. ———. LA: Vj/1, Episcopal Visitation Book, 1437–47.
———. ———. LA: L1/1/1/1, Lincoln Civic Minute Book, 1511–41.
———. ———. LA: L1/1/1/2, Lincoln Civic Minute Book, 1541–64.
———. Lincoln Central Library. Cordwainers' Guild Account and Minute Book, 1527–1772. LCL: MS 5009.
Maddison, A. R. Lincolnshire Pedigrees. Vol. 3. London, 1904 [vol. 52 of the Harleian Society].
Owen, Dorothy. M. "Lincolnshire Women in History." The Lincolnshire Historian. 2.6 (1959): 31–45.
———. Church and Society in Medieval Lincolnshire. History of Lincolnshire, vol 5. Lincoln: Society for Lincolnshire History and Archaeology, 1971; rpt, 1990.
Rogers, Alan. "Late Medieval Stamford: A Study of the Town Council 1465–1492." Perspectives in English Urban History. Ed. Alan Everitt. London: Macmillan, 1973.
Sanders, Eve Rachele. Gender and Literacy on Stage in Early Modern England. Cambridge: Cambridge University Press, 1998.
Stokes, James. "The Wells Cordwainers Show: New Evidence of Guild Drama in Somerset." Comparative Drama 19.4 (Winter 1985–6): 322–46.
———. "Women and Mimesis in Medieval and Renaissance Somerset (and Beyond)." Comparative Drama 27.2 (Summer 1993): 176–96.
———, and Stephen K. Wright. "The Donington Cast List: Innovation and Tradition in Parish Guild Drama in Early Elizabethan Lincolnshire." Early Theatre 2 (1999): 63–83.
Thompson, A. H. Visitations of Religious Houses in the Diocese of Lincoln. Vol 2. London: Canterbury and York Society, 1919.
———. Bishop Alnwick's Visitations. Lincoln Record Society 30 (1933).
Thompson, Pishy. The History and Antiquities of Boston. London: Longman, 1856.
Westlake, H. F. The Parish Guilds of Mediaeval England. London: Society for Promoting Christian Knowledge, 1919.

Chapter 3

Payments, Permits and Punishments: Women Performers and the Politics of Place

Gweno Williams, Alison Findlay and Stephanie Hodgson-Wright

In her book *Outside Belongings*, Elspeth Probyn discusses "the desire that individuals have to belong, a tenacious and fragile desire" that is "increasingly performed in the knowledge of the impossibility of ever really and truly belonging" (5). Probyn is concerned here with social and geographical identity, but the pattern of frustrated desire for inclusion also speaks to the position of women's drama in early modern English theater history. The endeavors of feminist scholars to recover women's drama are characterized partly by a wish for its inclusion in that history. At the same time, our need to acknowledge the differences of women's dramatic production means that this project is increasingly performed in the knowledge that these texts do not truly "belong" in the established narratives of early modern theater. Accounts of drama in the period have been dominated by a focus on the professional companies and theaters in the metropolis, in which women writers and performers had no place. Studies of the masque have broadened the metropolitan arena to include women's participation in court performances, but a truly inclusive "national" history of early modern drama calls for a more radical devolutionary process.

The regional studies pioneered by the Records of Early English Drama (REED) project have broadened the picture of dramatic activity in England. We draw on this impressive scholarship, taking a deliberate step away from metropolitan, commercial theater to attend to regional female performances in the period 1500 to 1645. Focusing on the regions allows historians of women's drama to create a dramatic tradition that can address the tensions outlined by Probyn. It opens up a larger geographical space and a range of venues in which women produced very different performances. It can thus accommodate the tenacious desire to belong to a national tradition, and simultaneously acknowledge the impossibility of full incorporation, which would eliminate regional and gender differences. Parallels can be drawn between the elite Catholic masquing tradition of the Jacobean and Caroline courts, where women silently figured idealized versions of the nation, and regional performances by noblewomen and commoners, but the distinctions are as important as the similarities. By examining the English regions where we live and work, we here explore three different geographical and cultural spaces that shaped women's performance opportunities. In the City of York (Gweno Williams), elaborate civic structures create a close-knit framework within which, and occasionally against which, women produced performances. In contrast, Lancashire, in the northwest of England (Alison Findlay), represents a rural environment that was geographically and culturally remote enough from the center of government to foster performances that were subject to careful surveillance. The varied climate and natural resources of Gloucestershire (Stephanie Hodgson-Wright) made it distinctively self-sufficient. Nevertheless, its excellent communications allowed for a particularly close relationship with central government. Its records detail a range of dramatic activities involving women, yet the absence of leading noble families and the dominance of Puritan influences are perhaps both factors contributing to the absence of large numbers of female performances from the historical records.

The nature of those records frequently implies a dynamic relationship between the centralizing tendencies of state policy and local customs and practices, which we explore. The documentary evidence constitutes, in the main, some kind of invocation of authority, to command, suppress or permit a performance to take place. On fewer occasions we find other types of authoritative documentation, such as a script or a letter. The nature of the written evidence already suggests limits to the picture of women's theatrical activity we can build, but it still allows us to redefine our perceptions of dramatic production by speculating on regional and gender differences. Place is an important defining feature, down to the immediate locales in which various female performances were enacted. Venues such as courtrooms, halls, churchyards, and town squares or streets inevitably raise questions about what constitutes theater; an outside venue, while appearing to offer more flexibility than the rigid architectural structure of a building, is equally subject to the process of cultural construction. Examination of these localized physical and cultural surroundings allows us to outline a picture of women's theatrical activity which supplements and so destabilizes the traditionally exclusive, centralized picture of early modern theater as a professional, metropolitan activity.

The City of York (Gweno Williams)

William Camden's *Britannia* (1586) described York as rich and populous, the second city and the fairest in England. Prosperous and politically significant as the home of the Council of the North, York maintained its religious status as second ecclesiastical center of England during the turbulent sixteenth-century transition from Catholicism to Protestantism. These factors helped to establish York's theatrical importance; the city remains highly significant in the history of drama because it was home to "the most lavish, long-lasting, and complex form of collective theatrical enterprise in English theater history" (Beckwith, xv). From 1376 to the 1580s, the annual Corpus Christi cycle of religious plays or "padgeants" and later variants, combining religious, secular, and commercial interests, was collaboratively staged by the numerous York craft guilds. Corpus Christi cycles or "mystery plays" were an important element of early national dramatic culture, with scripts surviving from locations including Chester, Lincolnshire, Wakefield, Coventry, and Cornwall,[1] but the wealth of the York records is unsurpassed. Texts of the plays and associated material constitute the richest documentary records of early theater activity, prompting the REED project's selection of York as the subject of one of its earliest volumes, published in 1979.

Accordingly, evidence from York can offer helpful insights into the range and variety of female participation in early theater culture nationally. In Pageant 9 of the York cycle, the Fishers and Mariners' *The Flood*, Noah's gregarious wife responds to the cataclysmic disappearance of her female friends with the question: "Wher are nowe all oure kynne / And companye ...?" (Beadle 1982, 89). Her inquiry appositely draws attention to the submerged status of women in accounts of early theatrical activity in York, their various roles effectively overlooked due to the unsubstantiated assumption that there was no female participation in the Corpus Christi cycle. In fact, documentation reveals that women engaged in a wide range of key activities for this major annual collective theatrical enterprise, including finance, planning, production, staging and audience management. Where some references are tantalizingly imprecise, analogies from other cycles or locations can inform the inquiry, importantly extending the range of what has hitherto been understood as women's dramatic activity.

Logically, the sheer scale of the Corpus Christi production required maximum involvement from all active sections of York's population, with particular responsibility falling on guild members, both men and women. Beckwith conservatively estimates that at performance time, at least 10 per cent of the city's inhabitants were directly involved in production of the plays, while Beadle counts over 300 speaking parts in the cycle, together with an "undoubtedly much larger" number of supernumeraries, including musicians, stagehands and other assistants (Beckwith, xvi; Beadle 1994, 88). The York Corpus Christi cycle comprised a chronological sequence of self-contained verse pageants based on Biblical and apochryphal episodes, performed

---

1 See regional essays in Beadle (1994).

outdoors from dawn to nightfall on wheeled pageant wagons, at up to sixteen traditional performance stations across the walled city.[2] More than fifty craft guilds funded and organized sequential performances of the cycle in mid-summer, on the feast of Corpus Christi or other religious holidays.

It is important to emphasize that this annual performance represented only the visible part of the ongoing civic and community energy devoted to the cycle. Medieval scholar Chris Humphrey and performance theorist Richard Schechner usefully draw attention to the extensive and invisible production framework underpinning any performance (Humphrey, 5; Schechner, xiii). York's ambitious theatrical undertaking was truly a cycle in the sense that it required almost continuous planning and pre-production as well as actual production. Multiple REED references to "pagiaunt" funding, negotiations and arrangements can be found dating from every month of the year, confirming that, for around two centuries, theater production was an ongoing year-round preoccupation in York.

Women's direct involvement with the guild infrastructure of funding, supporting and producing the plays is clearly recorded in REED documents. Financial contributions from women appear in accounts of payments and receipts enabling annual production of each guild's own pageant in the cycle. The Drapers' Guild received "paiaunt money" from "dame margaret dawson wydo" in 1523 (Johnston and Rogerson, 231).[3] The Bakers' Guild recorded contributions of "pagaunt money" from a suburban "clyffton wyffe" in 1547 and from two wives, "uxor burnleder" (literally, "the wife of a water-drawer") and "uxor Thomson" in 1571 (291, 364). Working women not registered as guild members also made involuntary financial contributions to pageant production since each guild was assigned additional pageant funding from fines paid by those in relevant occupations. For example, in 1564, "Inholders" who had paid fines that contributed to "the sustentacion of the ... pagiant" are specifically identified as both females and males (344).

Women's engagement in the mechanics of pageant production and staging is also recorded. Women were certainly accorded responsibility for stage properties; a dispute between the linen and the woollen weavers in 1540 named the wives or widows of the woollen weavers in joint financial considerations for the provision of torches (J&R, 269). These stage properties were crucial to successful atmospheric night-time performance of both guilds'

---

2 The plays ran from *The Creation of Heaven and Earth* to *The Last Judgement*. Particular pageants were permanently assigned to individual guilds, apparently according to congruence of topic and guild means.

3 Unless otherwise stated, all references to the York records are to page numbers in Alexandra Johnston and Margaret Rogerson's REED volume for York, hereafter called J&R.

pageants, *The Burial of the Virgin* and *The Assumption of the Blessed Virgin*, staged at the end of the cycle. This example also reinforces an emerging national pattern of evidence identifying plays about the Virgin Mary with "women's guilds," meaning those with high female membership (Goldberg 1997; Ryan).

The inhabitants of York also played key roles as spectators. A wagon-based restaging of the Cycle in 2002 confirmed the intensity of the city's transition into an open-air polyphonic dramatic arena whose dense medieval urban topography affords pre-eminence to performances in progress along the winding ceremonial route. Women played an important documented role in the annual reception of performances. Reimbursement in 1552 to Isabell Ruttre of Conystreet (a central performance station) "fir hous dressing" (J&R, 305) illustrates women's financial and artistic involvement with set dressing, open-air staging and audience placement. Invested with dramatic, religious, and civic significance, the Corpus Christi cycle offered the opportunity for highly visible audience engagement. Important women spectators were literally on show during performances, when overhanging upper house storeys provided superior viewpoints. Pageant protocols gave special priority to the "Lady Mayoress and her sisters," as significant civic audience members, by assigning them to a particular performance station at no charge every year (224, 228, 264, 314).

It was more common for spectators to pay for the privilege of a good view. Probable financial advantage as well as prestige accrued to citizens who could afford to invest in leasing a performance station at which each pageant would stop. Women who successfully leased stations include "the wife of Wharton" in 1506 (J&R, 202); "Dame Agnes Staveley, widow" in 1522 (228/823); "Widow Bekwyth" in 1526 (240/831) and "Wydoe Glasyn" in 1541 (278). Performance stations were usually fixed and defined by street location, so the 1538 performance station designation "at my lady wyldes" suggests particular female influence (264).

Other appearances of the term "wife" (Latin, *uxor*) in York records may offer potential evidence of further female dramatic activity (Goldberg 1992, 319). Variously indicating civic, employment, or marital status, "wife" appears to elide identities including: female dignitary, working woman, widow who continued her husband's trade, widow, or married woman (Goldberg 1992, 319). The term might therefore indicate a wider range of female pageant involvement consequent on guild membership than hitherto recognized, helping to illuminate references such as the Bakers' guild's repeated gratuities for unspecified reasons to "thold wyffes [the old wives]" (J&R, 559, 562). The term "wives" appears most suggestively in relation to female pageant production in the Chester play cycle's (now lost) *Annunciation* pageant, sponsored by the unidentified "Worshipful Wives," which may exemplify women's overall responsibility for a particular play.

Denise Ryan speculatively identifies these Chester wives as civic figures (Ryan, 149–76).

As these examples suggest, theatrical and civic events shared certain overlapping performative features. Civic ceremonies such as processions appear increasingly to have occupied a partial interface between performance and ceremonial, as the Corpus Christi cycle declined. York records of women's regular involvement in formal public processions and feasting on pageant and saints' days, evidenced by refreshments provided "aswell to the ladies as to the men" (J&R, 327) suggest some commonalities between cultural and civic stagings (310, 321, 326). It is often unclear in York records whether the term "procession" is primarily performance-oriented or ceremonial. Close congruence between women's roles in both is suggested by the fact that, in Winchester, the "wives" processed with the craft guilds at Corpus Christi (Ryan, 151–2). Similarly, in Lincolnshire, Stokes characterizes women as "integral participants in the mimetic civic spectacle" (Stokes, this volume, 32).

Scholars continue to debate whether women performed in medieval drama. Despite a lack of conclusive evidence that only men acted, musicologist Richard Rastall and performance historian and practitioner Meg Twycross support the longstanding critical view that women did not perform in medieval cycle plays (Rastall, 308–27; Twycross, 43). Urban historian Jeremy Goldberg argues against this presupposition. He posits an active interrelationship between women's economic roles and status as workers and craft guild members, both as wives and widows, and their consequent involvement with the pageants which constituted the important public and ceremonial face of the guilds (Goldberg 1992, 145–8; 1997, 145). Since guild membership in York expressly included annual commitment to pageant production, female guild members would also have participated in a variety of ways, in addition to the range of documented examples already discussed. By way of useful comparison, in the nearby county of Lincolnshire's less lavish pageant production tradition, Stokes cites examples of women's "co-equal" involvement in both guild activities and performance (this volume, 25). Goldberg identifies significant congruence in York between patterns of female guild membership and the inclusion of women's roles in pageants produced by particular guilds as a basis to argue for the possibility of women performing. He tabulates female roles within each pageant, arguing that the number of these roles "whether played by males or females, reflects the actual profile of women within the crafts and craft gilds" (Goldberg 1997, 147–8).

Recent research-based stagings of medieval drama have significantly advanced understanding of the plays in performance (Beadle 1982, 363–4). In such productions, women actors' successful and moving portrayals of gender-sensitive scenarios, such as pregnancy or maternal bereavement, further invite speculation that women may have acted. Childbirth and related matters were sharply designated female spheres in medieval culture; consequently, it may have been indecorous for a male actor to play either the pregnant Virgin Mary or Mary the Mother, who makes frequent reference to her womb. In the Lincolnshire town of Boston, a woman played "Regina" (possibly Mary, the Queen of Heaven) in the pageant by the Guild of the Blessed Virgin Mary (Stokes, this volume, 32). Undoubtedly, plays about the Virgin Mary were consistently associated nationally with women's guild involvement. For example, the York Drapers' Guild, with exceptionally high female membership, was responsible for the femino-centric *Death of the Virgin* (Goldberg 1997, 161–3).

The tumultuous religious reforms of the period enforced the end of the York Corpus Christi cycle; the last recorded complete performance was in 1569, though pageant traditions continued for a while in different forms. A "Paternoster" play (now lost) was performed until 1572; in 1584 and 1585 a Midsummer "play" or "interlude" integrating selected Corpus Christi pageants was watched by a civic party including "Ladys" (J&R, 410). Community commitment is emphasized by the city council's unsuccessful 1579 petition for revival of the cycle (Beckwith, 124). Women were involved in the dramatic transition as evidenced by payment in 1594 "to the minstrelles at my Ladye Richardson house where the old Searchers [Pageant masters] made their last feast" (460). Though cycle performance eventually ceased, it is important to stress the considerable length of time both the texts and associated production traditions might survive in individual and in community memory. Two factors seem important here: the active training of memory through oral learning and transmission of the rhyming speeches of the plays by actors, and the massive collective experience of, and investment in, the coordinated city-wide theatrical enterprise. Michael O'Connell uses Shakespeare, who is most likely to have known the Coventry cycle, as a possible measure for the impact and survival of mystery plays after the Reformation: "Shakespeare's references to elements of the plays suggest that they remained a general cultural memory some two or three decades after they ceased being performed" (484). Arguably the shared culture and first-hand pageant experience of the citizens of York generated profound and long-lasting memories over a significant period.

Alison Findlay has argued that "in Lancashire, the most Catholic county in England, women's performance often had a specifically spiritual dimension" (see this essay, 51). York also became a significant center of gendered recusancy, resistance, and performance in the 1570s and 1580s. York Castle became a major prison center where recusants from the Yorkshire region were held, tried and executed. Instead of the annual pageant cycle that had formerly filled the streets of York and engaged the energies of its citizens, the regular arrival, sensational activities, and punishment of Catholic recusants became the new spectacle. Many local citizens were active in resisting the new religion, women to a greater extent than men. The Jesuit priest Father John Mush, Margaret Clitherow's biographer, wrote "the gentlemen hereabouts had fallen away from the priests but the gentlewomen stood steadfastly to them" (40). Religion generated household gender divisions as men converted to Protestantism, while their wives remained Catholic and were fined accordingly. An intriguing variety of domestic dramas around household authority played out in York's churches, law courts, streets and prisons. In 1577, Ann Kitchinman attended church only when her husband "dragged her thither by force" (Aveling, 187). In Lord Mayor John Dineley's case, the court's public response to his wife's recusancy comprised a didactic comedy when he was "lectured on his position; a man who is set to govern a city and cannot govern his own household" (Aveling, 176).

Taking two Catholic recusant women of York, Margaret Clitherow and Anne Foster, as brief case studies, I suggest that dramatic influences and performance strategies from the plays explicitly and intentionally survived in the public behavior of women in York after the cycle was banned. Whether or not women performed in the cycle, a number of Catholic recusant women appear to have self-consciously refashioned the immediate memory and theatrical inheritance of the Corpus Christi cycle, particularly the Passion sequence of plays, as a script to enact their own forms of public bodily resistance to Protestantism and actively to generate a paradigm for martyrdom. Many of these women experienced imprisonment, in dreadful conditions, in Ouse Bridge prison, which stands on the traditional Corpus Christi pageant route. They appear to have figured this central symbolic location as a fortuitous and congruent staging element in their collective re-enactments of dramas of martyrdom.

Religious martyr and butcher's wife Margaret Clitherow (c.1556–86), who was executed at York Castle, is probably the best known York Catholic, but many other local women were punished, imprisoned or died in captivity, including Dorothy Vavasour, Anne Foster, Isabel Foster, Anne Tesh, Mary Hutton, Anne Launder, Elizabeth Cottard, Eleanor Hunt, Anne Thwing, Anne Warcup, and Margaret and Frances Webster. Like Clitherow, many of these women had Protestant husbands. Margaret Clitherow's story was most fully and immediately publicized, through the hagiographic life written and published within a year of her execution by Father John Mush. Clitherow was prosecuted for recusancy and refused either to conform or to plead; in 1596 she chose to be pressed to death rather than recognize the court's authority. Mush insistently structures his biography around dramatic metaphors which explicitly invoke memories of the Corpus Christi cycle: "this tragedy," "this pageant." Furthermore, Clitherow's stylized quasi-theatrical behavior involving costume, flamboyant gesture, and verbal defiance through silence during her trial, imprisonment and execution offered a self-conscious theater of sacrifice which also appears consciously modelled on elements of the York cycle, specifically Christ's trial and Passion.[4] Clitherow had multiple opportunities for contact with plays from her childhood to the cycle's final performances in the 1570s. Both her birth family and her husband John Clitherow held civic roles directly connecting them with the cycle.[5] As a butcher, her husband was eligible to act or involve himself directly in a production of *The Death of Christ on Calvary*.[6] Their home in the Shambles was very close to the Pavement, the final performance station.

In the final stages of her life, Clitherow seems to have become increasingly confident about transcending gender through the religious symbolism of her death. She repeatedly refused a reprieve offered because of her possible pregnancy. Instead, she engaged proactively with the physical staging of her own death, adopting masculine symbolic roles. She sewed her own costume for her execution "like to an alb" (a male priest's vestment) with tapes to secure her hands in a cruciform position in which she chose to lie to be pressed to death, thereby literally re-enacting *Corpus Christi* – the body of Christ.

Other Catholic women enacted and staged visible bodily resistance in a range of strikingly theatrical ways, in life and even in death. Anne Foster, wife of the York Coroner and friend of Margaret Clitherow, was imprisoned for recusancy with her daughters in 1577. She died in Ouse Bridge prison in 1578, whereupon her body, in a manner which she must have pre-scripted with the support of her fellow female prisoners, became an extraordinary public spectacle. Her corpse was found holding in its hands a written document professing the Catholic faith, demanding Catholic burial, and refusing Protestant rites. This ingenious act of posthumous self-excommunication enraged and confounded the religious and civil authorities as it effectively prevented them from disposing of her body in any way.

In response to this religious stalemate, the Protestant authorities "most inhumanely caused the dead corpse to be brought out of prison and laid openly on the bridge in the common street for all the world to gaze and wonder at." In doing so they placed the body directly on the Corpus Christi route, close to one of the central traditional performance stations, which could not help but reactivate people's memories of the "Catholic" dramas staged there so recently.

---

4 See my detailed discussion of Clitherow's case in Findlay and Hodgson-Wright with Williams, 25–6.

5 Her father was appointed Sheriff of York in 1567; her stepfather subsequently held civic office and eventually became Lord Mayor of York. In 1571 she married John Clitherow, who became a bridgemaster, responsible for collecting pageant rents.

6 Historians have been puzzled by the exceptionally high incidence of recusancy and martyrdom among York butchers and their families (Aveling, 59, Connelly, 62–3; also see Caraman, 3–4). The intense familiarity of the butchers (and their wives) with the dominant Passion motif in the York cycle (Beckwith, 23) may well have influenced their symbolic actions and choices.

When summoned to answer for his dead wife, John Foster used his legal knowledge to successfully argue his own innocence, his loving duty to bury her, and her insignificance, seeing that "she was but a woman, and being now dead never could offend them anymore." Daringly, Foster then arranged for her to be secretly buried in the grave of a recent Catholic martyr, the Earl of Northumberland (Connelly, 80–1).

These case studies of two Catholic women powerfully suggest how the York cycle endured in memory to offer important and widely understood symbolic analogies and resources at a time of religious crisis. A fascinating aspect of female reappropriation and adaptation of the Passion is the way it allowed liberation from gender roles: in her dying, the female martyr could assume the privileged role of Christ, the role she could never play in live performance.

Given its spectacular longevity and centrality in York, the Corpus Christi cycle has tended to dominate both the records and research into early theater there. Accordingly, there is much less known about folk plays, civic ceremonials, and outdoor public performances, such as "ridings." Sometimes authorized, sometimes not, ridings were public processions on horseback, often involving costume or other symbolic display; these appear to have partially filled the gap left by the Corpus Christi cycle after 1569. Sheriffs' ridings and spectacular civic armored ridings during religious festivals or saints' days functioned as ceremonial displays of civic or territorial authority, but they could also embody elements of carnival or misrule.[7] In 1554, "The Riding of St George" had included payments to "the king & Quene that playd" (J&R, 318). Archbishop Grindal's religious injunctions in 1570–6 against lay dramatic activities were tailored to local circumstances, prohibiting particular regional practices. Accordingly, in addition to the national prohibition of "sommer Lords or ladyes," the York ban specifically indicts the "notable and antient spectacle" of Yule and Yule's wife, a "very undecent and uncomely" riding which was flourishing around 1570, presumably, when the text was published in broadsheet, but which was banned as "a very rude and barbarouse custome" by 1572 (J&R, 358, 359–62, 369; White, 28). Whether "Yule's wife" was played by a woman is unclear; Eileen White suggests that both actors were disguised men (28). Notably, however, narrative commentary incorporated into the Yule broadside pays particular and sympathetic attention to the symbolism of the spectacle in relation to women's roles: "The very Rocke [distaff], sheweth that women laying aside their seruile works, must make good preparation for this solemne feast" (J&R, 359–62). As it becomes available, further evidence will

---

7   See Humphrey, chapter 3, for a very full discussion of different ways of reading and understanding ridings, taking "Gladman's riding" of 1443 in Norwich as a case study.

contribute to a fuller picture of women's participation in early dramatic activity in York.

Lancashire and the Northwest (Alison Findlay)

The Lancashire records contain no payments to women performers in their own right, although Ellen Nowell and "the wife of John Clarke, piper" were paid fees for his playing (George, 14–15), and there is a single, intriguing reference to the burial of "Ellen Thropp, Mr Atherton's fool" (244).[8] Women from the great houses, such as Lady Shuttleworth and Lady Charlotte Strange, made payments to players they appointed, but for evidence of female performances we must look beyond the commercial arena. This may be typical across England, but in Lancashire, the most Catholic county in England, women's performance often had a specifically spiritual dimension. We glimpse their participation in community dramas through the records of punishments and permits produced by a bureaucracy striving to keep the peace between different religious groups, and with the Crown.

Rushbearing, a ceremonial decoration of the Church on the patronal Saint's day, was associated with the female community and with the Old Religion. In 1603 in Burnley "the maid servantes and women Children within the said Chappellries ... have used and still doe use upon some sonday or holiday in the sommer tyme yerly to Carie and bring burdens of Rushes into there masters ffathers mothers mistresses and dames seates" (Baldwin, 32). As a legacy of Catholic holy days, these ceremonies, often accompanied by music, dancing, and refreshments, frequently angered Puritan reformers and brought punishments until they were re-authorized in 1617–18. In 1590, for example, Margaret Yat and Contance Eccles were presented at the Preston Sessions for rushbearing on 12 July (George, 297–8). Clerical Visitation articles by Archbishop Grindal and his successors forbade "sommer Lordes, or Ladies," and "disguised persons" at "Rishbearings," or at May Games, "or at anye other times, to come unreverently into the church or churchyard, and there to daunce, or playe any unseemely partes" during services (212). Women's participation in Sunday folk entertainments was read as recusancy. In July 1588, a group including eight women (a wife, four sisters named Goddard, and three individuals), were presented for leading "a Lamentable spectacle in the place of a preachinge ministry" in Bury (8–9). Details of the "spectacle" are not clear from the tangled account, but since it happened at the time of divine service, it clearly constituted sabbath-breaking. In neighboring Cheshire, where

---

8   Unless otherwise stated, all references to the Lancashire Records are to page numbers in George, *Records of Early English Drama: Lancashire*.

surveillance was more lenient (probably because recusancy was less of a problem), the extent of women's subversive participation can be seen. Elizabeth Symme, aided by David Wilkinson, dressed one Richard Coddington in women's apparel in her father's alehouse and then made him process through the streets, accompanied by a "great trayne" of people, to bring a present of cherries to Church Hill, "where shee sate as Ladye of the game ready to receive them" (Baldwin, 37). These are precisely the "unseemly parts" Grindal's directive was designed to eliminate.

James I noted the deadlock between "Papistes and Puritanes" with which the county was "infected" on his progress through Lancashire in 1617, and attempted to amend the abuse of orders by granting permission for "lawfull recreations" on Sunday afternoons (after divine service) and holidays. His "Declaration Concerning Lawful Sports" granted "the women leave to Carrie rushes to ye Church for the decoringe of it according to theire ould Custome," but carefully pointed out "wee barr from this benifitt & lib[ertie] all such knowne recusants" (qtd in George, 229–30). The Westminster declaration of 1618 also permitted May Games and maypoles, Whitsun ales and morris dancing. Presumably the "Country song" with its detailed picture of May-time dancing where "maydes buttocks quaked / lyke Custards new baked" recalls the restoration of this "harmeless mirth of Lancashyre" (32–5).

Cunning women often adopted Catholic terminology in their charms and, at the extreme of the spiritual spectrum, their performances were labelled as witchcraft (Bardell, 2002). Like Margaret Clitherow's trial in York, the 1612 Lancashire witch trial was a gruesome form of theater in which women played center stage in a courtroom. Nine-year-old Jennet Device gave a bravura performance, standing on a table to testify against her family, and reciting a thirty-one-line incantation supposedly used by her mother, Elizabeth Device, to cure those bewitched. As Jonathan Mumby observes, the prayer's form "is that of a religious drama," replaying Catholic rituals for Maundy Thursday, the "White Pater Noster" and Good Friday (Mumby, 97). In Jennet's performance it was reiterated as incriminating evidence. She heightened the drama by picking out those she accused in identity parades. Their confessions, read back like a script in the courtroom, are a dramatized example of what Carolyn Steedman has called "the autobiographical injunction," an enforced self-narrative built on a history of expectations, orders and instructions (28).[9]

In contrast, a clear example of woman's power to claim a public stage and defy official attempts to criminalize her performance is seen in the Quaker prophet Dorothy Waugh. She was moved by the spirit to appear alone on the market cross in Carlisle, "to speak against all deceit and ungodly practices,"

---

9   For discussion of the second witch craze of 1634, see Alison Findlay, "The Late Lancashire Witches: Sexual and Spiritual Politics in the Events of 1633–4," in Poole.

but was imprisoned by the Mayor, forced to wear a scold's bridle as punishment for her inappropriate oration, and then offered as a form of entertainment to those willing to pay two pence to see her in prison (Waugh, 1656). As Hilary Hinds has shown, although the Mayor tried to confine and commodify Waugh as spectacle, he lost control of the drama when her pitiful appearance moved her audience to tears. The sorry sight she presented implicitly demonized him instead of her, and in an attempt to counter this paradoxical reading, he was obliged to expel her from the city wearing the bridle.

At the top of the social scale in Lancashire, women's performances rivaled those of their contemporaries in London. The Stanley Household was popularly known as "the northern court," patronizing two groups of professional players, and acting as a touring stop for other all-male professional troupes. As in the royal court, however, there was a tradition of female performance in masques.[10] The French Huguenot Charlotte de la Tremouille, wife of the seventh Earl, brought with her the continental tradition of female performance and played one of Chloris's nymphs in the Queen's masque, *Chloridia* (1631). Charlotte's Huguenot background distanced her from Henrietta Maria, however, and the Stanley homes in Lancashire provided an alternative court for masquing (Bagley, 78–80). A Christmas masque by Sir Thomas Salusbury was performed for the royalists Lord James and Lady Charlotte at Knowsley House on Twelfth Night 1641 by their children, members of the household and neighbors. In the words of the masque, the performance represented the triumph of "hollidayes" in the face of Puritan attempts to banish such "superstitious raggs of Popery," so echoing the Lancashire tradition of summertime community performances associated with the Old Religion (George, 257, lines 20–2).[11]

The ladies of the household enacted the summer months of the New Year, beginning with James and Charlotte's eldest daughter, Henrietta Maria. Her role as Aprill, "evergrowing blisse, perpetuall springe" (263, line 31), was well suited to her state as a virginal child-bride, betrothed to Lord Molyneux (who performed February). The masque celebrates female fertility as a means of renewal in the uncertain days of strife between King and Parliament. Aprill says her parents bless the household "as the teeminge earth / now glads the halfe starv'd world, with a new birth / of long lost sweets" (263, lines 33–5). The

---

10 Countess Alice (married to Ferdinando, fifth Earl of Derby, and then to Sir Thomas Egerton) and Countess Elizabeth (née Vere and wife of the sixth Earl) both performed in royal masques.

11 "A Masque as it was presented at ye right honourable ye Lord Strange his at Knowsley," lines 20–2. The masque is printed as Appendix 4 in George, 252–66. For further discussion see Dutton, Findlay and Wilson.

figures of May, June and July, enacted by friends of the family, expand the scope of warm praise and adoration to the neighboring community: "All seasons bee to you as faire as wee" (264, lines 4, 8). The Stanleys' role in providing "bounteous hospitality" (264, line 27) is imaged in specifically maternal terms in the role of August, acted by Mrs. Mesieur, a French companion of Lady Charlotte. August's abundant harvest ensures "the Seasons all by mee are fed" (264, line 21), while September, the "Ladie of the Vintage," pours blessings on the couple, cursing any who "doe not say Amen" (265, line 1). In spite of class differences, the aristocratic female performers articulate the spirit of traditional communal festivity that fueled their lower-class counterparts in summer rites such as rushbearings and May Games.

The ladies' words were penned by Sir Thomas Salusbury, but the masque is particularly fascinating since it contains an example of active female intervention. The manuscript records "Iulyes part chang'd at the request of the faire representer of that Month" (264). Mrs E. Duckenfield, who played July, originally had only a couplet where she "bestowes / her best and earliest fruits" on spectators (264, lines 18–19). We do not know what hand she had in the new lines, but they provide a striking contrast to the rather bland blessing of the original:

> Bright Summers glory, July comes to pay
> Her full ripe Cherryes, those of June and May
> that did prevent her gift, and came before
> were taken pale, halfe colour'd from her store
> But theise are red, sweete, swelling in theire pride
> As tempting lipps of the expecting Bride,
> Or those that open to pronounce you blisse
> Then seale it with a chast, and mutuall Kisse.
>   (265–6, lines 39ff.)

Whether these lines were intended to allude to Henrietta Maria Stanley, the "expecting Bride" or to the performer herself, their candid eroticism is remarkable. They suggest the self-confidence of regional noblewomen, a willingness to exploit their physical attributes in performance.

The Stanleys' second court on the Isle of Man was also the site of entertainments following the royal model, even more appropriately so since the title of King of Man was held by the successive Earls of Derby. Thomas Parr's account of the Twelfth Night masque of 1644–5 at Castle Rushen indicates that the performers were a dazzling spectacle of royalist wealth. Lord Strange and his courtiers and "the right honourable Ladies with theire attendance were most gloriously decked with silver and gould broidered workes & most Costly ornaments bracelletts on there hands chaines on there neckes Jewels on there foreheads, earrings in there eares & Crownes on their heads" (George, 281). Given that the Stanleys were forced to retreat to the Isle of Man as Lancashire was lost to the Parliamentarian forces (Bagley, 99), the masque with its "gloriously decked" ladies was a deliberate political intervention. Their display of pomp, especially the jewels and "Crownes on their heads" constituted an arrogant, beautiful and fragile reassertion of royalist courtly culture.

The Castle Rushen masque may tempt us to regard the drama of noblewomen as utterly different from the practices of their non-elite sisters, but a final example from the end of the period reminds us that it is unwise to make absolute divisions. Quaker Margaret Fell transformed her patriarchal family household at Swarthmoor into a center for Friends' meetings, in which men and women had equal freedom to speak. Alongside such radical independence, Margaret exploited traditionally feminine, spectacular methods of self-presentation, not dissimilar from the masquing ladies in Castle Rushen.[12] In 1658, John Thurloe noted that she "hath liberty to were satins and silver and gold lase, and is a great gallant" (Thurloe, 165). In spite of the plainness associated with the Quaker calling, Margaret Fell invoked the power of upper-class identity to help her speak for the Quaker people, presenting herself to Charles II with the declaration "And now I am here to answer what can be objected against us on the behalf of many thousands ... who was moved of the Lord to leave my house and family, and to come two hundred miles to lay these things before you" (Fell, 1660). Although not moved by the same spirit, women across a range of geographical and religious positions in Lancashire and the northwest, produced performances in which recreation was bound up with the practice of belief.

Gloucestershire (Stephanie Hodgson-Wright)

Gloucestershire's varied geography meant that its development in the medieval and early modern period was somewhat precocious. The Cotswold Hills were given over to pastoral farming, and the Stroudwater Valleys were ideally suited to the various processes involved in cloth manufacture. In our period the region was the foremost in the manufacture of and trade in cloth. Furthermore, the Forest of Dean was a site of early mining, charcoal production, and produced a significant proportion of England's iron (Rollison 1992, 22; see also Johnson 1985, 14–28). John Wycliffe and William Tyndale were both highly influential Gloucestershiremen, and, as Rollison argues, the early processes of industrialization and commercialization "were related to the rise of Puritan pastoral disciplines. They were developments of the principle that the function

---

12   See Davies, 225–8 on this contradiction.

of industry was to provide work for, and thus to provide a means of disciplining, the burgeoning class of landless people" (Rollison 1992, 37; see also Johnson 1989, 28–76)[13]. The strongly reformist character of the region played a key role in making female performance more rarely documented than in post-Reformation York or Lancashire.

Lack of patrons was also a factor. Early records of dramatic activity in Gloucestershire feature women prominently: the Berkeley household gives us the earliest evidence of patronage of drama in the county, when in 1420–1421 Elizabeth, Countess of Warwick paid players from Slimbridge and Wotton and "two minstrels of Lady Abergavenny" to play at Berkeley Castle (Douglas and Greenfield, 395),[14] and a century later, at Thornbury Castle, seat of Edward Stafford, Duke of Buckingham, a lavish Christmas entertainment included "certain frenshe men and ij frenshe women playing afore the said Duc the passion of oure lord by a vise and also to a yong maide a Tumbeller" (359). However, it is only in the early part of our period that women enjoy such prominence. By the mid-sixteenth century their involvement is less apparent, possibly because the nobility was poorly represented in the county, hence little local patronage was forthcoming and opportunities for elite household performances were limited. The Duke of Buckingham removed from the county altogether after his disgrace in 1521. Only the Berkeley and Brydges households kept companies of players, and neither appeared to involve women as patrons or players. The lack of resident noble families, together with Gloucestershire's religious and political tendencies towards Puritanism and the Parliamentary cause,[15] probably meant that there was neither means nor motivation to produce self-affirming entertainments such as those staged in more northerly counties (as discussed by Alison Findlay, above), and which give evidence of female involvement in performance.

Royal progresses, which might also afford women creative and performative opportunities, were also somewhat compromised by the county's lack of suitable hosts. Queen Elizabeth visited Gloucestershire on three occasions, the first in 1572, involving a stay at Berkeley Castle. There is no record of a dramatic entertainment; hunting seems to have been the main attraction. In 1574 the record of the Queen's entertainment in the city

---

13 I am indebted to my PhD student, Sarah Lowe, for drawing my attention to this
    important work.
14 All references to Gloucestershire records, unless otherwise noted, are from the
    REED volume edited by Audrey Douglas and Peter Greenfield, hereafter D&G.
15 Johnson argues that the county was fairly evenly divided by the outbreak of war,
    and that both sides were anxious to control it, hence armies from both sides were
    heavily present (1989, 77).

is confined to a list of payments, totalling £128/3s/3d (D&G, 305), none made to a female worker. The county found the next progress less expensive; in 1592 Lord Chandos was paid £6/13s/4d for relieving the city of the cost of receiving Elizabeth during her progress (312). The Queen's stay with Lord Chandos at Sudeley Castle leaves us the only text of a dramatic performance in the county. Whether the entertainment was performed by Lord Chandos's own players, or by members of his household, is unclear. However, we must consider the likelihood of the latter, especially in light of similar entertainments at Harefield in 1602, given by Alice, Countess of Derby for Elizabeth I's last progress, and at Ashby in 1607, given for the Countess herself by her daughter, the Countess of Huntington (see Erler, 4–21 and Knowles, 489–90). At Sudeley, Elizabeth heard a play that mixed folk custom and local knowledge with classical mythology: an Old Shepherd welcomes the Queen on the first day and presents her with a "lock of wooll, Cotsholdes [Cotswolds] best fruite" (D&G, 349). Next, another Shepherd narrates a dumbshow of Daphne fleeing from Apollo and turning into a tree, adding his own lament that the god is encroaching upon his territory. He asks the Queen to look upon the tree so that her gaze will restore Daphne and revive Apollo's sense of justice; this duly happens and Apollo resigns his right to the Shepherd. But Daphne refuses to be given away, and runs to the Queen for protection, saying "whether should chastety fly for succour, but to the Queene of chastety, by thee [spoken presumably to Apollo] was I enterred in a tree, that by crafte, way might be made to lust, by your highness [to Elizabeth] restored, that by vertue, there might be assurance to honor" (352).

The focus on chastity is not especially surprising in an entertainment for Elizabeth I; nor is the illusion of continuity between simple shepherds and the elaborate entertainment in which they are represented. This sense of organic wholeness is challenged when Daphne emerges from the tree and claims this has been a *means to facilitate* Apollo's use of her body rather than prevent it. She is changed from one commodity with use-value into yet another, as any resident of the county boasting the Forest of Dean would be only too well aware. That this territory was simultaneously an exclusive royal hunting ground, but also occupied and worked by numerous unauthorized "foresters," makes the dispute between Apollo and the Shepherd particularly pertinent. Anxieties over political, economic and social control are metaphorically brought together in a reworking of the Daphne myth which judiciously maintains the royal privilege over the land, but subversively confounds the actual exchange of the female body between men. The dramatic *frisson* would have been heightened if one of the women of the Sudeley household had played Daphne. To some extent the performance would have dramatized her own status in the dynastic marriage market, in a manner similar to (if less complex than) the self-dramatization of Elizabeth Brackley and Jane Cavendish in *The*

Pastorall (see Findlay and Hodgson-Wright with Williams, 72–4), thereby giving Daphne's plea to Elizabeth a potential relevance beyond the immediate theatrical context.

Of course such a dramatic gesture is only possible when Queen Elizabeth is the monarch, but perhaps this is an indication of the extent to which her presence in the county disrupted its dominant practices and ideologies, especially the use of the marriage market to further the ambitions of local families. Anxiety about control over women's bodies is the feature that links the few instances in which women are cited in the records. In the case of Katherine Haselton against Dorothy Dorney for defamation in 1611–12, the witness Alice Arthure deposed that Dorney said Hasleton "was naught at Harsecome vpon a Bedd and that one Bond a Musitian did play at the bedes feete in the meane tyme" (D&G, 331). In Tewkesbury in 1600–1601, the occasion of the Christmas play is the context for an assignation between Margery Hodges and John Hazard; on discovery she offers to pay £5 or £3 and a gold ring "to saue her honestye" (342). The behavior of Hodges and Hazard may have been especially worrying because Tewkesbury's drama is exclusively associated with the Church. Singularly, apart from a large theatrical event in Whitsun week of 1600, at which several plays were staged in the abbey (now the cathedral) (340–2), the evidence mainly comprises records of payments to the churchwarden for the hire of the abbey's own costumes by external parties. This may indicate a flourishing tradition of local drama in Tewkesbury, and one in which women may have participated. If, as Stokes argues we should, we extrapolate evidence from other nearby counties, such as Somerset and Lincolnshire, then women's involvement as players can be considered *probable* as opposed to merely possible.

While we can assume that women participated in Christmas celebrations, May Games, and Whitsun ales throughout the county, the extent of such activities is unclear. In Littledean in 1601–2, eight women and three men were cited for dancing during the church service, and two men for playing the pipe and tabor to accompany them (D&G, 331–3). In light of the Visitation Articles of 1607, 1612, 1622, and 1624, which seem more concerned with entertainment of any kind encroaching upon Church property or time (345–6), we may conclude that the Littledean citation results from the inappropriate time of the dancing, rather than the participants or the dance itself and therefore that such activities occurred unnoticed at other times. Stokes reminds us that "[r]esistance to the traditional involvement by women in parish drama and play seems only to have begun gradually after the onset of the Reformation" (Stokes 1993, 184). Clearly, the particular conditions obtaining in Gloucestershire meant that the county had experienced such a shift in attitudes relatively early. The records show three clerics, Christopher Windle, Michael Hyndemer and John Wilmot, falling into disfavor for their more liberal views. Wilmot is cited for taking part in a cushion dance (usually part of a wedding celebration)[16] in which he "kneeled downe as the order of the dawnce is, and kissed one goodwife Hickes" (D&G, 343). Once again a woman's reputation is compromised, and entertainment is associated with lewdness.

While locally provided entertainment seems scant in the period, during the sixteenth century Gloucester received visits from numerous professional troupes from around the country. From 1550 to 1602 there are records of at least one performance per year taking place at the Bothall. Women's recorded involvement here is as patrons; visits by the Duchess of Suffolk's players in 1562–3 (299), Lady Manche's (Mountjoy's) players in 1571–2 (302), the Countess of Essex's players in 1578–9 (306) are recorded, as are frequent visits by Queen Mary's and Queen Elizabeth's players. Such visits were carefully regulated, as indicated by ordinances of 1580–1581 (307) and 1590–1591 (311). In his *Mount Tabor, or Private Exercises of a Penitent Sinner* (1639), R. Willis gives an account of seeing a stage play in Gloucester when he was a child; he also summarizes the usual practice of civic regulation:

> When Players of Enterludes come to towne, they first attend the Mayor to enforme him what noble-mans servants they are, and so to get licence for their publike playing; and if the Mayor like the Actors, or would shew respect to their Lord and Master, he appoints them to play their first play before himselfe and the Aldermen and common Counsell of the City. (quoted in D&G, 362–3)

Significantly, the play approved in 1580–1581 involves a Prince led astray by three ladies who turn out to be Pride, Covetousness, and Luxury (363–4). While this performance is clearly given by professional players, the anxieties about women that it dramatizes are entirely in keeping with the attitudes displayed in the records of locally produced entertainments discussed above.

Commercial theatrical activity in Gloucestershire declined with the increasing centralization initiated by James VI and I and continued by Charles I, and there is no record of any company of players from the Stuart royal household visiting the city. Furthermore, the particular nature of the records may also determine the paucity of recorded female involvement. Gloucestershire was dominated by the highly bourgeois city of Gloucester (as opposed to the county nobility) and sustained by a combination of well-developed industrial and commercial bases; these factors, together with the county's early and comprehensive acceptance of the Reformed Church, meant that Gloucestershire was relatively homogeneous and modernized in our period. One of the consequences appears to be a documentary privileging of the economic and legal aspects of dramatic activity; as women's economic and legal status was

---

16   As defined by Stokes (1993, 178).

usually that of object rather than subject, their presence in such records is inevitably less apparent.

An interesting conundrum cited by Douglas and Greenfield provides an appropriate conclusion to this section. In 1574, Michael Hyndemer, rector of Weston Subedge, admits to the accusation by John Castle that "in a Christmas Hollydayes he went a masking & yat there was ann egge brok" (344). Intriguingly, the editors of the volume suggest two interpretations of "ann egge brok": a woman's name, Anne Edgebrook, or an indication that an egg was broken in the proceedings (430). That one piece of evidence might equally signify a woman's presence at a masking or the destruction of a foodstuff returns us to that interpretative battleground on which the categories of woman and commodity are confused and conflated; other than at Sudeley in 1592, in Gloucestershire it seems that Daphne remained stuck in her tree.

Conclusion

In spite of the differences between our three locations, it is clear that religion was a key feature governing women's involvement with dramatic production. York's civic productions constituted an imposing religious celebration which officially involved female members of the community in the production, and possibly, performance of the plays. In contrast, the examples from Lancashire and Gloucestershire are of rituals and related performances marginalized by the official authorities of Church and local government after the Reformation. Women's participation in ales, rushbearing or sabbath-breaking festivities brought punishments encouraged by the more extreme Protestant factions in these regions.

Our lines of enquiry into a range of different performances have also raised common questions about performance spaces. The examples of Margaret Clitherow, Jennet Device, and Dorothy Waugh demonstrate how courtrooms, the prison, and even the marketplace could be constructed as theaters by women. Outdoor performances such as dancing, or Elizabeth Symme's costumed procession to a Cheshire churchyard, remind us that women's dramatic activity was not confined to the closet or household. At the same time, they show how these open spaces – undoubtedly because of their public character – were the subject of critical surveillance.

We also need to take into account the importance of women's role as producers rather than performers. The examples of royal or noblewomen as patrons of professional companies in the records remind us that regional touring was an important means of projecting a powerful female image. Although nothing held the same power as the Queen's physical presence, as in her visit to Sudeley, Gloucestershire, the arrival of a company of players patronized by a woman effectively advertised her influence and prestige. In the case of the Corpus Christi plays in York, we have an impression of female producers with a close knowledge of the material workings of theater.

When comparing the studies of the three individual locations, it becomes clear that women's involvement in dramatic activity in England between 1500 and 1645 is inextricably connected to the politics of place. The legacies of local performance traditions are affected not only by broad national or international Reformation and Counter-Reformation movements, but also by the material circumstances and sympathies of members of the local communities. Alliances to a region could be far more compelling to early modern women than the abstract appeal of national identity. Examples from the City of York, Gloucestershire, and Lancashire all raise intriguing questions about female performances in group festivities, including the tantalizing possibility of their roles in Corpus Christi plays and local dramas. The encouragement or suppression of local drama was also dependent on the particular temper of those exercising authority: to patronize, license, permit, or punish the participants. Further research on evidence from other regions is now required to provide a much broader context of examples with which individual cases can be compared. Obviously regional differences must be taken into account, and we must acknowledge that lack of evidence may accurately reflect the absence of women from performances, but the advantages of building up a nationwide survey of women's regional dramatic activity are significant. It would allow us to develop a fuller picture of the shadowy figure of the female performer.

Works Cited and Consulted

Aveling, J. C. H. *Catholic Recusancy in the City of York*. Durham: Catholic Record Society, 1970.

Bagley, J. J. *The Earls of Derby 1485–1985*. London: Sidgwick and Jackson, 1985.

Baldwin, Elizabeth. "Rushbearings and Maygames in the Diocese of Chester before 1642." *English Parish Drama*. Ed. Alexandra F. Johnston and Wim Hüsken. Amsterdam: Rodopi, 1996, 21–40.

Bardell, Kristeen Macpherson. "Beyond Pendle: The 'Lost' Lancashire Witches." In Poole, 105–22.

Beadle, Richard, ed. *The York Plays*. London: Edward Arnold, 1982.

———. "The York Cycle." *The Cambridge Companion to Medieval English Theater*. Ed. Richard Beadle. Cambridge: Cambridge University Press, 1994, 85–108.

Beckwith, Sara. *Signifying God: Social Relations and Symbolic Act in the York Corpus Christi Plays*. Chicago and London: University of Chicago Press, 2001.

Caraman, Philip S. J. *Margaret Clitherow*. Parish of St. Wilfrid, York: Incorporated Catholic Truth Society, 1986.

Connelly, Roland. *Women of the Catholic Resistance in England 1540–1680*. Durham: Pentland Press, 1997.

Davies, Stevie. *Unbridled Spirits: Women of the English Revolution 1640–1660*. London: Women's Press, 1998.

Douglas, Audrey and Peter Greenfield. Eds. *Records of Early English Drama: Cumberland, Westmoreland, Gloucestershire*. [D&G.] Toronto: University of Toronto Press, 1986.

Dutton, Richard, Alison Findlay and Richard Wilson. Eds. *Region, Religion and Patronage: Lancastrian Shakespeare*. Manchester: Manchester University Press, 2004.

Erler, Mary C. " 'Chaste Sports, Juste Prayses, & all softe Delight': Harefield 1602 and Ashby 1607, Two Female Entertainments." *The Elizabethan Theatre: XIV*. Ed. A. L. Magnuson and C. E. McGee. Toronto: P. D. Meany, 1991, 1–25.

Evans, Ruth. "Body Politics: Engendering Medieval Cycle Drama." *Feminist Readings in Middle English Literature*. Ed. Ruth Evans and Lesley Johnston. London and New York: Routledge, 1994, 112–39.

Fell, Margaret. *A Declaration and Information from Us, The People Called Quakers, delivered by hand to Charles II, 22 April, 1660*. qtd. in *A Sincere and Constant Love: An Introduction to the Work of Margaret Fell*. Richmond, Indiana: Friends United Press, 1992, 49–55.

Findlay, Alison and Stephanie Hodgson-Wright, with Gweno Williams. *Women and Dramatic Production 1550–1700*. Harlow, UK: Pearson, 2000.

Fisher, Sheila and Janet E. Halley. "The Lady Vanishes: The Problem of Women's Absence in Late Medieval and Renaissance Texts." *Seeking the Woman in Late Medieval and Renaissance Writings: Essays in Feminist Contextual Criticism*. Ed. Sheila Fisher and Janet E. Halley. Knoxville: University of Tennessee Press, 1989, 3–17.

Forest-Hill, Lesley. *Transgressive Language in Medieval English Drama: Signs of Challenge and Change*. Aldershot, UK and Burlington, VT: Ashgate, 2000.

Gardiner, Harold C. *Mysteries' End*. New Haven: Yale University Press, 1946.

George, David. *Records of Early English Drama: Lancashire*. Toronto: University of Toronto Press, 1990.

Goldberg, P. J. P. *Women, Work, and Life Cycle in a Medieval Economy: Women in York and Yorkshire c. 1300–1520*. Oxford: Clarendon, 1992.

Goldberg, Jeremy. "The Craft Guilds, the Corpus Christi Play and Civic Government." *The Government of Medieval York: Essays in Commemoration of the 1396 Royal Charter*. Ed. Sarah Rees Jones. York: University of York, 1997, 141–63.

Hinds, Hilary. "Sectarian Spaces: The Politics of Place and Gender in Seventeenth-Century Sectarian Writing." *Literature and History* (forthcoming).

Humphrey, Chris. *The Politics of Carnival: Festive Misrule in Medieval England*. Manchester and New York: Manchester University Press, 2001.

Johnson, Joan. *Tudor Gloucestershire*. Gloucester: Alan Sutton & Gloucestershire County Library, 1985.

———. *The Gloucestershire Gentry*, Gloucester: Alan Sutton, 1989.

Johnston, Alexandra F. and Margaret Rogerson. Eds. *Records of Early English Drama: York*. [J&R.] Toronto: University of Toronto Press, 1979.

Knowles, James D. "Identifying the Speakers: 'The Entertainment at Ashby' (1607)." *Notes and Queries* 35.4 (1988): 489–90.

Mumby, Jonathan. *The Lancashire Witch-Craze: Jennet Preston and the Lancashire Witches, 1612.* Lancaster: Carnegie Publishing, 1995.

Mush, Father John. *A True Relation of the Life of Mrs Margaret Clitherow 1586.* In *The Troubles of our Catholic Forefathers Related by Themselves.* Ed. John Morris. London: Burns and Oates, 1877.

O'Connell, Michael. "Continuities between 'Medieval' and 'Early Modern' Drama." *A Companion to English Renaissance Literature and Culture.* Ed. Michael Hattaway. Oxford: Blackwell Publishing, 2000, 477–85.

Poole, Robert. Eds. *The Lancashire Witches: Histories and Stories.* Manchester: Manchester University Press, 2002.

Probyn, Elspeth. *Outside Belongings.* London: Routledge, 1996.

Rastall, Richard. *The Heavens Singing: Music in Early English Religious Drama.* Cambridge: D. S. Brewer, 1996.

Rollison, David. *The Local Origins of Modern Society: Gloucestershire 1500–1800.* London: Routledge, 1992.

Ryan, Denise. "Women, Sponsorship and the Early Civic Stage: Chester's Worshipful Wives and the Lost *Assumption* Play." *Research Opportunities in Renaissance Drama XL* Ed. Peter H. Greenfield. n.p.: University of Puget Sound, 2001, 149–75.

Schechner, Richard. *Performance Theory.* rev. edn. New York and London: Methuen Drama, 1988.

Smith, Brian and Elizabeth Ralph. *A History of Bristol and Gloucestershire.* 2nd edn. Phillimore & Co: Chichester, 1982.

Steedman, Carolyn. "Enforced Narratives: Stories of Another Self." *Feminism and Autobiography: Texts, Theories, Methods.* Ed. Tess Cosslett, Celia Lury and Penny Summerfield. London and New York: Routledge, 2000, 25–39.

Stokes, James. "Women and Mimesis in Medieval and Renaissance Somerset (and Beyond)." *Comparative Drama* 27.2 (1993): 176–96.

Thurloe, John. *State Papers of John Thurloe,* VIII (4), *Journal of the Friends Historical Society,* October, 1911.

Twycross, Meg. "The Theatricality of Medieval English Plays." *The Cambridge Companion to Medieval English Theater.* Ed. Richard Beadle. Cambridge: Cambridge University Press, 1994, 37–84.

Waugh, Dorothy. "A relation concerning Dorothy Waughs cruell usage by the Mayor of Carlile." *The Lambs Defence Against Lyes.* London: 1656.

White, Eileen. *Elizabethan York.* York: Yorkshire Architectural Society and York Archeological Society, 1989.

Acknowledgment: Gweno Williams wishes to thank Mike Tyler, Director of 2002 Guild Mystery Plays in York.

PART II
BEYOND ELITES

PART II
BEYOND ELITES

Chapter 4

The Case of Moll Frith: Women's Work and the "All-Male Stage"

Natasha Korda

Recent scholarship on women's involvement in theatrical production in early modern England has begun to question the paradigm of the "all-male stage." In focusing primarily on aristocratic women's roles as patrons, playwrights, and performers in court masques, however, such scholarship has left largely unexamined the roles of ordinary women in theatrical production, having considered such women mainly in their status as playgoers or consumers of theatrical commodities (see Bergeron, Howard, Levin, Neill, Nelson, and Westfall). A notable and oft-cited exception to this tendency is the historical figure of "Moll" or Mary Frith, who is recorded in the *Consistory of London Correction Book* in 1612 as having made an appearance "at the ffortune [theater]," where she sat "vppon the stage in the publique viewe of all the people there presente in mans apparrell & playd vppon her lute & sange a songe" (Mulholland, 31).[1] Moll, of course, had been the subject of Middleton and Dekker's *The Roaring Girl, or Moll Cut-Purse*, published in 1611, whose Epilogue famously promises the Fortune's audience, "The Roaring Girl herself, some few days hence, / Shall on this stage give larger recompense" (lines 35–6). While Frith's appearance at the Fortune provides a remarkable instance of an ordinary woman performing in a public theater, in retaining its exceptional status, this instance leaves undisturbed the generalized conception of an all-male stage.

In this paper, I would like to challenge Moll's exceptional status by suggesting that her classification as a player, cutpurse, and roaring-girl (the terms ordinarily used to situate her within the social order) only serves to mystify her quite unexceptional status as a worker within the networks of commerce surrounding early modern London's public theaters. Insofar as women appear to have worked within these networks in significant numbers

---

1 In original documents quoted here some words appear in abbreviated form, for example. "p[rese]nte." I have silently expanded such words rather than using italics or brackets.

(Lemire; Korda 1996, 2002), consideration of Moll's status as a "worker" may allow for a more thoroughgoing critique of the all-male stage than has that of her status as a "player." Such a critique will require that we broaden our focus beyond the purview of traditional stage history, however, to examine not only players and playhouses, but the heterogeneous forms of commerce that lent them support. For if we take into account the full range of social and economic interdependencies and collaborations that went into theatrical production, what emerges is a nexus of commerce between active economic agents of both genders. Within this nexus Moll is but one of many.

The title-page of the 1611 quarto edition of *The Roaring Girl* displays a woodcut of Moll in lavish "male" attire accompanied by the caption, "My case is alter'd, I must worke for my living." Critics of the play have hitherto read Moll's altered "case" in reference to her complex sexual and gendered identity as a cross-dressed player, but have neglected the ways in which that identity might be shaped by her stated exigency to work for her living. Within such readings, Moll stands as a figure for the practice of cross-dressing and for the gendered and sexualized discourses that subtend this practice (see Rose; Garber).[2] What such readings fail to address, however, is the relationship implied in Moll's motto between her altered case or cross-dressed persona, on the one hand, and her necessity to work, on the other. What, we might ask, moreover, *is* the nature of Moll's "work"? To begin to answer this question we will need to examine more carefully the relationship of the fictional "Moll" to the historical figure of Mary Frith, and the latter's place within the commercial landscape of early modern London. For it seems likely that the title-page motto, like the play's Epilogue, aims to capitalize on the notoriety of the historical Moll, and thereby to invest the fictional Moll with particular significance. If this is indeed the case, then the significance of Moll's motto (and in particular the relationship between her altered case and her exigency to

---

2   This is certainly not to suggest that Moll's reference to her "case" carries no sexual innuendo: the term was common slang for the female genitals in the period. The play repeatedly suggests that Moll's anatomical sex has been altered by her male apparel, as when Sir Alexander Wengrave declaims "Heyday, breeches! What, will [my son] marry a monster with two trinkets?" (2.2.76–7). Such lines indeed seem to beg for a Butleresque reading in which Moll's "sex" is constructed from the outside in and clothing is constitutive of identity. Garber offers such a reading when she argues that the play "theorizes the constructedness of gender in a disconcertingly literal way through the construction of bodies – and of clothes. The tailor makes the man (and the tail)" (224). In reading Moll's altered "case" in exclusively sexualized and gendered terms, however, criticism risks replicating the troubling sexualization of female labor that is so rampant in *The Roaring Girl*, and in early modern culture at large. Such readings thereby participate in the occlusion of the diverse forms of female labor that contributed to early modern theatrical production.

work) may be illuminated by the economic circumstances that led Mary Frith to perform "vppon the stage ... in mans apparrell."

Our knowledge of the particular characteristics of early modern women's work, Beverly Lemire argues, has been hampered not only by a dearth of documentary evidence but by our own unwillingness to look beyond "the standard male paradigms of employment" dictated by the guilds (118). Yet "historical evaluation should not end with the guildsman's assessment," for early modern working women "found work where they could, flourishing in *ad hoc* businesses" that were disapproved of by the guilds. These "'disorderly' commercial practices were as common as they were reviled," and formed a "vast network of commerce, which must be integrated into our concepts of the market" (Lemire, 120). The prominence of women working outside the guild structure within the informal networks of commerce that flourished in London's suburbs and Liberties is particularly intriguing in the present context, if we consider the importance of such commerce to the rising entertainment industry.

Recent scholarship has highlighted the commercial theaters' and playing companies' peculiar status as transitional economic formations, in certain respects retaining the residual structure of the guilds, while at the same time assuming the emergent form of innovative capital ventures (see Bristol, Ingram, Orgel, and Jones and Stallybrass). While many of those involved in the early entertainment industry sought status and protection by gaining their freedom from the established guild companies, Bristol argues, they were also "freelancing entrepreneurs in an underground economy" who took maximum advantage of the many forms of "de-racinated" and *ad hoc* economic activity thriving in early modern London (38). Yet scholars have yet to determine the extent to which the public theaters' dependence on such informal commerce rendered them open to women's economic participation. The high levels of female employment in these unregulated industries in the sixteenth and seventeenth centuries are generally attributed to increasing restrictions placed on female labor in the licensed guilds. In the case of the clothing guilds, limitations imposed on female sempstresses, bleachers and dyers applied only to their work on *new* cloth and clothing; articles of clothing that were already used and were being re-made or altered were generally not covered by these restrictions (Weisner, 179–80). In the face of such restrictions on their work by the guilds, women "frequently depended on a judicious cobbling together of opportunities, taking advantage of the commercial niches in the urban landscape" (Lemire, 114); such women played a vital role in London's shadow economy of unregulated crafts and trades, becoming second-hand clothing dealers, pawnbrokers, peddlers, hawkers, tipplers, victuallers, and so forth (see Lemire, Spufford, and Walker).

Wealthy widows frequently turned to pawnbroking in the period, as a "business, open to, and fit for, single women with cash in hand to use for stock in trade" (Holderness, 439). Yet the trade was carried out on a more informal level as well by the wives of landlords, inn- and tavern-keepers, theater people, and by single women involved in unlicensed retailing, victualling, and tippling.[3] Ingram cites the case of William Downell, a tailor, who with his wife had taken up lodging with John Singer (one of the twelve original members of the Queen's Company) and his wife, Alice. Downell brought a complaint against the Singers in the Court of Requests, claiming that Alice Singer had taken several pounds out of a chest in which he had stored the £200 dowry he had just received from his wife's family. Alice maintained that "shee had leant" the money "to a Neighbour of hers upon a good quantitye of plate pawned and engaged for that money," and assured him that "the daye followinge or not above two or three dayes at the most he should have it againe" (Ingram, 58). Insofar as Alice needed to "borrow," if not steal, money from her tenant in order to subsidize her pawnbroking activities, hers was most probably a small-scale, *ad hoc* operation.

This kind of illicit brokering of second-hand, and sometimes stolen, goods between women was quite common in the period. Walker maintains that we should not separate analyses of early modern women's work and economic status from a consideration of the forms of female criminality in the period. Indeed, she argues, insofar as women were often excluded from the "skilled, paid work defended by urban guilds," and "their appearance in records was usually as transgressors of the guild and borough regulations which sustained the male monopoly ... our definition of 'criminality' must surely be redefined ... to include female participation in the various economic and social networks of exchange and interaction which provided the backdrop to prosecutions for property crime" (98). Viewed from this perspective, the many forms of unregulated female labor, ranging from the licit to the illicit, may be better understood if placed on a continuum. Such a continuum would enable us to make sense of the fact, for example, that women were more likely than men to steal cloth, clothing, and household goods, including linen, plates and other utensils; for the very same expertise was required in assessing the value of such objects in both licit and illicit markets (Walker, 85–90; Weisner, 238). This

---

3   Henry Chettle, in his *Kind-Hartes Dreame*, speaks of landladies who, if their tenants "wanted money" would "on munday lend them ... uppon a pawne eleven pence, and in meere pittie aske at the weekes end not a penny more than twelve pence" (47). Garthine Walker cites many instances of women acting as informal, neighborhood pawnbrokers, and maintains that "small-scale pawning was commonplace" in alehouses and inns by women (91–3).

revisionist view of female criminality is crucial to an understanding of women's informal commerce generally, and of Moll Frith's participation in such commerce more particularly.

Frith's extraordinary appearance on the stage of the Fortune theater in male attire takes on new significance, I would like to suggest, when viewed within the context of the day-to-day commerce that surrounded that theater, as detailed in the "diary" or account-book of its owner, Philip Henslowe, and in relation to the many ordinary women who worked within these informal networks of trade. Some thirty pages of the manuscript are devoted to records of a pawnbroking business Henslowe managed from 1593 to 1596.[4] The great majority of customers listed in the pawn accounts were women: of the 312 loans in which the debtor's identity is known, 244, or 78 percent, were made to women, and 68, or 22 percent, to men. The accounts provide a fascinating glimpse into the day-to-day economic activities of ordinary women in and around the theater, and help to remind us that the sphere of commerce in which the theaters were intertwined was hardly an all-male preserve. The high incidence of women in Henslowe's pawn accounts may be attributed not only to the needs of market women to find ready cash, or of housewives to balance the household economy; for it is clear that some of these women had a financial interest in the pawnbroking business themselves. A "goody Watson," for example, is listed 53 times in the accounts, often pledging more than one, and sometimes up to four, items in a single day. In the four-month period between September 1594 and January 1595, she is listed 46 times – or once every two and a half days, on average. She was thus most likely herself a broker who was either hired by Henslowe as an agent or as a partner in his business. She is also listed as selling clothes for Henslowe in the second-hand clothing market, which may indicate she had expertise in this area (fol. 19v). There are several other women in addition to Goody Watson who likewise appear to have

---

4   The bulk of these records may be found on fols. 55r-61r, 73r-81r and 133r-136r; however, there are other references to actors pawning their costumes with Henslowe scattered throughout the "diary," some dated well after 1596 (see 19v, 28v, 37r, 41v), one as late as 1602. For a more extended discussion of Henslowe's pawnbroking records, see Korda (1996) and Jones and Stallybrass, esp. chapters 1 and 7.

worked with Henslowe in his pawnbroking business.[5] Such arrangements between large-scale pawnbrokers and female agents or intermediaries were quite common during the period (Lemire, 114; Walker, 91). Male brokers probably relied on female intermediaries because of their expertise in assessing the value of such goods, and because of their knowledge of the community of female borrowers.

Other women listed in Henslowe's accounts may have turned to pawnbroking on a more *ad hoc* basis, such as "goody harison," who is listed five times in a single day pawning a diverse range of goods (fo. 79r; see also 57v, 78v, 79v and 133v). There is also a "mrs Rysse a tayllers wiffe," who appears to have been in the practice of pawning remnants of cloth and other clothing from her husband's business, such as "A lynynge for a clocke of branched velvet" and "a manes gowne unmade up." Mrs. Rysse, the *ad hoc* pawnbroker, and her husband, the licensed tailor, provide an excellent example of the division between regulated male labor and unregulated female labor in the clothing trade. There is evidence as well that Henslowe's wife Agnes was actively involved in his pawnbroking and money-lending activities; she is listed several times lending money to actors (as well as friends, family, and other employees). An entry for 13 March, 1601/2, for example, reads: "Lent unto Thomas towne by my wiffe ... upon a payer of sylcke stockens tenneshellens [ten shillings]" (fo. 28v; see also 28r, 38v, 83r and 124r). Such accounts make clear the extent of women's economic participation in the shadow industries that surrounded the commercial theaters, and that may have helped to supply playing companies with costumes and properties (see Jones and Stallybrass, 30–2, 181–93; see also Korda 1996, 2002).

It is against this backdrop that I propose to read the historical case of Mary Frith, whose work as both a receiver and broker of second-hand and stolen goods may well have brought her into contact with Prince Henry's Men and the Fortune theater. Piecing together the precise contours of her career from the tantalizing shreds of historical evidence is no easy task. The "hard" evidence provided by scattered court records and other historical documents, together with the "softer" evidence provided by popular literary sources, suggests a career trajectory that began with the kind of *ad hoc* illegal activity to which a woman in desperate circumstances may have turned, and ends with the organization of a successful business enterprise that capitalized on the commercial opportunities afforded by London's expanding informal economy. Frith's performance at the Fortune is situated at the midpoint of this career

---

5   There was an "anne nockes" who appears often in the accounts from 9 December, 1593 to 9 December, 1594 (perhaps under an agreement to work for one year), and a "mrs grante" who reckons accounts for him from January through May of 1594 (Henslowe, fols. 73r–81r, 133r–135v, 136r, 73r–81r; see also Carson, 23).

trajectory, midway between her notoriety as a cutpurse and her celebrity as a broker, inviting us to consider what role it may have played in this transition.

A record in the Middlesex Sessions Rolls indicates that in her early years, Frith may have resorted to criminal activity in league with several other female accomplices. In 1602, she was indicted with two other "spinsters," Jane Hill and Jane Styles, for stealing the purse of an unknown man at Clerkenwell, although according to Mark Eccles a trial jury found her not guilty (Eccles, 66; Ungerer, 62–3). The popular pamphlet biography published in 1662, *The Life and Death of Mrs. Mary Frith, Commonly Called Mal Cutpurse*, likewise mentions her involvement with a group of such women, although it describes them not as thieves but rather as receivers of stolen goods: "Their Trade [was] to receive Goods which were lifted: that is to say, Stollen by Thieves, and so in a fair way sell them again" (sig. B12v). The phrase "in a fair way" suggests that like many brokers of stolen property in the period, these women were "strategically placed to funnel the[ir] 'takes' into wider legitimate markets" (McMullan, 24), serving as intermediaries between licit and illicit forms of trade. Receiving and brokering stolen goods was "an offence that was usually perceived and prosecuted as a crime of women" (Wales, 79; see also Sharpe, 156), as is evidenced by the scores of women charged with such crimes in the Middlesex Sessions records (Jeaffreson ed., 2: 149, 168; Le Hardy ed., 8, 160, 168, 200, 231, 257, 294–5, 299–300, 310, 365–6, 373–4, 377, 382). These records likewise show that female thieves, receivers, and brokers of stolen property frequently acted in consort with other women, as did Frith.[6] Because there was no effective statute against receiving stolen goods until 1691, however, the crime was prosecuted only infrequently, and "remained an offence that was notoriously difficult to prosecute" (Walker, 91), rendering it a relatively safe means of income for poor women who turned to crime.

The available evidence suggests that by the second decade of the seventeenth century, Frith had herself become a successful broker of stolen goods. According to a case brought in the Court of Star Chamber, in February 1621, one Henry Killigrew, gentleman, while "in priuate familiarity" with a prostitute, had his pocket picked and purse stolen by her. Having "heard howe ... many that had had their pursses Cutt or goods stollen, had beene

---

6   A "spinster" named Elizabeth Arnold, for example, stole jewelry, plate, "together with divers articles of wearing apparel" in 1589/90 and distributed the goods to two other women, Elizabeth Hawtrey and Elizabeth Jonson (Jeaffreson ed., 1: 192). The "world of stolen clothes, linens and household goods," according to Walker, "was populated by women: women stealing, women receiving, women disposing, women searching, and women passing on information, as well as goods, to other women" (97). Her study of Cheshire finds that in the late sixteenth and early seventeenth centuries, "most women committed burglaries either alone or in league with other women" (85).

helped to theire goods againe and diuers of the offendors taken or discouered" by Mary Frith, he went to see her. With Frith's help, one Margaret Dell was arrested, brought to Frith's house by the constable of St Bride's in Fleet Street, where she was identified by Killigrew as the perpetrator (P. R. O. St. Ch. 8/124/ 4; cited in Dowling, 67–71; see also Ungerer, 68–9). This practice of returning stolen articles to their owners for a fee was a common and lucrative one among receivers, brokers, and what were termed "thief-takers" during the period (Beattie, 55; Johnston and Tittler, 246; McIntosh, 258; McMullan, 71; Sharpe, 161; Wales, 68–70). In the absence of a modern police force, most prosecutions of crime in early modern England were brought by the victim, and were therefore "very dependent upon private initiative" (Sharpe, 10). Professional "thief-takers," who often were or had been thieves themselves, drew on their extensive knowledge of criminal networks to present victims of property crimes with an attractive alternative to expensive and lengthy litigation, compounding with thieves for the return of stolen property to its rightful owners for a fee. Compliant criminals were thus rewarded and relieved of the burden of fencing their pilfered goods, while recalcitrant ones could be punished by blackmail and extortion, or by being turned over to magistrates, who also depended heavily on the services of thief-takers (Beattie, 58; McMullan, 151; Sharpe, 161–3; Wales, 74, 77) – as it appears the constable of St Brides, Giles Allen, did on the services of Frith, according to the Star Chamber bill.

Women, according to Walker, frequently "engaged in quasi-official activity in the return or custody of stolen goods" (98). Their involvement in the disposal of stolen goods, she maintains, "placed them in a strong position to detect and deal with thefts – especially those by other women" (93).[7] What distinguishes Frith from other female informants is that she parlayed the knowledge gleaned in her early days as a thief and/or receiver of stolen goods into a successful business enterprise. In the "diary" portion of *The Life and Death of Mrs. Mary Frith*, she describes the workings of this enterprise as follows:

> In my house ... I set up a kind of *Brokery* or a distinct factory for *Jewels, Rings* and *Watches*, which had been pinched or stolen .... I might properly enough call it the *Insurance Office* for such Merchandize, for the Losers were sure upon Composition [payment of a fee] to recover their Goods again, and the Pyrates were as sure to have good ransome, and I so much in the Grosse for Brokerage [a percentage of the whole for acting as agent] without any more danger; the *Hue and Cry* being always directed to me for the Discovery of the Goods not the *Takers*. A Lawless Vocation yet bordering between the illicit and convenient, more advantageous by far to the injured, then the Courts of Justice and benefits of the Law, and more equal to the wrong-doers .... My House was the *Algiers* where they traffiqued in safety ... and

---

7   Walker cites numerous instances of women acting in this capacity in Chester (93–4).

publiquely exposed what they got without the danger of Inquisition .... I may be said to have made a perfect regulation of this *thievish Mystery*, and reduced it to certain rules and orders, which during my administration of the Mistresship and Government thereof, was far better managed then afterwards it was .... (sigs C10r–C11r)

While we have no way of determining the accuracy of this account of Frith's "Brokery," it does seem largely to correspond with the evidence provided by the Star Chamber bill: both suggest a successful business venture that had attained a relatively high level of organization and public reputation under Frith's management.[8] While it is certainly true that popular criminal literature of the period tends to exaggerate the complexity and coherence of the criminal "underworld" (Archer, chap. 6; Beier; Slack), the shadow economy in second-hand and stolen goods does appear to have achieved some degree of organization by the early seventeenth century (see McMullan, esp. chap. 1; Sharpe, 163).[9] That Frith's commercial activity included trade in fashionable apparel in addition to jewelry and watches is evidenced by a suit brought by a hatmaker named Richard Pooke in 1624 in the Court of Requests to recover the unpaid portion of a bill for some beaver hats, which were then in fashion and exorbitantly expensive, upon which she had made a downpayment of £3 in 1616 (Eccles, 66). While the title-page woodcut of *The Roaring Girl* depicts Moll herself sporting such a hat, the large expense and number of hats involved in the transaction with Pooke suggests that they were not solely for her personal consumption.

The markets in second-hand and stolen goods and clothing appear to have been thoroughly intertwined: frippers (used clothing dealers) worked as pawnbrokers (and vice versa), pawnbrokers as receivers of stolen goods, and receivers as "thief-takers." Not all brokers had the wherewithal (the knowledge of criminal networks or level of organization) to return stolen

---

8   As such, Frith's business appears to have been an early antecedent of the system developed in the late seventeenth and early eighteenth centuries by such famed thief-takers as Jonathan Wild (see Howson, esp. chap. 9; Lemire, chap. 5; McMullan, 153; Sharpe, 161–2; Wales, 70). The term "Thiefetaker" first appears in the Middlesex Sessions rolls as early as 1609 (Johnston and Tittler, 246). The practice became far more widespread after 1693 with the passage of an Act of Parliament by which "the government embarked on a new policy of offering rewards for the capture of thieves" (Howson, 36).

9   The commercial growth of London fostered "a lucrative market for the disposal and distribution of stolen property" that allowed the more organized brokers to "open permanent offices and warehouses for the recovery of stolen property" (McMullan, 23–4, 105). In 1585, some eighteen such "Harboringe Howses" were raided in London, Westminster, and the suburbs, including Southwark (Tawney and Power eds, 338–9).

property to its owners, however; instead, they altered the goods beyond recognition for resale, or sold "the stolen goods vnto duchmen, Scotts and French Brokers," as a letter from the Lord Mayor and Aldermen of London to the Queen's Attorney General complained in 1601. The letter describes the growing numbers of such "Brokers," and of their location in the Liberties, which afforded them protection from the law: "those Brokers are nowe of late growen soe manie and soe dispersed into priviledged and exempt places in and nere vnto this Cittie of verie purpose to auoide the entry into the Register of suche parcells of goods as they buy or take or pawne: By meanes whereof manie times suche goods as are stollen are neuer found" (Aydelotte, 164–5). The registry of pawned goods to which the letter refers had been established in 1594/5, when city authorities began to take a strong interest in controlling the informal commerce of such brokers. The Court of Common Council instituted two Acts aimed at "diuers persons, called Retayling Broggers, Brokers or Hucksters, and others, such as use to ... receiue, buy, and take to pawne, at the handes of base, shifting, and suspected persons ... diuers Plate, Jewels, Goods, Wares, Merchandises, Apparell ... and other such like thinges, whereof the greatest part are stolne" (Corporation of London, 1).

Although the explicit aim of such legislation was to prevent the circulation of stolen property encouraged by such brokers, the "reformation" it proposes is not outright prohibition but rather a series of measures aimed at regulating and even, through the extraction of various fees and penalties, profiting from what had clearly become a highly lucrative form of trade. By the first year of James's reign, the expansion of such commerce was sufficiently worrisome to authorities as to become the focus of Parliamentary legislation, and a statute was passed instituting new fees, penalties, and regulations against "upstart Brokers" who, it proclaimed, had impertinently "assum[ed] unto themselves the name of Brokers and Brokerage, as though the same were an honest and a lawfull Trade Misterie or Occupation ... findinge thereby that the same is a more idle and easier kinde of Trade of livinge, and that there riseth and groweth to them a more readie more greate more profitable and speedier Advantage and Gaine then ... manuall Labours and Trades did or coulde bringe them" (1 James I, c. 21; *Statutes of the Realm*, 4: 1038–9).

Philip Henslowe, who started his pawnbroking business in 1593, would seem to have been precisely the sort of "upstart Broker" targeted by the abovementioned legislation. Whether or not Henslowe himself dealt in stolen goods and apparel, it seems likely (given the amount of stolen property in circulation among pawnbrokers and frippers) that theater people, in their commerce with such "retailing brokers," wittingly or unwittingly participated in the exchange of stolen, as well as used, costumes and props. Such was the case with John Shank, Sr, a member of the Prince Henry's-Palsgrave's company,[10] who in 1614 was accused by a linen-draper named Henry Udall of "buying four network bands and a pair of cuffs at the [Fortune] Playhouse at an under-rate, being part of the goods which were stolen from the said Henry" (Bentley, 564).[11] Bentley surmises that Shank procured costumes for the company, a practice which his will suggests he continued for the King's Men, whom he joined shortly thereafter (562).[12] The geographical proximity and economic ties of such informal brokers to the commercial theaters may well have brought Moll Frith into contact with Prince Henry's Men and the Fortune theater, if not with Philip Henslowe himself. Court records from her early years (between c.1602 and c.1614) place Moll in St Giles Without Cripplegate, near the Fortune theater, and in Southwark, near the Bankside theaters.[13]

The careers of Philip Henslowe, John Shank, Sr, and Mary Frith are each in different ways demonstrative of the mixture of economic ingenuity and performative strategies deployed by those who sought to make a living in the informal sector surrounding the commercial theaters. Theater historians have not always been kind to Henslowe on precisely these grounds, as though the opportunistic flexibility that characterized his career was an aberration, rather than representative of wider social and economic phenomena (Fleay thus referred to him as an "old pawnbroking, stage-managing, bear-baiting, usurer" [94]). Less well-known, though no less representative in this regard, is the career of Shank. Renowned as a jig-maker (Bentley, 563), Shank was forced to give up this specialty, if only temporarily, it appears, shortly after the

---

10 Formerly Prince Henry's Men, which Shank joined c.1610 (Chambers, 188).

11 The playhouse in question was undoubtedly the Fortune theater, which was the company's ordinary venue according to its patent (Chambers, 190).

12 Shank's will, dated 31 December, 1635, refers to "Sixteene pound*es* and Twelve shillings which they [his Maiesities servants the players] owe me for Two gownes" (Honigman and Brock, 188).

13 According to a record in the Middlesex Sessions Rolls, in 1602 a cordwainer, Thomas Dobson, and silktwister, William Simons, from the parish of St Giles Without Cripplegate, gave bonds that "Marya FFrithe" should appear at the next sessions of jail delivery on suspicion of having taken "a purse with XXVs of Richard Ingles" (Eccles, 66; Ungerer, 63–4). On 23 March, 1614, Mary Frith was married to a Lewkenor Markham in the parish of St Saviour's in Southwark (Eccles, 66; Ungerer, 68). She later moved to Fleet Street, which bordered on the Liberty of Whitefriars, a notorious criminal sanctuary and home to the Whitefriars theater, where she set up shop as a broker. The Star Chamber Bill of 1621 cited above locates Moll's brokerage and receiving house in Fleet Street, as does The Life and Death of Mrs. Mary Frith (sig. C12r). We know from a transcript of the will of "Mary Markham, alias FFrith" of 1659 that she resided in "the parish of St Bride, alias Bridgett, in FFleetstreet, London" when she died, and was buried there in the church of St Bridget's (Ungerer, 72–5).

performance of *The Roaring Girl* in 1611 at the Fortune, when the Middlesex Bench instituted "An Order for suppressinge of Jigges att the end of Playes" in October of 1612, citing "certayne lewde Jigges songes and daunces vsed and accustomed at the play-house called the Fortune in Gouldinglane" that had attracted "divers cutt-purses and other lewde and ill disposed persons in greate multitudes" (Jeaffreson ed., 83). A ballad of the same year entitled "The Common Cries of London" or "Turner's Dish of Lenten Stuff" suggests the impact the Order may have had on Shank's career: "Since Shancke did leave to sing his rimes," it says, "he is counted but a gull" (Collier ed., 212). The term "gull" may refer either to a trickster or to one who is tricked (*OED*); the ballad's reference to Shank as a "gull" suggests both meanings, for it depicts the commercial landscape of early modern London as a site of ingenuity and deception, in which one must either learn and practice the tricks of one's trade, or be tricked oneself. "I doubt it is a bodge," the balladeer sings of a female hawker whose "measure is too little," and warns "Thus all the City over / the people they do dodge" (Collier ed., 208). The term "dodge," which means "To move to and fro, or backwards and forwards; to keep changing one's position or shifting one's ground" so as to "elude a pursuer," "change about deceitfully," "haggle," or "avoid discovery" (*OED*), perfectly describes the flexibility, ingenuity, and strategies of evasion, that characterize informal commerce. The protean character of such commerce is likewise reflected, quite literally, in the shifty etymology of the term "bodge," which has been variously linked by philologists to the terms "badge" (a "badger" was a hawker, peddler, or regrator [reseller]) and "botch" (a "botcher" was a mender or patcher of old garments), and as such, incorporates many of the shifty occupational identities that define the informal sector.

   Within the commercial landscape of London's suburbs and Liberties, as described in Turner's ballad, women trick and trade, dodge and bodge, as actively as men, and workers and players are placed on a continuum. The "wench that cries the kitchin stuff" and "sings her note so merry" belongs to the same nexus of performative commerce as the "players on the Banckeside" who "sing [their] rimes" (Collier ed., 208, 212); both depend upon a tactical mix of publicity, performance, and flexible commerce to earn a living. As such, both are subject to shifts in legislation or civic regulation that may precipitate a sudden slide from duper to dupe. Against this background of informal commerce, Frith's performance at the Fortune begins to look considerably less exceptional. Unraveling the precise nature of her own motivation and agency in mounting this performance, however, remains a far from simple matter, as does the relationship of that performance to Middleton and Dekker's play. The play capitalizes on Frith's notoriety as a "cutpurse drab" and "roaring girl," on the one hand, while suggesting that this notoriety is ill-founded "slander" (2.2.10), on the other. In Act 5, scene I, however, Moll is revealed to be a thief-catcher, not a thief. She boasts of having taken one cutpurse "i' the twopenny gallery at the Fortune" (283–4), and compounds with another for the return of a purse ("Heart, there's a knight, to whom I'm bound for many favours, lost his purse at the last new play i' the Swan – seven angels in't: make it good, you're best: do you see? – No more" [303–6]). Such a revelation would undoubtedly have provided valuable publicity to Frith, who was in the process of refashioning her own public persona along these lines.

The fictional "Moll" likewise restores her reputation in Act 5, scene 1 by discovering the tricks of two "base rogues" (107), Trapdoor and Tearcat. Their encounter is particularly intriguing in the present context, in that the part of Tearcat may well have been played by none other than John Shank, Sr, who specialized in clown roles requiring dialect and song (Bentley, 563). Tearcat not only displays his knowledge of thieves' cant or "peddler's French" (5.1.179) as does Trapdoor, he also speaks pidgin Dutch, and sings a bawdy, canting, drinking song with Moll. Frith's own performance on the stage of the Fortune, as described in the *Consistory of London Correction Book*, suggests that it may have been part of a post-play jig (she "playd vppon her lute & sang a songe" and spoke "immodest & lascivious speeches" [Mulholland, 31]), in which case it may have been negotiated, if not performed, with Shank. If Shank had earlier played Tearcat, the jig would have been an effective reprise of the scene in which the fictional "Moll" negotiates their performance of a duet, substituting "the Roaring Girl herself" (Epilogue, 35) for the actor who had impersonated her. Such a substitution would have been an equally effective reversal of the substitution of the "real" Moll for Moll Fitzallard that takes place in the final scene of the play (5.2.186ff.).

Whether or not this coupling of Shank and Frith ever actually took place at the Fortune, juxtaposing them in thought may help us to unthink some of our assumptions about the "all-male" stage. The fluid occupational identities of both figures blur any rigid boundaries between worker and player. In this they were hardly exceptional; those who worked in the informal sector in the suburbs and Liberties of London relied on both economic ingenuity and a variety of performative tactics to cobble together a living. Shank supplemented his jig-making career by working as a broker of used and stolen attire; Frith furthered her reputation as a broker by appearing on the stage of the Fortune (and other public sites around London, including St. Paul's) in lavish attire.[14] Both, it would seem, had a talent for tailoring their performative tactics to their economic circumstances, and vice versa: when their cases were altered, they

---

14 According to the *Consistory of London Correction Book*, Frith was "taken in Powles Church with her peticoate tucked vp about her in the fashion of a man with a mans cloake on her" and "frequented all or most of the disorderly & licentious places in the Cittie as namely she hath vsually in the habite of a man resorted to alehowses Tavernes Tobacco shops & also to play howses" (Mulholland, 31).

knew how to make a living. Frith's public display of extravagant attire upon the stage of the Fortune theater would have served as an effective advertisement for her brokerage, particularly if her business catered to other women who participated in the fashion of cross-dressing. This method of advertising would have made good sense if, as the *Hic Mulier* pamphlet attests, such women were known to frequent the theaters (they are described as "the gilt durt, which imbroders Play-houses" [sig. A4r]).

When viewed in relation to her status as a worker, Frith's altered "case" points not only to the sexualized and gendered codes within which her clothing might have been read in the period, but to the volatile networks of informal commerce through which such attire made its way onto the public stage, and to the important role that women played within this world of sartorial work. The dedicatory Epistle to the 1611 Quarto text immediately points to the "alteration in apparel" as the proper context within which to read the altered "case" of its title-page, while famously linking the clothing trade to the theater: "The fashion of play-making I can properly compare to nothing so naturally as the alteration in apparel: for in the time of the great-crop doublet, your huge bombasted plays, quilted with mighty words to lean purpose, was only then in fashion; and as the doublet fell, neater inventions began to set up" (Epistle, 1–6). I do not mean to suggest that the "alteration in apparel" does not include reference to Moll's cross-dressing; indeed, the Epistle goes on to describe her as "a woman, [who] passes through the play in doublet and breeches" (14–15). Rather, I am proposing that Moll's sexualized and gendered attire takes on new significance when viewed within the larger context of the "alteration in apparel" – the fabrication and refabrication, sale and resale, loan and theft, of apparel that fuelled the clothing and entertainment industries, and in so doing, gave employment to so many "distressed needlewomen and trade-fallen wives" (3.1.95). That is, the "alteration" in question may be read in very material terms as pointing simultaneously to the work necessary to produce the latest trends in fashion (including the fashion of cross-dressing) and to the incessant change of fashion that created the demand for such work.

The work of alteration, as we have seen, frequently fell to women, particularly when it involved remaking rather than making up new, as was often the case with the production of costumes for the public theaters. While there is no evidence that Frith ever worked as a needlewoman or sempstress (her pamphlet biography professes "she could not endure that sedentary life of sewing or stitching, a Sampler was as grievous [to her] as a Winding-sheet, her Needle, Bodkin and Thimble, she could not think on quietly, wishing them changed into Sword and Dagger" [sig. B3v]), it is possible that such work was carried out by other women in her employ, as early modern brokers were known to hire sempstresses and other artisans to make alterations in used or stolen wares (those, presumably, that could not be returned for a fee to their owners) for resale (McIntosh, 260). The pamphlet *Hic Mulier* suggests further that the labor of alteration was in increasingly high demand as a consequence of the fashion of cross-dressing; it impugns city tailors for "metamorphos[ing] ... modest old garments, to this new manner of short base and French doublet" (sig. C1v). Thus, whether or not Frith herself ever worked as a sempstress, her work as a broker clearly profited from the "alteration in apparel" or ever-changing fashions.

In conclusion, Moll Frith's economic ingenuity is crucial to an understanding of her cross-dressed persona, and vice versa, for the two are inextricably intertwined. To view Moll in her status as a worker as well as a player is not to diminish the importance of the latter, but rather to suggest that the significance of her exceptional appearance "at the ffortune ... in mans apparell" can best be understood when viewed against the backdrop of the unexceptional women who worked in large numbers within the networks of commerce surrounding the early modern public theaters.

Works Cited and Consulted

Archer, Ian W. *The Pursuit of Stability: Social Relations in Elizabethan London.* Cambridge: Cambridge University Press, 1991.

Aydelotte, Frank. *Elizabethan Rogues and Vagabonds.* Oxford: Clarendon, 1913.

Beattie, J. M. *Crime and the Courts in England, 1660–1800.* Princeton: Princeton University Press, 1986.

Beier, A. L. "Social Problems in Elizabethan London." *Journal of Interdisciplinary History* 9 (1978): 203–21.

Bentley, G. E. *The Jacobean and Caroline Stage.* Vol. 2. Oxford: Oxford University Press, 1941–68.

Bergeron, David. "Women as Patrons of English Renaissance Drama." *Patronage in the Renaissance.* Ed. Guy Fitch Lytle and Stephen Orgel. New Jersey: Princeton University Press, 1981.

Bristol, Michael. *Big-Time Shakespeare.* London and New York: Routledge, 1996.

Butler, Judith. *Gender Trouble: Feminism and the Subversion of Identity.* New York: Routledge, 1990.

Carson, Neil. *A Companion to Henslowe's Diary.* Cambridge: Cambridge University Press, 1988.

Cerasano, Susan P. and Marion Wynne-Davies, eds. *Renaissance Drama by Women: Texts and Documents.* New York and London: Routledge, 1996.

Chambers, E. K. *The Elizabethan Stage.* Vol. 2. Oxford: Clarendon, 1923.

Chettle, Henry. *Kind-Hartes Dreame.* Ed. George Bagshawe Harrison. New York: Barnes and Noble, 1966.

Clark, Alice. *Working Life of Women in the Seventeenth Century.* New York: A. M. Kelley, 1919.

Collier, John Payne ed. *Roxburghe Ballads.* London: Longman, 1847.

Corporation of London, Court of Common Council. *Retailing Brokers.* Acts & Orders, April 9, 1595. London: J. Windet for Iohn Wolfe, 1595. STC 16715.

Dowling, Margaret. "A Note on Moll Cutpurse – 'The Roaring Girl.'" *Review of English Studies* 10 (1934): 67–71.

Dunlop, Jocelyn O. *English Apprenticeship and Child Labor*. London: Unwin, 1912.

Eccles, Mark. "Mary Frith, The Roaring Girl." *Notes and Queries*, n. s., 32 (1985): 65–6.

Erickson, Amy. Introduction. *Working Life of Women in the Seventeenth Century*. By Alice Clark. Ed. Amy Erickson. New York and London: Routledge, 1992.

Feuillerat, Albert, ed. *Documents Relating to the Office of the Revels in the Time of Queen Elizabeth*. London: David Nutt, 1908.

Fleay, Frederick. *Chronicle History of the London Stage 1559–1642*. London: Reeves and Turner, 1890.

Garber, Marjorie. "The Logic of the Transvestite: *The Roaring Girl* (1608)." *Staging the Renaissance: Reinterpretations of Elizabethan and Jacobean Drama*. Ed. David Scott Kastan and Peter Stallybrass. New York and London: Routledge, 1991, 221–34.

Henslowe, Philip. *Henslowe's Diary*. Ed. R. A. Foakes and R. T. Rickert. Cambridge: Cambridge University Press, 1961.

Hic Mulier: Or, The Man-Woman: Being a Medicine to Cure the Coltish Disease of the Staggers in the Masculine-Feminines of our Times. London, 1620.

Holderness, B. A. "Widows in Pre-Industrial Society: An Essay Upon Their Economic Functions." *Land, Kinship, and Life Cycle*. Ed. R. M. Smith. Cambridge: Cambridge University Press, 1984.

Honigmann, E. A. J. and Susan Brock. *Playhouse Wills 1558–1642*. Manchester: Manchester University Press, 1993.

Howard, Jean E. "The Materiality of Ideology: Women as Spectators, Spectacles, and Paying Customers in the English Public Theater." *The Stage and Social Struggle in Early Modern England*. London and New York: Routledge, 1994, 73–92.

Howson, Gerald. *Thief-Taker General: The Rise and Fall of Jonathan Wild*. London: Hutchinson, 1970.

Ingram, William. *The Business of Playing: The Beginnings of the Adult Professional Theater in Elizabethan London*. Ithaca and London: Cornell University Press, 1992.

Jeaffreson, John Cordy, ed. *Middlesex County Records*. 4 vols. London: Middlesex County Records Society, 1886–92.

Johnston, Alexandra F. and Robert Tittler. "'To Catch a Thief' in Jacobean London." *The Salt of Common Life: Individuality and Choice in the Medieval Town, Countryside and Church*. Ed. Edwin Brezette DeWindt. Kalamazoo, Michigan: Western Michigan University Press, 1995.

Jones, Ann Rosalind and Peter Stallybrass. *Renaissance Clothing and the Materials of Memory*. Cambridge: Cambridge University Press, 2000.

Korda, Natasha. "Household Property/Stage Property: Henslowe as Pawnbroker." *Theatre Journal* 48:2 (1996): 185–95.

———. "Women's Theatrical Properties." *Staged Properties in Early Modern English Drama*. Ed. Jonathan Gil Harris and Natasha Korda. Cambridge: Cambridge University Press, 2002, 202–29.

Le Hardy, William, ed. *County of Middlesex: Calendar to the Sessions Records*. Vol. I. London: Guildhall, 1935.

Lemire, Beverly. *Dress, Culture and Commerce: The English Clothing Trade Before the Factory, 1600–1800*. New York: St. Martin's, 1997.

Levin, Richard. "Women in the Renaissance Theater Audience." *Shakespeare Quarterly* 40 (1989): 165–74.

The Life and Death of Mrs. Mary Frith. Commonly Called Mal Cutpurse. Ed. Nakayama S. Randall. 1662 Reprinted New York and London: Garland, 1993.

McIntosh, Mary. "Thieves and Fences: Markets and Power in Professional Crime." *British Journal of Criminology* 16 (1976): 257–66.

McMullan, John L. *The Canting Crew: London's Criminal Underworld 1550–1700.* New Brunswick, NJ: Rutgers University Press, 1984.

Middleton, Thomas and Thomas Dekker. *The Roaring Girl.* Ed. Paul Mulholland. The Revels Plays. Manchester: Manchester University Press, 1987.

Mulholland, Paul. "The Date of *The Roaring Girl.*" *Review of English Studies,* new series, 28 (1977): 18–31.

Neill, Michael. "'Wit's Most Accomplished Senate': The Audience of the Caroline Private Theaters." *Studies in English Literature* 18 (1978): 341–60.

Nelson, Alan H. "Women in the Audience of Cambridge Plays." *Shakespeare Quarterly* 41 (1990): 333–6.

Orgel, Stephen. *Impersonations: The Performance of Gender in Shakespeare's England.* Cambridge: Cambridge University Press, 1996.

Rose, Mary Beth. "Women in Men's Clothing: Apparel and Social Stability in *The Roaring Girl.*" *English Literary Renaissance* 14 (1984): 367–91.

Sharpe, J. A. *Crime in Early Modern England 1550–1750.* London and New York: Longman, 1984; reprint 1999.

Slack, P. A. "Vagrants and Vagrancy in England 1598–1664." *Crisis and Order in English Towns 1500–1700.* Ed. Peter Clark and Paul Slack. London: Routledge and Kegan Paul, 1972.

Spufford, Margaret. *The Great Reclothing of Rural England: Petty Chapmen and their Wares in the Seventeenth Century.* London: Hambledon Press, 1984.

Stallybrass, Peter. "Worn Worlds: Clothes and Identity on the Renaissance Stage." *Subject and Object in Renaissance Culture.* Ed. Margreta de Grazia, Maureen Quilligan, and Peter Stallybrass. Cambridge: Cambridge University Press, 1996.

Statutes of the Realm. Vol. 4. London: G. Eyre and A. Strahan, 1819.

Sugden, Edward H. *A Topographical Dictionary to the Works of Shakespeare and His Fellow Dramatists.* New York: Longmans, Green & Co., 1925.

Tawney, R. H. and Eileen Power. Eds. *Tudor Economic Documents: Being Select Documents Illustrating the Economic and Social History of Tudor England.* Vol. 2. London: Longmans, 1924.

Ungerer, Gustave. "Mary Frith, Alias Moll Cutpurse, in Life and Literature." *Shakespeare Studies* 28 (2000): 42–84.

Wales, Tim. "Thief-takers and their Clients in Later Stuart London." *Londinopolis: Essays in the Cultural and Social History of Early Modern London.* Ed. Paul Griffiths and Mark S. R. Jenner. Manchester: Manchester University Press, 2000.

Walker, Garthine. "Women, Theft and the World of Stolen Goods." *Women, Crime, and the Courts in Early Modern England.* Ed. Jennifer Kermode and Garthine Walker. Chapel Hill: University of North Carolina Press, 1994.

Weisner, Merry. "Spinning Out Capital: Women's Work in the Early Modern Economy." *Becoming Visible: Women in European History.* Ed. Renate Bridenthal *et al.* Boston: Houghton Mifflin Co., 1987.

Westfall, Susan. *Patrons and Performers: Early Tudor Household Revels.* Oxford: Oxford University Press, 1990.

Chapter 5

"Quacking Delilahs": Female Mountebanks in Early Modern England and Italy

Bella Mirabella

Although it is common knowledge that women rarely appeared in the theaters in England before the Restoration, there were other non-traditional stages upon which women could perform. These stages – sometimes only a few boards and a curtain set up in public places, in squares, or piazzas, at fairs, church ales, on street corners, in the courtyards of inns, outside storefronts, and occasionally inside shops – were the theaters of the mountebanks. And it was on these makeshift stages that women had the chance to participate in two important and interconnected spheres of early modern life: medicine and performance. Although women were usually not the lead mountebanks, these "quacking Delilahs" (as one critic called them) were nonetheless crucial members of these troupes, acting as performers and healers and often responsible for the very success of these medicine shows. However, it is not easy to uncover their traces; one must seek out the flicker, the brief mention of the female performer, added often as an aside by the male writers of the day, who do not present her as a primary player, and who often do not even mention her name. Nonetheless, by examining these traces, we discover many references which reveal a rich and vibrant picture of the role of women as performers and healers.

Although mountebanks were like other itinerant entertainers, moving from town to town, or country to country, the singing, dancing, juggling, musical, vaudeville-like routines of the mountebanks had as their aim the selling of folk remedies. In fact, it is the selling of these remedies and the promise of healing in a theatrical setting that distinguishes these entertainments. Although this concept of public healing and performance may not coincide with our modern notion of privacy and secrecy between patient and doctor, medicine is often described in performative terms even today. The operating room is often called a theater, and doctors still "perform" operations. My own dentist displays an old-fashioned sign – "Dentistry Performed Here" – reminding us that indeed the dentist will perform certain acts and the patient, hoping to heal, will participate in the long tradition of medicine as performance. In the mountebank entertainments, the performance space is not an operating room or a doctor's office but the open square, piazza or mountebank shop where medicine becomes drama, the promise of healing is entertainment, and audience and actors participate in a dramatic spectacle.

This spectacle, lively, charged and humorous, left the audience spellbound, thrilling with the anticipation of healing. Peter Burke's idea of a "social drama" involving "elaborate rituals" is a useful way to describe the electric combination of healing and entertainment, characteristic of the mountebank performances (95).[1] In this social drama, medicine becomes performance and performance medicine. And it is in the intersection of these two discourses that women had a chance to perform in the theater of the streets. Within the frame of medicine as performance, this essay examines the role female mountebanks played as performers and healers in Italy and England, despite those critics who felt that a woman's silent domesticity was all she should perform.[2]

But before highlighting the women, it is important to set the stage, as it were, for their performances and to imagine what these entertainments were like. Mountebank performance characteristically included dancing, acrobatics, elaborate gesture, music-making, and mimicry. The word "mountebank" comes from the Italian *montimbanco* and *saltimbanco*, meaning to mount or jump on a bank or stage; this well describes the physicality of these itinerant players, who were ready to set up their stages at any opportunity. In Italy the *montibanchi* were also called *ciarlatani*, from the verb *ciarlare*, meaning to speak idly, to chatter.[3] Linguistic display was vital to the spectacle:

---

1   The term "social drama" is pertinent here since these performances were not detached from everyday life. Rather, their intimate connection to medicine and healing distinguish them from any other dramatic presentation. Those on the stage as well as those in the audience are all performers in a drama that takes place in the public arena.

2   Focusing on England and Italy allows a broad consideration of the different possibilities open to women as part of the mountebank tradition. However, women appeared in mountebank shows all over Europe; see Julie Crawford's discussion of Margaret Cavendish's fascination with them in Antwerp, in this volume (241 n.1). On female medical performers in Germany and France, see Katritzky 2000, and Klairmont-Lingo 1999.

3   The noun *ciarla* means loquacity as well as gossip and false report, and *ciarle* means nonsense, indicating that what *ciarlatani* had to say was idle, false, perhaps to be enjoyed, but not to be believed. In England the word "mountebank" was used interchangeably with terms like "quack," "quacksalver," and "empiric." Quack, derived from the Dutch *quacksalver*, describes persons who are untrained yet pretend to have knowledge of herbal or home remedies. In the 1600s the Dutch word *kwakken* meant to brag and show off.

mountebanks were glib, smooth talkers who wooed audiences with glittering, usually humorous speeches. In fact, the humor of the mountebank harangues was thought to have its own healing powers. In his dedication to *The Harangues or Speeches of Several Famous Mountebanks*, the author "D.G." writes that reading the speeches will bring back to life "the gaping crowd ... gull'd by the enchanting tongues of quack and zany," and this memory will be a "pill to purge melancholy" and "revive former mirth" (6). However, medical showmanship was not limited to language. Through gesture as well, the dramatics of healing went beyond the selling of a remedy to the performance of its powers. Coryat, for example, witnessed a mountebank who cut himself, then quickly applied a "certain oil," which immediately stopped the blood and healed the wound. He also describes another mountebank, who, because of his anti-venom medicine, was able to hold a viper, play with it, and "receive no hurt" (410).

The mountebanks' free open-air entertainments took place in any space where people might congregate, such as a fair, church-ale, harvest celebration, or carnival (Morley, 295). In some piazzas or squares, mountebank performers were daily attractions. While mountebanks worked all over Europe and England, some of the most vivid descriptions come from Italy. In the late 1590s, Fynes Moryson wrote about "a generation of empirics" who haunt marketplaces in Italian cities: these are called "montibanchi of mounting banks ... and ciarlatani of prating" (424–5). Mountebanks rarely performed alone and were usually accompanied by other performers, male and female, who worked as clowns, musicians, dancers, actors, or acrobats. Many traveled with a female companion, often depicted dancing or playing an instrument (see figs. 5.1, 5.2; also see M. A. Katritzky's essay in this volume, fig. 6.6, for a woman dancing on a mountebank stage). Some had performing apes and buffoonish sidekicks, called a Merry Andrew in England or a *zanni* in Italy. Women often took part in the comic action: Moryson describes how the mountebanks "proclaim their wares upon these scaffolds, and to draw concourse of people, they have a zani or fool with a visard on his face, and sometimes a woman to make comical sport" (425).

Venice was famed for its mountebanks. A fascinated Coryat watched them putting on their performances twice a day in the Piazza San Marco, where a "whole rabble" of performers shares the stage: "some wear visards being disguised like fools in a play, some that are women (for there are divers women also amongst them) are attired with habits according to the person that they sustain" (273). Once the stage is set up, the supporting players sing and play instruments while the "principal Mountebank" opens the trunk bursting "with a world of newfangled trumperies." When the music ceases, the mountebank "makes an oration" for almost an hour wherein he "extol[s] the virtue of his drugs and confections." Coryat marvels at the glittering oratorical skills of the *ciarlatani*:

5.1 Charlatans on Piazza San Marco, from Giacomo Franco, *Habiti D'Huomini e Donne Venetiane*, **1609.**

5.2 *A mountebank couple on a trestle stage*, from the friendship album of
Sigmundus Ortelius (dated 20 March 1574).

For they would tell their tales with such admirable volubility and plausible grace, even extempore, and seasoned with that singular variety of elegant jests and witty conceits, that they did often strike great admiration into strangers that never heard them before. (273)

Any respectable mountebank was known for glib, entertaining loquacity. One English mountebank, Thomas Rand, targeting older women, promises a cure for

those troubled with the pimple pamplins,
Whose skin is too short for the bodies,
That cannot sleep for farting.

He also vows to "purge the Brain from all graffick cloudifying humors which obstruct the senses of all superanuated maids" (*Harangues*, 2–3).

Volpone's impersonation of the famed mountebank Scoto in Ben Jonson's play opens a window into what these entertainments must have looked like, revealing both their audience appeal, and linguistic gyrations. Volpone, hoping to seduce Celia, the merchant Corvino's wife, comes into Piazza San Marco and sets up his stage under her window. The moment the skit begins, Sir Politic claims that mountebanks are "the only knowing men of Europe!" And although Peregrine counters with "And, I have heard, they are most lewd impostors" (2.2.9, 14), the crowd is clearly with Politic. Thrilled by the arrival of the mountebank, the people run after him shouting "Follow, follow, follow" (2.2.28). Attacking his competitors as "turdy-facy-nasty-paty-lousy-fartical rogues," Volpone/Scoto sounds very much like the printed harangue of T. Jones, an English mountebank, who launches a diatribe against an "Upstart, Glister-Pipe, Bum-Peeping Apothecary" who prescribes "Vomit" (*Harangues*, 19).[4] Volpone is so clever and witty that Sir Politic, positively delighted, remarks: "Excellent! Ha' you heard better language, sir?" (II.2.68). In a paradoxical moment, Jonson congratulates himself for his perfect imitation of linguistic duplicity, while also poking fun at it.

---

4   See this collection of harangues for more glib sales pitches. One mountebank promises a "neverfailing stiptick, corroborating, odiferous, anodinous, balsamic, balsam of balsams, made of dead men's fat, rosin, and goose-grease, which infallibly restores lost maidenheads, raises demolished noses, and by its ... cosmetic quality, preserves supernatural bawdy from wrinkles" (*Harangues*, 14) and cured the Duchess of Boromolpho of "cramp in her tongue" (18). Another promises to cure a hurt caused by lifting a "dung pot" by using a "medicating unguent, being properly used by friction, and by the hand of a maid of fifteen" (3). A bit of doggerel ends with "And if you die / Never believe me more" (12).

When Volpone's long oration is complete, he begins his selling pitch, lowering his price, because "I despise money," (2.2.181) he says. Soon after, Celia throws down her handkerchief and buys Volpone's remedy; this matches Moryson's description, in which people pass along their "handkerchers with money" to the mountebanks who would cast them back "with wares tied in them, which some buy for use, others only to have more sport from the fool" (425). The folk remedies for sale, "distilled water, and divers ointments," or secret oils or powders like Volpone's were for common ailments like catarrh, "burning Aches and stitches ... the Itch and scabs" (Moryson, 425). But the theatrics and speeches did not end when the selling began. On the contrary, as we see in *Volpone*, Nano and Mosca, Volpone's sidekicks, sing throughout the sales pitch. Preying on the fears of the audience, they ask, "Would you be ever fair? And young? / Stout of teeth? And strong of tongue?" (2.2.195–6). According to Coryat, while the lead performer handed out the remedies, he would continue to deliver an "extemporal speech" festooned with "savory jests" ministering "passing mirth and laughter to the whole company, which perhaps may consist of a thousand people that flock together about one of their stages" (274).

Sometimes the sales oration could be followed by a comic play. An Italian writer, Domenico Ottonelli, reported that after the remedies were sold, and the money collected, the head charlatan cried out: "Let the comedy begin!" At this moment all the charlatans would change their costumes, take on comic roles and present a full-length play, "filling people with laughter and delight" (Eamon, 239). The entertainments needed to be enticing enough to insure that an audience would gather and continue to gather each time the mountebanks arrived. Those who purchased a remedy, in essence, paid the price of admission while treating the onlookers to a free entertainment.

The fame of the mountebank shows indicates that the performers were fairly talented actors and musicians, and the performances, ranging from skits and vaudeville-like routines to full-length plays, must have been humorous enough to secure return customers. In England, for example, the slapstick antics of a Merry Andrew at Wisbech fair enthralled Thomas Holcroft as soon as the clown jumped onstage,

> alighting half upright, roaring with pretended pain, pressing his hip declaring he had put out his collar-bone, crying to his master to come and cure it, receiving a kick, springing up and making a somersault; thanking his master kindly for making him well, yet the moment his back was turned, mocking him with wry faces. (Thompson, 75)

These theatrical skits probably provided ideas and inspiration for the more professional theater. William Eamon, for example, writes that the "slapstick comedy" of the mountebanks used "the characters, devices and gigs of what would later be called (in politer circles) the commedia dell'arte" (238).[5] Characters such as Dottore Graziano, lawyer, university don, sometimes quack doctor; Franceschina, the pretty young maid, and the *zanni* often appeared on the mountebank's stage. In one skit, Graziano advises a patient how to cure a toothache: "Hold a ripe apple in your mouth and put your head in the oven; before the apple is cooked your toothache will be gone" (Eamon, 241). The tricks of Franceschina and her fame in England is evident by the passage in *Volpone* in which Corvino, outraged to find Celia looking out her window at a mountebank troupe, beats the entertainers off, crying "What, is my wife your Franciscina, sir?" (2.3.4).

The absurdly humorous quality of these skits probably explains in part why these performances were very entertaining. But the popularity of these shows was also due to the presence of the women. Ottonelli observed that the "comici ciarlatani" would not be so well received without their women (Lea, 311). In Thomas Platter's visit to Avignon in 1598, he records seeing the Italian mountebank troupe of Zanni Bragetta that had seven performers, two of whom were women. These female performers could act, play music, dance, or perform acrobatic feats. The international crowd in the foreground of figure 5.1 forms the border of a famous scene depicting the Piazza San Marco in Venice. Two of the three stages feature women performers; the richly dressed lute player in the center may be a courtesan figure, an *innamorata*, or even a cross-dressed male (Henke, 7); the bearded man in the long coat may be Doctor Graziano, and the player to his right, the *zanni*. Note that the older mountebank is holding a snake in his hand, while the other holds up a remedy for sale.

The woman player could become a spectacular draw. The Italian mountebank, Girolamo Ferranti, famous for his "orvietan," a remedy for poison and other illnesses, had a young female called La Vettoria in his troupe. In Florence in 1616 La Vettoria performed every evening in the piazza with eight other men and women. They made money from their sales and, as the Florentine *Avvisi* reports,

> keep giving pleasure to the people assembled there, who spend to their hearts' delight. The shapely Vettoria, dressed like a trim and neat boy, packs in large crowds with her dangerous leaps, her divine dancing, her sweet singing, and her beautiful gaze, that by its sweetness softens and lulls her audience, who sing and cry out: "O, my heart, what is this marvel?" Of course, there are certain old men who keep gazing at her with their mouths open, because they want to play games with her and have a taste themselves. (Henke, 27)

---

5   The precise relationship of mountebank performances to commedia dell'arte is a much debated issue. See, for example, Katritzky (2000), Gentilcore (1998), and Henke (1997).

Vettoria had to be "accompanied home each day after her work by four policemen lest she be crushed by the crowds who seek her" (Henke, 27). In this description Vettoria seems to be the extra, added pleasure one might potentially possess along with the herbal remedies; she is a delight the men would devour if the police were not there.

Like the description of Vettoria, many references to these women players are erotic. Garzoni reports that a mountebank called "Il Toscano" had in his group a female acrobat, a "putta" (whore), who "elicits a strange desire in the people with her lascivious graces" (Henke, 8). In the Zanni Bragetta troupe, the women were not only performers, but were responsible for collecting the money for the cures. According to Thomas Platter, in passing wares and money back and forth in handkerchiefs, the women sometimes "added a little note to the tin, detailing where they could be met, and at what hour" (Katritzky 1998, 114). In *Volpone* it is the possibility of such an assignation that enrages Corvino when Celia drops her handkerchief to Volpone/Scoto. Believing she has become part of the entertainment, Corvino scolds his wife for behaving like the "tumbling whore" (2.6.14) he has seen perform with the mountebanks: "You were an actor with your handkerchief! / Which he, most sweetly, kissed in the receipt" (2.5.39–40).

Mountebank performances themselves were thought to be breeding grounds for lechery, and both weak-willed women and men could easily be corrupted. Corvino believes that Celia is so taken with the mountebank performance because she is a whore, eager to "mount," like all women easy prey to sexual advances. When he challenges his wife with, "Would you not mount?" (2.5.18), he attacks what he sees as her desire to sexually mount Scoto *and* her desire to mount the stage. In effect, as Peter Parolin writes, Corvino is threatened by Celia's "theatrical agency" (115), the fear that she will become a performer. The threat that Corvino feels about Celia mirrors what the larger male society felt about female mountebanks – that their role as performers (and as healers) gave them a certain amount of agency in the world beyond the enclosure of the home, in which Celia is expected to remain confined.

In other references to mountebank women the emphasis is not on their "lascivious" charms, but their status as performers, peddlers, and healers. Ottonelli, for example, describes a "zanni," playing a musical instrument, who is then joined by other performers, "often a woman." Later in the selling portion of the entertainment, another woman is mentioned, "La Signora," who "sells her dainties or whatever delicacies she has" (Lea, 311). What is important in this instance is that La Signora seems to be selling a remedy of her own making, revealing that the female members of the troupes could also be the ones who created the cures.

Often the women who performed in these troupes were the wives of the head mountebank (fig. 5.2, for example, may well represent a husband-and-wife team). In 1609 a mountebank called Talavino requested permission from the

Grand Duke Cosimo of Tuscany to perform "with his wife and company" and to be allowed to sell *olio distillate*, or distilled oil (Henke, 10). When Girolamo Ferranti died, his wife Clarissa maintained control over the famous formula for "orvietan" and used it to secure her own successful performance career. Retaining the secret of the formula, she married two other husbands, both mountebanks, and acted in their shows from the 1620s through the 1640s. Clarissa, apparently quite talented, was described by a French writer as "that gallant and superb actress Clarice" (Marks, 137). In seventeenth-century Paris, Clarissa and many other mountebanks performed on the Pont-Neuf, a gathering place like the piazzas of Italy and the squares of London (Marks, 136).

In England, during the latter end of the seventeenth century, Joseph Haines, a well-known mountebank, was accompanied by his wife, who had her own area of expertise. Working in partnership with her, Haines tells the women who are reticent about consulting him to seek out his wife, an "expert on all feminine Distempers" who has "Cosmetic Water" that promises to remove freckles, "Sunburns, or Pimples." She also offers a "famous never-failing remedy for offensive breaths, [and] a famous essence to correct the ill scent of the arm pits." Along with her other miracles, she can change hair color, "shape the eyebrows to a miracle," make "low foreheads as high as you please" and "remove all warts, from the face, hands, fingers, and privy parts" (*Harangues*, 40).

In such roles, these female performers seem fully engaged in the enterprise, not relegated to the inferior position of sidekick. These women not only performed on the mountebank stages in a variety of ways, as singers, actors, musicians, or dancers, they were also involved in the creation and selling of their own remedies. Although David Gentilcore writes that women played only a "limited," "secondary role ... as members of established troupes, acting alongside their husbands or performing dances and songs to draw in crowds" (1995, 307), I would argue that the very act of being on the stage made these women performers and granted them a certain amount of economic and theatrical agency. The wives of the mountebanks were not only performers, but, as these examples indicate, were also engaged in "commercial partnership" with their husbands, "equal business partners, with shared responsibilities" (Katritzky 2001, 144). These women were "traveling, healing, entertaining, and risking litigation along with these men" (Klairmont-Lingo 1986, 594). Here we have an example of what Natalie Zemon Davis calls "shared work identity," where women worked alongside of their husbands doing the exact same work, but not always getting the same recognition (174–5; also see Klairmont-Lingo, 1999).

In the sixteenth and seventeenth centuries there were so few doctors and so many poor people who could not afford their care that many healers who were on the margins were allowed to practice and take care of the medical needs of people. For example, in 1542 the third of Henry VIII's Medical Acts was passed allowing "divers honest persons, as well men as women, whom God hath endued with the knowledge of the nature, kind and operation of certain herbs, roots and waters, and the using and ministering of them to such as be pained with customable diseases." This permission came in response to the paucity of medical care and to the accusation that doctors and surgeons neglected people's health needs, while "minding only their own lucres" (Poynter, 153–4). Further, according to English Common Law, "anyone could practice medicine as long as the patient consented" (Cook, 28).

During this period, as recent scholarship has shown, many healers, whether part of mountebank troupes or not, were often women. The very real need for medical care and the fact that women played a role in healing may help explain why some of them were involved in these entertainments.[6] Most ordinary people put their faith in folk medicine and often looked to members of their community who were steeped in traditional lore. These folk practitioners were thought to possess "secrets," or familiarity with cures that the doctors did not have (Eamon, 259). It is likely that most male and female mountebanks had some medical knowledge of this sort. In fact, according to Brockliss and Jones, the "ranks of the traveling mountebanks were full of practitioners struggling to be regarded as part of the orthodox medical community" (279). The mountebank healers often cared for people who could not afford aid from the regular doctors. In a 1578 trial, for example, Jean L'Escalier, a female empiric, defended herself by saying that she did not take away from the practice of the doctors in the Angevin countryside since she treated those whom the medical community ignored (296).[7]

The great popularity of the mountebanks as both multi-media performers and peddlers of simple remedies drew them into the debate about medical care and made them subject to attacks from physicians as well as critics of the theater. Subject to the condemnation, laws, and regulations that hounded other

6 With the introduction of the Elizabethan Poor Laws, for example, parishes paid local "wise women to look after the sick poor." As Cook surmises, this arrangement would indicate that even those who could pay would seek health care from women (32–3). In England, it was apparently not until the eighteenth century that male practitioners dominated in this sphere (Cook, 33n.22); also see Pelling, Pomata, Klairmont-Lingo (1999), and Wyman. Patients and practitioners could also consult medical and herbal books by women, such as Mrs. Corylon, *A Book of Divers Medicines, Broths, Salves, Waters* ... (1606); Jane Jackson, *A Very Short and Compendious Method of Physic and Chirurgery* (1642); Joan Gibson, *A Book of Medicines* (1632).

7 Examples such as this indicate that the "corporative community's hatred of the medical penumbra" was primarily a moral one rather than an economic one since healers like L'Escalier were filling a healthcare vacuum (Brockliss and Jones, 296).

traveling performers, the mountebank troupes had to receive permission and be granted a license in order to perform in safety; without a license they were considered rogues (Chambers, 1: 280).[8] Many English laws from 1531 to 1598 stipulated that players who did not enjoy the protection of a rich patron could be arrested, imprisoned, or in the case of a 1547 law, "branded and put to forced labor as slaves" (Chambers, 1: 270). In order to control the number of mountebanks under James I, the College of Physicians was empowered to "fine or imprison" mountebanks or "bring them to trial," if necessary (Sloan, 140). In 1588 a female mountebank, Tomazine Scarlet, who "confessed she knew nothing of Physick," and who could neither "read or write, yet had hundreds under her cure to whom she gave medicines," was fined "ten pounds and was committed to prison for her misdeeds" (Thompson, 29–30). In Italy as well laws were passed trying to suppress the actors, and licenses were required for traveling performers (Gentilcore, 1995; Henke, 9–12; Lea, 314).[9]

Although a medical establishment comparable to what we have today did not exist during the sixteenth and seventeenth centuries, an elite group of male doctors tried to establish itself as the exclusive medical authority. In England, for example, the College of Physicians, founded in 1518, continually struggled to defend its position against mountebanks and any other groups who dared to practice medicine without the required university education. In *The Piss-Prophet* (1637), Thomas Brian attacks those men and women who have not been "authorized" by the College of Physicians or the universities (107), or who have not been "lawfully" "qualified with that knowledge and those arts that necessarily" make a physician (104). In Montpellier, the medical establishment declared its intention to "exterminate all empirics from the city" in 1573 and 1580 (Klairmont-Lingo 1985–6, 583).

Doctors and other critics attacked mountebanks as quacks, fakes, and worse: "the very scum of the Earth" bent on destroying "the noble art of medicine" (Turner, 33). James I's *Daemonologie* (1597) associates them with devils and witches, comparing Satan – who uses tricks and "innumerable" false practices – to "that Italian Scoto" (232), the famous mountebank who was Volpone's model. One London observer writes in 1602 that "quack-Salvers" are drawn from the "abject and seditious scum and refuse of the people" who "get their living by killing men." Pull off their masks, and "they will appear to be runagate Jews, the cut-throats and robbers of Christians, ... shifting and outcast pettifoggers ... stage players, jugglers, peddlers, prittle-pratling

---

8   In *Mount Tabor*, for example, Willis writes that when players came to Gloucester they needed to "attend the Mayor to inform him what noble-man's servants they are, and so to get a license for their public playing" (10).

9   See Matthews for mountebank licenses in Britain.

barbers ... toothless and tattling old wives, chattering char-women, long-tongued mid-wives, dog leeches and such like baggage" (Thompson, 34).

As this catalogue makes clear, women were an essential part of the mountebank world, as healers and entertainers, and as such were subject to attack. In his *Observations ... With an Useful Detection of the Mountebanks of Both Sexes* (1653), Richard Whitlock attacks women as "she empirics" and "Quacking Delilah's," "Quacking Hermaphrodites" who are like their "Grandmother Eve" except that Eve killed "us all at once," and the female mountebanks "kill us one by one" (52, 45). Another critic, Daniel Turner, in his *Apologia Chyrurgia* (1695), writes these "ignorant" women use cures "as make the devil in hell dance for joy" (17) "Whipping is not good enough for these women," he concludes: "capital punishment is the only way" (124).

Such fulminations did not stop customers from seeking out female practitioners and mountebanks who, excluded from formal education, relied on practical knowledge and folk experience. Turner laments that "it is said that women," along with weavers and cobblers, "did cure more people than Chyrurgions" (16). At the hands of these "petticoat pretenders," people fall under the spell of a

> continual delusion practiced by ignorant women in the heart of their metropolis, the city of London, where there are such prodigious numbers, who take upon them to practice both physic and chyrurgery that [there is] scarce a street, lane, court, alley, or other building [wherein] you shall not walk far before you meet with some bawdy doctress ready to entertain you and administer to your infirmities, be they ever so obscene. (107)

Richard Whitlock complains that people readily believe in the efficacy of such women, spreading the word that "such a good woman, gentlewoman, or Lady, gave me that did me good" (54). In shocked disbelief, and without any apparent irony, Turner contemptuously writes that people prefer the female mountebanks, who "endeavor" with "Ointments and precious Salves" to "remove disorders" over the more dangerous medicine of the surgeons who "cut" their clients or use "searing irons" (118).

Further, critics found it particularly irksome that women would even presume to speak, to make judgments, to "discern" (Whitlock, 75). Turner is dismayed that "an ignorant Woman's Judgment" should be held to "surpass that of the most eminent artist" (121). The presumption of female mountebanks to quote "ancient authors" angered doctors such as John Cotta. In his *Short Discourse of the Unobserved Dangers* (1612), he warned men not to consult with women whose "authority in learned knowledge cannot be authentical" because neither God nor nature "made them commissioners in the sessions of learning and understanding" (25). Whitlock complains that women, ignorant of Latin, "only know nicknames of diseases." Unable to "diagnose," they can only "pronounce" (46, 47). Yet their quick tongues turn the heads of the "unwary" that choose to "embrace the Poison of a Woman's Speech, while they neglect and contemn the Counsel of a legal artist" (125).

These women, who dare to transgress their prescribed gender roles, need to know their place, and remain there. Since, as Cotta writes, they "profess no arts" and cannot "prove their rules, let them with sobriety govern the great rule of themselves," and be free from "the dishonor of womanhood" (26). Like Cotta, Whitlock invokes heavenly authority to reassure himself that women are ill-suited to discern anything. God destined women to be "semsters and cooks;" thus they need to set themselves on "proper works as making shirts and smocks for the poor ... employments commendably within their sphere" (Whitlock, 56, 55). But these ambitious women, not content with "comforting" people with food, want "fame," and it is this which is the "principal" desire of these "she doctors" (55).

These attacks rehearse the usual complaints about women – they are incompetent, ignorant, proud, prone to evil, and have the audacity to speak. As females, they ought to practice silence and remain at home, "within their sphere," in the very way that Corvino wishes Celia to behave. Since the very fabric of society rests on women fulfilling their designated duties, by leaving the home and choosing public roles as performers, speakers, and healers, they threaten to destabilize the social order. Whitlock's phrases "Quacking Hermaphrodites" and "Quacking Delilahs" express the collective fear the female mountebanks aroused, while attempting to demolish their authority. Delilah was after all the femme fatale of the Bible who deceived Samson and took away all his strength, just as the female mountebanks pretend to heal but really offer harm. "Quacking" underscores the insignificance of female speech, poking fun at the female voice, reducing it to the quacking of a duck – noisy, insignificant gibberish. Further, women who abandon their established gender roles lose their feminine nature, becoming hermaphrodites, or worse, becoming like men.

What is apparent from these attacks is the *dis*-ease that female mountebanks engendered in those trying to shore up the medical profession for their own. And while it is serious business if the remedies proffered by the mountebanks were dangerous, most of the cures, like blackberry, mint, lemon waters, or ointments of balsam or marshmallows, seem harmless enough (Turner, 108). But the simplicity and cheap accessibility of these remedies, combined with the transformation of medicine into a performance art, probably made it difficult for the doctors to compete with the mountebanks.

Yet while bitterly attacking the female mountebanks for performing cures, the licensed doctors rely on theatrical tropes that stress the connection between medicine and performance, describing women who mount "the public stage of ... Ambition," where music is the "bait" that draws people in. Some "bawdy Doctress ready to entertain" will certainly lead to a "fatal Performance," laments Turner (20, 107, 11). In his warning about the perilous "dance" of the "she practitioner" (50), Whitlock figures the female mountebank as a medical Salome whose performance will kill. Yet Cotta, for example, who has a chapter called "The True Artist," seems to admit that medicine is an art, a performance. But if medicine is an art, it is up to the doctors to define it as such. And if medical doctors are going to perform cures, they will do so in a venue under their control, not public and certainly not calculated to provoke laughter.[10]

In a similar vein, the mountebanks, mimicking the private venues of the doctors, did not always present their performances on a public stage: some "performed" their cures in front of and within shops. These mountebanks could be "sedentary, selling their remedies from their homes or workshops," and then traveling part of the year (Gentilcore 1998, 313). Some of the female mountebanks fell into this category and had shops as well. According to Whitlock, these "Petticoat Practitioners" and "Piss-pot Waterologists" with their "tricks" make "people believe they can discern" (75). He describes one "old Tart" who "boasted of her giftishness in Waterology," sitting in her "chamber next to the street door" ready to analyze urine and offer advice (78). In Bologna, Caterina Cattani Greca petitioned the Protomedicato to put up a sign outside her door indicating her treatments, since "as a well-born woman she [was] not allowed to mount platforms in public squares" (Gentilcore 1995, 307). As performance spaces these shops, as one might imagine, could be exotic and fantastic. Turner describes one shop in London festooned with the skeletons of dogs, rabbits, stuffed crocodiles, human bones, and teeth (29). In the same ways that the colorful spectacle of the outdoor performances lured people, so did the remarkable dwellings of the mountebanks bring people in for the entertainment of healing. The orations of these shop mountebanks, their analysis of urine, the selling of remedies, and the offer of prescriptions for maladies, are indoor versions of the open-air performances of the mounte-banks, while such a shop could be considered a performance space, a type of stage. Here the patient enters to be entertained and cured by the antics and remedies of the mountebank. In fact, in this venue, the female mountebanks could more safely occupy center stage, unlike some of the other public performances where they may not have been the lead act.

This narrative of female mountebanks on public and private stages makes it clear that throughout Europe they were well known as both healers and entertainers. What emerges in seeking out the "Quacking Delilahs" is that their presence, far from minor, was actually quite important. The audiences of the day embraced the mountebanks. And in those fleeting moments high up on

---

10   One Italian critic complained that "if medicine is a virtue, to want to sell it by means of clowning is to butcher it" (Gentilcore 1995, 308).

their makeshift stages or in their storefront theaters, the mountebanks played on the notion of medicine as performance and sometimes cured people with age-old remedies and with laughter in the community of shared experience. And in the midst of this medicine show, women played their part.

Works Cited and Consulted

Brian, Thomas. *The Piss-Prophet of Certain Piss-Pot Lectures*. London, 1637.

Brockliss, Laurence and Colin Jones. *The Medical World of Early Modern France*. Oxford: Clarendon Press, 1997.

Burke, Peter. *Popular Culture in Early Modern Europe*. Hants, UK: Scolar Press, 1994.

Chambers, E. K. *The Elizabethan Stage*. 4 vols. Oxford: Clarendon Press, 1923.

Cook, Harold. *The Decline of the Old Medical Regime in Stuart London*. Ithaca: Cornell University Press, 1986.

Coryat, Thomas. *Coryate's Crudities*. New York: Macmillan, 1905.

Cotta, John. *A Short Discoverie of the Unobserved Dangers of Several Sorts of Ignorant and Unconsiderate Practicers of Physic in England*. London, 1612.

Corylon, Mrs. *A Book of Diverse Medicines, Broths, Salves, Waters* ... [1606]. Wellcome Institute MS 213.

Davis, Natalie Zemon. "Women in the Crafts in Sixteenth-Century Lyon." Ed. Barbara A. Hanawalt. *Women and Work in Preindustrial Europe*. Bloomington: Indiana University Press, 1986.

Debus, Allen G. *The English Paracelsians*. New York: Franklin Watts, 1965.

Eamon, William. *Science and the Secrets of Nature*. Princeton: Princeton University Press, 1994.

Frost, Thomas. *The Old Showmen and the Old London Fairs*. London, 1874.

Garzoni, Tomaso. *La Piazza universale di tutte le professioni del mondo*. In Tomaso Garzoni, *Opere*. Ravenna: Longo Editore, 1993.

Gentilcore, David. "'Charlatans, Mountebanks and other Similar People': the Regulation and Role of Itinerant Practitioners in Early Modern Italy." *Social History* (1995): 297–314 .

———. *Healers and Healing in Early Modern Italy*. Manchester: Manchester University Press, 1998.

Gibson, Joan. *A Book of Medicines* [1632]. Wellcome Institute MS 311.

The Harangues or Speeches of Several Famous Mountebanks in Town and Country. By "D.G." London: T. Warner, 1700.

Harrison, G. B. *James I, Daemonologie* and *News from Scotland*. London: Bodley Head Quartos, 1924.

Henke, Robert. "The Italian Mountebank and the *Commedia Dell'Arte*." *Theater Survey* 38.2 (1997): 1–29.

Jackson, Joan. *A Very Short and Compendious Method of Physic and Chirurgery* [1642]. Wellcome Institute MS 373.

Jonson, Ben. *Volpone*. New York: W. W. Norton, 1968.

Katritzky, M. A. "Was *Commedia dell'arte* Performed by Mountebanks? *Album amicorum* Illustrations and Thomas Platter's Description of 1598." *Theatre Research International*, 23: 2 (1998): 104–25.

———. "Gendering Tooth-Drawers on the Stage." *Ludica* 5–6 (2000): 144–81.

———. "Marketing Medicine: The Image of the Early Modern Mountebank." *Renaissance Studies* (2001): 121–53.

Klairmont-Lingo, Alison. "Empirics and Charlatans in Early Modern France: The Genesis of the 'Other' in Medical Practice." *Journal of Social History* 19 (1985–6): 583–603.

———. "Women Healers at the Hotel-Dieu Oflyon: Poverty and Disease in the Early Modern Era." *Dynamis. International Journal of History and Science and Medicine.* 19 (1999): 79–94.

Lea, K. M. *Italian Popular Comedy: A Study in the Commedia dell'Arte 1560–1620.* 2 vols. New York: Russell and Russell, 1962.

Marks, Jonathan. "The Charlatans of Pont-Neuf." *Theatre Research International* 23. 2 (1998): 133–41.

Matthews, Leslie. "Licensed Mountebanks in Britain." *Journal of the History of Medicine and Allied Sciences* xix (1964): 30–44.

Morley, Henry. *Memoirs of Bartholomew Fair.* London: Chapman and Hall, 1859.

Moryson, Fynes. *Itinerary* (1617). New York: Benjamin Bloom, 1967.

Ottonelli, Domenico. *Della Christiana moderazione del teatro.* Florence: Stamperia di G. A. Bonardi, 1652.

Parolin, Peter. "'A Strange Fury Entered My House': Italian Actresses and Female Performance in *Volpone*." *Renaissance Drama* XXIX (2000): 107–35.

Pelling, Margaret. "Compromised by Gender: The Role of the Male Medical Practitioner in Early Modern England." *The Task of Healing: Medicine, Religion and Gender in England and the Netherlands, 1450–1800*. Ed. Hilary Marland and Margaret Pelling. Rotterdam: Erasmus Publishing, 1996.

Platter, Thomas. *Thomas Platter d. J: Beschreibung der Reisen durch Frankreich, Spanien, England und die Niederlande 1595–1600.* Ed. Rut Keiser. Stuttgart: 1968.

Pomata, Gianna. "Practicing Between Earth and Heaven: Women Healers in Seventeenth-Century Bologna." *Dynamis* 19 (1999): 119–43.

Poynter, F. N. L. "Medicine and Public Health." *Shakespeare in His Own Age*. Ed. Allardyce Nicoll. London: Cambridge University Press, 1976, 152–67.

Sloan, A. *English Medicine in the Seventeenth Century*. Durham: Durham Academic Press, 1996.

Thompson, C. J. S. *The Old Quacks of London.* Philadelphia: J. P. Lippincott, 1929.

Turner, Daniel. *Apologia Chyrurgica, A Vindication of the Noble Art of Chyrurgery, from the Gross Abuses Offered Thereunto by Mountebanks, Quacks, Barbers, Pretending Bone-setters and Other Ignorant Undertakers.* London: J. Whitlock, 1695.

Willis, R. *Mount Tabor.* London, 1639.

Whitlock, Richard. *Observations on the Present Manners of the English Briefly Anatomizing the Living by the Dead With an Useful Detection of the Mountebanks of Both Sexes.* London, 1653.

Wyman, A. L. "The Surgeoness: The Female Practioner of Surgery 1400–1800." *Medical History* 28 (1984): 22–41.

PART III
BEYOND THE CHANNEL

Chapter 6

Reading the Actress in Commedia Imagery

M. A. Katritzky

There is a venerable tradition of scholarship on the pioneering actresses of the early modern Italian stage. But mainstream theater history has been slow to absorb its findings, and many studies of the commedia dell'arte focus primarily on its comic male "masks." Only recently has emphasis on the colorful and distinctive stock roles given way to wider recognition that studying female roles and players is not an intriguing sideline, but essential to understanding the importance of the commedia to Western theater.[1] The spectacular success of early prima donnas created a radical change in theatrical gender dynamics that transformed the art of the *comici*, profoundly influenced the English theater before the advent of actresses, and paved the way for the modern professional stage.

Women had been performing in Europe and England long before the commedia dell'arte created the first female stars.[2] Nonetheless, commedia troupes are rightly credited with pioneering the systematic promotion of

---

1 This chapter is dedicated to the memory of Elizabeth Howe, whose contribution to the history of women on the stage is an inspiration to her former colleagues and students in the Literature Department of The Open University, and to theater historians worldwide. I wish to thank Pamela Allen Brown for motivating, and radically shaping, this adaptation of several sections of my 1995 DPhil thesis, and the Trustees of the Elizabeth Howe Fund for research support during the period 2002–2004. Translations, unless otherwise noted, are mine. The author of this chapter has made every effort to contact the copyright holders of the photographs here reproduced.

2 Modern scholarship dates the introduction of actresses into Italian troupes to the early 1560s, often citing the remark by renowned actor Pier Maria Cecchini in 1614 that "it was less than 50 years ago that women appeared in costume on stage" (Lea 114; Falconieri 1954, 41; MacNeil 2003, 2). Amateur all-female acting had a long tradition in European convents. Vigil Raber, director of the 1514 Bolzano Passion Play, assigned virtually all its female roles to local women amateurs (Katritzky, 2004, 105–106). Neither were amateur actresses unknown in sixteenth-century

professional actresses as celebrity performers. By the 1560s, prima donnas were a star attraction of the Italian companies, contributing significantly to their tremendous audience impact. The reconstruction of these women's contributions through written documents is far from straightforward, however, and the surviving visual material can greatly extend our understanding of early actresses and female roles. The commedia's transitory nature, with its reliance on improvisation, non-verbal entertainment, and scenarios or plot summaries, in addition to plays based on fully written-out scripts, makes visual records particularly important. Until comparatively recently, "the systematic codifying, dating and interpretation of the prints, drawings, paintings and frescos relating to the [commedia]," which are fundamental to assessing how far the visual record reflects early modern stage practice, had "barely begun" (Heck, 293). This essay examines commedia dell'arte actresses in the context of the pictorial record. Still under-researched by comparison with the textual documentation, these images indicate that the advent of the women player was a key catalyst in the expansion of the commedia beyond its dual roots in theater, especially humanist comedy, and in popular culture, including mountebank activity and carnival ritual. The visual record, which depicts female *comici* in a rich diversity of performance types and places, vividly suggests the widening impact of female stage roles and women's increasing integration into the acting profession.

The earliest formal record of an Italian actress joining a professional troupe is a Roman contract of 10 October 1564, in which Lucretia of Siena and six men agree to form a company to perform comedies (Re, appendix). Mixed gender troupes such as Lucretia's burst onto the mid-sixteenth-century European stage with a hybrid vigor and fertile creativity achieved by fusing the disparate skills of amateur actors, professional fools and buffoons, carnival revellers, courtesans, and street performers, such as mountebank troupes, acrobats, musicians, and dancers (figs 6.1–6.7). Although improvisation is often singled out as the defining characteristic of commedia dell'arte players, they presented fully scripted plays, *intermedi* and other musical theater by leading writers and composers, in addition to fully or partially improvised comedies, pastorals, tragedies and melodramas, shorter *bufonarie* and *momarie*, and set pieces based on instrumental music, singing, mime, dancing, and acrobatics.

England in cycle drama, Lord Mayor's shows, and elsewhere (Bevington 166; also see essays in Part I of this volume). French professional actresses are recorded from 1545, when Marie Ferré [or Fairet] first trod the boards (Scott).

6.1 Pieter de Jode after Lodewyk Toeput (*c.*1550–*c.*1603/5), *Masquerade*.

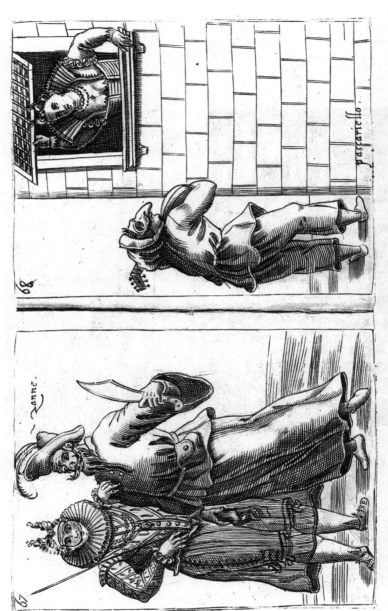

6.2   Pietro Bertelli, *Zanne with a courtesan, Pascariello with a courtesan* (1591), from Bertelli's *Diversaru[m] nationum habitus, iconibus in ære incisis.*

6.3   Julius Goltzius, *Magnificus larvatus, Scoztum Venetu Larvatum, il Zani famulus* (1581).

6.4   *A masked woman flanked by two men in Zanni costume* **(1596).**

6.5 *Freund sein khan nit schaden [it can't hurt to be friends]*, from the friendship album (1583–1601) of Hans Jakob Wintholtz (*c.*1583).

6.6   Joseph Heintz II (c.1600–78), *Carnival in Venice* (detail: dancing *Zanni* and woman on a mountebank stage).

6.7   *A feast*, by or after Marten de Vos (1532–1603).

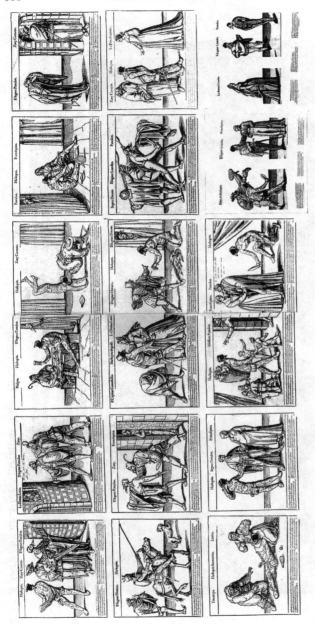

6.8   *A commedia dell'arte performance*, an arrangement of eighteen woodcuts from the *Recueil Fossard*.

6.9   *Harlequin disguised* (late sixteenth century).

6.10 *Italian comedians on stage* (late sixteenth century).

6.11   Ambrose I Francken, *Italian comedians* (late sixteenth century).

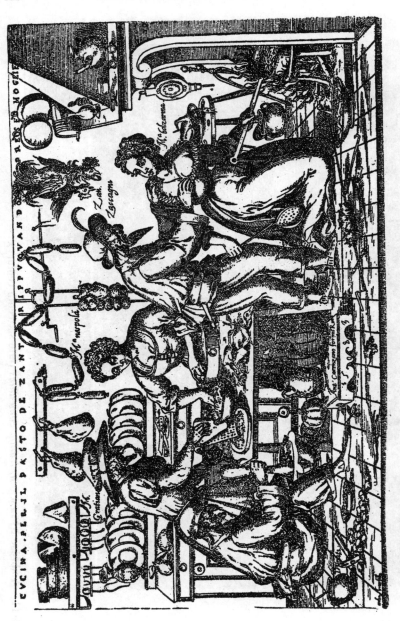

6.12   Ambrogio Brambilla, *Cucina per il pasto de Zan Trippu* (1583).

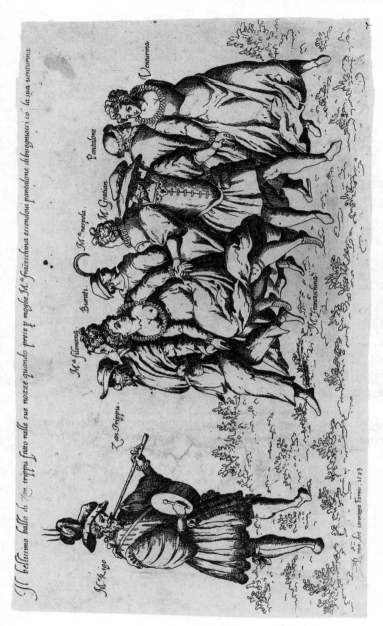

6.13   Ambrogio Brambilla, *Il bellisimo ballo di Zan Trippu* (1583).

6.14   Title pages to two commedia scenarios in the early seventeenth-century manuscript *Raccolta di scenari più scelti [...]*.

6.15 *Scene from the Italian comedy (c.1600?).*

Actresses competed for the part of the *innamorata*, the literary, educated, agile, beautiful, elegant, and performatively skilled romantic heroine, capable of declaiming, singing, dancing, jesting, miming, and memorizing (figs 6.8–6.11).[3] Talented women soon vied with actors in all theatrical spheres, as performers, leading stage attractions, and sometimes even as the writers and troupe leaders responsible for the major artistic and business decisions governing their companies. Vittoria Piisimi of Ferrara, who took the stage name "Fioretta," followed Vicenza Armani of Venice (fatally poisoned in 1569) as *prima donna* of the Gelosi troupe, and combined acting with a highly successful career as a troupe leader. Thomaso Porcacchi praised Piisimi in 1574 as "a most unique woman," and a decade later Tomaso Garzoni called her the "divine Vittoria, a compendium of all the arts, a perfect actress." While that encomium would seem hard to outdo, Garzoni reserves his highest praise for "the gracious Isabella," referring to Isabelli Andreini of the Gelosi (Baschet, 61; Garzoni, 753–4). Adding to the luster of Isabella's stage persona was her literary talent: her polished literary output gained her international renown as a playwright, poet and correspondent (see fig. 7.1 in Julie Campbell's essay, this volume). Like Vittoria, Isabella's daughter-in-law Virginia Andreini ("Florinda") and Drusiano Martinelli's wife Angelica Alberghini led early troupes. From the 1580s to at least 1605 Diana Ponti of Ferrara – one of several actresses who took the stage name "Lavinia" – led the Desiosi troupe, whose actresses so impressed Montaigne that he visited them in 1581 after their shows in Pisa, and arranged for them to receive presents of fish (Lea, 269).

Seeing women play women quickly became fashionable at the upper reaches of society. When Henri III of France came to Venice in 1574, he expressed the wish to see "the woman named Vittoria" act with her troupe, the Gelosi (Baschet, 57–8). Soon the *comici* were drawing Italian audiences away from the amateur players of the regular comedy, who always used males for women's roles. Their popularity made it commercially viable for them to earn a year-round living from performing, at court, in private houses, in the *stanze* they rented for semi-public performances, and in the new theaters then being built. Despite this temporal expansion, carnival remained their most profitable season, creating such demand that even the nobility often had difficulty in persuading their favorite troupes to serve them. Even dukes routinely experienced refusals that would be hard to imagine at the equivalent social level

---

3   See Brown, 403. Taviani and Schino speculate that early commedia actresses were learned courtesans with skills suited to theater (335). Their view is challenged by McGill, who argues women may have acquired performance and improvisation skills orally (59–61), and Scott, who proposes a multiplicity of models for the emergence of actresses (152).

in England.[4] The Medici took no chances for the spectacular 1589 wedding of Ferdinand de' Medici and Christina of Lorraine, which featured entertainments that constituted a "transitional landmark in the increasing role of women" in Renaissance theater (Saslow, 53). Hundreds of musicians, dancers, and singers were hired to perform in five *intermedi*, musical entertainments performed between the acts of plays. Although men were cast in the overwhelming majority of female and male roles, these *intermedi* broke new ground by starring three women. Two of the composer-performers, Antonio Archilei and Giulio Caccini, cast their wives, respectively the dancer, instrumentalist, and singer Vittoria Concarini and the singer Lucia Caccini, as *prima* and *seconda donna*. "Margherita," who was Archilei and Concarini's pupil, sang several supporting roles, and more women may have joined the cast at a later stage (Saslow, 54). These *intermedi* framed the acts of Girolamo Bargagli's scripted play *La pellegrina*, performed by all-male amateur actors, and two commedia plays, both staged by the Gelosi troupe. In these plays, *La Zingara* and *La pazzia d'Isabella*, the rival prima donnas Vittoria Piisimi and Isabella Andreini strove to outdo each other, and their brilliant performances as the gypsy (Piisimi) and the madwoman (Andreini) became a highlight of the wedding festivities.

While highly complex and luxurious, the Medici wedding was certainly not the first royal entertainment to employ professional actresses. Less than a decade after the advent of women players on the Italian professional stage in the 1560s, the mixed-gender companies were traveling beyond Italy to display their skills before the courts of northern Europe, including that of Elizabeth I. In the late 1570s, Drusiano Martinelli of Mantua led a troupe across the Alps. They played a nine-month season in Antwerp to October 1577, before traveling on to Paris and, in January 1578, England. Here, in spite of the plague prohibitions, the Lord Mayor and Privy Council of the City of London granted permission for "one Drousiano, an Italian, a commediante, and his companye" to perform within the city from January 1578 until the first week of Lent (Schrickx, 803). Flemish documents relating to this tour name all eight men of the troupe of eleven, including Drusiano's brother Tristano, depicted in the *Recueil Fossard* woodcuts and their iconographic derivatives (figs. 6.8, 6.9) as

---

4   In 1580, the Duke of Ferrara had trouble luring the best Gelosi players back from the Venice carnival, and Vittoria Piisimi and her husband Giovanni Pelesini wrote him letters of apology for being unavailable to entertain at two court weddings, including the Duke's own to Margherita Farnese (Solerti and Lanza, 165, 168). In 1583, Francesco Andreini wrote to Vincenzo Gonzaga, apologizing on behalf of himself and his wife Isabella for declining the Duke's invitation to perform at his forthcoming wedding to Eleonora de' Medici. Andreini cites prior obligations, being "bound by faith to the Gelosi, and in particular to Sig. Alvise Michiel, patron of the hall in Venice" (Lea, 308; MacNeil 2003, 6–7, 272–3).

Harlequin, the role he was to create around the year 1584 (Schrickx, 798). The troupe's three women, noted but not named by the documents, precede the official sanctioning of actresses on post-Restoration London stages by over eighty years (Howe, 20). Although the personnel of troupes often fluctuated rapidly, Spanish documents of the following decade are pertinent to the identities of Martinelli's actresses, who are significant for being among the first, and perhaps *the* first, women to feature in full-length plays on the English stage. These records are special licenses of 1587 allowing Drusiano, his wife Angelica Alberghini, his brother Tristano, their companions Angela Salomona and her (unnamed) husband, and "La Franceschina" to perform in Madrid (Falconieri 1957, 74–5).[5] In doing so, they identify the women of "Los Confidentes Italianos" as the first actresses in full-length plays on the Spanish stage – and their troupe as including veterans of the English tour of 1578.

Humbler female players also left their mark on foreign audiences. Prince Ferdinand of Bavaria was greatly impressed by the tumbling skills of a "young girl aged eleven or twelve," the star of a troupe of four Italian acrobats who performed for him in Trent in 1565 (fos. 42v–43r). Several years before Drusiano's troupe came to England, Italian women acrobats crossed the Channel to perform, scandalizing Thomas Norton, who in 1574 inveighed against "that unnecessarie and scarslie honeste resorts to plaies ... and especiallie the assemblies to the unchaste, shamelesse and unnaturall tomblinges of the Italion Woemen" (Lea, 354). English writers generally treated female players, regardless of whether they had speaking parts, with mocking contempt, degrading them by associating them with prostitutes. Thomas Nashe famously dismissed the celebrated Italian actresses as "whores and common Curtizens" and reduced their plays to the antics of "a Pantaloun, a Whore, and a Zanie" (Nashe, 215; see figs. 6.3 and 6.7 for such trios). The actor and troupe leader Dionisio, who, as "Scoto of Mantua" conjured, and possibly performed with a troupe, before Queen Elizabeth I in 1576 (Herford and Simpson, 704), is branded by Ben Jonson's Corvino as a "damned mountebank ... a common rogue ... fiddling in ... the *osteria*," his actress as a "tumbling whore," and their repertoire as "forcèd tricks" (*Volpone*, II.6, 10–16). John Marston's 1599 reference to a "nimbling tumbling *Angelica*" is taken by some as evidence for Angelica Alberghini's presence during the Martinelli brothers' 1578 English tour, or even as an indication of an otherwise undocumented later British visit by the troupe (110). More relevant to the presence of Italian actresses in Elizabethan England is a passage in John Day's *The Travailes of The Three English Brothers*, a play of 1607 that draws on the

---

5   Franceschina here may refer to the stage name of Silvia Roncaglia of Bergamo or, more likely, to the male actor Carlo or Carletto, who played the servetta Franceschina in Angelica's troupe throughout the 1590s.

overseas adventures of Anthony, Robert, and Thomas Shirley. In a much-quoted scene, Sir Anthony Shirley, to whom a visit by the English stage clown William Kemp in Rome is historically documented for 1601, invites Kemp and "an Italian Harlaken" to improvise a performance at his Italian residence (Lea, 350). The two clowns launch into an extended dialogue – with sexual innuendo robust enough to suggest that pictures such as figure 6.5 may have more than tenuous links to actual stage practice:

KEMP.   Now, Signior, how many are you in companie?
HARL.   None but my wife and my selfe, sir.
K.   Your wife! Why hearke you, wil your wife do tricks in publique?
H.   My wife can play.
K.   The honest woman, I make no question ... Your wife plaid the Curtizan.
H.   True.

(Nicoll 1931, 280)

English travelers' accounts of European performances emphasize the rarity of women performers back home. Actresses are treated as a newsworthy attraction and a significant innovation that was changing the theatrical landscape of early modern Europe. Fynes Moryson, who went to Italy in the 1590s, reports that "in Florence they had a house where all the yeare long a Commedy was played by professed players once in the weeke and no more, and the partes of wemen were played by wemen, and the cheefe Actors had not their parts fully penned, but spake much extempory or upon agreement betweene themselves, espetially the wemen, whose speeches were full of wantonnes, though not grosse baudry" (631). In 1608 Lord Herbert of Cherbury noted as a novelty that Italians performing in Paris featured "women [who] play boys" (Lea, 179). That year, in Venice, Thomas Coryat "saw women acte, a thing that I never saw before, though I have heard that it hath beene sometimes used in London, and they performed it with as good a grace, action, gesture and whatsoever convenient for a Player, as ever I saw any masculine Actor" (386).

For some actresses, superb musical gifts and a phenomenal ability to memorize quickly were the graces underpinning their success. In 1574, Vittoria Piisimi starred – at a week's notice – in the most demanding singing role of the Gelosi's production of Cornelio Frangipani's *Tragedia* (MacNeil 2003, 11–12). In 1608, the professional singer Caterina Martinelli, engaged for the title role of Monteverdi and Ottavio Rinuccini's opera *Arianna*, died just before the Mantuan wedding festivities of Francesco Gonzaga and Margherita of Savoy, for which the opera was written. Her replacement was Virginia Andreini, the *prima donna* of the Fedeli troupe, already engaged to perform in Giambattista Guarini's scripted drama *L'idropica*, the main play of the festivities. She mastered this demanding additional role in the astoundingly short span of six days. Virginia ("La Florinda") had performed well under pressure before, having achieved a stunning success in the title role of her husband Giovanni Battista Andreini's 1606 play *La Florinda*, which includes an elaborate sung lament. Her performance of *Arianna*'s lament represents both a key date in the development of opera and a defining moment in the history of women on the stage.[6] *Arianna* cemented her international reputation and became a routine feature of the repertoires of professional actresses.

Despite these successes, the mixed-gender troupes did not meet with universal acceptance. Their welcome varied widely from nation to nation. Even within the borders of Italy, the leading companies could be lionized in one region and shunned in another. Plays continued to be performed in which the lovers stayed off-stage entirely, and even in commedia dell'arte troupes, men played some female servant roles well into the seventeenth century. As late as 1588, for example, Diana Ponti's Desiosi troupe was licensed to play in Rome only without women (Lea, 270). Often this patchwork pattern of acceptance and exclusion arose from clerical opposition to theater in general and to actresses in particular. Scandalized by the growing power and success of the professional troupes and their intriguing actresses, prelates and theologians denounced the commedia's introduction of women onto the stage. In calling for a ban on all theater in 1578, Cardinal Gabriello Paleotti of Bologna specifically targets the *comici*'s "infamous women of ill repute," censuring actresses for earning their living through skills that exert a devastating effect on the morals of their audiences, and especially married men who fall for their charms (Taviani 1969, 39). Nonetheless, by the end of the century actresses were a standard feature of the professional Italian stage, inclusively implicated, rather than singled out, in Juan de Pineda's 1599 long-winded denunciations of the theater as a "devil's workshop" (Taviani 1969, 122). Five years later the Dominican monk Domenico Gori made renewed attempts to rid the stage of "the obscene antics" of the "commedie di Zanni." He warns men of the grave spiritual dangers of marrying an actress, and reminds actresses who perform in lewd comedies that their public words and gestures are as mortally sinful as the private deeds of prostitutes (Taviani 1969, 136–43).

Despite continuing clerical fulminations, there was no going back. The visual records chart the growing confidence of actresses in terms of costume and roles, sphere of action, and stage presence, and confirm the increasing indispensability of women performers at every level of theatrical activity.

---

6   According to MacNeil, in this performance "the combination of ... rhetorical gesture, seconda pratica music, and commedia dell'arte performance results in a radically new style of music theater that is representational in all its aspects" (2002, 403).

The Visual Record

Scholars studying women performers have a wide range of two-dimensional art to consider: paintings, drawings, and prints – some belonging to series, others created as single images – as well as rarer examples of three-dimensional art. These images are an invaluable evidential source for the appearance, costume, gestures, and props of early actresses, their stock roles and stage business. Early studies of actresses tended to interpret the iconography literally and to generalize broadly from a limited range of images of often uncertain date or provenance. While the pictorial record is important in assessing women's contribution to early modern theater, effective identification and interpretation require a critical approach to using pictures as historical evidence (as Leik for one points out), and an understanding of the complex issues surrounding gender representation on the early modern stage.

Only rarely does the pictorial record offer a straightforward reflection of early modern performing women. Most obviously, some pictures are modern forgeries, while others have suffered from unreliable restoration or dating, or have been altered by later additions, including texts.[7] Even in a genuine, reliable, and clear picture, women may be cross-dressed or otherwise disguised, and female stage roles are not necessarily played by women. A picture may not necessarily reflect a "historically authentic" performance event; if it does, there may be considerable variation in the degree of authenticity. All early modern pictures are subject to an array of contingencies that include artistic fantasy, iconographic precedents or commissioning pressures, and distortion for stylistic, moralistic, allegorical, satirical, or other reasons. Some depictions of actresses have no known visual precedents; many are pastiches, copies, or adaptations based on earlier works. Such factors are integral to the use of images as historical documents. They do not disqualify a picture from contributing to our knowledge of female performance, and an informed awareness of them can greatly enhance its theater-historical potential. Only a limited amount can be achieved by considering them in isolation. A better approach is to "read" individual pictures of actresses within the context of a wide array of relevant documentation, textual as well as visual.

---

7   A prime example is the famous "Bayeux painting," showing a crowded stage scene, which traditionally but erroneously has been held to record one of the first northern tours of the *comici*, to France in 1571 and 1572. An unreliable post-sixteenth-century caption identified some of its figures as ten members of the French royal family in the early 1570s collaborating with members of a commedia troupe (Duchartre, 86; Katritzky *Thesis*, 108–11; Leik, 190–6).

Among the best-known images of early actresses are those of the *Recueil Fossard*. The surviving sections of this dispersed and largely lost collection of miscellaneous early modern prints, now mainly in Scandinavia, include a much-reproduced sixteenth-century series of eighteen woodcuts of Harlequin with his Italian troupe of actors and actresses. Elsewhere I discuss the reasons for arranging these eighteen woodcuts to reflect episodes in the three acts of a particular commedia performance (Katritzky 1989). In total, nine male and five female characters, all named, are featured in these eighteen prints (fig. 6.8). My own reading of the plot tentatively distributes these fourteen characters between the household of the two older men, as follows: Segnor Pantalon has two male servants, Harlequin and Zany Cornetto; the female characters are his maid Francisquina (top, second from right; also in bottom row), and his wife, Dona Lucretia (center row, last on right). Donna Cornelia (bottom right) could be their daughter or a courtesan; such ambiguity of status is frequent in the iconography. The other older man, Segnor Dotour, has two menservants, Francatripa and Philipin; his maid is Licetta (third row, first image). Donna Lucia, either an *innamorata* or a courtesan, is courted illicitly by Pantalon (top, second from left), and officially by Segnor Horacio, the friend of Capitan Cocodrillo. Like practically all the males, the Doctor's son, Segnor Leandro, dallies with Francisquina, but his wooing of a more credible marriage partner, his social equal Donna Cornelia, in the final picture seems to suggest that this performance will end, as many did, with a marriage. Of the fourteen parts, four are featured in all three acts, and only one of these, Francisquina, is a female role. The other three are principal masks, Pantalone and his comic servants Harlequin and Zany Cornetto. Lucia, who is depicted in acts 1 and 2, and Lucretia, who is depicted in act 2, could double with Cornelia and Licetta, who feature only in the last act. Pantalon, Harlequin, and Zany take part in all three acts, and Leandro in the last two, but the other five male roles could be doubled by three players. Over a third of the players in this performance – five out of fourteen – are women. More significantly, the maid Francisquina is one of four major roles, and women feature in over half of the eighteen pictures which make up this series.

Two prints by the Milanese artist Ambrogio Brambilla represent a compact print series offering valuable visual evidence concerning the gender make-up of commedia dell'arte troupes. One shows five commedia characters in a kitchen, making preparations for a wedding (fig. 6.12). In the second, six newcomers join three of them, namely the comic manservant Burati, Doctor Gratian, and Nespola, in a celebratory wedding dance (fig. 6.13). The six men are three comic servants, two old masters, and a German captain who plays the pipe and tabor. It is harder to categorize the five young women, but they are possibly two maids, Nespola and Balzarina, and three courtesans, Filomena, Venturina, and Franceschina. Five of the eleven characters are women, and they are central to the narrative (Katritzky 1987).[8]

The best-known series of commedia-related colored drawings is in the undated (probably early seventeenth-century) *Corsini Album* manuscript collection of commedia dell'arte scenarios, probably the working collection of a troupe, or plots poached from the professional stage by some amateur. Whatever its exact theatrical status, it is unique in that each of its 101 scenarios has been provided with its own individual illustrated title page, depicting one scene, or composite scene, from that scenario, enabling the roles of many of the depicted actors and actresses to be identified (fig. 6.14). Another significant, if much less well known category of colored drawings, in the half-century from around 1570 to 1620, is found in albums of a very different type. Genre scenes of mountebank and carnival activity in series of plates depicting Venetian costume were produced for manuscript costume books and *alba amicorum*, pocket-sized friendship albums in which friends and patrons could be requested to enter their names and titles accompanied by short texts, and sometimes suitable illustrations (figs. 6.4, 6.5; also see Mirabella, this volume, fig. 5.2). To create such images, early illustrators looked to sources in art, as well as on the stage itself, to build up their own increasingly strong iconographic traditions and conventions.

While many attempts have been made to identify specific actresses with depictions of performers, only a few sources have any claim to reliability. One of them is McGill University Library's *Featherbook*. This unique album contains pictures painstakingly built up *c*.1615–18 in mosaic fashion, using small pieces of feather, by the Duke of Milan's head gardener Dionisio Minaggio.[9] Most feature birds and other natural history subjects, but there are also twenty-six human subjects, including fourteen pictures of *comici*. Seven show one actor, two feature two actors, one is of one actress ("Florinda") and four show an actor and an actress (labeled "Trastulo, Ricolina," "Mario, Flavia," "[S]chapin, Spineta," and an uncaptioned pair). The named women bear the stage names of commedia actresses. "Rizzolina" was taken by at least two early actresses, Angela Lucchese and Marina Dorotea Antonazzoni. "Florinda" is Virginia Andreini; "[S]chapin, Spineta," are Francesco Gabrielli and his wife Maria Teresa Gabrielli; and "Flavia" is perhaps Margherita Garavini (Corrigan).

8   Another important series (*c*.1576–9) survives as fresco paintings on the thirty walls of a winding staircase at the Castle Trausnitz in Landshut, Germany. Many scenes feature women players. Sixteen commedia scenes were also depicted on a ceiling frieze, which has been destroyed by fire (Katritzky 1996, 137).

9   The website http://digital.library.mcgill.ca/featherbook.html depicts all the *Featherbook* pictures in color.

Such identifications are far more reliable than those made for some of the better-known paintings featuring commedia actresses. Early modern images of actresses labelled "Isabella" cannot always be identified as Isabella Andreini, who popularized this stage name for female lovers, sharing it with, for example, the Uniti's Vittoria degli Amorevoli. The routine association of the woman standing in the foreground in figure 6.10 with Isabella Andreini remains conjectural. Accepted images of Andreini, possibly dressed in her stage role of the *innamorata* Isabella, include the portrait busts on the title-page woodcut of the 1601 edition of her *Rime* (see Campbell in this volume, fig. 7.1) and the commemorative medal struck after her death in 1604, and a full-length likeness in the right-hand background of a fresco depicting members of the Medici court, formerly in Sta Annunziata, Florence.[10]

Women's Stage Roles in the Visual Record

Portraits or assumed portraits of commedia players are vastly outnumbered by pictures showing unidentified performers, both on- and off-stage. Analysis of the visual record has the potential for clarifying the players' costumes and stage presence and their contribution to the dramatic effect at hand. The task is more difficult for actresses than actors, for several reasons. On the all-male stage, the presence of men playing women was conventionally limited to a minimum. Men playing men dominated the stage, and their roles were distinguished by easily recognizable stage costumes. Male stock roles rapidly developed stylized stage names, costumes, masks, and other distinguishing characteristics which aid their identification in pictures, even where the context is not obviously theatrical. In contrast, early actresses honed their skills in arenas in which overtly theatrical costume was rarely worn, such as the marketplace, oral tradition, and festivity. Depictions of female carnival masks and mountebanks suggest that even in stage contexts, female performers habitually wore less stylized costumes than men (figs. 6.2–6.4, 6.6). The visual and textual documentation suggests considerable overlap in the names, costumes and social classes of early modern female stock roles, both with each other and with the real-life types they represent. Perhaps because visual recognition is less straightforward for early female players than for actors, there are no detailed studies of female commedia costume comparable to those of its male roles.

For basic classification purposes, my reading of the visual evidence identifies four main categories of costume, none of which is foolproof as a sorting device. They are the elegant upper-class garments worn by the fashionable young

---

10   MacNeil 2003, 30–1, 48–50, 117–20, reproduces all three, and several derivative images.

innamorata and the respectable married woman; the servant's simpler and plainer outfit, worn by most maids, nurses, and crones; the provocative and showy costumes of courtesans; and the exotic, usually "Oriental," garb of the foreign or disguised woman. As with male roles, the majority of female commedia roles fall into the category of servant or served. Often imperious as a mistress to servants and suitors, the *innamorata* featured large in most commedia dell'arte plots, and the actress playing her often dominated the stage and eventually the troupe itself. Typically, the *innamorata* was a marriageable young daughter of Pantalone, Dottore, or other old masters of the *comici*. Many plots concern her complicated, but ultimately successful, search for appropriate marriage partners. Although the *innamorata* generally wore opulent gowns in the height of court elegance, no hard-and-fast rule may be used to separate her role from those of other young females, unlike the distinction between menservants and their masters. The *innamorata's* costume was particularly flexible, spanning a wide range of garments from the everyday wear of maids and elegant gowns of respectable upper-class women, to the overt stage costume of professional entertainers, such as exotic acrobats, dancers, and musicians, including the dancing, singing *cantarina* (figs. 6.7, 6.8). It is also hard to tell *innamoratas* apart from female mountebanks, who wear elegant gowns in images depicting them playing "respectable" stringed instruments such as violins, in contrast to male musicians on mountebank stages (usually theatrically dressed as commedia menservants and depicted playing many types of instruments) (fig. 6.6; also see Mirabella, this volume, fig. 5.2). This type of gown is worn by many of the Corsini women whose roles can be associated with named female lovers, by reference to the scenarios they illustrate (for two of these, see fig. 6.14). But others wear simpler dress appropriate to pastoral plays, and in the Corsini illustrations, Flaminia, Doralice, and Isabella, while in standard *innamorata* gowns, betray their madness through wild gestures and unkempt hair.

Female servants are as essential to commedia plots as the ubiquitous menservants, typically attending the lovers, performing household chores, transporting messages and objects, or fending off unwanted attentions of the *zanni* and the old men. Maids are more often depicted with props, such as a purse, scissors, dish of food, basket of vegetables, or spindle, that powerfully evoke their sphere of domestic activity and indicate potential or actual stage action. The maids Nespola and Balzarina in figure 6.12 are depicted in their kitchen, one preparing food at a table, the other tending a pot over the fire while repelling a manservant with a draining spoon, actions that suggest their involvement in extended comic stage business, or *lazzi*. Identified by their aproned dresses with neck-ruffs and head-cloths, maids are often depicted hovering behind their mistresses (figs. 6.9, 6.10). Its underplayed theatricality makes the stage maid's costume especially hard to identify where actresses are not explicitly depicted in performance contexts, or contextualized by male companions in the strikingly distinctive costume of commedia menservants.

Whether courtesans or not, the stage costume of female lovers was more dependent on context than on role. In the public arena, even the *innamorata* whose reputation is not respectable may wear a respectable, elegant gown (for an *innamorata* who could be a courtesan or a respectable woman, see Donna Cornelia in fig. 6.8, bottom right). The plot summary of scenario 15 of the *Corsini Album* suggests that the female depicted on the right of the title-page illustration is Cintia, a widow who became a courtesan before remarrying. Bare-headed and unmasked, she wears an elegant gown typical of those worn by female lovers of the *Corsini Album*, as does Goltzius's "Venetian Courtesan" (fig. 6.3), whose performative context is given by her male companions Il Magnifico and Zanni, stock commedia roles. This depiction is particularly valuable in specifying the exact profession associated with the depicted woman's costume, and in giving a detailed impression of the type of stage costume associated with the courtesan at a given date, in this case 1581. Notable are the high plumed bonnet, light full-face mask, high, sheer collar, waist sash, richly brocaded floor-length gown, short cape, gloves, and ample range of jewelry. The wide range of dates of related depictions of similar women, evidently also courtesans, by much less gifted friendship album artists, from the 1570s onwards (fig. 6.4) suggests that Goltzius's courtesan is based on a still earlier joint iconographic antecedent. They also demonstrate the difficulty of dating images of this type, because of the longstanding popularity of this costume, originally adapted with only minor modifications for the stage, but increasingly removed from the typical outfit of real-life courtesans as it became a traditional stage costume. Nudity is sometimes associated with the servant role, as with Franceschina's exposed breasts or legs (figs. 6.8 [top row, fifth scene], 6.13), but more often with that of the courtesan, especially in conjunction with opulent clothing, jewelry, or elaborate hairdressing, such as the bleached, curled styles favored by Venetian courtesans (figs. 6.2, 6.5, 6.7).

Despite its popularity in art, it is unclear how much nudity there was on the commedia stage itself. By its nature far less easily identified in pictures, cross-dressing (another form of erotic costuming) was certainly a significant stock-in-trade of the *comici*. Although the visual record is especially hard to interpret in this respect, it is well known that actresses, no less than genuine courtesans, frequently and elaborately disguised themselves as men. "The Harlotts called Cortisane," as Fynes Moryson notes, "commonly weare dobletts and Breches under their wemens gownes, yea, I have seene some of them goe in the Company of young men to the Tennis-Court in mens Apparrell ... most commonly wearing doblets and Hose of Carnation Satten, with gold buttons from the Chinne round to the waste behinde, and silke stockings, and great Garters with gold lace both of the same color" (628–9). In figure 6.2 the courtesan, with elaborate horned Venetian hairdo, wears breeches under her dress, as does many an *innamorata* in the scenarios. In the invaluable *Corsini Album*, the plot spelled out in the text of *L'Innocente Rivenduta* (scenario 61) makes possible the identification of a cross-dressed actress onstage (fig. 6.14, left). Doralice, the boyish, diminutive *innamorata* at the right, has exchanged clothes with the Turk next to her. She wears typical male Turkish costume (slippers, loose knee-length, long-sleeved robe gathered in at the waist, white undershirt, and simple turban). He wears Doralice's dark-sleeved gown with high collar, but betrays himself visually by his beefy physique.

Exotic Dress: "Turks" and "Gypsies," with Caveats on Reading Iconography

Turkish costume was more usually associated with stage or carnival disguise by both men and women than a stock type in its own right. A frequent disguise, especially for female lovers and maids, was some form of exotic stage dress of more or less Eastern flavor, often Turkish- or gypsy-inspired (fig. 6.1). In addition to its purely visual appeal, Turkish costume carried vivid military and religious connotations.[11] The Corsini illustrations demonstrate the popularity of orientalizing costume in a performance context. While costumed slaves, gypsies, and Turks of both genders are depicted, these pictures show that these costumes are also favorite disguises of female lovers. Doralice's assumed "Turkish" costume in figure 6.14 is similar to that worn by the *innamorata* Elisa after her capture by the Turks; it is also similar to the garb of Coviello's daughter, an *innamorata* masquerading as the slave-girl Turchetta, whose even shorter version of the "Turkish" tunic is further dramatized with an iron neck-collar (Corsini scenarios 53 and 98).

Artists also used the Turkish look for showy, exotic costumes for comic female types in depictions of outdoor parades and carnivals. The curious raised headgear of these women often resembles the Turkish *kashbasti*, introduced to the Turkish harem by European concubines in the mid-sixteenth century and featured in the highly influential late sixteenth-century costume plates of Cesare Vecellio (Katritzky *Thesis*, 194). Pictures such as figure 6.1, which shows nine performers, all masked, in exotic costumes with an unmistakable Oriental flavor, suggest that such disguises raise questions that are not adequately addressed by dismissing them as amateur carnival revellers. Where such players appear to be members of a troupe, performing in the open or parading to publicize their skills, it seems plausible to consider the possibility that these women have, as a publicity exercise, substituted exotic disguise for

---

11   Comedians who experienced the Turkish threat at first hand include Isabella Andreini's husband Francesco, who spent seven years in Turkish captivity before starting his acting career (Duchartre, 231).

the costumes appropriate to their stage roles. Exotic costume would have been the most gorgeous and eye-catching garments possessed by the troupe. By raising more interest with the public than the commonplace costumes of respectable female lovers and maids, while fitting in with the constraints of public decency better than courtesan costume, it would have effectively fulfilled the aims of the parade or open-air performance, which was to attract custom. But even if the comic types depicted are based on real troupes, the artists may have seen them years, even decades, before depicting them. The commedia dell'arte characters featured in such works follow iconographic precedents, sometimes resembling each other down to their individual groupings, gestures, and costumes. Thus, even fairly precise dating of these paintings on stylistic grounds does not always enable the players themselves to be accurately dated.

By the mid-sixteenth century, gypsies were popular stage characters. The illustration to Corsini scenario 21 resembles depictions in costume books of the period. But the appearance of gypsies alongside commedia dell'arte stock types in another painting may have a less straightforward explanation, demonstrating some of the complications involved in using early modern depictions of comic types as documentary information (fig. 6.15). It depicts two Zanni, a ragged child, and three women whose flowing, fringed cloaks and loose, striped robes and circular headdress with chin-cloths correspond to the traditional costume of the female gypsy. The exotic look and the symbolic, allegorical, and moral possibilities of gypsy culture attracted late Renaissance artists. Renowned for their skill in entertaining, fortune-telling, and cheating the gullible, gypsies were pagans who (according to legend) refused to help the Holy Family on their flight into Egypt, then thought to have been their country of origin. In Caravaggio's influential early seventeenth-century painting, *The Gypsy Fortune-Teller*, the gypsy plies her craft, using a flirtatious gesture to cover up the fact that she is subtly teasing a young soldier's ring from his finger. Figure 6.15 also shows a gypsy simultaneously telling and illicitly diminishing the fortunes of her client. Its modern title, *Scene from the Italian Comedy*, has been accepted without question as being an appropriate and adequate description of its subject by the many art and theater historians who have written about it. Barry Wind, who mistakenly identifies the central Zanni as a Pantalone, cites this painting as direct evidence for "the popularity of the fortune telling theme in the [commedia]" and interprets it as depicting "the gulling of Pantaleone by a gypsy" (32).

Investigation suggests a more complex link with the late Renaissance stage. The possibility that the painting constitutes a documentary record of an actual stage performance cannot be entirely discounted. The outfits look authentic, so the question of whether they are real, carnival, or stage gypsies is not resolved on the basis of costume. I would argue that rather than illustrating a dramatic episode played by costumed actors and actresses, the artist may have combined disparate elements from different sources as a suitable vehicle for his visual message. The painting can be closely associated with a number of interrelated allegorical and popular messages. It comments on Fortuna, the goddess of fortune, and her well-known fickleness. The child holds the whipping rod to a spinning top, associated in Dutch emblem books both with sloth and with the spinning wheel of fortune, also indicated by the central activity of the fortune-telling gypsy women. They dupe the Zanni by their outrageous flirting, which is a cover-up to rob him, thus paradoxically diminishing his fortune in the very act of telling it. Religious, allegorical, and popular, as well as dramatic, readings of the picture are possible. They are not necessarily equally valid, mutually exclusive, or incompatible with the possibility of a relationship between figure 6.15 and the professional stage. The ambiguity of its subject makes this work a particularly clear example of a painting whose use as a visual source for the history of performing women is far from straightforward, despite depicting recognizable stock types and costumes associated with the commedia dell'arte.

Masks Worn by Actresses

Richards and Richards are among many theater historians who suggest that the women of the commedia dell'arte were only rarely masked in performance (112). Examination of the iconographic material, however, reveals that a significant number of early female commedia characters are depicted with their faces wholly or partially covered by a veil or mask (figs. 6.1–6.4, 6.7). With the male characters, masks are predominantly worn by the old masters and their menservants. With the female characters, too, their range appears to be confined largely to particular types, although unlike the males, the female masked types are by no means exclusively depicted masked, and the wearing of masks appears to be dependent on performance situation as well as role. No masked females are depicted, for example, in *Recueil Fossard* woodcuts or Corsini illustrations, and only very few in peasant or servant dress. In general, the female types depicted with face masks wear the type of rich clothing associated with the *innamorata* or courtesan and appear in outdoor or informal, private indoor settings rather than on the public dramatic stage. At its most discreet the female stage mask is, like the loup, little more than a black eye-mask (fig. 6.2), prompting arguments that such masks are not genuinely theatrical. According to Duchartre, "the tiny black velvet mask, or *loup*, which the women of the *commedia dell'arte* sometimes wore cannot be considered a true mask, for it was used outside as well as inside the theater. The *loup* was as much a part of a woman's dress as her brocade and lace" (266). But the visual record shows that some actresses wore masks that differed from those worn by other richly dressed women. The theatrical mask often covered considerably more of the face than the loup. In numerous pictures the females wear types of black three-quarter masks, more substantial than the elegant loup, typically covering the nose as well as the eyes, sometimes also extending over the cheeks and upper lip, and often with a moustache attached to it (see fig. 6.4). Although its uneasy contrast to the feminine gown of its wearer provides the modern eye with gender-ambiguous cues, these "twiskes of downy or woolly stuffe covering their noses" (Coryat, 386) may have been intended primarily as germ filters.

More difficult to distinguish in the iconography than black face-masks are pale or flesh-colored face-masks (6.1–6.4, 6.8), and the most discreet form of mask depicted, the veil. Numerous images depict commedia actresses in a full or three-quarter-face flesh-colored moulded mask, veil, or thick make-up, although it is not always easy to distinguish between such facial disguises. In figure 6.1, the women's pale full-face moulded masks are secured by tapes running under their noses, the right hand woman's additionally looped below her ears. Others are fastened with tapes tied behind the ears (figs. 6.2–6.4). Courtesans frequently sported masks and veils. The exposed breasts and explicit gestures of the female in the middle of the left-hand performing trio of figure 6.7, who wears a full-face veil, mark her out as a courtesan. Textual records suggest actresses wore veils for their sexual allure, and were found provocative on stage. Members of the Confidenti troupe sent a plea to Ferdinando de'Medici in 1581 to waive certain laws regarding forbidden props and items of costume, and to release one of their actresses, arrested for wearing silver-colored veils, from prison (MacNeil 2003, 210).

Conclusion

The pictorial record both broadly supports textual evidence that women's participation varied widely from troupe to troupe, with between a third and half being women, and confirms the increasing prominence of the *prima donna* over the course of the sixteenth century. In erudite comedy, female parts were always played by boys and men, and the plays written for these all-male casts generally held to the convention that wives and romantic heroines should appear as little as possible during a performance, with much of their action related at second hand by maids and servants. Playtexts indicate that the respectable female roles only rarely break free of this convention before the advent of the commedia dell'arte. If they appear on stage at all before the mid-sixteenth century, female characters tend to hover well in the background, preferably framed by a window or door of their own private domestic interior. This theatrical device was extensively developed by commedia dell'arte actresses. Despite Church opposition, they turned the same doors and windows that had marked boundaries for their cross-dressing male colleagues into stepping stones onto center stage (Tylus). On the late sixteenth-century professional stage, although some maids continued to be played by men, key scenes involving the *innamorata* were increasingly no longer reported at second hand by the maid, but conducted in full view of the audience.

Commedia dell'arte actresses consolidated their on-stage presence by developing sophisticated strategies for circumventing the prejudices against women, and especially against women in public, on the late Renaissance stage, and for overcoming the challenges posed by the heritage of a theater dominated by the need to minimize on-stage female roles. Women players reinforced an increasingly vital and compelling stage presence through audience-pleasing devices such as improvised rhetorical set-pieces, musical virtuosity, and alluring costumes, and by developing a wide variety of both stock and occasional roles, whose costumes, gestures, and theatrical action are reflected in the pictorial record. As the commedia dell'arte *prima donna* became an essential stage presence, artists began to make actresses the focal point of theatrical compositions (figs. 6.9, 6.10, 6.14). Regardless of how closely male artists' focus on beautiful *innamoratas* reflected the priorities of stage practice, it is clear that the rise of the commedia dell'arte and its actresses promoted the emergence of female stage roles from the margins to the center of theater. Italian women of abundant talents, equal to the challenge of wholeheartedly grasping and exploiting these new theatrical opportunities, stepped triumphantly into the limelight of public acclaim. The visual record complements the textual documentation in confirming that commedia dell'arte actresses became increasingly adept in deploying youth, beauty and talent to successfully negotiate their fair share of the early modern stage.

Works Cited

Baschet, Armand. *Les comédiens italiens a la cour de France sous Charles IX, Henri III, Henri IV et Louis XIII.* Paris: Plon, 1882.

Bevington, David. "The Popular Troupe (1962)." *Medieval English Drama, a Casebook.* Ed. Peter Happé. London: Macmillan, 1984, 162–71.

Brandt, Britta. *Das Spiel mit Gattungen bei Isabella Canali Andreini,* I: *Zum Verhältnis von Improvisation und Schriftkultur in der Commedia dell'arte,* II: *"Lettere" (1607).* Wilhelmsfeld: Egert, 2002.

Brown, Pamela. "The Counterfeit Innamorata, or, The Diva Vanishes." *Shakespeare Yearbook* 10 (1999): 402–26.

Corrigan, Beatrice. "Commedia dell'arte Portraits in the McGill Feather Book." *Renaissance Drama* n.s. 2 (1969): 167–88.

Coryat, Thomas. *Coryate's Crudities: Hastily Gobled Up ...* [1611] 2 vols. Glasgow, 1905.

Duchartre, Pierre-Louis. *The Italian Comedy.* New York: Dover, 1966.

Falconieri, John. "The commedia dell'arte, the Actors' Theater." *Theater Annual* 12 (1954): 35–47.

————., "Historia de la commedia dell'arte en España," *Revista de literatura* 11 (1957): 3–37 & 12 (1958): 69–90.

Ferdinand of Bavaria, Prince. MS Korr.Akt 924 [manuscript travel diary of his 1565–6 journey to Italy]. Munich, Bayerische Hauptstaatsarchiv, Geheimes Hausarchiv.

Garzoni, Thomaso. *La piazza universale di tutte le professioni del mondo*. Venice, 1585.

Heck, Thomas F. *Commedia dell'arte: A Guide to the Primary and Secondary Literature*. New York and London: Garland, 1988.

Herford, C. H. and Evelyn Simpson, eds. *Ben Jonson. An Historical Survey of the Text. The Stage History of the Plays. Commentary on the Plays*. Vol. IX. Oxford: Clarendon, 1950.

Howe, Elizabeth. *The First English Actresses: Women and Drama 1660–1700*. Cambridge: Cambridge University Press, 1992.

Katritzky, M. A. "Italian Comedians in Renaissance Prints." *Print Quarterly* IV (1987): 236–54.

————. "The *Recueil Fossard* 1928–88: A Review and Three Reconstructions." *The Commedia dell'arte from the Renaissance to Dario Fo*. Ed. Christopher Cairns. Lewiston: Edwin Mellen Press, 1989, 99–116.

————. "A Study in the Commedia dell'arte 1560–1620, With Special Reference to the Visual Records." (=*Thesis*.) DPhil thesis, University of Oxford, 1995. Forthcoming from Rodopi Press.

————. "Orlando di Lasso and the Commedia dell'arte." *Orlando di Lasso in der Musikgeschichte. Bericht über das Symposion der Bayerischen Akademie der Wissenschaften München, 4–6 Juli 1994*. Ed. Bernhold Schmid. Munich: Bayerische Akademie der Wissenschaften, 1996.

————. "What did Vigil Raber's Stage Really Look Like? Questions of Authenticity and Integrity in Medieval Theater Iconography." Vigil Raber: zur 450. Wiederkehr seines Todesjahres (Akter des 4. Symposiums des Sterzinger Osterspiele, 25.–27. 3. 2002) K. Eds. Michael Gebhardt and Max Siller. Wagner: Schlern-Schrifter 326, 2004, 85–116.

Lea, Kathleen Marguerite. *Italian Popular Comedy: A Study in the Commedia dell'arte, 1560–1620*. 2 vols. Oxford: Clarendon, 1934.

Leik, Angelika. *Frühe Darstellungen der Commedia dell'arte. Eine Theaterform als Bildmotiv*. Neuried: ars una, 1996.

MacNeil, Anne. "The Nature of Commitment: Vincenzo Gonzaga's Patronage Strategies in the Wake of the Fall of Ferrara." *Renaissance Studies* 16 (2002): 392–402.

————. *Music and Women of the Commedia dell'arte in the Late Sixteenth Century*. Oxford: Oxford University Press, 2003.

Marston, John. *The Scourge of Villainie* [1599]. London: Bodley Head, 1925.

McGill, Kathleen. "Women and Performance: The Development of Improvisation by the Sixteenth-Century Commedia dell'arte." *Theater Journal* 43 (1991): 59–61.

Moryson, Fynes. "The fourth Part of an Itinerary ..." Manuscript; dated in pencil 1595. Oxford, Corpus Christi College MS. CCC 94.

Nashe, Thomas. "Pierce Penilesse his supplication to the Divell." [1592]. *The Works of Thomas Nashe*, vol. I. Ed. Ronald McKerrow. Oxford: Blackwell, 1966.

Nicoll, Allardyce. *Masks, Mimes and Miracles*. New York: Harcourt Brace, 1931.

————. *The World of Harlequin: A Critical Study of the Commedia dell'arte*. Cambridge: Cambridge University Press, 1963.

Re, Emilio. "Commedianti a Roma nel secolo XVI." *Giornale storico della letteratura italiana* 63 (1914): 291–9.

Richards, Kenneth and Laura Richards. *The Commedia dell'arte: A Documentary History*. Oxford: Blackwell, 1990.

Saslow, James. *The Medici Wedding of 1589: Florentine Festival as Theatrum Mundi*. New Haven: Yale University Press, 1996.

Schrickx, Willem. "Italian Actors in Antwerp in 1576: Drusiano Martinelli and Vincenzo Beladno (sic=Belando)." *Revue Belge de philologie et d'histoire* 50 (1972): 796–806.

Scott, Virginia. "'La Virtu et la volupté.' Models for the Actress in Early Modern Italy and France." *Theater Research International* 23 (1998): 152–8.

Solerti, A. and D. Lanza. "Il teatro ferrarese nella seconda meta del secolo XVI." *Giornale storico della letteratura italiana* 18 (1891): 148–85.

Taviani, Ferdinando, ed. *La commedia dell'arte e la societá barocca. La fascinazione del teatro*. Rome, 1969.

————, and Mirella Schino. *Il Segreto della Commedia dell'arte: La memoria delle compagnie italiane del XVI, XVII, e XVIII secolo*. Florence: La Casa Usher, 1982.

Tylus, Jane. "Women at the Windows: Commedia dell'arte and Theatrical Practice in Early Modern Italy." *Theater Journal* 49 (1997): 323–42.

Wind, Barry. "Pitture Ridicole: Some Late Cinquecento Comic Genre Paintings." *Storia dell'arte* 20 (1974): 25–35.

Chapter 7

"Merry, nimble, stirring spirit[s]": Academic, Salon and Commedia dell'arte Influence on the *Innamorate* of *Love's Labour's Lost*

Julie D. Campbell

More than an acerbic commentary on political events, the French court, or philosophical pursuits, *Love's Labour's Lost* (1594–5)[1] is a play that engages its audience in meta-academic discourse regarding these topics. It does so by having as its chief interlocutors four pairs of lovers who debate the ways of acquiring knowledge and an understanding of true love, but who leave the questions open at the end in order to inspire the audience to continue the conversation. Like the romantic couples in the *contrasti scenici* of the commedia dell'arte, the male and female characters take opposing sides on the issues, adding a fillip of sexual tension to the entertainment. Also, like the famed conversationalists of sixteenth-century French salon society, the couples engage in witty badinage, even while the play as a whole is addressing important philosophical issues, such as those addressed in academic settings.[2] To comprehend these references, we must first recognize and understand the ways in which Continental female performance invaded the English stage via many of Shakespeare's provocative female characters. In this case, the ladies of *Love's Labour's Lost* instigate the action of the play, direct the debates, and control the ending, suggesting that Shakespeare was inspired by the roles for actresses popularized by Italian troupes, as well as the reputations of the learned *académiciennes* and *salonnières* associated with the French court.

Scholars routinely draw readers' attention to the historical French elements of the play, with most focusing on the name recognition of the male characters and the association of the princess and her ladies with Marguerite de Valois

---

1   I refer throughout to *Love's Labour's Lost* in *The Norton Shakespeare*.
2   By "academic settings," I mean those for the meetings of the groups of Renaissance intellectuals who attempted to imitate the academies of classical antiquity.

and her attendants. Although scholars usually mention the risqué reputation of the group of ladies-in-waiting close to Marguerite de Valois and Catherine de Medici called the *escadron volant*, few have explored the performative talents associated with them and others of their milieu who were connected to the court. These women were known for their bawdy, witty, and erudite discourse in salon and academic settings, as well as their performances in court entertainments.[3] Since praise of the learnedness and writing of some of them also abounds in contemporary sources,[4] it appears that Shakespeare capitalizes on multiple facets of these women's reputations in this play that unfolds through dance, disguise, wordplay, and critique of poetry and letters.

Italian female performance also resonates in *Love's Labour's Lost*. In recent years, Louise George Clubb, Frances Barasch, and Pamela Brown have written about the influence of Italian actresses on plays for the English stage. Most recently, Brown has underscored the point, also noted by Clubb and Barasch, that "the impressive comic skills of the foreign actress during the golden age of commedia (roughly 1590 to 1650) may help account for the sudden appearance of the witty, willful, and elegant Beatrice, Rosalind, and Viola" (409).[5] The ladies of *Love's Labour's Lost* appear around 1594–5, placing them squarely in the midst of the period in question. In introductions to the play, however, editors inevitably comment on the commedia dell'arte characters reflected in Holofernes, Costard, and Armado, but seldom point out the ways in which the roles of the female characters resemble those of commedia actresses.[6] Such an

---

3　Richard David reviews the historical backdrop of the play regarding two embassies to the King of Navarre conducted by Marguerite de Valois in 1578 and her mother, Catherine de Medici, in 1586: "[On] both occasions the royal envoy, reinforcing diplomacy by coquetry, was supported by that famous bevy of ladies-in-waiting who for their grace and flightiness were known as 'l'escadron volant' "(xxii–xxxiii). Hugh M. Richmond discusses the women's probable identities, focusing especially on their alleged sexual prowess and the scandals they provoked (193–216).

4　See Théodore Agrippa d'Aubigné, "Á mes filles," regarding the Maréschale de Retz and Madame de Lignerolles debating before other members of the Académie du palais (851–4). Jacques Lavaud quotes such contemporaries as Philippe Desportes, Pierre de Ronsard, La Croix du Maine, Marie de Romieu, Nicolas Rapin, Jean de la Jessé, Flaminio de Birague, and Etienne Pasquier, regarding the learnedness, wit, and writing of Madeleine de l'Aubespine, Madame de Villeroy, and Claude-Catherine de Clermont, the Maréschale de Retz (58–60, 72–95, 122–3, 503–4, 516).

5　Frances Barasch notes that the "creative work of Vincenza Armani and Flaminia of Rome ... revolutionized Italian improvised theatre by introducing a new Renaissance heroine, not unlike Shakespeare's Juliet, Beatrice, or Rosalind" (2000, 5; also see Barasch, 2001). For an earlier discussion of this issue, see Louise George Clubb, 23–24, 67–89, 264–9.

6　See David, xxxv–xxxvi. See also Felicia Londré, 14–15, and Frances Yates 1936, 18, 173–82.

oversight is particularly problematic since in this play the main female characters behave much like commedia actresses – both in performance and reputation. In addition to their quick wits and ability to dissemble, Shakespeare's princess and her ladies sweep onto the scene, wreaking havoc on the male characters' ordered existence, in much the same way that commedia actresses reportedly took towns by storm in which they were performing. Although often considered to have a status similar to that of courtesans and to be disruptors of the peace because male spectators became infatuated with them and behaved in an unruly fashion (not unlike Navarre and company), such actresses amazed audiences with their performances of exquisitely refined, articulate *innamorate*, as well as their use of trickery and disguise.[7]

In *Love's Labour's Lost*, then, we have a fascinating palimpsest of Continental female performance to consider: women of the French court, known for their skilled discourse in academic and salon settings, their literary activities, their performances in court entertainments, and their risqué reputations, are portrayed, or written over, in roles that look suspiciously like those created for commedia dell'arte actresses.[8] That Shakespeare chooses to use female characters that strongly recall both types of female performers, in a play that ends, not in marriage, but in iconoclastic suspense about the future of the relationships raises important questions. What traits did these two groups of female performers share that so easily facilitated Shakespeare's conflation of them? Did the mélange of scandalous references provided by female characters who are both Catholic and foreign hold a special appeal for Shakespeare's audience? And, especially of interest, what should be made of the allusions to these types of female performers in connection with the debate format?

The answer to the first question opens the way for consideration of the next two: both groups of women were known for their wit, dancing, and accomplished verbal performances. The appearances, risqué reputations, and actions of both the Italian actresses and the French noblewomen surely inform Shakespeare's shaping of Rosaline who, like his dark lady, is "made to make

---

7   See Rinaldina Russell on the reputation of Italian actresses (6); also Rosalind Kerr on the association between courtesans and actresses (40–3).

8   It should be noted that there were also French actresses in France, but the Italian commedia troupes seem to be responsible for the spread of the popularity of using women on stage. Michael Shapiro writes, "In France, there is evidence of actresses even before the arrival of Italian popular troupes. An actress named Marie Fairet and her manager signed a contract at Bourges in 1545, but the use of actresses on a regular basis followed the arrival of the Italian popular companies, which played at court and publicly in Paris in the early 1570s. A French troupe introduced actresses in Bordeaux in 1598 and shortly thereafter in Paris" (180).

black fair" (4.3.259), and the other ladies of her company who are capable of dance, disguise, and dissembling at a moment's notice.[9] His use of *double entendres*, sharp retorts, and obscenely nuanced references in his female characters' repartee also recalls the verbal gifts of such women. "The tongues of mocking wenches are as keen / As is the razor's edge invisible ...," pronounces Boyet, "Their conceits have wings / Fleeter than arrows, bullets, wind, thought, swifter things" (5.2.256–61). Shakespeare's conflation of outlandish yet eloquent Continental female types, then, would have provided his English audience much diversion, especially, perhaps, at the expense of the French nobles, who were rumored to be so enamored with the performances of Italian players that they had begun to imitate them.

Concern about the influence of the Italian *comici* upon the French is voiced by Pierre de l'Estoile, an *audiencier* or "clerk-in-chief" for the Parlement, who, in his *Mémoires-Journaux* (1574–1611), writes on 26 June, 1577, that "the Court assembled and issued an order forbidding the Italian comedians, *I Gelosi*, to perform any more in Paris. Some said ... that their comedies taught nothing but fornication and adultery, and served as a school of debauchery for the youth of Paris of both sexes. And in truth their influence was so great, principally among the young ladies, that they took to showing their breasts – like soldiers – which shook with perpetual motion and served as a bellows to their forge"(60).[10] This trend, albeit sensationalized by L'Estoile, of French women imitating Italian actresses may be reflected in Shakespeare's blending of the two types in his female characters in *Love's Labour's Lost*.

The French noblewomen in question, like "the youth of Paris," had ample opportunity to become acquainted with Italian performers. They would have witnessed many performances by the Gelosi, whom Henri III had "imported from Venice" to entertain him in a variety of venues numerous times, as well as the Confidenti (L'Estoile 58; Boucher 3:1,019). In *Société et mentalités autour de Henri III*, Jacqueline Boucher notes that traces of relationships between French noblewomen and Italian comedians may be seen in the letters and poems that the Italians sent to their patronesses, as well as in the writings of the noblewomen themselves. She cites cases in which the Duchess de Nemours and Mademoiselle de Beaulieu, the natural daughter of the Maréschal de Brissac,

---

9   Pamela Brown discusses these and other famous skills of the Italian actresses (408–9, 411–13, 416).

10 On July 27, L'Estoile writes that the Gelosi "were refused appeal and charged not to bring the question up again on pain of a fine ... but at the beginning of September following they opened again at the Hotel de Bourbon in defiance of the court, with the express permission of the King, the corruption of the times being such that clowns, buffoons, prostitutes, and *mignons* have all the credit and influence" (60). For a description of L'Estoile's position and proximity to the court, see Nancy Roelker, 3–27, who also translated these passages from his journal.

exchanged verses with Isabella Andreini (fig. 7.1), the most famous *prima donna* of the Gelosi, and she draws attention to a letter signed, "La Franceschina," addressed to Nemours, noting that "La Franceschina" was typically an audacious servant's role. She speculates that the Italian author of the letter was perhaps "un acteur travesti," a cross-dressed actor (3:1,024–5).[11] Boucher also points out that Italian dancers were hired to perform the most difficult parts in court entertainments, as well as to give dancing lessons to the French nobles and royals who took part in these performances (3:1,054–6). She thus concludes that "[u]ne certaine familiarité" with Italian culture evinced by French noblewomen is easily explained (3:1,025).

Although specific lines of influence between French noblewomen and Italian actresses regarding performance practices are difficult to trace, it is easy to see that performances by French noblewomen mirror both the lowbrow, titillating aspects of performances by Italian actresses (and perhaps actors), as well as the highbrow eloquence associated with them. Shakespeare's conflation of both types of practices in *Love's Labour's Lost* would easily reference both groups of women for his audience.

A possible echo of the *escadron volant* imitating the more risqué maneuvers of Italian actresses, who frequently cross-dressed as men to participate in various onstage escapades (as do several of Shakespeare's heroines),[12] appears in L'Estoile's entry for 15 May, 1577, in which he notes that "at Plessis-les-Tours, the King gave a festive party in honor of M. le Duc, his brother ... at which the ladies of the court waited on table dressed as men in green silk suits" (59). In the same entry L'Estoile also mentions the queen's banquet at Chenonceaux, which was rumored to have been financed in part by "the Italians," at which "the ladies of the court appeared half naked ..." (59). (Both spectacles were organized by one of Catherine de Medici's favorite ladies of the court, Claude-Catherine de Clermont, the Maréschale de Retz ([St-John, 88]), who is discussed further below.) Regarding displays of nudity, Clubb – commenting on Andreini's acclaimed mad scene, *La Pazzia d'Isabella*, performed in 1589 for the wedding entertainments of Ferdinando de Medici and Christine de Lorraine – points out, "A contemporary French spectator of the Gelosi company's performances in the generation just before those of the Andreini observes that mad scenes were popular with the professionals because they gave actresses an excuse for ripping up their clothes to show off their

---

11   The translations from Boucher are mine.

12   Regarding similar cross-dressing escapades by English noblewomen, it is difficult to say whether art inspired life or vice versa, but such women as Mary Fitton (1578–1647) and Arbella Stuart (1575–1615) made use of the practice (Roberts, lxxxiii; Orgel, 114). Stephen Orgel comments at length on issues involved in women's use of "masculine apparel" during this period (83–105).

Con Priuilegio del Stato di Milano, & d'altri Principi.

7.1   Isabella Andreini, from *Rime d'Isabella Andreini Padovana, Comica Gelosa* (Milan, 1601).

breasts and the skillful undulations of their flesh" (264). As for Isabella herself, Clubb comments: "None of the accounts reveals how much of herself Isabella revealed, but as she was considered an uncommonly grand and moral sort of actress, it may be that she relied more on [her] talents for music, mimicry, and interpretation ... than on topless exhibitions" (265). In any case, in some dramatic scenes Italian actresses topless displays were standard practice (see Katritzky, this volume), while cross-dressing and eroticized costuming were common at the French court during this period.

Henri III's penchant for cross-dressing and disguise, as well as that of his *mignons*, has long been noted by historians. It is illustrated in instances of the king dressing as a woman during carnival time, as well as the king and his courtiers masquerading as Amazons or shepherds (L'Estoile, 58; Boucher, 3:1,106–7, 1,110–15, 1,181). Women of the court, too, as noted above, cross-dressed and wore various costumes for festive occasions. Other examples include their dressing as flagellants in an entertainment for the queen (3:1,153) and as shepherdesses to serve at a banquet (3:1,181). Boucher argues that the ladies' affinity for cross-dressing and disguise is not solely a sign of their lasciviousness, as L'Estoile insinuates, but rather an illustration of the "mentalité baroque" that characterized the court as a whole – a court that was wholly obsessed with theater, disguise, and masquerades (3:1,148–88) and so enamored with Italian actors that for the Mardi Gras celebrations of 1585, the king and his "troupe" of a hundred men "portaient des pantalons de diverses couleurs, comme en revêtaient les acteurs de la comédie italienne" [wore pants of diverse colors, like those worn by the actors of the Italian comedy] (3:1,184). Although scandalous deportment and *outré* costuming were *de rigueur* among some French noblewomen, the court's obsession with Italian comedians suggests that behaviors gleaned from the commedia actresses infiltrated the repertoire of the *escadron volant*, as did the sophisticated oratory skills associated with commedia performers.

The ladies of the French court displayed their dancing and oratory skills to celebrate the marriage of the Duc de Joyeuse and Marguerite de Vaudemont in 1581. Dressed in fantastic costumes, they portrayed naiads and dryads who shared the stage with sirens and satyrs in the *Balet comique de la Royne* (fig. 7.2).[13] The Italian director of the ballet, Baltasar de Beaujoyeulx, né Baldassare

---

13 Beaujoyeulx writes that the roles of the naiads belong to "mes dames la Princess de Lorraine, Duchesses de Mercueil, de Guyse, de Neuers, d'Aumalle, & de Ioyeuse, Mareschalle de Raiz, & de l'Archant: & mes Damoyselles de Pons, de Bourdeille, & de Cypierre." The women wear rich gowns of "argent & incarnat," silver and a deep cherry or rose color, and in their hair are "petits triangles enrichis de diamans, rubis, perles, & autres pierreries," little triangles enriched with diamonds, rubies, pearls, and other jewels (15v). They dance to the music of violins, moving through

Belgiojoso, records that Circé was represented by "la damoyselle de Saincte Mesme," who spoke her part "with a dolorous voice and a grace that few young women could imitate and none could surpass" (7, 10; Boucher, 3:1,053). He also writes that "la damoyselle de Beaulieu" played the role of Tethys, taking part in a dialogue with Glaucus (played by "le sieur de Beaulieu," her husband) (16). Moreover, "la damoyselle de Victry" recited verse to the king with such grace and "modeste asseurance" that the learned guests judged her capable of understanding the most exalted things "en toutes sciences & disciplines" (37v). Like the actresses of the commedia dell'arte, the women of the French court knew how to captivate and intrigue their audiences with their verbal prowess. Shakespeare's palimpsest, then, has roots in female performance from a variety of entertainments for the French court.

The *Balet comique* is one of the most elaborate examples of the masque genre, which was rapidly gaining favor in England, where it would reach its zenith in the productions of Ben Jonson and Inigo Jones during the reign of King James. Walter Cohen points out that the "symmetries" that shape *Love's Labour's Lost* "reinforce the work's formalized, dance-like structure and give it an aristocratic feel" (734). The "dance-like structure" of the play alludes to the popularity of the masque, and, since *Love's Labour's Lost* so heavily references the French court, it is not surprising to find this resonance in the play. Also not surprising is the fact that Shakespeare's Navarre would have Armado and the other commedia-style male characters stage *The Nine Worthies* (5.1.99–132), as his desire for this sort of entertainment reflects the taste of the French court. The same is true of his willingness to disguise himself and his noblemen as Muscovites (5.2.120–1). Likewise, *Love's Labour's Lost* clearly references the doubly nuanced reputations of French courtly women who performed in court masques and other entertainments. Shakespeare's ladies are remembered and praised for their prowess at dancing (2.1.114–15, 5.2.218–29), they carry off disguise with great ease (5.2.265), and they are accused of being "Light wenches" who have a history of sexual indiscretions (5.1.359; Cohen, 737). "Perchance light in the light," quips Longueville as he jokes about Maria's potential wantonness upon first meeting her (2.1.198). Paradoxically, these ladies are also eloquent spokeswomen on the subject of true love, as the princess, turned queen, and Rosaline illustrate in their moving speeches about what Navarre and Biron must do to earn their love near the end of the play (5.2.760–94; 5.2.818–31, 835–46). These facets of *Love's Labour's Lost* suggest

---

"douze figures de Geometrie," twelve geometric figures, before the king and his mother (22v). Beaujoyeulx notes that the four dryads are "les damoyselles de Victry, Surgeres, Lauernay, Estauay la ieune"(37v–39v). The goddess Minerva is played by the "damoyselle de Chaumont" (44). Translations from Beaujoyeulx are mine.

Figure des Sereines.

7.2 Sirens, from *Balet Comique de la Royne* (Paris, 1582) by Baltasar de Beaujoyeaulx. Reproduced by permission of the Harvard Theatre Collection, the Houghton Library.

that Shakespeare's portrayals of French courtly women, who shadow Italian actresses, are indeed based on intriguing precedents in Continental female performance.

Regarding the second question concerning the English fascination with Continental women, it is important to recall the ideological distance between Catholic Europeans and Shakespeare's Protestant audience, whose hostility toward Catholicism and aversion to English women performing before the general public no doubt shaped their response to *Love's Labour's Lost*. This ideological distance provided a buffer that permitted the English to find performances by such Continental female figures titillating and thought-provoking, yet allowed them to scoff at their lax manners and mores. Shakespeare's audience must have realized that these female characters could easily reflect women of the English court,[14] but on the surface, they were appraising the behavior of foreign "others." Insights into English opinion of the Italians and the French may be found in a variety of sources; however, some particularly relevant to notions about Continental women as they are characterized in *Love's Labour's Lost* may be seen in the works of Thomas Nashe and John Lyly.

In *Pierce Penilesse* (1592), Nashe underscores the prevailing notion that actresses are women of ill repute when he criticizes the Italian players who have "whores and common courtezans to play women's parts, and forbear no immodest speech or unchaste action that may procure laughter." He compares Italian performers to the players of England, noting, "but our scene is more stately furnished ... our representations honourable, and full of gallant resolution, not consisting, like theirs, of a pantaloon, a whore, and a zany, but of emperors, kings and princes ..." (90–91). Shakespeare's plays, of course, were to profit from imitation of Italian theatrical traditions, illustrating the competitive edge that tinges Nashe's point of view. In *Love's Labour's Lost*, Rosaline's quip about horns, followed by her bawdy bout of singing the "hit it" song with Boyet (4.1.11–124), clearly resonates with Nashe's scurrilous description of Italian actresses, as does Shakespeare's use of male characters that resemble the braggart (Armado), the pedant (Holofernes), the zany (Costard), and the parasite (Nathaniel) (David, xxxvi). In this play, Shakespeare's scene may be "stately furnished" to resemble a French court, but his players belie Nashe's protestations as they distinctly recall Italian comedians, no doubt to the delight of the English audience.

John Lyly, like Nashe, is also compelled to make comparisons between the Italians and the English. In *Euphues and His England* (1580), a work virtually

---

14   Yates suggests that the Devereux sisters, Penelope and Dorothy, inspired the female characters in (1936, 102–51, 174). Maurice Hunt perceives reflections of Queen Elizabeth in the play (173–92).

constructed upon comparisons of English and Italian culture, Lyly has the English Camilla haughtily state to her Italian lover, "I am *Philautus* no *Italian* Lady, who commonly are woed with leasings, & won with lust, entangled with deceipt, & enjoyed with delight, caught with sinne, and cast off with shame" (2:128). Instead, she protests – too much, it must be said – that her innocence should not be so assaulted by his Italianate wooing practices, which include visiting her masked and sending a love letter concealed inside a pomegranate, strategies echoed in *Love's Labour's Lost* (5.2). In *Euphues' Glass for Europe*, dedicated to "the Ladyes and Gentlewomen of Italy," Lyly continues the assault on Italian as well as European women in general, noting that the "Gentlewoemen" of Greece and Italy use "sonnets for psalmes" and "pastymes for prayers," and may be found "reading ye Epistle of a Lover, when they should peruse the Gospell of our Lord" (2: 198–9). Regarding the Englishwomen he holds up for comparison, he notes they

> ... use their needle to banish idleness, not the pen to nourish it, not spending their times in answering ye letters of those that woe them, but forswearing the companie of those that write them, giving no occasion either by wanton lookes, unseemely gestures, unadvised speech, or any uncomly behauiour, of lightness or liking. Contrarie to the custome of many countries, where filthie wordes are accompted to sauour of a fine witte, broade speach, of a bolde courage, wanton glaunces, of a sharpe eye sight, wicked deedes, of a comely gesture, all vaine delights, of a right curteous curtesie. (2: 201)

In describing this "custome of many countries," Lyly seems to nod slyly toward the mores of French salon society, as well as those of Italian actresses, courtesans, and noblewomen, all the while insisting that proper Englishwomen scorn the pen, preferring to stitch away their passions, while exulting in their piety. His descriptions of Continental women foreshadow those in *Love's Labour's Lost*, in which the princess and her ladies do, in fact, pass the time reading "ye Epistle[s] of a Lover" (5.2.1–78), are practiced at "broade speach," and accused of "light" behavior (2.1.112–26, 4.3.359). Nashe and Lyly, then, deride the mores of such women for their audiences while praising those of Englishwomen who live under the rule of "a young and tender Maiden" (2: 209), illustrating a common view of Continental women in these works popular on the Elizabethan literary scene shortly before the appearance of *Love's Labour's Lost*.[15]

Felicia Hardison Londré hypothesizes that the play was "originally written as a playful spoof of Euphuism combined with a tribute to the French manners and fashions admired at the English court in the 1570s" and that it was "later

---

15 Attempts have been made to identify Nashe as Moth and Lyly as Armado (see Hibbard, 52–3).

revised to tie the attractive leading characters to actual historical figures who were sympathetically regarded by the English" (329). Such sympathy, however, rested precariously upon public opinion of the French, which at court was especially based on political contingencies. French visitors to the English court were welcomed warmly, in the interest of maintaining a sound political alliance. The rest of the populace, however, did not necessarily concur with the court. Londré summarizes the situation by suggesting that Queen Elizabeth "would have realized that the ordinary Englishman would view it as satire on the effete, frivolous, Catholic French. This would serve to reinforce Protestantism among the citizenry while she herself, above the fray, could maintain strong diplomatic ties with France" (331). Thus, on the surface, at least, the female characters of *Love's Labour's Lost* could remain scandalous foreigners conveniently portrayed by English male actors, who were probably quite eager to prove that they could hold their own against the reputations of polished French courtly performers and accomplished Italian troupes.[16]

To address the third question, the resonance between Italian players, French noblewomen, and the characters of *Love's Labour's Lost* is especially underscored by the debate or dialogue-like nature of the play. In "The Play of the Courtier: Correspondences between Castiglione's *Il libro del Cortegiano* and Shakespeare's *Loves' Labour's Lost*," Donatella Baldini points out that in addition to having an open ending that mimics that of *The Courtier*, the play seems deeply indebted thematically to Castiglione's work in a number of ways (18). She writes,

> Shakespeare dramatizes an understanding of the relation between the sexes close to the one presented in the *Courtier*, where, in the frame, the male and female characters entertain each other with dances and games. In fact, the courtiers' dialogue itself is a game, set in a hall where women and men sit in an alternating seating arrangement. Within the dialogues the speakers represent courtship as a stylized ritual, a series of moves on the man's part and responses on the woman's part, and discuss each kind of move for its effectiveness in gaining the woman's favor. Thus courtship becomes almost a game to be won or lost, depending on the man's ability but also, as with games, on fortune: "every one of us have seene most noble yong men, discreete, wise, of prowesse, and well favoured spend many yeares in loving, sparing for nothing that might entice, tokens, sutes, teares: to bee short whatsoever may bee imagined, and all but lost labour" (*Courtier* 223; 3.41). The correspondence between the Courtier's expression and Shakespeare's title phrase bespeaks an analogous view of courtship as the most refined and emblematical of social games. (11)[17]

---

16 Brown points out, "Citations in plays concerning the Italian actors per se indicate more malign envy than open admiration" (406).

17 Baldini quotes from Sir Thomas Hoby's translation, *The Book of the Courtier* (1561).

Beyond suggesting a source for Shakespeare's title and themes, Baldini's observations bring into focus the ways in which Shakespeare's play exhibits hybridity of genre – it is both play and dialogue, a play in which the game of courtship is enacted in a dialogue on the nature of love. Near the end, Biron reminds us that this is clearly a play: "Our wooing doth not end like an old play" (5.2.851), but the open ending suggests otherwise.

For an audience familiar with dialogues generated by salon or academic rituals, a play about an academy that ends with the debate in question still open would not be considered unusual. It would be recognized as a meta-academic touch that mimics the endings of such dialogues as *The Courtier*, as well as Tullia d'Aragona's *Della infinità di amore* or Louise Labé's *Débat de Folie et d'Amour*.[18] That these Continental women and many others were writing dialogues and participating in salon and academic circles suggests that Shakespeare had much more than specific topicality in mind when he decided that the princess and her ladies should crash Navarre's all-male academy.[19] Baldini notes that, compared to the women in *The Courtier*, "The women in *Love's Labour's Lost* play a more prominent and many-sided role in the social game – where they hold the rhetorical field with wit and outspokenness and participate in masculine pursuits such as hunting – but they too show their social competence mostly in their critical response to male initiative which is asserted in the initial exclusion from the space of the court and in the later pursuits of courtship" (13). The ways in which Shakespeare's female characters assert their agency as players or interlocutors in the games of love indicate his

---

18 H. R. Woudhuysen, who illustrates links between Shakespeare's play and potential English sources for it, argues that the "most obvious analogy for the play's open ending is Chaucer's *The Parliament of Fowls*" (8).

19 Women of various classes in Italy and France participated in academic and salon society during this period. A catalogue of these women would take up too much space here, but a good start may be found in *Women Poets of the Italian Renaissance: Courtly Ladies and Courtesans*, edited by Laura Anna Stortoni, translated by Stortoni and Mary Prentice Lillie (New York: Italica, 1997), and *Italian Women Writers: A Bio-Bibliographical Sourcebook*, edited by Rinaldina Russell (Westport: Greenwood, 1994). Vittoria Colonna, Laura Bacio Terracina, Veronica Gambera, and other noblewomen, in addition to numerous courtesans such as Veronica Franco and Tullia d'Aragona, participated in academies and salons in Italy. In France women of the royal family were associated with courtly, learned circles, but others, too, hosted and participated in salons. Louise Labé, Pernette du Guillet, and the Mesdames des Roches are some of the best known. Madeleine de l'Aubespine, Madame de Villeroy, and Claude-Catherine de Clermont, the Maréschale de Retz were celebrated for their salons in Paris, as well as their participation in the *Académie du palais*. Retz's mother-in-law, Marie-Catherine de Pierre-Vive, Dame du Perron, was renowned for her salon in Lyon. For more on these and other *salonnières* see Keating and Yates (1968).

engagement with such cultural phenomena as the *contrasti* popular on the Italian stage and the debates in Continental salons and academies which included women among the interlocutors.

The Italian actresses' performances in *contrasti*, the staged debates usually enacted by pairs of *innamorati*, recall the repartee between the women and the men in *Love's Labour's Lost*. Excellent examples may be found in the *contrasti scenici* of Isabella Andreini, which address "the passions of love and hate, love and death, love and vows, marital love, tragedy, comedy, [and] epic poetry ..." (Clubb, 267). These debates address numerous themes that Shakespeare explores in *Love's Labour's Lost* (and some clearly resonate with his interest in experimenting with genre). In the "Contrasto sopra le passioni dell'odio, e dell'amore," the lovers Tacito and Amasia discuss if and how love and hate may co-exist, which passion is stronger, and how these passions affect them (Andreini, 17–22). In the "Contrasto sopra la dignità de gli amanti," Attilio and Diotima debate which is more worthy, the lover or the beloved, and in the "Contrasto sopra le armi e le lettere," Alessandro and Corinna argue which path to immortal fame is more noble, the pursuit of martial victories or the pursuit of literary and philosophical endeavors (11–16, 41–8). Such *contrasti* recall the debate in *Love's Labour's Lost* that might be stated, which is more worthy, the pursuit of philosophical matters or the pursuit of true love?

Scholars have commented on the intertextual echoes in Andreini's and Shakespeare's works for some time.[20] Regarding echoes of academic or salon debate, Clubb notes that the "sexual game of parry and thrust, played with loosely grasped literary and philosophical weapons" undertaken by pairs of *innamorati* in Andreini's *contrasti scenici* is characteristic of that carried out by Beatrice and Benedick in *Much Ado about Nothing* (267), and Richard Andrews suggests that "the conceit-laden exchanges to be found in Isabella Andreini are not so different in kind from those in *Love's Labours Lost* or other admired Shakespearean dialogues" (194). The characteristics that Clubb and Andrews discuss are those that reflect behavior and activities gleaned from academic and salon society. In addition to the dancing and acting associated with the *escadron volant* and commedia actresses, ladies of the French court and the Italian actresses were also known for their ability to participate in learned discourse on numerous topics of interest to humanists as well as how to engage in ribald badinage. Thus, the sober and wise discourse of the ladies of *Love's Labour's Lost*, like their mischievous, sometimes lascivious, wordplay, has precedents in Continental female performance.

---

20 To take *Hamlet* as an example, Clubb (264, 267), Angelini (112–13), and Andrews (192) have all commented on similarities between Ophelia's mad scene and Isabella's in *La pazzia d'Isabella*.

In Italy, actresses such as Andreini and Vittoria Piisimi were lauded for their verbal grace. Tommaso Garzoni writes that Piissimi is "a beautiful sorceress of love, she entices the hearts of a thousand lovers with her words" (qtd. and trans. in Richards and Richards, 221). Erycius Puteanus, a Belgian humanist living in Milan, writes to Andreini, "On Monday, I am to give a public speech here entitled, 'On My Public Office.' Would that I might have recourse to your Persuasion and that I might speak boldly and felicitously!" On another occasion, he opens a letter to her, "That such eloquence, that such learning should fall to the part of a woman! Where does that sex which is mighty in writing, which sweats in public declamation, which grows old in literary studies – where does it show itself stronger than in you?" (qtd. and trans. in MacNeil, 306, 311). Italian actresses were often well educated or at least capable of appearing so because, in many cases, they are believed to have begun their careers as *cortigiane honeste*, that is, as courtesans celebrated for their learning and eloquence. Of the connections between Italian actresses, courtesans, and salon society, Rosalind Kerr writes:

> Salon performances featuring dance, improvised dialogues, recitation of love poetry were frequently given in this period by this class of women, the "honest courtesan" who had been in residence in Rome and other Italian centres since at least the beginning of the century (Taviana and Schino 1982, 358). These women, often multi-talented poets, singers, musicians, dancers, and rhetoricians who began their careers as "companions" to rich aristocrats, found that they could acquire a certain financial independence through their earnings as performers. (42)

Nashe's swipe at Italian troupes for having "whores and common courtezans" among them inadvertently alludes to the facets of such actresses' roots that are supposedly responsible for their successful training for their roles – training shadowed, perhaps, in the gifted verbal performances of the princess and her ladies in *Love's Labour's Lost*.

Another trace of the roots of verbal performance for Shakespeare's ladies may be seen in the accounts of French female academicians that arise during the time of the *Académie du palais* under the reign of Henri III (1574–89). Their participation in debates at court has been documented by their contemporaries. In his letter "À mes filles touchant les femmes doctes de nostre siècle," written in the late sixteenth century, Théodore Agrippa d'Aubigné reminisces about a meeting during which the discussion focused on the excellence of the moral and intellectual virtues. Of the Maréschale de Retz and Madame de Lignerolles,[21] he writes that the two gave proof of their great learnedness and explains that

---

21 Henri Weber, editor of D'Aubigné's *Œuvres*, identifies Lignerolles as Louise de Cabriane de la Guyonnière, a lady-in-waiting to Catherine de Medici renowned for her wit.

during their speeches, "elles furent antagonistes, et se firent admirer" [they were antagonists and aroused admiration] (852–3). Women's participation in academic debate over moral issues resonates strongly with the princess and her ladies' roles in the debate about the nature of true love in *Love's Labour's Lost*.

The princess, quick to denounce clichéd Petrarchan compliments, verbally accosts their givers, laying the groundwork for her invincible stance on what constitutes true love at the end of the play. To Boyet, she says, "my beauty, though but mean / Needs not the painted flourish of your praise. / Beauty is bought by the judgement of the eye, / Not uttered by base sale of chapmen's tongues" (2.1.13–16). In an exchange with the simple Forester, she inveighs against Petrarchan flattery: "Nay, never paint me now. / Where fair is not, praise cannot mend the brow" (4.1.17–18). In the scene in which the ladies read their missives, all mock the Petrarchan vows of their lovers, with Maria concluding, "Folly in fools bears not so strong a note / As fool'ry in the wise when wit doth dote" (5.2.75–6). At the beginning of the play, the princess stops her own spate of criticism of the king by saying, "But pardon me, I am too sudden-bold. / To teach a teacher ill beseemeth me" (2.1.106–7), but after the crushing failure of the Muscovites' masque, the king begs her, "Teach us, sweet madam, for our rude transgression / Some fair excuse (5.2.431–2). After the death of her father, the princess begins to teach in earnest as she instructs the king to go to "some forlorn and naked hermitage" where through "frosts and fasts, hard lodging and thin weeds," she hopes that the "gaudy blossoms" of his love – his light-weight Petrarchan infatuation – will turn to steady, true love (5.2.777–85). The women's arguments in favor of sincere love born of wisdom over imitative, idle swearing and boasts lay bare the crux of the play's debate and show the women themselves to be formidable interlocutors.

While recent scholarship such as that of Clubb, Barasch, and Brown has brought to light important connections between Italian actresses and Shakespeare's female characters, little has been said about the French women who shadow the ladies of *Love's Labour's Lost* that moves beyond issues of topicality. In "Shakespeare's Navarre," Hugh Richmond suggests that the female characters in the play represent specific ladies of the French court, and he hypothesizes that Catherine de Bourbon is "the very Katherine who figures in Shakespeare's play," that Marie de Nevers is Maria, and that Rose de Montal might be Rosaline, although toward the end of his study he suggests that she could also be "the Queen's alter ego in the play" (Richmond 202, 209). In spite of his close examination of the histories of some ladies who attended at Nérac, he cannot ultimately say with certainty whom the ladies in *Love's Labour's Lost* represent. Nonetheless, he argues that Shakespeare "was familiar with men intimately associated with Henri and his court, who could annotate from observation or gossip every episode of *Love's Labour's Lost*" (196). To prove that these characters indeed represent ladies of the French court, Richmond focuses especially on the lascivious tales circulating about them. He emphasizes the sexual prowess of the *escadron volant*, calling them a "team of sexual Machiavels" who were, according to their reputation, "wholly without prudery or inhibitions" (201). His colorful descriptions conjure a vision of Renaissance "Bond girls" who are in cahoots with the evil Catholic Catherine de Medici and Marguerite de Valois, arch enemies of the Protestant Henri de Navarre, and they reflect the gossip that circulated about these women, as exemplified in the diary entries of L'Estoile. Other period portraits, however, such as that of D'Aubigné, suggest that some were concerned with more than costumes and topless displays, and the gravity of the play's female characters when discussing the king and his men's shortcomings belie Richmond's assessment. Clearly, more than historical re-enactment is taking place.

First, there is the issue of identification. If the play were truly meant to be a *roman à clef*, identifying characters would not be so difficult, especially if, as Richmond puts it, "every episode" could be annotated by people in the know. Second, the emphasis on the women's sexual exploits to the exclusion of almost everything else does not exactly match up with the speeches and actions of the female characters. Instead of being simple, courtesan-like figures who are "free to do whatever they [want] as long as they [are] nice to strangers and [do] not get pregnant" (Richmond, 201–2), Shakespeare's ladies are sharp critics of Petrarchan nonsense and empty oaths. They especially press the questions, what is the nature of true love, and what constitutes true knowledge and worthwhile learning? These are the critical debate questions of the age. Tellingly, they understand that only "a merry, nimble, stirring spirit" (5.2.16) survives the vicissitudes of passion. If they are courtesan-like in any particular way, they are like Diotima who teaches Socrates "who Love is and what like, and then his works"(Plato, 97). In spite of their willingness to engage in bawdy repartee, the women, like Diotima, have the moral upper hand at the play's conclusion, as they charge the men to acquire an understanding of true love and to prove themselves worthy of marriage. Also, like Elisabetta Gonzaga and Emilia Pia from *The Courtier*, they direct the debate about love to higher planes, thus fulfilling the stereotypical role of female interlocutors in Renaissance dialogues. Third, the structure of the play, with its aberrant ending, does not resemble the typical comedy. Instead of being a tidy series of historical vignettes that concludes with matches made, perhaps reminiscent of Navarre's and Marguerite's brief reconciliation at Nérac between August, 1579, and May, 1580, the ending is left open, with the questions about the nature of love and marriage not answered but postponed for a year. The dialogue-like aspects of the play thus resist specific historical assessment.

Instead of attempting to name the historical figures that shadow Shakespeare's female characters, scholars might more profitably investigate the many roles and the dualities of the reputations of the women of the French court and Italian actresses, in order to better contextualize the play. By understanding the sorts of "press" such women received, we find that Shakespeare expands the notion of what Clubb refers to as "theatergrams."[22] In this case, Shakespeare uses not only the recognized types played by Italian actresses, but also intermingles them with aspects of his characters that reflect information circulating about women of the French court, information that illustrates their verbal prowess.

Examples of the activities of the women close to Marguerite de Valois may be gleaned from a look at two who were well known in France and whose reputations most likely spread abroad, thanks to the numerous dedications made to them by contemporary poets such as Pierre de Ronsard, Philippe Desportes, and Pontus de Tyard;[23] their husbands' involvement in French politics;[24] and their own salon and academic activities, which were likely discussed by travelers who either were fortunate enough to be invited to their homes or who encountered them at the French court.[25] Claude-Catherine de

---

22   Clubb defines theatergrams as the "units, figures, relationships, actions, topoi, and framing patterns" used throughout Renaissance drama; these were gleaned from classic examples and modified by players onstage until they became "streamlined structures for svelte play-making and elements of high specific density, weighty with significance from previous incarnations" (6).

23   Regarding Retz, Keating writes: "Besides Baif, all the living members of the Brigade addressed verses to either husband or wife, and the newer school of poetry was represented not only by Desportes and Bertaut but by a host of lesser lights" (107). Keating also notes the references to Retz in the poetry on Artémis of Amadis Jamyn (116). John C. Lapp points out that Retz is thought to be the "new Pasithée" of Pontus de Tyard's *Nouvelles œuvres poétiques* (1573) and that he dedicated the second edition of *Solitaire premier* to her in 1573 (xx–xxi). Regarding Villeroy, by 1570, Ronsard was writing a sonnet, "à Conflans, le VIII septembre, 1570," to celebrate the hospitality he received *chez* the Villeroys at Conflans, their country home (Keating, 84–5). For poetic tributes to Villeroy by Jamyn, Ronsard, and Desportes, see Sorg, 10–11, and Ronsard (2: 640).

24   Nicolas de Neufville, sieur de Villeroy, and husband of Madeleine de l'Aubespine, became Secretary of State in 1570 and served, with one brief hiatus in the position under Henri III, until his death in 1617. He was widely known throughout his career for his associations with the leading poets of the time, especially Ronsard (Keating, 82–102). Albert de Gondi, who became a Maréschal de France in 1573, and whose land was raised to a duchy in 1581, was the husband of Claude-Catherine de Clermont. He was intricately involved in the politics of the Valois court, and he was rumored to have been an accomplice in the St. Bartholomew's Day Massacre (Strage, 192–5; de Pommerol, 59–67). He was also involved in the marriage negotiations between Queen Elizabeth and the Duc d'Alençon (de Pommerol, 106).

25   One English traveler who may have had the opportunity to enjoy the famous Retz hospitality was Philip Sidney; see Osborn, 41–2. Although there is no evidence that

Clermont, the Maréschale de Retz, and Madeleine de l'Aubespine, Madame de Villeroy, were hostesses of Parisian literary salons frequented by members of the Pléiade and various courtiers and their wives. Retz was associated from girlhood with "the train of the Queen Mother" (Keating 105). Villeroy was the daughter of the Secretary of State, a position that her husband eventually inherited. She was well-known for her "beauty and her poetic talents at the courts of Charles IX, Henri III, and Henri IV."[26] Both women were praised for their skills as poets, musicians, and witty conversationalists. Retz was, in fact, one of the women who accompanied Marguerite de Valois and Catherine de Medici to Nérac,[27] and she also performed the role of a naiad in the *Balet comique* (Beaujoyeulx, 15v), as well as organizing and appearing in other court spectacles. We must wonder if it is coincidental that Shakespeare includes Retz's pastoral pseudonym "Dyctinne" in one of the numerous spates of wordplay in *Love's Labour's Lost*.[28]

In addition to being praised by D'Aubigné for her polished performance in a debate before the court academy, Retz was lauded for her oratory skills when ambassadors from Poland came to request the duc d'Anjou for their king in 1573. She responded to them publicly in Latin for Catherine de Medici, and it is noted that her discourse "l'emporta sur ceux du chancelier de Birague et du comte de Chiverny, qui répondirent pour Charles IX et le duc d'Anjou" [outshone those of the chancellor of Birague and the comte de Chiverni, who

---

Sidney visited either of the Villeroy houses, he may have known something of the Villeroy salon, not only through his exposure to courtly society in Paris, but also because in Vienna he became friends with Jean de Vulcob, the cousin of Madeleine and Claude de l'Aubespine. For an overview of the Vulcob and L'Aubespine family relations see Lavaud, 39–41.

26   Madame de Villeroy is so described in the *Nouvelle Biographie Générale* (Paris: Firmin Didot Frères, Editeurs, 1963), 3: 574.

27   See St-John, 89.

28   The passage reads as follows:

DULL: You two are bookmen. Can you tell me by your wit
What was a month old at Cain's birth that's not five weeks old as yet?
HOLOFERNES: Dictynna, Goodman Dull, Dictynna, Goodman Dull.
DULL: What is 'Dictima'?
NATHANIEL: A title to Phoebe, to *luna*, to the moon. (4.2.34)

Since Queen Elizabeth is often associated with the moon, it is not unusual to find such jests in Shakespeare's works, but in *Love's Labour's Lost*, packed with so many references to the French court, it is intriguing to find this particular one, associated with a woman well known for her oratory skills. Numerous poems refer to Retz as "Dyctinne," and it was common knowledge among French salon habitués that the name was associated with her.

responded for Charles IX and the duc d'Anjou].[29] Jacques Lavaud notes that her oration was so impressive that "presque tous les mémoires contemporains le mentionnent" (nearly all the contemporary memoirs mention it)(77).[30] Although there is no definitive list of those who frequented the *Académie du palais*, women mentioned as attendees along with Retz and Lignerolles are Villeroy and Marguerite de Valois (Keating, 79–80; Yates, *French Academies* 32–3). Such women's performances in debate and learned conversation became part of international courtly gossip, as D'Aubigné's letter to his daughters demonstrates. In it he praises Italian, French, and English women, including "la Marquise de Pesquiere" (Vittoria Colonna), "Izabella Andrei" (Isabella Andreini), Cornelia Miani, Olympia Fulvia Morata, and other learned ladies in Europe, as well as Queen Elizabeth of England (852). Clearly, by the late sixteenth and early seventeenth centuries, learned women across the Continent and in England had earned international reputations, and Shakespeare capitalizes on them as he fashions his female characters in *Love's Labour's Lost*.

Along with French noblewomen's engagement in formal academic situations, the combination of their taste for bawdy conversation and their astuteness in literary matters emerges in the action of the play, reflecting activities popular in sixteenth-century French literary salons. The badinage of the couples in the play seems especially related to salon society. Sources suggest that both Retz and Villeroy were accomplished wits, and contemporary accounts of their verbal performances in salon settings call to mind the sophisticated yet ribald jests of the ladies of *Love's Labour's Lost*. In his *Confession Catholique du Sieur de Sancy*, D'Aubigné recalls a conversation with Villeroy in which she delights in asking bawdy questions about the nature of a saint's confessions, such as requesting to know how he confessed his lewdness and how to say in Greek "cette huile legere" [that light oil] that Saint Dominique sowed between the thighs of a nun, calling it "huyle d'amour" [oil of love] (584). If D'Aubigné's memory of Villeroy's participation in bawdy salon banter is accurate, it appears that French courtly society's tolerance for ribaldry may have outstripped or at least rivaled that of Shakespeare's audience.[31] To turn again to Retz, we may look to the lawyer Estienne Pasquier who records his memories of her quick wit in a letter to "Monsieur Airault" (1591). He writes of an evening during which he dined at her home,

---

29 My translation. See the *Nouvelle biographie générale* (10:842). Edouard Fremy also gives an account of this event in his *Origines de l'Académie française: L'Académie des derniers Valois: Académie de poésie et de musique 1570–1576, Académie du palais 1576–1585* (154).
30 My translation.
31 See Keating's commentary on Villeroy's reputation for bawdiness (93–4).

and he recounts how, after exhausting the serious subjects, the group turned to "le discours de l'amour." The general discussion of love quickly becomes focused on the *questioni d'amore*, "who can better speak of love, a young man or an old one?" Pasquier notes that his adversary was Retz herself, who provoked him mercilessly by referring to him as a "bon-homme," an old man. Catching on to her game, he says, he took her words as a grave insult, "comme un huictiesme peché mortel" [as an eighth mortal sin], and then the war of wits broke out in earnest.[32] These vignettes of Villeroy and Retz verbally sparring with their companions illustrate their adroit wits and ribald senses of humor, which clearly impressed their contemporaries as much as their intellectual and literary endeavors. Such humor, as Shakespeare surely realized, easily lends itself to dialogue for comedies, especially one that showcases a "civil war of wits" (2.1.225) in which the male characters argue about the nature of women and love, sampling topics from the *querelle des femmes* and the *questioni d'amore* popular in academic and salon debate, and the women stoop to bandying about suggestive wordplay, such as when Catherine and Boyet move from "grappling" and "ships" to "hot sheeps" and the question of how "common" her lips might be (2.1.217–22).

In addition to trading witticisms with Navarre and his gentlemen in a manner that recalls salon behavior, the ladies of *Love's Labour's Lost* read and criticize the men's literary efforts. Catherine says that her verses from Dumaine are "A huge translation of hypocrisy / Vilely compiled, profound simplicity" (5.2.51–2). Maria notes that her missive from Longueville "is too long by half a mile" (5.2.54). Of Biron's verses, Rosaline says "The numbers true, and were the numb'ring, too, / I were the fairest goddess on the ground" (5.2.35–6). She then goes on to mock his attempts at Petrarchism with copious wordplay on images of fair and dark, showing herself to be the more accomplished wordsmith. Eve Sanders suggests that "[o]ne of the layered ironies of the men's monopoly on study is that the women are acute readers, in some cases more so than the men," and she analyzes the princess's critique of Armado's letter with its "modish language that had so charmed the King and courtiers," as well as Rosaline's critique of Biron's verse, noting that Rosaline, too, "demonstrates that she has the critical sensibility to judge a poem's prosody and the aptness of its imagery" (52). Sanders argues that in their use of reading and interpretation and in their "anti-masque" in which they "directly undertake to teach the teachers a lesson that will confound the terms on which the men have based their assertions of self-superiority," the women of the play "assert that each 'she' which the men read as a sign is a reader in her own right, one capable of construing meaning" (54). This ability to "construe meaning," to critique and pronounce judgments upon the men's writing (and acting: Rosaline reviles

32 See Estienne Pasquier, "A Monsieur Airault," 897–900.

their "shallow shows, and prologue viley penned" [5.2.305]), recalls literary salon activity. The women of French salon society such as Retz and Villeroy were sought-after patrons whose taste helped shape much of the poetry of the period.[33] Moreover, these women were writers whose works circulated in manuscript among their intimates.[34] Reading and critiquing the verse of one's fellow salon members were thus intrinsic parts of salon performance. In addition to "undermin[ing] the conventional justification of women's intellectual inferiority for the King's men-only admissions policy" (Sanders, 53), this allusion to learned women who critique literary efforts invokes the contemporary reality that certain women of the French court were well versed as readers and critics, which was also true of some English noblewomen of Shakespeare's time.[35]

The performances by Continental women in learned society – formal debates at court, less formal ones in salons, and the ability to write and critique the works of others – are important to consider when analyzing the women's part in the debate over love and philosophy in *Love's Labour's Lost*. Such women's associations with marriage, too, should be examined in conjunction with the play's ending. While the deferral of a debate resolution is a common device in dialogues, the deferral of marriage problematizes more than the genre of comedy in the play. It reflects the fraught state of matrimony over which the early modern church was concerned; therefore, Shakespeare's choice to include women in this debate in *Love's Labour's Lost* seems particularly relevant. Instead of putting the arguments about women and marriage in the mouths of male characters only, to reflect the traditional arguments about it by clergy and other male authorities, Shakespeare gives his female characters scope for voicing their judgments about what marriage should be. The deferred ending, however, suggests that there are no easy answers.

The sacrament of marriage was, from the highest levels of society, perceived to be in peril. In England, Elizabeth eschewed marriage, and conduct book writers were taking great pains to solidify the model of the patriarchal family, as Henry Smith's *A Preparative to Mariage* (1591) and John Dod and Robert Cleaver's *A Godlie Forme of Householde Government* (1598) illustrate. In France, Henri III surrounded himself with his mignons, seeming to prefer them

---

33 Lavaud argues that the Retz salon was especially influential in supporting a revival of Petrarchism (81).

34 Ronsard, in his "Sonnet à Madame de Villeroy," praises her as a poet, as does Philippe Desportes, who compares Villeroy to Myrtis, Corinna, and Sappho (Sorg, 28).

35 Englishwomen such as Mary Sidney Herbert, the Countess of Pembroke; Penelope Devereux, Lady Rich, and, of course, Queen Elizabeth, were known for their influential tastes in literature and for their patronage.

to his wife, and Henri IV's political marriage to Marguerite de Valois was a well-publicized sham that was eventually dissolved. Moreover, the behaviors of the women of the French court and Italian actresses reflected the problem. The dramatic palimpsest, at this point, is richly complex.

Italian actresses were accused of problematizing marriage with their portrayals of lustful and deceptive women in plays that illustrated, not the sanctity of marriage, but its worldly aspects. Kerr translates part of Antonio Seneca's sermon *Sulla soppressione degli spettacoli comici* (1597) in which he argues that plays make a mockery of the marriage sacrament because

> Characters playing the lovers come on stage, speak of lecherous things, and frequently mention unnamable parts of the body, and most shameful to say, prescribe love potions, which can remake virgins and remove impediment against changing women back into brides. (46)

The actresses' lifestyles were also perceived as threatening. Kerr notes that both "the nonconforming and obscene charges (against players) were heavily reinforced by another revolutionary change – the presence of women – whose addition to the companies created subversive households which travestied the traditional Christian family organization" (39). Women of the French court were accused of sexual machinations on behalf of the state and the church as Catholics and Huguenots vied for the throne. Richmond suggests that the espionage of the *escadron volant* "was more valuable to the Queen Mother than the victories of her army" (201). The array of references bound up in Shakespeare's female characters, then, would be intensely thought-provoking for his English audience, and the subject matter of the debate would be of the greatest interest to them on both the political and personal fronts.

Shakespeare presents his audience with controversial figures engaged in debate over the chief philosophical and religious issues of their times. Then he adds his final stroke of genius, the open ending that draws the audience into the debate, just as audiences for salon debates or court masques would be invited to participate at the end of a formal debate or a choreographed dance. Ultimately, he leaves the questions in the hands of his audience. The sober pronouncements by the female characters about what is required for true love leaves room for hope that the male characters will become the lovers that they should be, but Shakespeare's use of figures associated with nobles and royals of the French court, as well as Italian actors, who all reflect moral upheaval, resonates with the dismal aural images of cuckoldry sounded by the "Cuckoo, cuckoo – O word of fear" refrain voiced by Spring and the "coughing" that "drowns the parson's saw" lamented by Winter (5.2.876, 896) at the play's end. When the Continental female figures in *Love's Labour's Lost* are contextualized along with their male counterparts referenced in the play, we may see how Shakespeare synthesizes historical figures, players, characters, and conflicts into a richly suggestive debate format, one that invites his audience to join in the intellectual fray while entertaining them with its Continental sophistication.

Works Cited

Andreini, Isabella. *Fragmenti de alcune scritture*. Ed. Francesco Andreini. Venetia: Combi, 1627.

Andrews, Richard. *Scripts and Scenarios: The Performance of Comedy in Renaissance Italy*. Cambridge: Cambridge University Press, 1993.

Angelini, Franca. "La pazzia di Isabella." *Letteratura italiana*. Ed. Alberto Asor Rosa. Turin: Teatri moderni, 1986, 112–13.

Baldini, Donatella. "The Play of the Courtier: Correspondences between Castiglione's *Il libro del Cortegiano* and Shakespeare's *Love's Labour's Lost*." *Quaderni d'italianistica* 18.1 (1997): 5–22.

Barasch, Frances. "Italian Actresses in Shakespeare's World: Flaminia and Vincenza." *Shakespeare Bulletin* 18.4 (2000): 17–21.

———. "Italian Actresses in Shakespeare's World: Vittoria and Isabella." *Shakespeare Bulletin* 19.3 (2001): 5–9.

Beaujoyeulx, Baltasar de. *Balet Comique de la Royne*. Paris: Adrian le Roy, Robert Ballard, and Mamert Patisson, 1582.

Boucher, Jacqueline. *Société et mentalités autour de Henri III*. 4 vols. Paris: Champion, 1981.

Brown, Pamela. "The Counterfeit *Innamorata* or The Diva Vanishes." *Shakespeare Yearbook* 10 (1999): 402–26.

Buisseret, David. *Henry IV*. London: Allen and Unwin, 1984.

Clubb, Louise George. *Italian Drama in Shakespeare's Time*. New Haven: Yale University Press, 1989.

Cohen, Walter. Introduction. *Love's Labour's Lost. The Norton Shakespeare*. Ed. Stephen Greenblatt, *et al*. New York: Norton, 1997, 733–8.

D'Aubigné, Théodore Agrippa. "À mes filles touchant les femmes doctes de nostre siècle." *Œuvres*. Ed. Henri Weber *et al*. Bruges: Gallimard, 1969, 852–3.

———. *Confession Catholique du Sieur de Sancy*. *Œuvres*. Ed. Henri Weber *et al*. Bruges: Gallimard, 1969, 576–666.

David, Richard. "Introduction." *Love's Labour's Lost*. The Arden Edition of the Works of William Shakespeare. Cambridge: Harvard University Press, 1960, xxxii–xxxvii.

Dod, John and Robert Cleaver. *A Godlie Forme of Householde Government*. London, 1598.

L'Estoile, Pierre de. *Mémoires-Journaux. The Paris of Henry of Navarre as Seen by Pierre de L'Estoile*. Ed. and trans. Nancy Lyman Roelker. Cambridge: Harvard University Press, 1958.

Fremy, Edouard. *Origines de l'Académie française: L'Académie des derniers Valois: Académie de poésie et de musique 1570–1576, Académie du palais 1576–1585*. Paris: Ernest Leroux, 1887.

Hibbard, G. R. "Introduction." *Love's Labour's Lost*. Oxford: Clarendon, 1990, 1–83.

Hunt, Maurice. "The Double Figure of Elizabeth in *Love's Labor's Lost.*" *Essays in Literature* 19.2 (1992): 173–92.

Keating, L. Clark. *Studies on the Literary Salon in France, 1550–1615.* Cambridge: Harvard University Press, 1941.

Kerr, Rosalind. "The Actress as Androgyne in the *Commedia dell'Arte* Scenarios of Flaminio Scala." PhD diss., University of Toronto, 1993.

Lapp, John C. "Introduction." *The Universe of Pontus de Tyard.* Ithaca: Cornell University Press, 1950, xi–lx.

Lavaud, Jacques. *Un poète de cour au temps des derniers Valois: Philippe Desportes (1564–1606).* Paris: Droz, 1936.

Londré, Felicia Hardison. "Introduction." *Love's Labour's Lost: Critical Essays.* New York: Routledge, 1997, 3–37.

―――. "Elizabethan Views of the 'Other': French, Spanish, and Russians in *Love's Labour's Lost.*" *Love's Labour's Lost: Critical Essays.* New York: Routledge, 1997, 325–41.

Lyly, John. *Euphue's Glass for Europe. Euphues and His England.* The Complete Works of John Lyly. Ed. R. Warnick Bond. 3 vols. Oxford: Clarendon Press, 1967, 2: 1–228.

MacNeil, Anne. *Music and Women of the Commedia dell'Arte in the Late Sixteenth Century.* Oxford: Oxford University Press, 2003.

Nashe, Thomas. *Pierce Penilesse, His Supplication to the Divell.* [1592]. Ed. G. B. Harrison. Elizabethan and Jacobean Quartos. New York: Barnes and Noble, 1966.

Nouvelle biographie générale. Vol. 10. Paris: Firmin Didot Frères, 1855; rpt. Copenhagen: Rosenkilde et Bagger, 1964.

Orgel, Stephen. *Impersonations: The Performance of Gender in Shakespeare's England.* Cambridge: Cambridge University Press, 1997.

Osborn, James M. *Young Philip Sidney, 1572–1577.* The Elizabethan Club Series 5. New Haven: Yale University Press, 1972.

Pandolfi, Vito. *La commedia dell'arte: storia e testo.* Vol. 2. Firenze: Casa Editrice le Lettere, 1988.

Pasquier, Estienne. "A Monsieur Airault." *Œuvres complètes.* Vol. 2. Amsterdam, 1723; rpt. Genève: Slatkine Reprints, 1971, 897–900.

―――. *Pastorale du vieillard amoureux. Œuvres complètes.* Vol. 2. Amsterdam, 1723; rpt. Genève: Slatkine Reprints, 1971, 903–8.

Plato. *Symposium. Great Dialogues of Plato.* Trans. W. H. D. Rouse. New York: New American Library, 1956, 69–177.

Pommerol, Marie Henriette Jullien de. *Albert de Gondi, Maréchal de Retz.* Travaux d'humanisme et Renaissance 5. Geneva: Droz, 1953.

Richards, Kenneth and Laura Richards. *The Commedia dell'Arte: A Documentary History.* Oxford: Basil Blackwell, 1990.

Richmond, Hugh M. "Shakespeare's Navarre." *The Huntington Library Quarterly* 42.3 (1979): 193–216.

Roberts, Josephine. Ed. Introduction. *The First Part of the Countess of Montgomery's Urania.* By Lady Mary Wroth. *Medieval and Renaissance Texts and Studies.* Vol 140. Binghamton. New York: Medieval and Renaissance Texts and Studies, 1995, xv–ciii.

Roelker, Nancy Lyman. "Introduction." *The Paris of Henry of Navarre as Seen by Pierre de L'Estoile.* Cambridge: Harvard University Press, 1958, 3–27.

Ronsard, Pierre de. "Sonnet a Madame de Villeroy." *Œuvres complètes*. vol. 2. Ed. Gustave Cohen. Bourges: Gallimard, 1950.

Russell, Rinaldina. *The Feminist Encyclopedia of Italian Literature*. Westport: Greenwood, 1997.

Sanders, Eve Rachele. *Gender and Literacy on Stage in Early Modern England*. Cambridge Studies in Renaissance Literature and Culture 28. Cambridge: Cambridge University Press, 1998.

Shakespeare, William. *Love's Labour's Lost. The Norton Shakespeare*. Ed. Stephen Greenblatt, *et al*. New York: Norton, 1997, 741–802.

Shapiro, Michael. "The Introduction of Actresses in England: Delay or Defensiveness?" *Enacting Gender on the English Renaissance Stage*. Ed. Viviana Comensoli and Anne Russell. Urbana: University of Illinois Press, 1999, 177–200.

Smith, Henry, *A Preparative to Mariage*. London, 1591.

Sorg, Roger. *Les chansons de Callianthe: fille de Ronsard*. Paris: Léon Pinchon, 1926.

St-John, Christie Ellen. "The *Salon Vert* of the Maréchale de Retz: A Study of a Literary Salon in Sixteenth-Century France," PhD diss., Vanderbilt University, 1999.

Strage, Mark. *Women of Power: The Life and Times of Catherine de' Medici*. New York: Harcourt, Brace, Jovanovich, 1976.

Taviani, Ferdinando and Mirella Schino. *Il segreto della Commedia dell'Arte*. Firenze: La Casa Usher, 1982.

Woudhuysen, H. R. Introduction. *Love's Labour's Lost*. The Arden Shakespeare. Walton-on-Thames, Surrey: Nelson and Sons, 1998, 1–106.

Yates, Frances. *A Study of Love's Labour's Lost*. Cambridge: Cambridge University Press, 1936.

———. *The French Academies of the Sixteenth Century*. Studies of the Warburg Institute 15. London: University of London, 1947; rpt. Nedeln, Liechtenstein: Kraus Reprint, 1968.

Chapter 8

Women Performing Homoerotic Desire in English and Italian Comedy: *La Calandria, Gl'Ingannati* and *Twelfth Night*

Rachel Poulsen

In *Twelfth Night* Shakespeare reveals a debt to two mainstays of the Italian Renaissance theater: the highly influential and durable comic formula of the cross-dressed heroine who sparks another woman's erotic desire; and the Italian actress herself, an iconic figure of desirable beauty, verbal agility, and rhetorical skill. Viewed from this perspective, *Twelfth Night* is a comedy about claiming power through appropriation and improvisation – not only in the world of the play, but in the metatheatrical sense of the English dramatic enterprise itself. As this essay will show, English playwrights muted but did not erase the overt lesbian eroticism that so deeply marks their Italian models, while creating scenes that summoned up the foreign actress and drew on her celebrated skills.

In *Twelfth Night*, acting and seduction proceed in tandem. In the first encounter of Viola and Olivia, they instantly draw attention to their status as players, and to their craft. Both wear costumes that signal histrionic display: Viola in her sexy page's suit, Olivia in her showy black veil. As Cesario, Viola implores Olivia to let her recite Orsino's love-message: "I have taken great pains to con it" (1.5.153–5). When Olivia asks about her origins, she demurs – "I can say little more than I have studied, and that question's out of my part" (158–9). Her recourse to a script prompts Olivia's tart demand: "Are you a comedian?" (161). But Olivia profoundly distrusts the "poetical" speeches of actors – they are "more the like to be feigned" – and requests that her visitor speak extemporaneously (172–3). Going out of her text, Viola/Cesario asks to see Olivia's face, a daring challenge that leads to a dramatic unveiling and open flirtation. A tour de force of "improvised" yet highly literary wit follows, an exchange of banter skewering Petrarchan conventions and classical love narratives, culminating in Olivia's stagy ring trick. Viola's nimble acting works all too well, for Olivia falls madly in love with her Cesario. Viola proves to be so brilliant that she shocks herself: "I am the man." (2.2.23).

Since its beginnings in plays like *La Calandria* (1513) and *Gl'Ingannati* (1531), Renaissance comedy employed similar situations of female homoeroticism, and in ways that transcended mere plot devices. In the useful term invented by Louise George Clubb, the topos can be seen as a "theatergram," or structural unit that occurs in many kinds of plays, in many places. The theatergram is perhaps the best way to appreciate Renaissance drama as an art form dependent on re-using and exploring the permutations of its own content. Clubb defines theatergrams as "interchangeable structural units," such as "characters, situations, actions, speeches, thematic patterns," that are then "combined in dialogue and visual encounters to act out the fiction with verisimilitude" (2002, 35). The plots and theatergrams of seminal Italian comedies, such as *Gl'Ingannati*, were most widely circulated through Europe in the plays of the commedia dell'arte. As with many other theatergrams, that of "mistaken" female homoerotic desire was performed by commedia performers in professional touring companies whose stock-in-trade was recombination and improvisation. These professional troupes, some led by women actors, were crucial to the transmission of continental dramatic developments to England. There the fame (and notoriety) of Italian actresses proved irresistible to English playwrights, many of whose works exhibit a kind of "actress effect" that, rather than inhering in a single character, explored the limits of female behavior and charisma in terms both admiring and critical. The "actress effect" in *Twelfth Night* is split between the deft wit of Olivia and Viola, and the homoerotic energy they mobilize reflects Shakespeare's regard for his textual and cultural sources. Viewed through this genealogy, *Twelfth Night* explores ideas about class and power through an idiom of female performance.

Shakespeare's source material for *Twelfth Night* can ultimately be traced to two of the most influential and widely adapted plays of the Renaissance. Both sixteenth-century examples of Italian learned comedy, Cardinal Dovizi da Bibbiena's *La Calandria* and the Sienese Accademia degli Intronati's *Gl'Ingannati* are the basis of countless commedia scenarios and analogues in early modern English drama. Originally performed by all-male amateur companies, the plays made their way into England via printed copies, translations, prose variations, and performances by professional actors. As they rapidly fanned across Europe, the plays popularized the cross-dressed heroine who repeatedly comes into erotic contact with other women on stage. The stylization and repetition of staging female homoerotic desire point toward its entertainment value to audiences, as well as its larger cultural significance. What rapidly becomes clear is that female homoeroticism is not an aberration in the dominant heterosexual teleology of early modern English comedy, but is rather constitutive of the genre.

Commedia erudita is a vital part of English dramatic history, stylistically, formally, and topically. However, a crucial aspect of textual study and reception history has been undervalued in Shakespeare criticism: the impact of Italian commedia troupes, and especially their women players, on the transmission of *erudita* plots to England. The professional companies presented scripted plays along with improvisational works and propagated the use of cross-dressing plots in early modern comedy.[1] What does it mean that actresses functioned as cultural go-betweens, connecting all-male transvestite theaters in two different countries? And what can the Italian actress tell us about intertextual relationships between *La Calandria, Gl'Ingannati*, and Shakespearean comedy?

"Learned comedy" built on the comic models of Terence and Plautus in occasional productions throughout Italy. Its features, repeated and stylized by commedia companies arising in the mid-1540s, spread all over Europe, including the English court.[2] David Orr postulates, "by virtue of these troupes' playing *erudita* drama in England to unrestricted audiences, they acted definitively as intermediaries in transmitting the learned drama of Italy to the English stage" (13).[3] Transmission of *commedia erudita* through performance, with its emphasis on female lead characters, shaped the knowledge and experience of playgoers and playwrights alike.[4] In a very short span of time, actresses became crucial to the diffusion of humanistic Renaissance stage practice from Italy to England.

---

1   Although the commedia dell'arte companies are best known for their improvisational virtuosity, Robert Henke notes that their work encompassed "practically all the scripted forms of the *commedia erudita*," and also incorporated other classical and Renaissance literature (12). Performances of scripted plays were popular, "especially after the advent of the actress around the mid-1560s" (6). In addition, the actors themselves published original speeches and plays – several of them female-authored, such as Isabella Andreini's pastoral *Mirtilla* (1588).

2   Kathleen Lea cites the Revels Accounts of 1573–4 as evidence of the early presence of the *comici* in England (353). Smith notes that the Drousiano troupe received a license to play publicly in London in 1577–8, and that Elizabeth witnessed an Italian masque in 1579 (556). Clubb records "seven visits to England by Italian players between 1546 and 1578" (1989, 50).

3   Some scholars disagree: Kenneth Richards for example, pronounces, "Quite clearly the 'Commedia dell'arte' was known in Elizabethan England, but it is difficult on the evidence available to see its influence on early English theatre as very significant" (242).

4   Andrews stresses the dependence of commedia dell'arte on *commedia erudita*: "All the 'comic' scenarios which have come down to us ... base their plot schemes and characters on conventions established by the *commedia erudita* between 1508 and the 1550s" (171).

In addition, the most popular plays were printed, circulated, and sometimes translated.[5] These several routes reveal that female homoeroticism, modified and continually reinterpreted from Italian sources, is present in all stages of cultural transmission. It may be impossible, then, to overstate the importance of the Italian example for English drama. According to Louise George Clubb and Robert Black, "Shakespeare's narrative material was disposed, cut and augmented according to the theatrical structures of Italian comedy, which was being disseminated as a repertory of combinable parts in printed texts and commedia dell'arte performances" (172). Early *commedie erudite* practiced many of the same formal and stylistic conventions as their classical sources, including stereotypical characters such as separated twins, witty servants, insufferable pedants, misguided fathers, thwarted yet determined lovers, and foolishly amorous old men. The plots, as well as the setting – always an exterior urban scene – came from ancient Roman precedents. However, the enterprise diverged with classical tradition in some key points. In *La Calandria* Bibbiena takes the long-lost twin plot of Plautus's *Menaechmi* and makes one of the siblings female.[6] The Intronati add a romantic underpinning to their heroine's struggles.

It is hardly coincidental that the most robust commedia plots are also the ones most suited to adaptation by female performers. Kathleen Lea remarks, "According to the conventions of the Commedia erudita young women appear very seldom: their affairs and affections are described by the Nurses or their maids; it is not uncommon for the girl about whom the plot revolves to have no speaking part at all. Professional actresses soon changed this convention" (175–6).[7] Clearly, the most propitious way to showcase the traveling companies' female stars was to play material featuring roles for them. The cross-dressed heroine, when played by a male actor, presents the image of a

---

5   These modes of transmission are relevant for the development of all Renaissance romantic comedy, although the majority of source studies have focused on Shakespeare. Clubb singles out printed editions as the most reliable form of evidence for influence, but not necessarily the greatest in impact (1977, 111 n.6). There are no extant records of any *commedie erudite* having been performed by English actors, which emphasizes the importance of the Italian companies' role in spreading the form. The closest English example is Gascoigne's *Supposes* (1556), first played at Gray's Inn – a closely adapted version of Ariosto's *I Suppositi*.

6   Bibbiena's innovation of a female central character also departs from the classical Roman depiction of male cross-dressing. In Plautus's *Casina*, for example, a male slave dresses as the eponymous maiden to dupe "her" husband and his master, who both attempt to sleep with her on the wedding night. Casina herself, however, is never represented onstage at all.

7   Clubb concurs, arguing further that professional actresses influenced not only performance conventions, but playwrights themselves: "The result was that the

quick-witted, capable woman adept at maintaining the illusion of another identity. The rise of female performers on the popular stage in the 1560s amplified the role's transgressive potential and its erotic volatility, because the actress herself, and more specifically, the persona of the *innamorata*, or lover, was controversial and hyper-visible.[8]

Although the commedia contained several supporting female parts, including the servant (*servetta*), the courtesan (*cortigiana*), and the bawd, the most prominent and virtuosic character was the *innamorata*. She embodied the full range of emotion, from joy to madness; her attributes, such as self-conscious literariness, eloquent speech, and aristocratic bearing, were those of the actresses themselves. The doubling of characteristics between the performer and her role was stressed even further in the many comedies that starred two *innamorate*, one or both of whom claimed the added erotic agency and mobility granted by male disguise. "In the professional theater," Peter Parolin remarks, "the actress disrupts a previously all-male domain; in society, the actress is the theatrical woman who lays claim to the power of autonomous self-fashioning that male figures sought to reserve for themselves" (108). The extratextual social meaning of the actress necessarily compounds the dramatic effect of the independent cross-dressed heroine, as well as her experience of same-sex intimacy. It is reasonable to suppose, then, that simply by virtue of their bodily presence, Italian actresses would have magnified the social transgression within the two most influential Italian Renaissance plays.

The first, *La Calandria*, was originally performed by an all-male amateur troupe in 1513 in Urbino, and played in Rome the following year to honor the wedding of Isabella d'Este. A performance in Lyons in 1548 for Catherine de Medici is the first recorded instance of female players in *commedia erudita* (Andrews, 154). Between its first publication in 1521 and 1600, the play went through twenty-six editions, its circulation making an impact on the theater traditions of all nations it touched.[9] In the play, the heroine Santilla has lived for twelve years as "Lidio," working for a Roman merchant who wants her to marry his daughter. However, unbeknownst to her, Santilla's long-lost brother, the real Lidio, is alive and has also settled in Rome. His lover Fulvia is married, and Lidio trysts with her by taking his missing sister's name and wearing

---

ingénue of Counter-Reformation written comedy also became a more articulate, heroic, generally noteworthy figure than her prototype in early *commedia erudita*" (1968, xxii).

8   Andrews declares that "the *arte* genre, once we find it established and documented, always uses female as well as male performers," and that "the first woman to appear in any surviving document as a full partner in a professional company of actors" dates from Siena in 1564 (154).

9   On the play's performance history see Andrews, 48–63; Herrick, 71–5; Melzi; Ruffini; and Radcliff-Umstead, 143–55.

women's clothes. His presence emphasizes Santilla's indeterminate gender identity and erotic potential, for unlike many later cross-dressing plays, *La Calandria* does not overlay the heroine's erotic ambiguity with heterosexual romance.

The device of identical twins who eventually discover one another was to become a familiar, even hackneyed comic practice; the one of the resourceful cross-dressed heroine, even more so. But at the time Bibbiena was writing, the two Lidios (male and female) were innovative and required explanation. Because Lidio and Santilla are distinguishable only by their clothing, Lidio's servant Fessenio explains that "God himself could not have made them more alike" [gli dèi non gli ariano potuti fare piú simili] (1.1): the only way they seem to differ is genitally.[10] Raising the issue of twins' difference only to thwart it with their apparent indistinguishability, Fessenio invokes gender as a transitive, alterable idea governed by a principle of supplementarity. *La Calandria* underscores the uncertainty of appearances by including hermaph- roditism and sex-changing in the play's fascination with mistaken identity.

Other characters repeatedly mistake the twins for one another. When Santilla ventures out in the city, Fulvia's maid approaches with a sexual proposition from her mistress, but Santilla (logically) acts as though they have never met. Fulvia, fearing rejection, sends the charlatan magician Ruffo to seduce "Lidio" with magic, a scheme to which Santilla acquiesces, because she is trying to evade her master. This places Santilla in a distinctly unusual position for a comic heroine: in order to avoid marriage to one woman, she agrees to a romantic assignation with another. Plus, as her servant Fannio remarks, "You are sure to gain some pleasure from it" [Se ne trarrà piacere] (3.17). The undefined "pleasure" of the encounter, sexual or financial, seems a forgone conclusion.

Fannio lies to Ruffo that "Lidio" is a hermaphrodite, which will explain the reality of Santilla's body once she is in a sexual situation with Fulvia. Since Fulvia has specified that Lidio must be conjured "in the form of a woman," [in forma di donna (2.3), Fannio assures him he "will use only the woman's organ with Fulvia" [userà con Fulvia solo il sesso feminile] (3.17). What exactly the "female organ" was, and how it could be used to please another woman, was a question debated by contemporary ecclesiastical and legal authorities alike. As Katharine Park argues, the "rediscovery" of the clitoris by anatomists in the mid-sixteenth century led to heightened anxiety about female sexual pleasure, since according to the Galenic model, women possessed genitalia complemen- tary to men's. The clitoris, considered a supplementary penis, "meant that all women were in some sense hermaphrodites." Moreover, "it suggested that

---

10   All English quotes are from Oliver Evans's translation "The Follies of Calandro." Passages from the original are from Bonino.

many more women than previously thought – indeed perhaps every woman – could potentially penetrate and give pleasure to another woman" (Park, 178). Since *La Calandria* appeared over forty years before the rediscovery of the clitoris, we are left to wonder what the pleasure-giving "female organ" is that Ruffo takes for granted.

Clearly, in a play so concerned with anatomy and exploring the idea of female potency, the body of the actor will be the object of scrutiny. Women playing female roles would lend them a greater degree of verisimilitude and, due to the mystique and controversy surrounding actresses, excitement. Both disguising and accentuating female characteristics, male dress could lend the performers a fresh range of behaviors to exploit, all new to an audience. Perhaps the level of decorum expected of women would elevate the bawdy scenes to new heights; certainly the scenes of homoeroticism between them, like Santilla's dilemmas, were theatrically unprecedented.

Santilla remains an erotic cipher throughout the play. She does observe that it is better to be a man (2.1), because it confers safety and status that she never could have attained as a woman. Santilla never denies that she wants to marry the maiden Virginia; nor does she bemoan an essential femininity chafing under male clothes, or having to act strong when she feels weak, as Shakespeare's cross-dressed women often do.[11] Rather, she focuses on the material and social constraints both genders place on her as conditions of survival. Santilla exclaims:

> I am a woman, yet I must also be bridegroom! If I marry Virginia, they will find out I am a woman and not a man: they will turn me out and might even have me put to death … If I reveal myself now to be a woman, I would only bring harm upon myself. [Femina sono, e conviemmi esser marito! Si io sposo costei, subito cognoscerà che io femina e non maschio sono; e, da me scornati, el padre e la madre e la figlia porriano farmi uccidere … Se paleso esser femina, io medisma a me stessa fo il danno.] (2.8)[12]

---

11 *The Merchant of Venice* (2.6.34–9) and *As You Like It* (2.4.3–6).

12 Judith C. Brown notes that while female-female sex acts were proscribed in Christian penitentials as early as the seventh century, the 1532 statute enacted by the Holy Roman Empire advocated the death penalty: "if anyone commits impurity with a beast, or a man with a man, or a woman with a woman, they have forfeited their lives and shall, after the common custom, be sentenced to death by burning" (7, 13). Louis Crompton likewise points out that "in countries such as France, Spain, Italy, Germany, and Switzerland, lesbian acts were regarded as legally equivalent to acts of male sodomy and were, like them, punishable by the death penalty" (11). Simons (85–6) notes that three Italian jurists wrote capital punishment for female sodomy into the most influential penitential codes of the Renaissance.

Santilla cannot comfortably be a woman or a man; both are dangerous. She is most concerned, however, with the family's reaction to her deceit. If a cross-dressed woman was not prosecuted for sexual misconduct, the attempt to pass permanently as male, especially if she married a woman, made her eligible to be prosecuted for fraud. Women were rarely subjected to capital punishment for homoerotic behavior *unless* other transgressions elevated it to the category of sodomy (Brown, *Immodest*, 134). Punishment was different for appearance and behavior. "But judgments in Medieval and Renaissance Europe," Patricia Simons explains, "did not carefully distinguish between 'lesbianism' and 'gender-crossing,' for either activity usurped social roles and physical signs (including costume and phallus) granted only to the privilege of masculinity" (87). Thus, the sexual threats and confusion Santilla faces in her impending marriage to Virginia are profoundly social, rather than personal.

The potential for same-sex acts is never far from the action of *La Calandria*. Santilla's unfixed erotic desires, like her initial willingness to go to Fulvia's bed, verge between comedy and blasphemy. When Fulvia dons a male disguise in 3.5, it is a provisional maneuver, worn with the sole purpose of going out to pursue Lidio – an expression of unambiguous heteroerotic desire. However, Fulvia's temporary claim of masculine privilege merely accentuates Santilla's manly status, which, in its permanence, is closer to a gender "identity."

The play's conclusion does little to alter Santilla's polymorphously erotic capacity: it keeps both siblings in their cross-dressed roles and refuses to reverse the play's gender switch. Santilla saves her brother's life by changing back into a dress and sneaking into Fulvia's house, smuggling out Lidio and thereby absolving him of adultery charges. Grateful, Fulvia offers her son Flaminio as a reward. Santilla says, "Now I understand why, when we were in the room together, she kissed me tenderly and said: I don't know which of us three is happiest; Lidio has found a sister, I a daughter, and you a husband" [Or mi fai chiara perché ella, là in camera, teneramente baciandomi, disse cosí a me: – Chi di noi piú contento sia non so. Lidio ha trovata la sorella; io la figliuola; e tu il marito –] (5.12). With this gesture, Fulvia transmutes their bond from that of potential sexual partners to mother and daughter. Her earlier passionate caresses – when she vainly groped under Santilla's skirts looking for "the dagger for my sheath" [il coltel della guaina mia] (4.2), but found only the "woman's organ" – give way to a chaste kiss. This tactic develops into a pattern in later comedies: women joining as relatives, with a man as an intermediary, allay homoerotic tension between female characters. Santilla gains a brother, a mother, and a husband by accepting Fulvia's generosity, and instantly changes from an orphaned child to a woman thoroughly enmeshed in a social network. In *Twelfth Night*, Olivia welcomes Cesario's female persona in a similar manner: rather than renouncing her earlier professed love or attempting to account for her "mistaken" attraction (as both Orsino and Sebastian do), she simply says, "A sister, you are she"

(5.1.315). Such arrangements can function not as a repudiation of homoerotic feeling, but as means to legitimate and institutionalize it.

If *La Calandria* was the first Renaissance play to turn a classical plot into a vehicle for a female lead character, *Gl'Ingannati* was the first to give that heroine her own romantic desires (Salingar, 188). Staged female homoerotic desire was crucial to this pattern. Clubb and Black point out that the "theatergram of the heroine cross-dressed for love unintentionally arousing love in a lady is common ... to a score of other *commedie erudite,*" and *Gl'Ingannati*, as perhaps the most influential play in Italian Renaissance drama, was the most famous example (173).[13] Following its initial printing in 1537, it went through fifteen editions before the end of the century. Its 1543 French version by Charles Estienne (*Les Abusez*) was the first translation of an Italian play into another language. *Gl'Ingannati* was the Intronati's first full play, and exhibited what would become thematic hallmarks. According to Clubb and Black, "All the plays of the Intronati ... manifest the family characteristics – the romantic demonstrations of constancy, pathos, true love, vindicated feminine honor, and the representation of brave, devoted, strong-minded resourceful women, taking on disguises and undertaking journeys" (169). The plot details of *Gl'Ingannati*, however, were adapted and reproduced in different genres and languages over the course of the century. These analogues include a tale in Bandello's prose *Novelle* (1537/54); Estienne's French translation; Lope de Rueda's Spanish variation, *Los Engañados* (1539–58); Niccolo Secchi's plays, *L'Interesse* (1549) and *Gl'Inganni* (1547); Pierre de Belleforest's story in

---

13   Later plays apply the theatergram of female same-sex attraction in every imaginable form. *L'Anconitana* (1534) by Angelo Beolco (known as Ruzante) concerns a married woman named Ginevra, who falls in love with the young man Gismondo. She disguises herself as a man to pursue him, only to discover he is her missing sister Isotta in disguise. When the secret is revealed, Isotta exclaims, "I am not surprised that, stirred by a secret force, you felt so great and sudden a love for me, for it is your own flesh and blood that you love" (4.2). In Piccolomini's *L'Alessandro* (1543/44) Lucrezia is disguised as the young man Fortunio. She falls in love with Lampridia, and attempts to reconcile herself to the attraction: "it would give me great pleasure to be with her and to kiss the face and breast of such a lovely woman. After all, I'm not the first woman who has loved another woman. She'll forgive me and, if I ask her, she'll keep it a secret for my sake." Lampridia turns out to be Aloisio, her childhood love since they were both disguised for their own safety at the age of seven. Although shared history "rights" the homoeroticism of the couples at the end, both plays depend on the female-female attraction for pathos and emotional gravity as well as for laughter. The Italian text of *L'Anconitana* / *The Woman From Ancona* is reprinted from Ruzante, *Teatro*. *Alessandro* / *L'Alessandro is* translated from the 1966 edition, prepared by F. Cerreta.

Part IV of *Histoires Tragiques* (1570); "Appolonius and Silla" in *Barnabe Riche His Farewell to the Military Profession* (1581); Curzio Gonzaga's play *Gl'Inganni* (1592); *Laelia*, the title of two Latin verse translations of *Les Abusez* performed at Queens College, Cambridge in 1547 and 1595; and, of course, *Twelfth Night*.[14]

Gl'Ingannati shares with *Twelfth Night* the main plot of a marriageable young woman falling in love with the cross-dressed woman sent to woo her, and both plays resolve the conflict with the miraculous reappearance of a male twin. In the Italian version, Gherardo, a citizen, wants to marry Virginio's young daughter Lelia. He sends Lelia to a convent, where she can be safe while he is away on business. The nuns teach her how to dress and act like a man, so she can leave the convent and move about the city.[15] Dressed as the servant Fabio, Lelia offers herself in service to her beloved, Flamminio, who employs her to woo Gherardo's daughter Isabella, causing Lelia great distress.

As a woman, Lelia has limited social prospects. She intimates that she was raped while a prisoner during the Sack of Rome (when she also lost her brother Fabrizio); because of it, she says, "I thought that I could never live respectably enough for people not to gossip" [né credevo poter vivere sí onestamente che bastasse a far che la gente non avesse che dire] (2.3.).[16] Her sexual reputation makes it difficult to resume her own identity, so the disguise gives her a respite from her troubles. Also, she points out, she may be invisible to Flamminio, but she can "see her lord all the time, to talk to him, to touch him, to hear his secrets" [veder di continuo il suo signore, parlargli, toccarlo, intendere i suoi segreti] (1.3.). As Fabio, she becomes his most trusted companion.

Soon, though, she must also contend with Isabella's affections. Lelia confesses, "She thinks I'm a boy, and she's fallen madly in love with me, and she showers me with affection" [Ella, credendo ch'io sia maschio, si è sí pazzamente innamorata di me che mi fa le maggior carezze del mondo] (1.3.). Lelia attempts to prolong the infatuation to draw Isabella's affections away from Flamminio, knowing even as she does that Isabella will desire progressively more serious romantic gestures in return. In a climactic threshold scene observed by the servants Scatizza and Crivello, Isabella draws Lelia/Fabio inside and kisses her in an unrestrained expression of erotic yearning.

---

14   Melzi, 70; Andrews, 93; Salingar, 188–9.
15   As Elissa B. Weaver has argued, theatrical productions in Italian convents were important vehicles for both entertainment and learning from about 1450 on. Their value as educational tools was questioned by critics who deplored the use of immodest male costumes, especially since most plays were performed by novices (184–5, 61). Thus, the Accademia's reference to nuns skilled at cross-dressing may be a satirical poke at the convent theater tradition.
16   All English quotes are from Newbigin's translation as "The Deceived" in Cairns, ed. Passages from the original are from Borsellino.

Isabella recognizes that her actions may be inappropriate, but defends her forwardness: "You are so beautiful and I love you so much. That's why I am doing something which you may judge unworthy of a young lady. But heaven knows, I couldn't help myself" [La vostra troppa bellezza e 'l troppo amor ch'io vi porto è cagion ch'io fo quello che forse voi giudicarete esser di poco onesta fanciulla. Ma Dio lo sa ch'io non me ne son potuta tenere] (2.6.). Isabella kisses her again before retreating further into the house, leaving a flustered Lelia just outside.

The erotic valences of this scene offer a number of possible viewing positions and pleasures. Isabella believes she is seducing a male servant, which is inappropriate for her gender and class position. The audience knows the "truth," that both the characters are really female. But while this same-sex kiss is dismissible as "innocent" by the viewer seeking to assuage sexual anxieties about propriety, the excited voyeurism of the servants gives rise to others by amplifying the scene's transgressive intensity. Their running commentary on the encounter ("This is just a bit too cosy"; "Where the devil has she put his hand?" ["Questa dimestichezza è troppa"; "Dove diavol gli tien la man, colei?"]) gives it a sense of escalating sexual power and intensity that culminates with Scatizza exclaiming, "For the love of God, I've got a hard on fit to burst" [Al corpo di Dio, che m'è infiata una gamba che par la voglia recere] (2.6.).[17] when Isabella abruptly returns inside. Scatizza's outburst mediates the audience's experience of imagining what Isabella and Lelia/Fabio are doing offstage, and implicates them in finding it arousing.

Scenes that depend on gender indeterminacy in sexual conduct for laughs are fairly common in both Italian and English comedy. Often, two women are engaged in what one thinks is heterosexual passion. Nevertheless, many critics have suggested that such scenes of female-female eroticism are undermined or ultimately effaced by several factors: the material reality of an all-male acting company; the surface appearance of male-female sex that the play will eventually reify and celebrate in the marriage conclusion; the rhetoric of contempt developing around same-sex attraction; or the manipulation of "lesbian" overtones for the delectation of male viewers.[18] It is important to remember, however, that the Intronati produced and dedicated plays to their primarily *female* audience, bourgeois women with discriminating tastes who participated knowingly in the Accademia's self-mocking courtly behavior.[19]

---

17 The phrase *m'è infiata una gamba* refers to an erection, but literally means a "swollen leg." Keir Elam translates *par la voglia recere* both as "I'm about to throw up" and "I'm about to come," highlighting the "frankly physical seduction scene" and emphasizing the vulgar language of the servants (23).
18 See, for example, Orgel 81; Goldberg 42; and Bruster.
19 Clubb and Black, 165; Newbigin, 259–61.

While the Intronati playwrights may have teased or condescended to their audience at times, they were also serious about pleasing them. We must ask, then, how and why scenes of female homoeroticism were appealing to this audience, and why they became a staple of Renaissance comic practice. The groundbreaking event Richard Andrews calls "the first staged love scene in Italian 'regular' comedy" is between two female characters (99). Perhaps the mediating effect of the servants' narration authorized the female audience members to act as voyeurs themselves, allowing them to imagine the love scene and identify with the peeping duo; perhaps they relished the maiden's transgression, or the heroine's freedom. Peter Parolin has affirmed the "transformative power attending audience membership; far from being the most passive aspect of the theatrical experience," it "encourages and enables agency" (118). Perhaps a play's own evaluation of same-sex erotic situations is less remarkable than the fact that they occur at all, and become available for reappropriation by spectators. As a motif in early modern drama, recurring pairs of female characters locked in erotic embraces refute the assumption that "lesbian" desire lacked representation. Rather, as Valerie Traub has ably demonstrated, the "discursive proliferation" of female homoeroticism is integral to Renaissance cultural production.[20]

With the arrival of Lelia's long-lost brother Fabrizio, the gender confusion escalates. His father sees him in male dress and assumes it is his disobedient daughter out gamboling, according to Gherardo, "like some disreputable whore" [come le disoneste donnacce] (3.6.). The old men punish "her" by locking Fabrizio in Gherardo's house with Isabella – not realizing that Isabella's unrestrained lust will enable the two to have sex immediately. By the time the men realize their error, it is too late to protect Isabella's virginity. In a broadly comic exchange, Pasquella tries to convince Gherardo that he has not witnessed his daughter's defloration, but only girlish play, which may be disturbing but is less threatening than the alternative:

PASQUELLA. What's the matter? Isn't it Lelia?
GHERARDO. I tell you, it's a man.
PASQ. It can't be. How do you know?
GHER. I saw it with my own eyes.
PASQ. How?

---

20   Traub traces representations of desire between women in Renaissance painting, music, medical texts, travel narratives, and poetry, in addition to drama.

GHER. On top of my daughter, heaven help me!
PASQ. Oh, [the girls] were just playing around.[21]

(4.8)

This dispute spirals out of Pasquella's control as she insists that Gherardo "merely" witnessed his child cavorting with his own half-naked fiancée, and not with a man. While the servant upholds the spectacle of two young women in this position as the more benign option, since it would render them nominally virgins and allow both of them to retain status as marriageable ladies, it raises other questions about the policing of physical behavior and pleasure. Why does Pasquella continue to insist that Fabrizio is a woman, even after Gherardo emphatically states that he has seen his daughter in a compromising position? Was such same-sex "play" completely non-threatening? This scene admits female-female eroticism as a physical possibility or reality, even as it attempts to minimize its importance as "sex." Very seldom in English drama are sexual misunderstandings this explicitly anatomized, but the same principle obtains in both traditions: a "lesbian" scenario is defended as harmless in the world of the play, but at the same time is embedded in other layers of transgression that signal its potentially disruptive power. Just as in *La Calandria*, characters who seek to stabilize notions of gender and sex instead find them to be insistently unstable.

La Calandria and *Gl'Ingannati* share a bawdy preoccupation with the physicality of romantic love, especially as it pertains to female bodies and desires. However, the social attitudes in the plays are indicative of a culture that closely regulated women's behavior. Both Lelia and Santilla initially put on male clothing not to pursue homoerotic desires, but for physical protection, mobility, and/or proximity to a man. They are aware of the harm they face by being outdoors alone, and speak of the dangerous consequences of being discovered. From a formal perspective, disguise was a dramaturgical tool that allowed female characters to move and speak freely while maintaining credibility. It also added urgent realism to the plights of the characters, because along with self-reflexive theatricality, cross-dressing brought believable opportunities and acute risks. In this sense, Italian comedies always contain tragic potential, simply because they take place in recognizable urban locales where young women alone are never safe.

Nevertheless, the tone of these plays is also more broadly comic and farcical, less "romantic," than the Shakespearean experiments that used their plots. The subtly shifting erotic energies fueling a play like *Twelfth Night* are broadly

---

21 PASOELLA Che cos'è? non è Lelia? / GHERARDO. Dico che gli è un maschio. / PASQ. Eh, non è vero! Che ne sapete voi? / GHER. L'ho veduto con questi occhi / PASQ. Come? / GHER. Adosso alla mia figliuola, trist'a me! / PASQ. Eh! che dovevano scherzare! / GHER. È ben che scherzavano. (4.8)

articulated in *Gl'Ingannati*. In the former, Olivia is a woman living on her own, without a man symbolically or literally regulating her desires. She is susceptible to lovesickness, but her intellect allows her to articulate her infatuation with Cesario in the structured language of love poetry. Though impulsive in showing her attraction, she is also self-aware and reflective: "Even so quickly may one catch the plague? / Methinks I feel this youth's perfections / With an invisible and subtle stealth / To creep in at mine eyes" (1.5.265–8). Her counterpart Isabella is also young and sexually desirable, but her feelings are manifested through bodily actions rather than speech. As her maidservant Pasquella announces, Isabella is a captive in her father's house, expressing her yearning for Fabio in masturbatory frustration:

> For the last few days she's been on heat, and she's so madly in love that she's on the go morning and night. She's [sic] scratches her fanny all the time, she rubs her legs together, she runs up to the loggia and down to the window, downstairs and upstairs ... [da certi dì in qua, è intrata in quanta frega ed in tanta smania d'amore che né dì né notte ha posa. Sempre si gratta in pettinicchio, sempre si stropiccia le cosce; or corre a le finestre; or si sotto, or di sopra] ... (2.2.)

Even a contemporary translation risks losing the bawdy force of such a passage. In his 1611 English-Italian dictionary, John Florio glosses *Smánia* as "rage, rashnesse, madnesse, furious chafing, angry fretting, raging passion, braine-sicknesse rising of too much abundance of bloud in the head, whereof follow such raging passions." When Pasquella confides in the audience about Isabella's "smania d'amore" she conveys an image bordering on the obscene (504, 408).

It should hardly be surprising, then, that when Fynes Moryson writes in his 1617 *Itinerary* about viewing a play in Florence, the most notably "foreign" markers are women, improvisation, and sexual bluntness, which he links in a typically English semantic chain: "the partes of wemen were played by wemen, and the cheef actours had not their parts fully penned, but spake much extempory or upon agreement betweene themselves, espetially the wemen, whose speeches were full of wantonnes" (qtd. in Lea, 343). Even Moryson's brief comment divulges how English audiences "explored what was forbidden in their own culture" through Italian counterparts, with an "unstable mixture of admiration and loathing" (Jones, 101). Nevertheless, the transgressive "field of fantasy" Italian drama provided, as an intensely coarse play like *Gl'Ingannati* confirms, was often grounded in time-tested stage practice (116).

Conversely, as Michael Shapiro has noted of *Twelfth Night*, the three scenes Olivia and Cesario share alone (in 1.5, 3.1, and 3.5) progressively deepen their relationship. He maintains, "In each of these encounters insistence on privacy leads one to expect physical intimacy, as in *Gl'Ingannati*, but Shakespeare dramatizes the emotional entanglements ... the audience witnesses an intense interaction between two women" (154). The radically different characterization of the couples is indicative of the tone of both plays as a whole: a corporeal focus in the former; a rhetorically centered, restrained mood in the latter.[22] For these reasons, most critics have favorably compared *Twelfth Night* with *Gl'Ingannati*. Despite overwhelming similarities in plot and structure, the two plays are drastically different in tone, especially in their treatment of sexuality. The Italian plays are more forthright about female homoeroticism in particular – not only because it was more closely policed in Italy, but also because a vocabulary, a legal category, and a system of punishment existed for female sodomy. It functions as a topic of comedy because it is acknowledged to exist. Although cross-dressing was a volatile topic in England when Shakespeare composed *Twelfth Night*, it did not carry the same associations with illegal sexual behaviors that it did in Italy. Maggie Günsberg notes, for example, that Aretino's 1525 *La Cortigiana* (5.12) links female cross-dressing with "the vice 'for which burning is the punishment,'" or sodomy (84). In spite (or perhaps because) of such prohibitions, the theatergram of female same-sex attraction enabled by a cross-gender disguise was incredibly popular; its proliferation undoubtedly contributed to its spread into England. Later plays apply it in all manner of permutations, and by the time Flaminio Scala recorded fifty *commedia* scenarios in 1611, over a third of them involved a cross-dressed heroine (Herrick, 225).[23]

Given the number of cross-dressing plots at his disposal, Shakespeare's adherence to the *Gl'Ingannati* story – and his departures from it – are conspicuous. Keir Elam remarks, "*Twelfth Night* ... does away with sodomitic fireworks, vengeful voyeuristic merchant fathers, erectile scopophilic servants, devouring whores, busybody bawds, and the whole commedia apparatus of more or less brutal physical engagement and crude sexual bartering" (30). What, then, remains? The elements unique to *Twelfth Night* deploy cross-dressing and female homoeroticism in order to make larger points about cultural anxieties regarding class mobility and overlapping forms of service. The most obvious alterations are in the character of Olivia. Unlike Isabella, she has control over her property and person, and is determined to keep it: Sir Toby remarks, "She'll not match above her degree, neither in estate, years, nor wit. I have heard her swear't" (1.3.90–91). Sebastian is impressed

---

22 This division is not at all distinct, especially if one reads *Twelfth Night* with an eye toward bawdy. Dympna Callaghan finds the play rife with "raw physical humor that often disconcerts critics who favor the ethereal lyricism held to be the definitive characteristic of romantic comedy" (435).

23 Eighteen of Scala's fifty *scenarii* feature a cross-dressed woman; many, such as "The Husband," "The Disguised Servants," "The Bear," and "The Mad Princess," also include the theatergram of female homoeroticism.

with her ability to maintain a household with "such a smooth, discreet, and stable bearing" (4.3.19). In addition, Olivia shares a number of important characteristics with Viola that heighten their resemblance and affinity: most notably, both women are in mourning for a father and a brother.

Olivia's authority extends to her rhetorical skill. In her first encounter with Cesario, she inverts typical poetic personae by extolling the boy's beauty: "Thy tongue, thy face, thy limbs, actions, and spirit / Do give thee five-fold blazon" (1.5.262–3). In addition, as Jonathan Sawday has observed, she blazons *herself* before Cesario may take the opportunity, vowing to make certain her face is "inventoried and every particle and utensil labelled to my will" (1.5.215–16). Their vying for discursive control, according to Sawday, "serves to underlie the complex erotic negotiations of 'mastery' and 'submission' which the play seems intent on exploring" (202). Indeed, Olivia's need to assert dominance over her wooer may be a greater determinant of her pleasure than object choice alone.

In her linguistic virtuosity, Olivia may represent the legacy of the Italian actress, and the *innamorata* in particular – a personage whose "glamour," as Pamela Brown argues, consistently "shadowed the English all-male stage" (402). A playwright adapting the blatant sexual humor of *Gl'Ingannati* could see the potential of deepening Isabella's character to give her greater nuance and authority. Whereas the earliest experiments in Italian *commedia erudita* kept women offstage, and later plays explored the possibilities of a cross-dressed heroine, *Twelfth Night* features two fully developed and articulate female lovers.[24] Adding complexity and charisma to Olivia *as a woman* – the same talents exhibited by commedia actresses – increases the seriousness of homoerotic possibility between her and Viola/Cesario, and likewise turns the plot toward Shakespeare's thematic concerns about power dynamics.

Other critics have pointed out the dynamics of love and service that subtend Olivia and Viola's richly homoerotic exchanges. From claiming to be and do something "as secret as maidenhead," to imagining building a "willow cabin" (1.5.190, 237), Viola attempts to serve Olivia in eroticized terms redolent of their shared womanhood.[25] Hutson posits, "The transgressive 'glimpse' being offered to a seventeenth-century audience here ... is less that of lesbian desire than that of the opportunity for social advancement and erotic gratification

---

24 A number of other English playwrights adopted this theatergram as well, including Lyly's treatment of Gallathea and Phyllida in *Gallathea*; Middleton's fascination with cross-dressed women and marriageable widows in plays such as *No Wit, No Help Like a Woman's* and *The Widow*; and Shakespeare's own earlier depictions of attraction between Rosalind and Celia (and Rosalind and Phebe) in *As You Like It*.

25 Jami Ake has argued that such imagery constitutes a pastoral idiom that counters Orsino's stale Petrarchanism and begins to articulate "an alternative poetics of female homoeroticism" (381).

... for any servant of ability entrusted with missions of such intimate familiarity" (160). That is, Shakespeare engages the highly charged and overdetermined theatergram of cross-dressed wooing to articulate the theme of class-crossing, a preoccupation in every plot strand and every one of the play's relationships.[26] This latter issue was arguably far more contested than "female sodomy" in early modern England, and hence apt material for comedy.

Twelfth Night borrows structurally from Italian comedies in other ways. Maria is a faithful rendition of the commedia's clever, ambitious *servetta*. Most comparative scholars agree that her gulling of Malvolio is a variation on the mocking jest, or *beffa*; I would add that Malvolio himself seems to be a conflation of two commedia character types: the fussy pedant, and the self-important old man convinced of his attractiveness to younger women.[27] Malvolio, "loving out of his class," is an amalgam of Italian theater practices, as are Viola and Olivia in sharing the mantle of the improvising actress (Clubb and Black, 173). Perhaps the character most influenced by the Italian tradition, however, is Olivia. With her social and economic freedom, as well as her desire for mastery, she is one of the most powerful persons in the play. Lisa Jardine has suggested that Olivia's desire for the young page is the most transgressive of all the drama's interpersonal crosscurrents (75); if this is the case, then *Twelfth Night*'s homoeroticism codes both her power and her potentially unruly sexual agency. According to Jean Howard, "It is Viola who provokes the love of Olivia, the same-sex love between women thus functioning as the marker of the 'unnatural' in the play and a chief focus of its comedy" (34). Howard argues that Olivia's infatuation is a form of ridicule and punishment for her own assumption of self-mastery.

But is this really a punishment? *Twelfth Night*'s own reluctance to unravel the networks of homoerotic affect that suffuse the play, seen in the deferred marriages and Cesario's retention of his male costume, keeps those relationships held in tension, even as the audience gets its happy ending in the twins' reconciliation. The refusal to "straighten out" the ending (or to subordinate its heroine) is a major intervention into a long theatrical tradition of same-sex attraction between women in the Renaissance and represents a major departure from the models of *La Calandria* and *Gl'Ingannati*.

Likewise, the transposition from the *arte* companies' woman-focused productions to the very different eroticism of the all-male English professional

---

26 Cristina Malcolmson makes a similar point, but does not extend her analysis to homoeroticism: she argues, "In *Twelfth Night*, the current and popular controversy over women mediates the dilemmas about social mobility" (39). Mary Ellen Lamb posits that the play's exploration of power differentials in love relationships dramatizes a particularly *heterosexual* erotics of service.

27 See Clubb and Black, 173; Hutson, 160; Newbigin, 266; Hurworth, 122.

stage accentuates the polyvalent eroticism of female seduction duets, by adding
to the mix the sexual appeal of boy actors. Perhaps *Twelfth Night* casts a
knowing glance at the stereotypical reputation of Italians for sodomy, at the
same time as it celebrates the *innamorata*. Perhaps it comments meta-
theatrically on the service young men rendered to acting companies, and
teases the anti-theatricalists who charged that the players offered sexual
"service" behind the scenes. Perhaps the play suggests that in early modern
households, gender is even more mutable than rank. Perhaps. What is certain is
that the play appropriates hallmarks of Italian stage practice into the English
tradition. Further, by drawing on established histories of female improvisation,
cross-dressing, and homoeroticism to create an "actress effect," *Twelfth Night*
multiplies the erotic, social, and linguistic positions open to female characters
and viewers.

   Michael Shapiro has used the metaphor of "italics" to describe the
phenomenon of cross-dressed gender on the early modern stage. In Shapiro's
reading, the actors' abilities, combined with the "oscillating" layers of disguise,
create "an impression of depth" (7). "Italics" convey difference as well as
emphasis; materials printed in italic type were usually meant to be set apart
from the body of a text as foreign, more prominent, or both.[28] It is precisely the
effect the Italian actress exerted on the dramatic material she circulated. This
metaphor is also apt for *Twelfth Night*'s use of the Italian comic topoi of female
homoeroticism and improvisatory female performance: by italicizing –
emphasizing and setting apart, via the use of Italian stylistic elements – gender
and eroticism, the play draws attention to the many levels of social tension
layered within.

Works Cited

Ake, Jami. "Glimpsing a 'Lesbian' Poetics in *Twelfth Night*." *Studies in English Literature* 43.2 (Spring 2003): 375–94.
Andrews, Richard. *Scripts and Scenarios: The Performance of Comedy in Renaissance Italy*. Cambridge: Cambridge University Press, 1993.
Beolco, Angelo (Ruzante). *L'Anconitana/The Woman From Ancona*. Trans. and introd. Nancy Dersofi. Berkeley and Los Angeles: University of California Press, 1994.
Bibbiena, Bernardo Dovizi. *La Calandria*. Ed. Guido Davico Bonino. In *Il teatro italiano: La commedia del Cinquecento*. Vol. 2. Torino: Einaudi, 1977, 3–88.
Brown, Judith C. *Immodest Acts: The Life of a Lesbian Nun in Renaissance Italy*. Oxford: Oxford University Press, 1986.

28   Pamela Brown makes a similar observation about the "sexual dynamics" of
     Othello, claiming they are "Italicized: stressed while being perceived as hyper-
     Italic" (416).

Brown, Pamela. "The Counterfeit *Innamorata*, or, The Diva Vanishes." *Shakespeare Yearbook* 10 (1999): 402–26.

Bruster, Douglas. "Female-Female Eroticism and the Early Modern Stage." *Renaissance Drama* n.s. 24 (1993): 1–32.

Cairns, Christopher, ed. *Three Renaissance Comedies: Ariosto's* The Supposes, *Machiavelli's* The Mandrake, *Intronati's* The Deceived. Trans. and introd. Jennifer Lorch, Kenneth Richards, Laura Richards, and Nerida Newbigin. Lampeter, Wales and Lewiston, New York: Edwin Mellen, 1996.

Callaghan, Dympna. "'And All is Semblative a Woman's Part': Body Politics and *Twelfth Night*." *Textual Practice* 7.3 (Winter 1993): 428–52.

Clubb, Louise George. *Italian Plays (1500–1700) in the Folger Library*. Firenze: Leo S. Olschki Editore, 1968.

———. "Woman as Wonder: A Generic Figure in Italian and Shakespearean Comedy." *Studies in the Continental Background of Renaissance English Literature: Essays Presented to John L. Lievsay*. Ed. Dale B. J. Randall and George Walton Williams. Durham, NC: Duke University Press, 1977, 109–132.

———. *Italian Drama in Shakespeare's Time*. New Haven: Yale University Press, 1989.

———. "Italian Stories on the Stage." *The Cambridge Companion to Shakespearean Comedy*. Ed. Alexander Leggatt. Cambridge: Cambridge University Press, 2002, 32–46.

——— and Robert Black, eds. *Romance and Aretine Humanism in Sienese Comedy, 1516: Pollastra's* Parthenio *at the Studio di Siena*. Siena: La Nuova Italia, 1993.

Crompton, Louis. "The Myth of Lesbian Impunity: Capital Laws from 1270 to 1791." *Journal of Homosexuality* 6:1–2 (Fall/Winter 1980–1): 11–25.

Elam, Keir. "The Fertile Eunuch: *Twelfth Night*, Early Modern Intercourse, and the Fruits of Castration." *Shakespeare Quarterly* 47.1 (Spring 1996): 1–36.

Evans, Oliver, trans. "The Follies of Calandro." *The Genius of the Italian Theater*. Ed. Eric Bentley. New York: Mentor Books, 1964, 31–98.

Florio, John. *Queen Anna's New World of Words*. London, 1611. Rpt. Scolar Press Facsimile. Menston, England: The Scolar Press Limited, 1968.

Gl'Ingannati. [Anon.] *Commedie del Cinquecento*, Vol. 1. Ed. Nino Borsellino. Milan: Feltrinelli Editore, 1962, 195–290.

Goldberg, Jonathan. *Sodometries: Renaissance Texts, Modern Sexualities*. Stanford: Stanford University Press, 1992.

Günsberg, Maggie. *Gender and the Italian Stage: From the Renaissance to the Present Day*. Cambridge: Cambridge University Press, 1997.

Henke, Robert. *Performance and Literature in the Commedia dell'arte*. Cambridge: Cambridge University Press, 2002.

Herrick, Marvin T. *Italian Comedy in the Renaissance*. Urbana: University of Illinois Press, 1966 [1960].

Howard, Jean. "Cross-Dressing, the Theater, and Gender Struggle in Early Modern England." *Shakespeare Quarterly* 39.4 (1988): 418–40. Rpt. in *Crossing the Stage: Controversies on Cross-Dressing*. Ed. Lesley Ferris. New York: Routledge, 1993, 20–46.

Hurworth, Angela. "Gulls, Cony-Catchers and Cozeners: *Twelfth Night* and the Elizabethan Underworld." *Shakespeare Survey* 52 (1999): 120–32.

Hutson, Lorna. "On Not Being Deceived: Rhetoric and the Body in *Twelfth Night.*" *Texas Studies in Literature and Language* 38.2 (Summer 1996): 140–74.
Jardine, Lisa. *Reading Shakespeare Historically.* New York: Routledge, 1996.
Jones, Ann Rosalind. "Italians and Others: Venice and the Irish in *Coryat's Crudities* and *The White Devil.*" *Renaissance Drama* n.s. 28 (1987): 101–19.
Lamb, Mary Ellen. "Tracing a Heterosexual Erotics of Service in *Twelfth Night* and the Autobiographical Writings of Thomas Whythorne and Anne Clifford." *Criticism* XL (Winter 1998): 1–25.
Lea, Kathleen M. *Italian Popular Comedy: A Study in the Commedia dell'arte, 1560–1620, With Special Reference to the English Stage.* 2 vols. New York: Russell & Russell, 1934; rpt. 1962.
Malcolmson, Cristina. "'What You Will': Social Mobility and Gender in *Twelfth Night.*" *The Matter of Difference: Materialist Feminist Criticism of Shakespeare.* Ed. Valerie Wayne. Ithaca: Cornell University Press, 1991, 29–57.
Melzi, Robert. "From Lelia to Viola." *Renaissance Drama* 9 (1966): 67–81.
Orgel, Stephen. *Impersonations: The Performance of Gender in Shakespeare's England.* Cambridge: Cambridge University Press, 1996.
Orr, David. *Italian Renaissance Drama in England Before 1625: The Influence of Erudita Tragedy, Comedy, and Pastoral on Elizabethan and Jacobean Drama.* University of North Carolina Studies in Comparative Literature v. 49. Chapel Hill: University of North Carolina Press, 1970.
Park, Katharine. "The Rediscovery of the Clitoris: French Medicine and the Tribade, 1570–1620." *The Body in Parts: Fantasies of Corporeality in Early Modern Europe.* Ed. David Hillman and Carla Mazzio. New York: Routledge, 1997, 170–95.
Parolin, Peter. "'A Strange Fury Entered My House': Italian Actresses and Female Performance in *Volpone.*" *Renaissance Drama* n.s. 39 (1998): 107–35.
Piccolomini, Alessandro. *Alessandro/L'Allesandro.* Ed. and trans. Rita Belladonna. Ottawa: Dovehouse Editions, 1984.
Radcliff-Umstead, Douglas. *The Birth of Modern Comedy in Renaissance Italy.* Chicago: University of Chicago Press, 1969.
Richards, Kenneth. "The 'Commedia dell'arte' and the Caroline Stage." *Italy and the English Renaissance.* Ed. Sergio Rossi and Daniella Savoia. Milan: Edizioni Unicopli, 1989, 241–51.
Ruffini, Franco. *Commedia e festa nel Rinascimento: La* Calandria *alla corte di Urbino.* Bologna: Il Mulino, 1986.
Salingar, Leo. *Shakespeare and the Traditions of Comedy.* Cambridge: Cambridge University Press, 1974.
Sawday, Jonathan. *The Body Emblazoned: Dissection and the Human Body in Renaissance Culture.* New York: Routledge, 1995.
Scala, Flaminio. *Scenarios of the* Commedia dell'Arte. Trans. Henry F. Salerno. New York: Limelight, 1989.
Shakespeare, William. *Twelfth Night, or What You Will. The Norton Shakespeare.* Ed. Stephen Greenblatt *et al.* New York: Norton, 1997.
Shapiro, Michael. *Gender in Play on the Shakespearean Stage: Boy Heroines and Female Pages.* Ann Arbor: University of Michigan Press, 1994.
Simons, Patricia. "Lesbian (In)Visibility in Italian Renaissance Culture: Diana and Other Cases of *donna con donna.*" *Journal of Homosexuality* 27:1–2 (1994): 81–122.

Smith, Winifred. "Italian and Elizabethan Comedy." *Modern Philology* V (1907–8): 555–67.

Traub, Valerie. *The Renaissance of Lesbianism in Early Modern England.* Cambridge: Cambridge University Press, 2002.

Weaver, Elissa B. *Convent Theatre in Early Modern Italy: Spiritual Fun and Learning for Women.* Cambridge: Cambridge University Press, 2002.

Chapter 9

Courtly *Comédiantes*: Henrietta Maria and Amateur Women's Stage Plays in France and England

Melinda J. Gough

Henrietta Maria, queen consort of Charles I of England, is known to literary and performance scholars primarily for her sponsorship of court masques and plays, spectacles through which she functioned as an "exigent mediatrix of her native [French] culture" (Peacock, 155). Bringing such general insights to bear on the question of material practices involving women actors, this essay focuses on French precedents for Henrietta Maria's English appearances, alongside her female companions, in private stage plays. In London prior to Henrietta Maria's arrival in May 1625, women's voices had rarely been heard on the stage. During her queenship this changed, however, particularly at court, where amateur women's theatricals became a regular pastime. Critics and biographers have often taken the queen's acting as a seemingly obvious consequence of French expectations that women acted on the professional and court stages.[1] But there was never any question of Henrietta or any other elite woman appearing on a "public stage" in the sense that uninvited individuals could pay to come in and view her. Further, early seventeenth-century French attitudes toward professional actresses were more complicated and ambivalent than English scholars have tended to assume. To better comprehend what precedents, precisely, enabled women at the court of Henrietta Maria's childhood to fashion their own amateur theatricals as socially acceptable, and to what ends, we must look more closely at that court's dealings with professional women actors, including actresses from Italy. The most logical

---

1 Suzanne Gossett, for example, explains Henrietta Maria's first decision to act on the English court stage, in the 1626 production of the French pastoral *Artenice*, with the quick aside that "Henrietta ... was used to actresses"(103), while Stephen Orgel, though briefly noting European censures against actresses, writes that "by Shakespeare's time they were a commonplace feature of the European stage – societies that maintained a public stage expected to see women on it" (1996, 1).

influence on Henrietta Maria's own acting in England, I argue, was a cosmopolitan French court milieu deeply sensitive to international fashion and in which, under the aegis of Henrietta Maria's mother Marie de Medici, elite young women actively participated in amateur private theatricals by modeling themselves on traveling professional actresses.

Unfortunately we have little direct evidence regarding Henrietta Maria's own personal history on the French court stage. It is often assumed that Henrietta Maria performed in amateur plays at the French court, but to date almost no concrete support for this notion has been uncovered. This essay offers new evidence proving that Henrietta Maria did, in fact, act on the French court stage before she crossed the channel to become queen of England. But even such additional documentary evidence teaches us little about the shape such performances may have taken; hence we are left with a very limited picture of the expectations that surrounded royal women's acting at the French court of Henrietta's girlhood. To partially fill this gap, this essay considers a performance in which Henrietta Maria, because still an infant, did not appear: a 1611 production of *Bradamante* directed and performed by her eldest sister Elisabeth. In this instance, a young princess of France modeled her own theatrical production on those of professional actresses from Italy. Italian singer-actresses such as Isabella Andreini had effectively united histrionic virtuosity with unassailable virtue, and had become famous in elite circles across Europe. Their example thus made it possible for socially elevated young girls of the court to reach for similarly skilled theatrical display without risking misprision of their own moral and hence social status. Indeed, when girls such as Henrietta's sister Elisabeth took speaking parts in private plays, contemporaries emphasized their skill in stage declamation (and the practice in memorizing lines that was essential to acquiring this facility). Such skillful elocution combined with graceful gesture was so noteworthy, I suggest, because play acting for invited, elite audiences allowed young royal women and their female companions to visibly exercise their most decorous socio-political function: the mirroring back to the court of its own graceful magnificence, as well as the possible enhancement of that court's prestige within the European court nexus as a whole.

Valuable in its own right, this sharpened picture of royal women's performance at the early seventeenth-century French court may also enable us to rethink Henrietta Maria's contributions as a theatrical producer and performer in England. In particular, it will help us to address two specific misconceptions: that Henrietta Maria's performances necessarily lacked skilled execution, and that they were merely frivolous pastimes.

The Royal Troupeau: Elisabeth's 1611 *Bradamante*

In the summer of 1611, when Henrietta Maria was only a year old, her eldest sister Elisabeth along with her "troupeau" of fourteen other royal and noble children, including Henrietta Maria's sister Christine, performed a play before select members of the French court. At the time, Elisabeth was nine years old; Christine was five. At three o'clock on August 2, their brother Louis XIII was taken by carriage to Saint Germain, the ballroom of which had been made over into a theatre "tout accommodé" for this performance.[2] Here, together with the queen regent Marie de Medici, Marguerite de Valois, and princes, princesses, and seigneurs of the court, the young king was entertained by "la comédie de Madame [Elisabeth]," a tragi-comedy derived from Robert Garnier's *Bradamante*.[3]

This play was acted and initiated by Elisabeth herself with direct encouragement from her mother Marie de Medici. This we learn from one of the queen regent's letters. Assenting to Elisabeth's request for permission to perform this "comédie," Marie also warns of her own intention to supervise directly the rehearsal process:

> I am very willing to give my eldest daughter the permission she has requested to recite her play, but she must learn her lines well; in a few days I intend to come to Saint-Germain in order to observe if she will have retained her verses; inform her of this in order that she will dispose herself to know her part well.[4]

---

2 This dating is New Style. Throughout this essay, unless otherwise noted in the text, New Style dating will be used for all events that take place in France and all letters written by continental authors (even if those persons are writing from England). Old Style dating will be used for events that take place in England and letters written by English authors.

3 For a list of audience members, see Héroard, 2: 392, and King, 157–8. Malherbe calls this "la comédie de Madame" (Lalanne, 3: 244). Lanson suggests that this production must have been an abridged version of Garnier's script; the youth of its actors, he argues, indicates that the play must have been turned into a ballet. However, given that Malherbe describes the actors' declamation, gestures, and action but makes no reference to any dancing, and given that all contemporary descriptions refer to it as a "comédie" (meaning "play") rather than a "ballet" (a term reserved solely for the French equivalent of the English masque), Lanson's suggestion seems erroneous.

4 "Je veux bien volontiers accorder à ma fille aînée la permission qu'elle désire pour réciter sa comédie, mais elle doit bien apprendre les vers; j'ai l'intention d'aller dans peu de jours à Saint-Germain pour voir si elle les aura bien retenus; vous l'en avertirez de ma part afin qu'elle se dispose à bien faire" (Batiffol, 295). The English translation is my own; cf. King, 156.

Marie not only planned a visit to Saint Germain in order to assess her daughter's success in memorizing her lines; four days before the final performance she facilitated in her own apartments a dress rehearsal put on by Elisabeth and her troupe (Héroard, II: 71). Marie also issued an invitation to the event in her own name and that of the players:

> You are invited in my name and in the name of the whole company of *comédiantes*, to be present at their play which will be given tomorrow, at one o'clock in the afternoon after dinner. Your pleasure in listening to them will countervail any trouble or inconvenience which you may suffer from the roads on your way.[5]

The event seems to have rewarded Marie's efforts. Indeed, in a letter written the next day, the queen regent singled out her daughter's abilities for special praise:

> ... my daughter's play was well recited in the presence of a goodly assemblage. She, as well as all the others, acquitted herself so well and so prettily that I listened with much satisfaction and contentment.[6]

Motherly pride alone does not account for this expression of pleasure at the play's execution, for the poet Malherbe, too, praised Elisabeth's acting, specifying that she not only appeared in Amazonian attire as befitted the role of Bradamante but went on to exceed general audience expectations, astonishing everyone with her gracefulness.[7]

---

5   "De ma part et de celle de toute la compagnie des comédiantes, je vous prie de venir voir leur comédie; elle sera demain récitée à une heure après dîner. Le plaisir que vous aurez à les entendre supassera la peine et l'incommodité que vous pourrez recevoir par les chemins" (Batiffol, 297). This English translation expands and slightly adapts King's (157).

6   "... la comédie de ma fille fut bien récitée en bonne compagnie et fit si bien et si gentiment et toutes les autres aussi qui en estoient que j'en demeurai avec beaucoup de satisfaction et de contentement" (Batiffol, 297); I have slightly modified King's English translation (157).

7   "Madame, qui étoit habillée en amazone comme représentant Bradamante, étonna tout le monde par sa bonne grace" (in Lalanne, 3: 244–7). For a contemporary commentary critical of the actors see King, 157. Although Héroard (2: 392) lists Mademoiselle de Vendôme in the role of Bradamante and assigns to Elisabeth the part of Marphise, Malherbe is likely a more reliable witness: given that he wrote the prologue's lines from heart in his letter to Peiresc, his memory of the event must have been strong. Cf. Wiley, 235, who seems to have used Héroard's journal as his source without accounting for Malherbe's identification of Elisabeth's role. Marphise and Bradamante were both leading parts, good vehicles for displaying theatrical virtuosity.

These contemporary assessments of Elisabeth's performance employ vocabulary like that used six decades earlier to describe the first ever recorded stage appearance of professional Italian actresses, also at the French court. This event was the 1548 performance of *La Calandria* by a troupe of professional or semi-professional actors at Lyons, as part of the celebrations for the entry into that city of Henri II and his new bride Catherine de Medici. The diarist Brantôme, recounting the performance, noted several women "comédientes" who were "très belle" and "parlaient très-bien et de fort bonne grace."[8] Several factors may account for the similar language used to describe this performance and Elisabeth's *Bradamante*. First, just as a commedia dell'arte troupe might frequently be directed and managed by its chief actress, who not only led the company by the magnetism of her acting but also selected and organized her company's dramatic repertoire (Nicholson, 248), so Elisabeth, as the *capocomico* of Saint Germain's royal "compagnie," initiated this production of *Bradamante* and took one of its leading female roles. Second, just as commedia actresses were renowned for their cross-dressing, so this production of *Bradamante* included some girls playing male roles, while Elisabeth, as one of Garnier's Amazonian heroines, also appeared in androgynous guise. Finally, Elisabeth's performance would have enabled her to display the kind of "protean virtuosity" that characterized the careers of commedia actresses. Diva-actresses such as Flaminia "Romana," as Eric Nicholson has shown (246–50), self-consciously revised the texts of chivalric romance for the stage and thus acquired star power by playing the role of love-struck heroine or innamorata, in one production, that of warrior woman in the next. Performing the eponymous lead character in this adaptation of Garnier's *Bradamante*, Elisabeth would have acted a similarly challenging part, for in adapting Ariosto's narrative Garnier had made his Bradamante both innocent lover and martial woman in one.

Such implicit emulation of Italian professional actresses can be accounted for in part when read against the history of contact between members of the French royal family and those troupes of foreign actors, particularly companies from Italy, in which women took leading organizational and dramatic roles. As early as 1548, as we have seen, an Italian group that included women actors performed for the French court at Lyons. Three decades later, Vittoria Piisimi, then prima donna of the Gelosi, performed for Catherine de Medici's son Henri III during his travels through Italy (Gilder, 63: Lacour, 63; MacNeil, 2003, 11, 15, 196–97 and in 1577 this troupe performed again for the French King, this time in France (MacNeil, 2003, 200–2001; cf. Boucher, 1016–18). Under Marie de Medici's queenship and regency,

8 Pierre de Bourdeille, Seigneur de Brantôme, as quoted in Henke, 86; see also Gilder, 56. For lengthier discussions of this performance see also Andrews; Bryce.

French royal sponsorship of Italian actors and actresses intensified. In late 1599, for example, Henri IV wrote to Tristan Martinelli, the Arlequin of the Accessi, asking that his troupe come to France in order to entertain his new queen (MacNeil, 2003, 249). Two years later, the Gelosi under the direction of Francesco and Isabella Andreini took up residence at the French court. Marie seems to have been particularly impressed by Isabella and other women actors; when the Gelosi left Paris in 1603, for example, they carried with them a letter of commendation from Marie to her sister the Duchess of Mantua asserting "that during the time Isabella Andreini has dwelt here, she and her company have given full satisfaction to the King, my lord, and to me, and for this reason I recommend her to you with all affection" (Gilder, 81; cf. MacNeil, 2003, 256–57). In 1608 Italian players were again present at the French capital, and in 1611, the year Elisabeth's *Bradamante* was mounted, Marie herself initiated written negotiations for the appearance in Paris of the Comici Fedeli, the troupe headed by Isabella Andreini's son, Giovanni Battista Andreini. In these communications, Marie asked specifically for two women actors: "Flavia" and "Florinda" (wife of Giovanni Battista Andreini).[9] When the troupe arrived, in 1613, it included not only Florinda and Flavia but also a third actress named Lidia (Lacour, 39).

Sponsoring professional actresses from Italy, the French monarchy also fostered amateur acting by royal women and their female companions. Earlier, under Catherine de Medici's influence, the *escadron volant*, a group of female courtiers "dressed and adorned like goddesses, but welcoming like mortals," had performed frequently (Yates, 251; see also Julie Campbell's essay in this volume). The royal children, girls included, also performed in tragedies and pastorals. In 1556 the elder daughters of Henri II – most notably the princess Elisabeth – played in Jodelle's *Sophonisbe* (Boucher, 1040). In addition, among the many spectacles, games, and *divertissements* for the 1564 fêtes at Fontainebleau was a play based on the story of Ginevra (taken from Aristo's *Orlando Furioso*) performed by "the late king Henri II's legitimized daughter Diane, later duchesse d'Angouilême, accompanied by 'the most noble and beautiful princesses, ladies, and girls of the court'" (Brantôme, 53, cited in Scott, 178). This production, as Virginia Scott suggests, was "performed largely, and probably exclusively" by young women (179); it also featured Italian *intermedii* between the acts (Prunières, 34). According to Rosamund Gilder (85), on one occasion Catherine's own daughter Marguerite, together with her brother Anjou (the future Henri III) performed a tragedy at Fontainebleau for the court. Gilder

9   Marrow (81 n. 63); see also Wiley (22–4); Gilder (31); Schwartz (47–49); Batiffol (122). By the winter season of 1613–14 Marie had arranged to rent for this troupe, at the cost of 200 livres per month, the Hôtel de Bourgogne; a lease shows them renting it again from October 16 to November 16, 1621.

does not substantiate her claim, but Marguerite's acting ability was certainly noted by contemporaries: describing the royal children performing in the various tournaments, jousts, banquets and plays that formed part of the 1564 festivities, Antoine Sarron, secretary to the Spanish ambassador, notes that "aussi a fort bien représenté personnages, Madame *Marguerite*, s[o]eur dudict Roy [Charles IX], aux Comédies, & avecq fort bonne grace & audace" (Scott, 178).

Among the many spectacles, games, and *divertissements* of the 1565 Fontainebleau fêtes, for example, was a *comédie* "sur le subject de la belle Genièvre de l'Arioste" with Italian *intermedii* between the acts, performed by "les plus honnestes et belles princesses, et dames et filles de la Cour" (Prunières, 34). And according to Rosamond Gilder (85), on one occasion Catherine's own daughter Marguerite, together with her brother Anjou (the future Henri III) performed a tragedy at Fontainebleau for the court.

I have not been able to ascertain the extent to which Catherine's daughters may have interacted with or modeled themselves on foreign actresses and actors, but there is substantial evidence by which to trace later interactions between Marie de Medici's children and traveling troupes from Italy. For example on numerous occasions commedia players acted before the Dauphin and his siblings, for example, while according to Louis Battifol (294) and Mary Anne Everett Green (4), the royal children themselves formed a "troupeau" that regularly emulated commedia performances at Saint Germain and Fontaine-bleau. Louis XIII's physician Jean Héroard reports, for example, that in 1608 when playing the role of Charlemagne in Garnier's *Bradamante* at Fontaine-bleau before his mother and father, the Dauphin had seven verses to speak and remembered none, "whereupon he marked tearfully, 'I have forgotten all my part.'" In 1610, Marie had her eldest son put on a costume "to dance Pantalone" before her. And in 1613 Louis, now king, followed the lead of Italian players in adapting Ariosto's chivalric romance for the stage: with his "little friends," he presented the tragedy of "Emon, tirée de l'Arioste" at the Louvre with his mother in the audience (Héroard 2: 118, 121; Wiley, 24, 235, 238–9).

The princesses, too, produced and performed "comédies" derived from Ariosto – such as the 1611 adaptation of Garnier's *Bradamante*. In this production, Elisabeth was not the only girl to take a speaking role. Héroard lists at least nine others, some in male roles. He also clarifies that Christine, Henrietta Maria's other sister, played the part of Charlemagne's daughter Léonor.[10] This amateur production, as we have seen, emulated the kinds of organizing efforts,

---

10 Héroard, 3: 392. Léonor's character appears only at the play's dénouement, and Malherbe states that Christine "did not appear on the stage until the end of the last act, at which point she spoke a word or two, so as not to be excluded" [Madame Chrétienne ne parut sur le theatre qu'en la fin du dernier acte, où elle dit un mot, seulement pour en être comme les autres] (Lalanne, 3: 244–7).

Italian epic-romance source material and graceful acting familiar to French court audiences through Italian professional actresses. Moreover, Marie de Medici's invitation to the play emphasizes such parallels by billing Elisabeth and her cohorts as a company of players ("compagnie des comédiantes"). By using not the French term "comédiens" but the word "comédiantes," a term derived from Spanish and/or Italian, this invitation further likened Elisabeth's company to foreign troupes – Henri IV had used precisely this term, it is worth noting, in a letter to the Governor of Lyon invoking his protection for "Isabelle [Andreini], comédiante, et sa companie" (Gilder, 81, 56).[11]

Why, we might ask, were Italian companies with their professional actresses – rather than, say, professional Frenchwomen actors – the working model for this 1611 royal production? One answer might be that at this time, native professional actresses did not yet enjoy the unassailable reputation for moral virtue, nor the international cachet, of their more famous Italian counterparts. Documentary evidence does show that in the provinces, amateur French-women had been acting for at least several centuries and that as early as 1545, at least one woman had acted in a professional capacity. But in Paris, it was not until the second decade of the seventeenth century that women appeared regularly on stage at the city's only legal commercial playhouse, the Hotel de Bourgogne. This discrepancy between the provinces and the capital was in part a question of genre: while French traveling companies performed various kinds of plays, including the tragicomedies and pastorals thought more fitting for women actors, bawdy farce largely ruled on the Parisian commercial stage until the second decade of the seventeenth century, thus making this venue seem incompatible with female chastity. Not coincidentally, it was a professional company particularly well known for its tragicomedies – not for farces – that first achieved significant success on the Paris stage with a woman actor, Marie Venier (dite Laporte), in the early seventeenth century.[12] Still, Parisian actresses do not seem to have achieved international fame, nor do they seem to

---

11   The Littré definition suggests that the French terms "comédien" and "comédienne" derived etymologically from "comédie; espan. Comediante; ital. commediante." The first recorded uses of the French words "Comédien" and "comédienne" are circa 1500 (*Grand Larousse*, 2: 803).

12   On amateur actresses in France outside Paris, see Bapst, 56–9; Gilder, 83–5; and esp. Lacour, 5–15. Marie Fairet [or Ferré], evidently the first professional French actress, performed in a provincial troupe not a Parisian one; see Bapst, 177; Gilder, 86–9; Shapiro, 180. Bapst says that women did not appear on a regular commercial stage in Paris until the second half of the seventeenth century (177). Yet one Marie Venier, dite Laporte, who performed with Valleran's troupe as early as 1598 in Bordeaux, seems to have acted in Paris as early as 1606 or 1610, though not yet at the Hotel de Bourgogne; see Lacour, 16–28; Rigal, 170–73; Gilder, 90–91; Shapiro, 180. On women's late entry into Parisian farce see Rigal, 173–82.

have enjoyed unqualified social and moral status at the French court even by the later 1630s: on one occasion, as Tallemant des Réaux recalled, when the courtier-playwright Boisrobert invited a young professional actress from one of the Paris troupes to a social event at which the king and his household were present, this was seen by the royal assembly as a social *faux pas*, and as a result Boisrobert fell from favor despite his subsequent attempts to distance himself, socially, from his actress companion and her alleged whoredom.[13] Negative views of the native French professional actress's morality persisted.

By the time that Elisabeth produced and performed in *Bradamante*, by contrast, Italian traveling actresses had gained legendary fame for both virtuosic skill and moral excellence not only in France but at courts across Europe. Vincenza Armani, for example, had been eloquently defended from anti-theatricalist attacks of alleged licentiousness in a published funeral oration that, as Robert Henke shows, praised her technical prowess as part of its moral defense. This encomium, Henke argues, employed strategies used by other actor-writers in support of their craft: "Seen in a neo-Platonic light, beauty generated by refined technical skills could not but produce the good," and this beauty included that produced by the technically skilled actress (Henke, 94–100, esp. 94). Following Armani, Isabella Andreini – who defined herself against charlatans and players of the piazza and aligned herself with high literature – provided Europe as a whole the example of a woman in whom humanist *virtú* might be reconciled, in life and in art, with virtuoso acting (Henke, 105; Gilder, 67–81; MacNeil 1994, 1995, 1999, 2003).

It was to foreign rather than native professional actresses, therefore, that French royal women such as Elisabeth turned in order to model before an elite, cosmopolitan court their own histrionic skill in ways that might enhance, rather than endanger, their reputations for chaste beauty. The question remains, though, as to what kinds of social or political utility might have attended such young royal women's self-fashioning through theatre. 1611, the year of *Bradamante*'s production by Elisabeth and her troupe, was the first year of Marie de Medici's regency, and already her power was threatened by revolt from the realm's most powerful factions, the Protestants and the Princes of the Blood. Marie as a result sought external support, from Spain, and it is this specific political context, I suggest, that can help us to assess the importance of Elisabeth's accomplished acting as the eponymous heroine of Garnier's play. It was in the summer of 1611 that an extraordinary ambassador from Madrid's first proposed a political alliance between Marie's government and that of Spain to be secured through Elisabeth's marriage to the Spanish king's heir apparent, the future Philip IV (Carmona, 226–45; Hayden). Acting for a court audience, Elisabeth could display moral virtue and graceful beauty through

---

13   Tallemant as cited in Wiley, 89–90.

theatrical skill, specifically verbal eloquence and its visual counterpart, the disciplined bodily comportment of theatrical gesture and movement. From Marie de Medici's interventions in the rehearsal process, her efforts to attract an elite audience, and her satisfaction with the end product, we may conjecture that in this performance of *Bradamante* Elisabeth did demonstrate the very kind of verbal and kinetic grace thought most appropriate to her social role as one of the most elevated marriageable women in Europe.[14] Confirming her own status, Elisabeth thus enhanced her mother's as well – courting Spain in defiance of French Princes of the Blood and Protestants alike.

Henrietta Maria as *Comédiante*

Regarding this 1611 performance of *Bradamante* Janet Mackay has written, "All the members of the junior Court had parts – excepting Madame Henriette, who was too young and flighty to be trusted" (10). As noted previously, the youngest daughter of Marie de Medici was only one year old when her sisters performed *Bradamante*, but this fact seems not to have deterred Mackay from repeating typical unsubstantiated assertions of Henrietta Maria's vapid frivolity. As an infant, Henrietta Maria could hardly have participated in Elisabeth's *troupeau*. Yet this youngest daughter of France would soon grow up to inherit her sister's love of theatricality, similarly displaying her own mastery of courtly eloquence and disciplined movement even when, in England, such activities invoked Puritan censure.

French and English scholars to date have provided little concrete information regarding Henrietta Maria's acting activities in France. But a closer look at the correspondence of Italian diplomatic representatives in Paris,

---

14 Similar skill in amateur female performance in the French provinces had been attested to earlier by at least one contemporary commentator, and in ways that suggest a relationship between an unmarried woman's theatrical virtuosity and her class mobility. In 1468, recording a young girl's performance of a mystery play on the life of Saint Catherine, the chronicler of Metz wrote: "The personage of Saint Catherine was performed by a young girl, about eighteen years old, who was the daughter of Dédiet the glazier, and she did her duty very well indeed, to the pleasure and delight of everybody. Though this girl had 2,300 lines in her part, she had them all at her fingers' ends, and this girl did speak so quickly and so pitifully that she made several people cry, and pleased everybody. And for this reason the girl made a rich match with a nobleman belonging to the hired troop of Metz, named Henrie de Latour, who fell in love with her because of the great pleasure he took in her playing" (Gilder, 84). On this occasion, a glazier's daughter enacted moral and religious virtue with theatrical virtuosity. And far from casting aspersions on her chastity, this performance enhanced the girl's marriageability.

and later in London, can help us fill this gap with new documentary evidence. In one of his weekly missives to the Grand Duke of Tuscany, written 5 October, 1623, the Florentine ambassador in Paris, Giovanni Battista Gondi, wrote that "Madame the king's sister [Henrietta Maria] with many other principal ladies of the court recited in the presence of their Majesties a very beautiful play."[15] This production seems to have taken place at Montceaux, one of Marie de Medici's palaces, in honor of a visit by her son Louis XIII and his wife Anne of Austria. Gondi's letters for that year are also full of news regarding possible suitors for Henrietta Maria, including Charles Prince of Wales. Thus, just as her elder sister Elisabeth had acted in a private court play under her mother's supervision at the moment when her future marriage to a foreign prince was being actively negotiated, so too Henrietta Maria took to the court stage, likely under her mother's aegis, at a time of heightened possibility for a prestigious match with a foreign prince – in this case the heir to the English throne.[16] Such acting, moreover, was worthy of note by a foreign ambassador, indicating its potential significance in the realm of European court politics.

The letters of Benedetto di Cize, representative of Savoy in London, provide additional documentary evidence that Henrietta Maria acted in Paris; Cize's correspondence also traces one concrete instance in which Henrietta Maria, as queen of England, actively drew on that history to mediate Anglo-French cultural crossings. In 1635, we learn, Henrietta Maria sponsored a production by her ladies based on a French play. In a letter dated 18 October, 1635, Cize writes:

> The queen told me that she was preparing a play for the king's birthday at the end of next month which she was having performed by the same ladies who were in the one that was staged before, being the same one that she had played in at the Louvre when she was a girl. (Orrell 1978, 91)[17]

According to John Orrell, such references to several different productions in the summer and fall of 1635 suggest "that Henrietta Maria's ladies acted more

---

15 "Madama sorella del Re con molto altre Signore principale recitò in presenza di loro M. M. una bellissima commedia" (Gondi, no pagination).

16 On the similar political context for Henrietta Maria's appearance in Anne of Austria's 1624 court ballet, see Gough, "A Newly Discovered Performance."

17 Professor Orrell's transcript for this document, which he has graciously sent to me in private correspondence, reads: "elle [the Queen] me dit comme elle preparoit une Commedie p. la Naissance du Roy, que seroit p^r. la fin du mois prochain qu'elle faisoit resiter par les mesme dem^{lles}. de laut^{r}e. [l'autre?] qui feust faitte estant la mesme quelle avoit faitte au Louvre estant fille."

often than has been thought hitherto" (91).[18] I would add that this correspondence provides further confirmation that just as her elder sisters Elisabeth and Christine had done in the 1611 *Bradamante*, so Henrietta Maria herself took speaking roles on the French court stage. Cize's correspondence also teaches us something quite important about the relationship between Henrietta's own acting history in Paris and her later proclivities, in England, as patron of other amateur actresses. The 1635 performance by Henrietta's ladies, we learn, was directly indebted to the queen's own performance history as a princess of France. In 1635, in other words, Henrietta Maria directed her ladies to act in a play that she herself had acted in, as a girl, at the Louvre. In this way, she personally facilitated the translation to England of French court customs with which she was directly familiar: traditions whereby royal women and their female companions might take speaking parts before invited members of the court and foreign representatives.

Women had danced and on occasion even acted at the English court long before Henrietta Maria's queenship, of course. Italian actresses, for example,

---

18   Orrell points out that Whitehall was prepared for a pastoral, perhaps an early production of *Florimène*, on 19 November, 1635, but that Cize on the other hand "twice calls the play intended for 19 November 'la Commedie', while he describes *Florimène* as a 'Ballet'." So it is possible that this November production was not *Florimène* but rather a separate play. This conjecture, then, sends us back to Cize's letter of October 18, which reports that according to the queen, this November production was to be performed by the same ladies who had performed "in the one that was staged before, being the same one that she had played in at the Louvre when she was a girl." That another play had indeed been "staged before" is substantiated by a different letter Cize authored that summer. Dated 22 August, 1635, this letter mentions a performance the previous day involving Henrietta Maria's ladies: "I must tell you that the comedy that was played yesterday before the queen by the ladies was very lovely ... " (Orrell's transcript reads: "il fault que je die que la Commedie qui feust joue hier advent la Reine par les damoiselles a esté fort belle ... "). It is this play performed on August 21 n.s., then, that Cize later refers to as "the one that was staged before, being the same one that she had played in at the Louvre when she was a girl." The 1634–5 sponsorship of several French plays by the queen may have been part of a more general strategy signaling her renewed allegiance to all things French, including French domestic and foreign policies. On the relationship between the queen and Richelieu during this period and its impact on our understanding of *Florimène*'s production in 1635, see Britland. Caroline Hibbard has suggested that in this instance Henrietta Maria need not necessarily have been softening her attitude toward Richelieu; rather, she may instead have been paying renewed attention to all things French given that England at this time was in deep negotiation with France for a possible alliance (private correspondence). For evidence of additional English court performances sponsored and performed by Henrietta Maria, see Ravelhofer.

had entertained Elizabeth I on at least one occasion (Gilder, 60; Barasch; Thompson, 104). And with the arrival in 1603 of Queen Anna, wife of James I (of England and VI of Scotland), royal and noble women became more frequent sponsors of masques, performing leading parts as silent dancers (Barroll, 75–6; Lewalski, 15–42; Thompson, 106; Tomlinson 1995, 28–73; Wynne-Davies 1996, 80). Clare McManus has recently traced numerous instances in which under Anna's influence, the Jacobean court was exposed to a female masquing tradition which "pushed upon constraints of genre and convention," thus forming a "constituent part of the progression of the early modern woman towards a less restricted stage performance" (McManus, 210–11). Anna and her ladies did not speak or sing in masques or plays, but as McManus argues, the masque genre's limits on aristocratic and royal speech for both men and women led to an increasing non-verbal expressivity of textualized dancing bodies, women's bodies in particular. And it was under Anna, as McManus has shown, that "the female masquing voice was first heard [in England] in White's 1617 *Cupid's Banishment*," a masque performed not at Whitehall before the king but in Anna's honor at Greenwich by pupils of a Deptford girl's school (McManus, 210, 164–201).

What changed under Henrietta Maria's influence, then, was not so much the fact of women's performance in England but its expanded scope at the very top of the social hierarchy. At the royal court after Henrietta's arrival in 1625, women's theatrical activity occurred with greater frequency and in new forms, for the young queen and her ladies not only danced but themselves took speaking parts in plays performed for the king. Before Henrietta became queen, the education enjoyed by women at the English royal court would not regularly have included that training in memorization, elocution, and gesture that came from rehearsing and performing in stage plays. Beginning with Henrietta Maria's first winter in her new country, however, the situation changed: under her aegis, female performance activities at court soon integrated practices formerly reserved, in London at least, for professional male actors and, occasionally, foreign actresses.

Elsewhere I have traced the ways in which one significant theatrical innovation in Henrietta Maria's English masques – her use of a virtuoso singer-actress in *Tempe Restored* (1632) – derives less from the fact that in the queen's native France, as opposed to England, professional actresses might be seen regularly on the public stage, and more from casting choices characteristic of queens' court ballets, practices with which Henrietta herself would have been familiar in France either personally or through knowledge of her mother's most famous ballets a generation previously.[19] But to what extent did Henrietta Maria's

---

19 Gough, " 'Not as Myself.' " On this singer-actress see also Gossett; Orgel 1996, 5–6; Tomlinson, 2003; and Knowles.

specifically theatrical (as opposed to masquing) activities draw on French performance traditions? More specifically, in what ways might the stage plays she acted in England – *Artenice* (21 February, 1626) and *The Shepherds' Paradise* (performed 9 January, 1633 and probably repeated on 2 February of that year) – witness similar practices to the ones we have traced in Elisabeth's *Bradamante*?

In February 1626, less than a year after she crossed the Channel, Henrietta Maria and her French ladies performed speaking parts in *Artenice*, a pastoral based on Racan's *Les Bergeries*. According to Caroline Hibbard (25), this production shows "how quickly and resolutely" the new queen embarked upon the project of mediating French customs for the English court. I would argue that such cultural work is evident in not only the play's national origins and language of delivery but also, less obviously, its organizing framework. The February 1626 production of *Artenice* exemplifies several characteristics that we have studied previously in connection with Elisabeth's *Bradamante*. First, just as Elisabeth's production was described by Malherbe as "la comédie de Madame" and by Marie de Medici as "la comédie de ma fille," so Henrietta's 1626 *Artenice* is described by Amerigo Salvetti, the Florentine agent in London, as "her beautiful pastoral" ("sua bellissima pastorale").[20] This does not mean, as Bentley and other scholars have assumed, that Henrietta Maria authored the play text – at least not in the modern sense of "authorship." What Salvetti's phrasing does indicate, however, is that like Elisabeth before her, Henrietta Maria actively initiated and shaped her own production.[21] Second, just as Elisabeth both headed her "compagnie" and acted a leading role in her play, so too Henrietta Maria organized her troupe and was its lead performer, a fact confirmed in a letter by Sir Benjamin Rudyerd: "The *demoiselles* mean to present a French pastoral wherein the Queen is principal actress" (Orrell 1979, 11). Third, the production process for Henrietta's *Artenice*, like Elisabeth's *Bradamante*, involved diligent rehearsal. From Rudyerd's letter we learn that *Artenice* was in preparation as early as 18 December, 1625; given its performance date of 24 February, 1626, we can therefore deduce a rehearsal period of at least two months. Moreover, Henrietta took a direct role in rehearsing her female companions; according to Salvetti, "On the day of carnival, for which Tuesday was set aside, she [the queen] acted in her beautiful pastoral, assisted

---

20 Letter dated 6 March 1626, as cited and translated in Orrell 1979, 11. I am grateful to Professor Orrell for sending me his transcript of this phrase in the original language.

21 For an explanation of how mistranslations of this phrase led to G. E. Bentley's erroneous attribution of this play to Henrietta Maria's authorship see Orrell, 1979, 11. For a helpful redefinition of masque authorship under the patronage of queens, see Wynne-Davies.

by twelve of her ladies *whom she had trained since Christmas*" (Orrell 1979, 10–11, emphasis mine).

Given such sustained training, it is not surprising that just as French spectators at the 1611 *Bradamante* described the princess's performance as having been executed "si bien et si gentiment" and with "bonne grace," so Italian observers described *Artenice*'s actresses in similarly glowing terms. The Venetian ambassador to London, for example, remarked on the "rich scenery and dresses" and Henrietta Maria's "remarkable acting" (Cotton, 39). Salvetti's letters are even more specific; having noted the queen's efforts in training her ladies for her "beautiful pastoral," this Florentine agent continues: "Everything went off very well, the decoration and the changing of the scene as well as the gestures and the elocution of the ladies, among whom the queen outdid all the rest" (Orrell 1979, 11). When female characters stepped into the public street, in comedies, they risked signaling their identity as courtesans (Henke, 101). By contrast, *Artenice*, with its rural, pastoral setting, enabled its actresses greater freedom of physical movement while avoiding association with prostitution. Like Garnier's *Bradamante*, moreover, Racan's *Artenice* was a tragicomedy designed, in part, to showcase the theatrical virtuosity of its eponymous female lead: moving from tragic impossibility to comic resolution in a plot focusing on the romantic trials of the princess Artenice, this play provided a useful vehicle by which its chief woman actor might, by acting a range of emotions, display that histrionic versatility for which commedia actresses were so famous.

Unlike foreigners present at the 1626 production of *Artenice*, however, English contemporaries write nothing of the women actors' skill or lack thereof. Instead, they focus on the challenge this production posed to prevailing English notions of courtly female decorum. In the words of John Chamberlain, "On Shrove Tuesday the Queen and her women had a masque or pastoral play at Somerset House, wherein herself acted a part, and some of the rest were disguised like men with beards. I have known the time when this would have seemed a strange sight, to see a Queen act in a play, but *tempora mutantur et nos* [times change and so must we]" (Orgel and Strong, 1: 384–5).[22] European courts had already changed with the times, it seems: for Elisabeth's 1611 *Bradamante*, as we have seen, royal and titled girls who took speaking parts (including those who played in masculine, martial attire) were received with admiration. It is not surprising, therefore, that foreign agents in London, while noting English reactions such as Chamberlain's, qualified such comments by adding their own more favorable judgments. These agents, after all, were part of the cosmopolitan European court culture to which Henrietta Maria's production of *Artenice* seems to have addressed itself. This was a world in

---

22 For other similar responses see Tomlinson 1992, 189.

which amateur women's performance was the rule rather than the exception; where women's histrionic activity could connote not just lasciviousness but also, thanks to the likes of Vincenza Armani and Isabella Andreini, its beautiful and virtuous opposite; and where, it seems, acting by elite women, modeling itself on such diva-actresses but in tragicomedies and pastorals for restricted audiences rather than commercial comedies and farces, seemed constitutive of, rather than a threat to, the graceful civility on which courts prided and defined themselves.

When in England Henrietta Maria performed the French play *Artenice* in her native language, she forcefully asserted her status as a daughter of France with all the associated prerogatives. In this way, she arguably deployed French traditions of women's courtly self-display both as a means of capturing the king's attention and as a vehicle for social, religious, and political defiance. That winter, the royal marriage had become stormy. Alarmed by his wife's independent mindset and actions, the king had begun taking steps to isolate her from the French members of her retinue. Her household's makeup was part of the queen's legal prerogative as agreed to in the marriage contract, yet Charles and Buckingham, determined to check what they perceived as her unfortunate willfulness, had begun to challenge her rights in this area. Caroline Hibbard has suggested that at this period in time, Henrietta saw herself as locked in competition with Buckingham for influence over the king; because Buckingham was famed as a dancer and general performer, the remarkable energies that Henrietta devoted toward plays and masques during the first years of her marriage may thus be seen as efforts to outdo her husband's favorite (Hibbard, 25). If, from a French perspective, as I have suggested, skilled amateur acting by royal women was seen to enhance, rather than diminish, their prestige, it is also plausible that from Henrietta Maria's viewpoint, producing and acting in a French play at this juncture was a useful vehicle through which she might forcefully assert the royal status she enjoyed not primarily as Charles I's queen but also *independently* of her married station, that is, as a member of the French royal family. The queen's Frenchified acting, then, may have constituted both a plea for Charles's attention and a kind of local resistance, an insistence on her prerogatives not only as royal consort but also as a French princess.

By 1633, the year in which Henrietta Maria produced and acted in *The Shepherds' Paradise*, her marriage had entered its halcyon days. This play, too, was a pastoral tragicomedy, and hence presumably showcased the actresses' skill in depicting a range of physical and emotional states. It was originally intended by the queen as a present for the king's birthday: her Frenchified theatrical prerogatives, formerly possibly a site of resistance to Charles, Buckingham, and Englishness more generally, were now exercised expressly to achieve what Castiglione had deemed a most praiseworthy aim for female courtiers: the entertainment of courtly men (Brooks, 193–4). It is particularly significant, therefore, that *The Shepherds' Paradise* was written and performed in not French but English – part of Henrietta's gift to Charles, perhaps, being this display of honoring the English tongue. To this task the queen seems to have applied herself with, ironically, a rather French courtly insistence on skillful elocution and gesture. In 1626 *Artenice* had been rehearsed for two months. *The Shepherds' Paradise*, though, was in preparation for approximately six, with frequent rehearsals – sometimes daily. Regarding these extended preparations we can learn much from Salvetti's letters. On 3 November, 1632 the Florentine agent writes that "[t]he queen, together with sundry Court ladies, is going to rehearse a pastoral in order to stage it at her palace in London when she has returned there. Her Majesty will take part in the pastoral herself, and without dispute it will be of the best, so great is the grace she shows in all her actions" (Orrell 1979, 17). On November 19 he continues: "Her Majesty the queen rehearses her pastoral every day. Nevertheless she will not be able to perform it on the 29th, the king's birthday, because none of the ladies performing in it with her are ready, neither is the apparatus for the scenery, and so on" (17–18). As of January 14, rehearsals were still underway, and Salvetti's letters of November 26 and December 3 further clarify that the queen's pastoral could not yet "be made ready" largely because "the performers [were] not all ready" (18).

As early as September, the cast had begun to receive daily acting lessons by Joseph Taylor. This we learn from John Pory's letter to Viscount Scudamore on 15 September, 1632: writing of the queen's daily rehearsals, Pory adds that "Taylor the prime actor at the Globe goes every day to teach them action" (Feil, 109–10; see also Poynting 1997, viii–ix). This arrangement, Melissa Aaron claims, testifies to an increased theatrical professionalism at the Stuart court due, in large part, to Henrietta Maria's influence. Such efforts to acquire histrionic virtuosity on the part of royal and noble female actors, I would add, may have been entirely new to England but not to Henrietta herself. In France, as I have argued, Henrietta Maria's sister Elisabeth had emulated professional commedia actresses in the amateur realm. Henrietta Maria's use of an *English* professional player to train herself and her fellow amateur actresses recalls such practices but takes them one step further, literally employing available professional expertise.

Contemporary discussions by foreign audience members suggest that her efforts paid off: the French ambassador, for example, reported that the queen "excelled really all others both in acting and singing" (quoted in Tomlinson 1995, 90), while Salvetti, describing the first performance on 9 January, 1633 in a letter written two days later, emphasized the production's virtuoso acting:

> Last Wednesday her Majesty the queen performed her pastoral; the scenic apparatus was very lovely, but so was the beauty of the performers, and of the queen above all the rest, who with her new English and the grace with which she showed it off,

together with her regal gestures and actions on the stage, outdid all the other ladies, though they acted their parts too with the greatest variety. (Orrell 1979, 18)

Salvetti here makes special note of the queen's newly demonstrated skill in English pronunciation while describing such on-stage linguistic display as full of "grace." Moreover, the queen's gestures and actions are here deemed "regal": the skilled and disciplined kinesis of the actor's craft is perceived not as contrary to her royal station but as thoroughly befitting her social role "above all the rest." And although Henrietta Maria's co-stars cannot touch her excellence, they too are described as having acted their parts "with the greatest variety": in this phrase we may detect echoes of the terms of praise typically given the leading ladies of commedia dell'arte companies, actresses whose fame derived in part from their remarkable, and remarkably virtuous, dramatic versatility.

Conclusion

As early as 1626 through till at least 1635, then, Henrietta Maria took nothing less than a central role in transplanting to English soil a vigorous tradition of women's performance at the French court, one that in turn had modeled itself on professional theater from Italy – particularly the organizational and histrionic roles such theater afforded its most talented women. Henrietta Maria's upbringing in a French court culture that fostered such opportunities for women's performance positioned her uniquely within her new English context.[23] As a result, while the theatrical activities on which she immediately embarked initially shocked her new countrymen, to the experienced eyes of Europeans these same performances appeared quite decorous, even beautiful.

---

23 Sarah Poynting notes that Henrietta Maria's arrival in England from a foreign court where women had long participated in political factionalism must have "increased the likelihood that women in her own court would follow suit" and, "talent aside," links such political self-confidence to the daring displayed by the actresses in *The Shepherds' Paradise* (2003, 180–811). Poynting also notes that the somewhat lower status of the particular court women who acted in this play, compared to that of the female courtiers in Henrietta's masques, indicates the relative respectability these two performance modes held (2003, 171). I agree with this assertion, but here attempt to further nuance current understandings of women's theatrical activity in the period by emphasizing the many ways in which royal and courtly women's stage plays associated themselves with the moral and intellectual prestige of professional Italian diva-actresses in order to more closely associate elite women's acting with "civility."

This argument, I hope, will serve to debunk claims that this Stuart queen with her frivolous pastimes presided over that decline of English drama that Alfred Harbage has attributed to the Caroline period. In 1936 Harbage described *The Shepherds' Paradise* as "the worst play in the language" and disparaged not only its male author but also its female actors: "One cannot believe that these fragile-brained ladies of the court committed to memory such limitless stretches of opaque prose" (14). According to Harbage, as we have seen, Henrietta Maria's amateur plays at court – most notably *The Shepherds' Paradise* – must have suffered from their actresses' lack of experience and histrionic ability. Information that the rehearsal period for *The Shepherds' Paradise* was extended in part due to lack of readiness no doubt led Harbage to conjecture that the play's final performance, too, was marked by poor acting. Yet if Henrietta Maria had not been particularly demanding regarding her troupe's histrionic skill, one might ask, why would she have prolonged the production past the king's birthday, the date on which she had planned to honor Charles with the performance?[24] Such extended delay, rather than supporting notions that *The Shepherds' Paradise* was poorly acted, may well point to the queen's enforcement of exacting standards, her unwillingness to perform this pastoral for the king until it could be done right.

As noted by Sarah Poynting, critics have typically dwelt on jokes and complaints about the length and intelligibility of *The Shepherds' Paradise* while slighting instances of praise for the play. Indeed, Poynting argues against the idea that contemporaries found this play dull (1997, xiii). Nonetheless, negative critical bias has, until recently, characterized assessments of not just this pastoral but also Henrietta's theatrical activities *tout court*. In 1967, for example, Jean Parrish and William Jackson cited as authoritative Harbage's comments about Henrietta Maria and her troupe in order to argue that an edition of *Artenice* printed in England in 1626 must have been used as a promptbook for its "frivolous" royal actress and her equally unskilled acting companions.[25] Such unsubstantiated assertions belie the increasingly sustained and serious nature of women's preparation for histrionic court performance during the Caroline period, itself a function, I have argued, of Henrietta Maria's French (or rather, Franco-Italian) heritage.

---

24 For this idea I am indebted to Peter Parolin.

25 Having discovered that an abridged edition of the play text, based on the 1625 Paris edition, was printed and bound in London, Parrish and Jackson posit that the purpose of this booklet was to act as promptbook for women performers untrained in memorization of lines (190). However, the edition might have been issued as a commemorative volume for the few invited spectators rather than as a prompt book, and the manuscript notes describing production elements that are found in the Harvard Library copy could well have been inserted by one such spectator.

Henrietta's motives for energetically sponsoring and performing in female court spectacle have, I argue, been misunderstood. Sophie Tomlinson (1992, 1995) has helpfully focused our attention on the body of satiric discourse denigrating women's cultural production and consumption in England during this period, the most infamous instance being William Prynne's jibe at "women actors, notorious whores." Still largely ignored, however, is the question of why the queen and members of her court might have insisted on exercising such theatrical prerogatives even in the face of aggressive mockery. Without such an explanation, the queen remains vulnerable to charges of frivolity, of imposing her love of acting out of mere personal whim.[26] It is here that French precedents can best help us. Henrietta Maria's English stage plays exemplified a mode of courtly pastime new to England but by this point familiar to France, one in which amateur women actors at court, through sustained rehearsal, sought to acquire for themselves and display before others a kinetic and verbal grace which we might otherwise associate only with professional actresses of the period, but which was in fact central to the self-understanding of European courts as centers of civility.[27] Untrained in continental codes by which such virtuosity might connote intellectual and moral *virtù* as well as elevated social status, English spectators were initially taken aback by the queen declaiming in plays, an activity which to them seemed incongruous with regal greatness. But for Henrietta Maria and members of foreign courts present at these English spectacles, a royal or noble woman's emulation of theatrical activities made famous throughout Europe by virtuous Italian diva-actresses – circumscribed within pastoral and tragicomic genres performed before elite audiences – constituted not a threat to that woman's social status but rather the opposite.

---

26 Tomlinson (2003) convincingly argues that Henrietta Maria's acting, together with her use of a professional singer-actress in the 1632 masque *Tempe Restored*, appealed to European aesthetics, most notably a desire for "theatrical vibrancy" and emotional depth in on-stage female characters. Stressing the concrete ways in which Italian singer-actresses served as models for this kind of amateur female performance, my argument here emphasizes the attention to skill and grace that defined this new theatrical aesthetic, as well as its international political consequences: the ways in which such performances of female "vibrancy" could function metonymically to signal a host court's own desirability and civility, reflecting that court's greatness not only back to itself but also to an audience of foreign ambassadors.

27 On skilled self-display in musical performance, its centrality to gendered definitions of courtliness, and the relationships that subsequently resulted between professional musicians and noblemen and women in late sixteenth-century France, see Brooks (150–67, 191–244).

Works Cited

Aaron, Melissa. " 'A Strange sight, to see a Queen act in a play': Henrietta Maria and Theatrical Professionalism in Early Stuart England." Unpublished paper, Shakespeare Association of America, Montréal, April 2000.

Andrews, Richard. "L'attrice e la cantante fra Cinquecento e Seicento. La presenza femminile in palcoscenico." *Teatro e Musica. Écritures vocale et scenique*. Ed. Margherita Orsino. Toulouse: Presses Universitaires du Mirail, 1999, 27–43.

Bapst, Germain. *Essai sur l'histoire du Théatre*. Paris: Hachette, 1893.

Barasch, Frances. "Italian Actresses in Shakespeare's World: Vittoria and Isabella." *Shakespeare Bulletin* 19.3 (Summer 2001): 5–9.

Barroll, Leeds. *Anna of Denmark, Queen of England*. Philadelphia: University of Pennsylvania Press, 2001.

Batiffol, Louis. *La Vie Intime d'une Reine de France au XVIIe Siècle*. Paris: Calmann-Lévy, 1906.

Boucher, Jacqueline. *Societe et Mentalites Author de Henri III*. PhD thesis, University of Lyon II, 1977. 4 vols. Lille: Atelier Reproduction des Theses Universite de Lille III; Paris: Librairie Honore Champion, 1981.

Britland, Karen. "*Florimène*: the Author and the Occasion." *Review of English Studies* 53.212 (November 2002): 475–83.

Brooks, Jeanice. *Courtly Song in Late Sixteenth-Century France*. Chicago: University of Chicago Press, 2000.

Bryce, Judith. "The Theatrical Activities of Palla di Lorenzo Strozzi in Lyon in the 1540s." *Theatre of the English and Italian Renaissance*. Ed. J. R. Mulryne and Margaret Shrewring. New York: St. Martin's Press, 1991, 59–63.

Carmona, Michel. *Marie de Médicis*. Paris: Fayard, 1981.

Cotton, Nancy. *Women Playwrights in England c. 1363–1750*. Lewisburg: Bucknell University Press, 1980.

Feil, J. P. "Dramatic References from the Scudamore Papers." *Shakespeare Survey* 11 (1958): 107–16.

Gilder, Rosamond. *Enter the Actress: The First Women in the Theatre*. Boston: Houghton Mifflin, 1931.

Gondi, Giovanni Battista. Letter to the Grand Duke dated October 5, 1623. Archivio di Stato, Florence. Mediceo del Principato, filza 4637.

Gossett, Suzanne. " 'Man-maid, begone!': Women in Masques." *English Literature Renaissance* 18.1 (Winter 1998): 96–113.

Gough, Melinda. " 'Not as Myself': the Queen's Voice in *Tempe Restored*." *Modern Philology* 101.1 (August 2003): 48–67.

———. "A Newly Discovered Performance by Henrietta Maria." *Huntington Library Quarterly* 65.3&4 (2003): 435–47.

Grand Larousse de la Langue Française. 7 vols. Paris: Larousse, 1972.

Green, Mary Anne Everett. *The Letters of Queen Henrietta Maria*. London: Richard Bentley, 1857.

Harbage, Alfred. *Cavalier Drama: An Historical and Critical Supplement to the Study of the Elizabethan and Restoration Stage*. New York: Modern Language Association, 1936.

Hayden, J. Michael. "Continuity in the France of Henry IV and Louis XIII: French Foreign Policy, 1598–1615." *Journal of Modern History* 45 (1973): 1–23.
Henke, Robert. *Performance and Literature in the Commedia dell'Arte.* Cambridge: Cambridge University Press, 2002.
Héroard, Jean. *Journal de Ma Vie.* 2 vols. Paris: 1868.
Hibbard, Caroline. "Translating Royalty: Henrietta Maria and the Transition from Princess to Queen." *The Court Historian* 5.1 (May 2000): 15–28.
King, Mary, trans. *Marie de Médicis and the French Court in the XVIIth Century: translated from the French of Louis Batiffol.* Ed. H. W. Carless Davis. London: Chatto & Windus, 1908.
Knowles, James. " 'Can ye not tell a man from a marmoset?': Apes and Others on the Early Modern Stage." *Renaissance Beasts: Of Animals, Humans, and Other Wonderful Creatures.* Ed. Erica Fudge. Urbana: University of Illinois Press, 138–63.
Lacour, Léopold. *Les Premières Actrices Françaises.* Paris: Librarie Française, 1921.
Lalanne, M. L., ed. *Oeuvres Complètes de Malherbe.* 5 vols. Paris: 1862.
Lanson, Gustave. "Etudes sur les origins de la tragédie classique en France." *Révue d'histoire littéraire* 10 (1903): 223–4.
Lewalski, Barbara Kiefer. *Writing Women in Jacobean England.* Cambridge, MA: Harvard University Press, 1993.
Littré, Émile. *Dictionnaire de la Langue Française.* Paris: Librarie Hachette, 1874.
Mackay, Janet. *Little Madam: A Biography of Henrietta Maria.* London: G. Bell and Sons, 1939.
MacNeil, Anne. *Music and the Life and Work of Isabella Andreini: Humanistic Attitudes toward Music, Poetry, and Theater during the late Sixteenth and Early Seventeenth Centuries.* PhD diss. University of Chicago, 1994.
———. "The Divine Madness of Isabella Andreini." *Journal of the Royal Musical Association* 120 (1995): 195–215.
———. "A Portrait of the Artist as a Young Woman." *Musical Quarterly* 83.2 (Summer 1999): 247–79.
———. *Music and Women of the Commedia dell'Arte in the Late Sixteenth Century.* Oxford: Oxford University Press, 2003.
Marrow, Deborah. *The Art Patronage of Maria de' Medici.* 1978; Ann Arbor: UMI Research Press, 1982.
McManus, Clare. *Women on the Renaissance Stage: Anna of Denmark and Female Masquing in the Stuart Court 1590–1619.* Manchester: Manchester University Press, 2002.
Nicholson, Eric. "Romance as Role Model: Early Female Performances of *Orlando Furioso* and *Gerusalemme liberata.*" *Renaissance Transactions: Ariosto and Tasso.* Ed.Valeria Finucci. Durham: Duke University Press, 1999, 246–69.
Orgel, Stephen. *Impersonations.* Cambridge: Cambridge University Press, 1996.
——— and Roy Strong. *Inigo Jones: The Theatre of the Stuart Court.* 2 vols. Berkeley: University of California Press, 1973.
Orrell, John. "The London Court Stage in the Savoy Correspondence, 1613–1675." *Theatre Research International* 4.2 (1978): 79–94.
———. "Amerigo Salvetti and the London Court Theatre, 1616–1640." *Theatre Survey* 20.1 (May 1979): 1–26.

Parrish, Jean, and William A. Jackson. "Racan's *L'Artenice*, an Addition to the English Canon." *Harvard Library Bulletin* 14.2 (Spring 1960): 183–90.

Peacock, John. "The French Element in Inigo Jones's Masque Designs." *The Court Masque*. Ed. David Lindley. Manchester: Manchester University Press, 1984, 149–68.

Poynting, Sarah, ed. *The Shepherds' Paradise by Walter Montagu*. Malone Society Reprints, 1997.

———. "'In the Name of All the Sisters': Henrietta Maria's Notorious Whores." *Women and Culture at the Courts of the Stuart Queens*. Ed. Clare McManus. Houndmills, Basingstoke, Hampshire; New York: Palgrave Macmillan, 2003, 163–85.

Prunières, Henri. "Ronsard et les fêtes de Cour." *La Revue Musicale* (May 1924): 27–44.

Ravelhofer, Barbara. "Bureaucrats and Courtly Cross Dressers in the *Shrovetide Masque* and the *Shepherd's Paradise*." *English Literature Renaissance* 29.1 (Winter 1999): 75–96.

Rigal, Eugene. *Le Théatre Français Avant La Période Classique*. Paris: Hachette, s.d.

Schwartz, I. A. *The Commedia dell'Arte and its Influence on French Comedy in the Seventeenth Century*. Paris: H. Samuel, 1933.

Scott, Virginia. "*Ariosto's Orlando Furioso*: Performance at the Valois and Bourbon Courts." *The Court Historian* 8.2 (December 2003): 177–87.

Shapiro, Michael. "The Introduction of Actresses in England: Delay or Defensiveness?" *Enacting Gender on the English Renaissance Stage*. Ed.Viviana Comensoli and Anne Russell. Urbana: University of Illinois Press, 1999, 177–217.

Thompson, Ann. "Women/'Women' and the Stage." *Women and Literature in Britain, 1500–1700*. Ed. Helen Wilcox. Cambridge: Cambridge University Press, 1996, 100–116.

Tomlinson, Sophie. "She That Plays the King: Henrietta Maria and the Threat of the Actress in Caroline Culture." *The Politics of Tragicomedy*. Ed. Gordon McMullan and Jonathan Hope. London and New York: Routledge, 1992, 189–207.

———. "Theatrical Women: The Female Actor in English Theatre and Drama 1603–1670." PhD dissertation, Darwin College, Cambridge University, 1995.

———. "Theatrical Vibrancy on the Caroline Court Stage: *Tempe Restored* and *The Shepherds' Paradise*." *Women and Culture at the Courts of the Stuart Queens*. Ed. Clare McManus. Houndmills, Basingstoke, Hampshire; New York: Palgrave Macmillan, 2003, 186–203.

Wiley, W. L. (David). *The Early Public Theatre in France*. Cambridge, MA: Harvard University Press, 1960.

Wynne-Davies, Marion. "The Queen's Masque: Renaissance Women and the Seventeenth-Century Court Masque." *Renaissance Drama by Women: Texts and Documents*. Ed. S. P. Ceresano and Marion Wynne-Davies. Routledge, 1996, 79–104.

Yates, Frances A. *French Academies of the Sixteenth Century*. London: The Warburg Institute, 1947.

PART IV
BEYOND THE STAGE

PART IV
BEYOND THE STAGE

Chapter 10

The Venetian Theater of Aletheia Talbot, Countess of Arundel

Peter Parolin

In April 1622, Aletheia Talbot, Countess of Arundel, the highest-ranking noblewoman in England, appeared twice in the *Collegio* of the Venetian Senate to defend herself against anonymous accusations that she had played a part in the Foscarini affair, a treason scandal that was rocking Venice.[1] Rumors were circulating that at her palace on the Grand Canal, the Countess had hosted illegal meetings where the Venetian diplomat Antonio Foscarini betrayed state secrets to the ambassadors of the pope and emperor. Foscarini was murdered in prison for his role in the affair, but was posthumously exonerated when the charges against him were found to be false.[2] Lady Arundel was more successful in her self-defense: after her two appearances before the Doge, the Collegio cleared her name, insisting that despite the rumors, they had never entertained any suspicion against her.[3] As proof of their good will, they sent the Countess gifts of confections and waxworks.

But while Lady Arundel did not abet treason, her presence in the Collegio established her as a player in this notorious Venetian drama. When reports of the affair reached England, John Chamberlain immediately cast it in theatrical terms, writing to Dudley Carleton that "sure in mine opinion yt was a play never plaide before to see a Lady of that qualitie go to justifie her selfe in the

---

1   My thanks to Pamela Brown, Susan Frye, and Ashgate's anonymous reader for commenting so astutely on this essay, as well as to David Howarth for generously sharing citations and advice, and to Sara Roger at Arundel Castle for graciously assisting me in the Castle's archives.
2   A chronology of the Foscarini affair, including the discovery of his innocence, can be found in Smith, 1:183–90 and Hervey, 201–19. Foscarini was strangled in prison and on 21 April, 1622 his body was displayed publicly, "hanging by one leg on the gallows in the Piazza" (Smith,1:184). The very next day, April 22, Lady Arundel made her first appearance before the Collegio of the Senate.
3   The Collegio was a committee within the larger Senate, "composed of the Doge and twenty-five principal senators, to whom foreign affairs and matters of general policy were entrusted" (Smith, 1:53).

college upon so little ground as ydle rumors" (2:435). While Chamberlain implied that the public theatricality of the affair discredited an elite woman like the Countess, I will suggest that Lady Arundel exploited the Foscarini affair as a theatrical opportunity that she could turn to her own advantage. Through performance, Lady Arundel sought in Venice not only to clear her name but also to assert a greater degree of personal control over her public identity and to gain access to a measure of participation in public affairs.

This essay will situate Lady Arundel's elaborately theatrical self-defense in the multiple contexts of early modern women's performance. From the Countess's perspective, the most important context may have been the English court, where she appeared in three of Queen Anna's masques and where effective theatrical self-presentation was an essential ingredient of political success. Equally relevant, if more suspect to Lady Arundel's English audience, was the context of Italian performance in which women featured prominently, from the professional actresses essential to the success of theatrical troupes to the *cortigiane oneste* who dazzled listeners with demonstrations of their rhetorical proficiency.[4] Finally, it is important to consider Lady Arundel's performativity in the context of popular performance spaces in England, from the stages of the public theaters with their dramas of women on trial to the urban neighborhoods where real women displayed their wit as a defense against misogynist commonplaces.[5] In all these contexts, women adopted the tools of the theater to promote their own agendas in the midst of complex situations. Lady Arundel's performance in the Venetian Collegio can thus be seen as an act of high-stakes theater in which she exploited elements of English and Italian theatrical experience to fashion herself into a representative of her husband and her country even as she asserted her independent right to pursue desired social and political goals.

If we look solely at Lady Arundel's exoneration by the Venetian authorities, we might conclude that theatrical techniques offered women an effective way to establish a desired public narrative of the self. However, Lady Arundel's performance in Venice elicited critical commentary as well as praise and it seems unlikely that her Venetian theater helped her achieve any larger political

---

4   For the centrality of the actresses to professional troupes in Italy, see McGill, especially p. 68; for the skills and the social world of the *cortigiane oneste*, see Margaret Rosenthal's rich analysis of Veronica Franco.

5   Not only did the theaters stage dramas of women on trial, but they presented those dramas to audiences that included substantial numbers of women. Scholars like Alison Findlay and Pamela Brown compellingly argue that our interpretations of early modern culture benefit from acknowledging the presence of women as audience members, auditors, and effective participants in cultural events (see Findlay; and Brown, esp. "Introduction," 1–32). For an analysis of non-elite women on scaffolds, see Dolan.

goals in England. From this larger perspective, the difficulties as well as the successes of women's public performance become apparent. In early modern England, there was hostility toward the theatrical woman, even though women's performance, as new research is making clear, was part of the cultural landscape on both the elite and popular levels.[6] A woman stepping into an explicitly performative mode could trigger criticism that she was threatening both her class position and gender identity; in the process her strategic purposes for performing could easily be lost. The example of Lady Arundel's Venetian theater is interesting, then, because it shows one woman attempting to negotiate this difficult cultural terrain, and it indicates that despite the practical and ideological impediments to women's performance, some determined women still sought to intervene in this field, poaching elements of the theatricality they knew from a variety of cultural milieux, adapting them, and putting them to use in unexpected contexts.

Lady Arundel's theatricality is rooted in the circumstances of her life and her continual search for avenues of self-expression. Yet Lady Arundel's accomplishments were long overlooked in favor of scholarly focus on the great art collection amassed by her husband, Thomas Howard, Earl of Arundel.[7] As early as 1911, Lionel Cust complained that "Arundel's biographers have hitherto done scant justice to the memory of [his] wife, Alethea Talbot, to whose wealth and energy the formation of the great Arundel collection must, to some extent, be attributed" (97). Only recently has the Countess begun garnering significant attention, with David Howarth calling her "co-creator of the most varied collection in early modern Europe" (1998, 132–3). She accompanied the Earl and Inigo Jones on a trip to Italy in 1613–14, where Jones instructed the Arundels in Italian painting and architecture. Lady Arundel's presence on the Italian trip is telling at a time when many writers discouraged women from traveling.[8] Further, the Arundels visited Rome, a suspect destination for English subjects in those years; indeed there was some

---

6 In this volume, see Stokes, Mirabella, and Korda for women's theatricality in a popular context and Campbell, Crawford, and Gough for elite women's theatricality.

7 For an interesting point of comparison on the subject of an elite woman's relationship with her husband, see Crawford on Margaret Cavendish in this volume.

8 See, for example, Thomas Palmer, who says in a treatise on travel that "[t]he Sex in most Countries prohibiteth women [from travel], who are rather for the house then the field; and to remaine home, then travaile into other Nations" (17). Lady Arundel's travels in particular occasioned critical commentary. When, after the Foscarini affair, she wished to travel from Venice to Spain to meet the Infanta, James I denied her request. The Florentine agent in London wrote to the Grand Duke with an account of the King's reaction: "Non essendo trovare da S.M. molto

talk at home that as prominent Catholics, the Arundels were up to no good in Rome (Howarth 1985a, 51). Yet, despite the climate of religious suspicion, the Earl never hesitated in bringing the Countess to Rome, writing to her that "I would wish you to see Rome well, for there are no more such places" (Howarth 1985a, 229). The Earl's letter expresses confidence in his wife's judgment and his delight in their shared pleasures.[9] Later his biographer would note that Countess sympathized "with her Lord in valuing all curious Arts" (Walker, 212). In the years following that early trip to Italy, Lady Arundel was actively involved in acquiring art treasures and cultivating relationships with artists and agents.[10] For her efforts, she was rewarded with dedications by artists and scholars: Tizianello dedicated to her his *Life of Titian* (Hervey, 200), and Francis Junius dedicated to her his English edition of *De Pictura Veterum* (Howarth 1985a, 80). Rubens and Van Dyck were among the artists who painted her portrait.[11]

For the Arundels, collecting no doubt expressed a genuine appreciation of art, but it also helped them create and maintain their pre-eminence among the Stuart aristocracy, efforts made all the more pointed by their sense of being unjustly denied the social position and material possessions they believed were rightly theirs. The Earl's grandfather, the fourth Duke of Norfolk, had been attainted and executed for his role in the Ridolfi plot against Elizabeth I. The Earl of Arundel worked unsuccessfully all his life to have his grandfather's dukedom restored; he also worked, more successfully, to reacquire the possessions that were historically attached to that title. Many of the Arundels' earliest purchases were the hereditary art treasures, houses, and lands forfeited in the attainder. Anastasia Novikova says of the Arundels that they spent "all

---

bene che una dama di questa qualita vada cosi vagando per il mondo" [Not being found very good by His Majesty that a lady of this quality should go wandering like this about the world] quoted in Howarth 1985b, 230 n.55).

9   In his draft will of 28 March, 1617, the Earl extravagantly professed his confidence in the Countess: "I must wth infinite humility & thankes unto Almighty God acknowledge that in her he hath given me more true happinesse & comforte then ever to any man wth a wife, for I doe publish & avowe unto the world that if I had all the wealth of a kingdome (I protest unto God) I durst as freely leave it all in her owne disposition as in my owne handes."

10 On Lady Arundel's influence in the world of fine arts, see Howarth 1998.

11 Daniel Mytens also painted companion portraits of the Countess and her husband. Analyzing the different gender codes governing these paintings, Anastasia Novikova concludes that the painting of the Countess limits Lady Arundel by defining her in terms of her husband, the primary focus of interest. Novikova's article is stimulating, although her focus is different from mine: where she explores the gendered conventions that circumscribe the Countess's portrait, I am interested in the way Lady Arundel exploited, recalibrated, and defied those conventions.

their lives trying to make their form match a content" (74); Stephen Orgel notes that their aggressive connoisseurship was designed to assert the Earl's status "as much by his taste as by his lineage" (2000, 259).[12] Lady Arundel was as protective of her status as her husband, insisting, for example, on her right to take precedence over the Countess of Nottingham as chief mourner at Queen Anna's funeral in 1619.[13]

The assertion of high status is always a largely theatrical endeavor: only by being performed can social forms produce political and cultural capital of the kind the Arundels desired. As David Bevington and Peter Holbrook put it, "status in a courtly society depends for its very existence upon display" (3). Unsurprisingly, then, the Arundels both appeared in the court masque, a central form of status performance, during the reign of James I. While the Earl performed in *Hymenaei, The Haddington Masque*, and *The Gypsies Metamorphosed*, the Countess played in *The Masque Of Beauty, The Masque of Queens*, and *Tethys' Festival*. (See fig. 10.1, Inigo Jones's costume sketch for the Countess of Arundel.) These masques propounded a powerful ideology in which aristocratic presence played an essential role in banishing discord and ensuring harmony: "the masquers are the noble ladies and gentlemen whose very presence provides the impetus for the idealized fictions of the usually slight plot" (Summers and Pebworth, 131).

Having performed in court masques, Lady Arundel drew on their tropes and techniques to defend herself years later when she was accused of involvement in the Foscarini scandal. Her virtue cast into question by unnamed rumormongers, she insisted on defending herself in front of the Venetian Senate; she insisted on receiving public vindication; and she insisted on humiliating Sir Henry Wotton, the English ambassador to Venice and the one man to whom she could trace the stories against her. Lady Arundel's public performance borrowed an ideology of aristocratic presence from the masques in order to counter what she claimed were scurrilous attacks. The fact that she was not wholly successful in dispelling criticism perhaps testifies to the limited scale of her version of the masque or to

---

12   Orgel's argument finds support in the 1617 version of the Earl's will, which stipulates, "that my sonne James Maltravers may succeede me in my love & reverence to Antiquities & all thinges of Art, I give unto him all my statues and pictures whatsoever wth all inscriptions." Later, Edward Walker wrote that during the Civil War, the Earl congratulated himself on having had the foresight to remove not only his family to the continent, away "from the Rage and Fury of the barbarous Multitude," but also "those rare and excellent Collections of Paintings and Designs, which by so long time and so vast Expence he had collected together" (Walker, 220). In both of these quotations, the Earl defines his lineage according to his taste; indeed the art objects themselves become a kind of posterity that he protects as carefully as he does his own family.

13   For an account of this episode, see Chamberlain, 2:232–3.

10.1   Atalanta in *Masque of Queens* (1609). Drawing by Inigo Jones. Reproduced by permission of the Duke of Devonshire and the Chatsworth Settlement Trustees. Photograph Survey, Courtauld Institute of Art.

its limited power outside of the protective environment of the English court. However, the fact that she succeeded to the extent she did suggests that court theatricals permitted the women who performed in them to imagine themselves as agents capable of acting independently on their own behalf, even in foreign cities and in the face of hostile accusers.

In using elements of the masque, Lady Arundel did more than simply assert her presence to dispel disruptive adversaries. Recent scholarship has suggested that even as the masques celebrated aristocratic community, they also provided room for competitive maneuvering within that community. Courtly entertainments, as Bevington and Holbrook note, were "attempts to garner, secure and enhance prestige at the heart of power"; the masque, "rather than being simply the expression of monarchical power, was available for use by other interests, and functioned at the intersection of rivalrous political discourses" (4, 9). In other words, the masques were an arena for the playing out of opposing ambitions within court circles. Martin Butler has called them "negotiations [that] can be understood as acts of accommodation or realignment, give and take between differently empowered participants in the political process, transactions that served to shift, manoeuvre and reshape the forms in which power circulated" (26). As a concrete example of the way women could engage in such negotiations, Leeds Barroll cites Anna of Denmark, who used her masques "to promote her circle, to establish her presence at court and to establish a context for the exercise of her own politics" (132). In *The Masque of Queens*, Lady Arundel witnessed Anna's use of the masque to promote specific ladies and specific interests. Summers and Pebworth point out that *Queens*, first scheduled for performance during the 1608–9 Christmas festivities, "was postponed until February 2, 1609, the Feast of the Purification of the Virgin Mary, a date of considerable significance to the Roman Catholic Anna, [who] insisted on including a number of her coreligionists as dancers" (139). As one of the Catholics invited to dance in *Queens*, Lady Arundel may have learned from Anna the way in which "the masque provided her with a special kind of political voice" (Barroll, 135). Given the nuanced politicking scholars have found in the court masques, it makes sense to read Lady Arundel's performance in the Venetian Senate Chamber not merely as a defensive assertion of her innocence, but as an opportunity that the Countess seized in order to authorize a particular narrative of the self.

When the Foscarini scandal broke in 1622, the Countess of Arundel had been living in Venice for a year and a half, having set up residence there ostensibly to be near her two eldest sons, who were studying in the city. As a Catholic, Lady Arundel may have found Italy a more congenial place than England, especially given the recent death of the Catholic Queen Anna.[14] Lady

---

14 In the 1640s, problems of religious difference contributed to the decision of the Earl and Countess to leave England, a final leave-taking for both of them.

Arundel had not followed her husband's conversion to Anglicanism in 1616, a conversion that many suspected was politically expedient and connected to the Earl's rising fortunes at court, where he became one of James I's most powerful advisers.[15] Yet the Earl's political standing was never entirely secure: he was briefly in the Tower in 1621 as the result of a quarrel in Parliament with Robert Lord Spencer and he was engaged in constant rivalry with James's favorite Buckingham. Indeed it is likely that Buckingham was involved in efforts to deny Arundel a much-needed 2,000 pound annuity that the King had granted him when he became Earl Marshal, also in 1621.[16] Against this backdrop of competitive politics, it may have seemed useful to Lady Arundel to find a way to assert her own personal power and prestige, to remind the King of her loyalty to him and her value as a kind of goodwill ambassador in Venice, and to stress the high esteem in which her husband was held abroad. So when the Foscarini scandal broke, the Countess was quick to use it to perform her own virtue and political value.

Lady Arundel was drawn into the scandal when the English ambassador, Sir Henry Wotton, informed her that rumors placed some of Foscarini's illegal meetings with foreign diplomats at her palace on the Grand Canal. As a result, Wotton told the Countess, the Senate was about to expel her from Venetian territories; he advised her to leave Venice immediately on her own initiative rather than face public humiliation. She decisively rejected his advice, denying the charges against her and determining to appear in the Venetian Collegio to clear her own reputation as well as England's. In the Collegio, Lady Arundel's performance instincts emerged strongly as she drew on her theatrical expertise to help turn a potentially damaging situation to her advantage. Chamberlain's comment that the Countess had appeared in "a play never plaide before" perhaps disguises his disapproval of her independent self-promotion in a criticism of her public theatricality per se.

Lady Arundel also likely saw the situation in theatrical terms, though without sharing Chamberlain's assumption that theatricality entailed degradation. Indeed her experience in Italy, where women were celebrated for their participation in the professional theater, would likely have fostered the opposite assumption. Assessing the leading actress Vittoria Piissimi, Tommasso Garzoni particularly praised her rhetorical strength:

> Above all worthy of the highest honours is the divine Vittoria who metamorphoses herself on the stage: a beautiful sorceress of love, she entices the hearts of a thousand lovers with her words; a sweet siren, she enchants with smooth incantations the souls of her devout spectators. (quoted in Richards and Richards, 221–2)

---

15 For the Earl's conversion, see Hervey, 113–19.
16 See Hervey, 190–5, for this period in Arundel's political life.

Adolfo Bartoli was equally enthusiastic in his praise of Isabella Andreini who, in addition to her fame as an actress, was a noted poet:

> Isabella was praised by the most famous pens of that golden century: Jacopo Castelvetro, Gabriello Chiabrera, Torquato and Ercole Tasso, Ridolfo Campeggi and others honoured her with their verses, bestowing great praise on her; to all of which praise she modestly responded with sonnets so distinguished that at times … the response was superior to what had prompted it in the nobility of feeling and grace of style that could clearly be heard between the sweetness and the robustness of the lines. (quoted in Richards and Richards, 224)

Not only did the Italian actresses earn great acclaim, but they also often managed their companies. As Kathleen McGill says, "when women began to perform on stage, they immediately assumed the direction of the troupes as well, and companies became known in reference to their female 'stars' " (68). The world of Italian performance thus offered Lady Arundel examples of women who occupied center stage, garnered adulation, and exercised institutional power in the theater. All of these aspects of the Italian actress's experience could have enhanced the Countess's confidence in confronting the Foscarini affair. From her perspective, the situation opened with unnamed persons trying to destroy her, so that her overarching goal in the Collegio would be to thwart their efforts, impose a clear understanding of the true nature of her role, and emerge triumphant herself. Not only does this trajectory mimic the role of the aristocratic figures in the masques Lady Arundel performed in at the Jacobean court, but it also shares affinities with many commedia dell'arte plotlines in which intrigue and mistaken identity give way to clear perceptions of the truth and in which the central female characters ultimately realize their desires.[17]

Although none could identify the origins of the rumors against her, Lady Arundel suspected that Wotton was behind them. As the secretary to the Venetian Council of Ten wrote, "she is not without reasonable suspicion that he had something to do with the origin of this false report, because he objected to her staying in this city, fancying that she watched his proceedings, and was a

---

17 Analyzing commedia plotlines, Louise George Clubb identifies the theatergram of "woman as wonder" in which the woman "functions as an example of virtue for imitation and admiration …. At her full development the figure is known by a hush that falls about her, a sense of her being a thing enskied and sainted" (68). Lady Arundel may fall short of becoming "a thing enskied and sainted," but she surely works to create a dramatic effect in her Collegio appearances. See Scala, in particular "Isabella's Fortune," and "The Jealousy of Isabella," for scenarios in which Isabella and Flaminia reveal hidden identities and attain their (romantic) desires against the obstacles that had threatened them.

weight on his arms, preventing him from acting with such freedom in public affairs as he desired" (*Cal. S.P. Ven., XVII*, 298). Perhaps the enmity between the Countess and Wotton can be traced to religious difference, she being a life-long Catholic and he an active Protestant; perhaps it stems from Wotton's loyalty to Buckingham, Arundel's rival politically at court and culturally in the quest for great art treasures.[18] Whatever the source of her dislike of Wotton, the Countess clearly saw him as the villain in this scandal. She determined to use the force of her aristocratic presence to humiliate him, both in Venice and at home. Here it is worth mentioning that the records in this case do suggest some kind of murky role for Wotton. Although he claimed that rumormongers had victimized him with bad information about the Countess, he never named his sources, an odd choice for someone trying to justify himself. His advice that the Countess flee Venice was also questionable: if she had followed it, she certainly would have stoked the rumors against her. Next, Wotton tried at every turn to prevent or at least delay Lady Arundel's appearance before the Senate: the ambassador "tried hard to dissuade her," said Lady Arundel's servant Vercellini, and Wotton revealed in his own statement that he had asked her to delay until he had "time to discover the origin of the rumour" (*Cal S.P. Ven., XVII*, 298, 302). When the Countess insisted on going immediately to the Senate, "Wotton resolved to accompany her, although very unwillingly" (*Cal S. P. Ven., XVII*, 302). Wotton's extreme discomfort suggests that he knew he was being drawn into a game he could not win, or in theatrical terms, that he was being forced into a play in which he would take the role of the villain, the disruptive antimasquer who must be brought into line.

Accompanied by the reluctant Wotton, Lady Arundel made her first Collegio appearance on 22 April, 1622. With Wotton translating, she denied the charges against her and declared that she would rely utterly on the Doge for "the acknowledgement of her sincerity and reputation, a matter concerning which she has great reason to feel extreme anxiety" (Hardy, 77). The Doge played his part perfectly: he immediately came to her defense, insisting that the rumors were false: Lady Arundel's name had never even come up at Foscarini's trial. Furthermore, the Doge flattered Lady Arundel in terms that only heightened the sense of her Senate appearance as an exclusive performance: "When your Ladyship sent this morning to demand audience of us, and made your appearance, we congratulated ourselves immensely on the visit of so meritorious a lady, who has favored this city with her presence, and we imagined it had been induced by a request for some courtesy or other, much to the delight of these noblemen" (Hardy, 77). Much gratified, the Countess hinted that she would also appreciate a public statement from the Collegio attesting to her innocence. Accordingly, the Collegio drafted a statement and

---

18   On the hostility between the Countess and Wotton, see Hervey, 203–4.

invited Lady Arundel and Wotton to return on April 29 to hear it read. At this second appearance, Lady Arundel presented the Doge with two documents, one a request that he would write to King James and "acquaint his Majesty with my innocence" (*Cal. S.P. Ven., XVII*, 301), and the other a formal narrative of the entire affair, drafted by Wotton. This narrative redounded against Wotton since it forced him to admit that he was the person who had first told the Countess of the rumors against her, a fact he had initially misrepresented.[19] In her own statement to the Doge, Lady Arundel employed dramatic language to publicize her gratitude to the man who had saved her reputation: "the favour and kindness with which your serenity has been pleased to honour me and my children your respectful servants, are beyond my power to portray in glowing colours, save in the recesses of my own heart, where they will ever remain indelibly engraved, and above all this last boon ... concerning as it did my honour and reputation" (Hardy, 80). The Collegio ended its session by expressing goodwill toward Lady Arundel, allocating 100 ducats to be spent on confections and waxworks for her and promising to provide her with a galley to attend the annual Ascension-Day ceremony of the Doge's marriage to the sea (Smith, 1, 186ff.; Hervey, 202 ff.).

That Lady Arundel saw her appearance in the Collegio as a *performance* is clear from her behavior throughout this affair. To her, the element of public show that a Senate appearance would entail was essential. In fact, she initially decided to go the Collegio because she was aware of "the publicity of this matter," and she wanted to receive "public satisfaction of her innocence and some public atonement for the wrong done to her" (*Cal. S.P. Ven., XVII*, 302). This public dimension of the Countess's performance was risky because it potentially evoked the same kind of self-defense that lowly women undertook

---

19   Initially, Wotton told the Senate that "Yesterday this most excellent lady returned from the country, and at her residence found a crowd of company, who ... [told her] that, according to general report, her ladyship was somewhat concerned in the catastrophe" (Hardy, 76–7). In the statement the Countess had him draft a few days later, "the crowd of company" disappears and Wotton himself is revealed as the first to mention the rumor: "Sir Henry Wotton, English ambassador at Venice, supposing the countess to be at her villa near Dolo, sent his secretary John Dynelei to her on the 21st April with a letter containing three points: (1) he had heard, and it was commonly reported in the city, that Foscarini had been condemned in part because he had met some public ministers several times in the countess's house on the Grand Canal ..." (*Cal. S.P. Ven. XVII*, 301–2). Members of the Collegio noted the discrepancy in Wotton's story in their statement to the Venetian ambassador in London: "some additional facts are inserted, whilst others differ from those alleged by the ambassador at the first audience ... Such discrepancies must naturally induce you to keep yet more on the watch, and to modify the communications enjoined you, according to your own ability" (Hardy, 83–4).

in the London courts of the day.[20] However, the Countess accepted the risk, clearly exploiting the power of her own presence to assert rather than undermine her elite status: just as the aristocratic body represents platonic ideals in the masques, Lady Arundel's presence in the Collegio underscores her high standing and her virtue. As Wotton explained to the Doge, the Countess, "jealous as she justly is of the maintenance of that decorum which becomes her noble birth . . . [and] aware of the purity of her own conscience, has determined on presenting herself before your Serenity" (Hardy, 77). Furthermore, the Countess took specific steps to protect her status. In her appearances before the Senate, she differentiated herself from the others in the room, offering herself as a text to be appreciated and praised. While Wotton and the Doge discussed her case, she presented herself visually as an emblem of wronged innocence. In exploiting the visual, the Countess drew adroitly on the representation of aristocratic women's bodies in the English masque. Generally avoiding speech, as the masquers did, Lady Arundel stood as a visual text whose meaning was elucidated by other people's commentary.[21] For example, the Senate's statement, read aloud, began, "Lady Countess! The mental purity and candour exhibited by your Ladyship in the worthy mode of life led by you here, neither can or may be in the slightest respect damaged by slanderous reports" (Hardy, 79); this endorsement would doubtless have gratified the attentive Countess as well as providing the audience with a spectacularly positive gloss on the aristocratic body before them.

Lady Arundel's control of the visual aspects of her performance is underscored in the physical orchestration of her Senate appearances. Wotton leads her into the Collegio as "her usher," supporting her arm with his right hand, and she then takes her seat at the Doge's right hand, a mark of great public honor (Hardy, 76–7). Impressed by the respect shown to his wife, the Earl of Arundel, far away in England, wrote to Dudley Carleton, a former English ambassador in Venice, observing that "*you* could never procure that my wife should sitte by the Doge in Collegio" (Hervey, 212; italics mine). In fact, the seat to the right of the Doge was customarily reserved for ambassadors themselves so Lady Arundel was upstaging Wotton from the start, usurping his place of honor. On her second Collegio appearance, Lady Arundel arrived as before with Wotton as her usher and was seated again at the Doge's right hand. This time, the Countess also brought two documents that she wished to be read aloud, and she drew attention to them by rising from her seat to present them to the Doge. When Wotton requested that the Doge

---

20   For an account of women's rhetorical strategies when facing execution in early modern England, see Dolan; for women's defenses against slander and libel, see Gowing.

21   On the aristocratic woman's body on display in the masques, see McManus.

dispense with reading the longer of these documents, "the lady signified with her gestures that she wished both to be read" (*Cal. S.P. Ven., XVII*, 301), and they were. Lady Arundel had the whole Collegio listening attentively to her version of the events in question.

The fact that Lady Arundel prepared statements in advance also suggests that she saw the entire affair as a theatrical event that she could script and stage-manage. Her personal statement explicitly constructs her meeting with the Doge as a theatrical process of showing, seeing, and appearing: "I have thought it necessary to procure a relation from the English ambassador which I hand to your Serenity, and which I desire my king to see and the rest of the world, so that the benignity of your Serenity and my innocence may both appear at the same time" (*Cal. S.P. Ven., XVII*, 301). Strategically, Lady Arundel positions herself as subordinate to the Doge, respecting his authority and subjecting herself to his judgment. As Wotton related to the Doge, Lady Arundel came to the Collegio "to receive your commands, which she is so far from wishing to avoid, that she, on the contrary, submits herself to them, for the acknowledgement of her sincerity and reputation" (Hardy, 77). In deferring so ostentatiously to the Doge, Lady Arundel was of course attending to the proper forms of diplomatic respect but within the confines of her own drama, she was also strategically establishing him as the central authority figure who would watch her, approve of her, and finally guarantee her innocence. In this respect the Doge became a figure like that of King James sitting in the audience of the English masques, the origin of the virtues that he then recognized in the aristocrats on stage. Yet in deferring to the Doge, Lady Arundel also circumscribed his apparently all-powerful position. In her carefully-orchestrated theatrical scenario, he had no option but to play the part she desired him to play. If he wished to avoid offending King James, he had to exonerate Lady Arundel fully.

Henry Wotton also had to play the role Lady Arundel scripted for him, although he participated reluctantly in her drama. After enduring one appearance with the Countess in the Collegio, he was dismayed when the senators invited them both to return for a follow-up meeting:

Lionello was sent yesterday to tell the English ambassador and the Countess of Arundel to come into the Collegio this morning. Lionello reported that on his doing so the countess welcomed the favour of an audience and the ambassador also, but when told that the countess also was asked he changed colour. He confirmed this by saying he had no business to treat with that lady before his Serenity, yet he would come and receive the public commands and she would enjoy this very great honour. (*Cal. S.P. Ven., XVII*, 300)

Wotton's evident discomfort enhanced Lady Arundel's performance, establishing him as the dishonest troublemaker who would wither in the presence of her superior virtue. Indeed, the second Senate appearance proved as unpleasant for Wotton as he had feared. He squirmed when listening to the senators exonerate the Countess, and he repeatedly interrupted during the reading of the narrative, saying "I have to justify myself also in this matter, because, as I told your Serenity, I also have been deceived" (*Cal. S.P. Ven., XVII*, 303). With Wotton's anxiety serving as a foil to the Countess's self-confident performance of her own innocence, the Venetians increasingly relegated the English ambassador to the sidelines. When Wotton spoke up with a theory of who was responsible for the rumors against the Countess, nobody even acknowledged him: "Ignoring [Wotton's] remark, the doge turned to the countess and said: We hope you will rest satisfied, as we shall always try to render you so" (*Cal. S.P. Ven., XVII*, 304). Lady Arundel may not have physically hounded Wotton out of the Senate, but she had surely outplayed him. Aletheia Talbot was firmly in control of her Venetian theater.

In terms of an English referent, the Countess's theatrical ascendancy over Wotton may recall the moment in *The Masque of Queens* when the "preposterous" dance of the hags is dispelled by the mere appearance of Heroic Virtue and the twelve aristocratic ladies in the House of Fame. Ben Jonson writes of this moment that "not only the hags themselves but the hell into which they ran quite vanished, and the whole face of the scene altered, scarce suffering the memory of such a thing" (Orgel 1969, 92). The court masque effects this transformation by asserting aristocratic power over those causing disruption. It is worth considering whether Lady Arundel did not see her performance in the Venetian Senate in similar terms. Certainly she received complete vindication from the Venetian authorities: in the concluding scenes of her drama, Lady Arundel left the Senate Chamber and returned to her private residence, where the Venetian secretary Lionello brought her the gifts of the republic, "which consisted of fifteen salvers containing wax and confections very gaily decked, the show being gazed on by the whole neigbourhood of the Mocenigo Palace" (Hardy, 83). The Venetian secretary Lionello further reported that "the Countess expressed herself as greatly obliged by the favours she had received and seemed entirely satisfied. When he went down the staircase, her steward confirmed this, saying that she appeared as contented as [Wotton] was confused, as he feared that he had utterly ruined his fortunes and his prospects at the court by this business" (*Cal. S.P. Ven., XVII*, 304). For the Countess, all the pieces were in place now: the scene had shifted to her own palace where an appreciative audience publicly admired the beautiful tokens sent her by the Republic. Wotton's utter frustration put the finishing touches on what seemed to be a spectacular theatrical success.

While all this drama was transpiring in Venice, accounts of it were reaching England fast and furious. From the language all the players used, it is clear that the Countess had outflanked potential critics by establishing herself as a symbol of her country. The Venetian Senate used the figure of the Countess to express its estimation of the English nation as a whole, as the following letter to Girolamo Lando, Venice's ambassador in London, makes clear:

> We charge you to speak to the lady's husband so that he entertain no doubt of the invalidity of the report and remain convinced of the affection and esteem of the republic for him ... Should other noblemen of the Court discuss the topic, you will repeat these assurances, which by admitting the news to be false and announcing our regret will clear the private character of the countess and that of the entire English nation (*Cal. S.P. Ven., XVII*, 298)

The Senate clearly understood that the Countess's involvement in the Foscarini affair had the potential to affect court politics in London. Guided partly by Lady Arundel's determined performance, the Senate sent documents to Lando that would corroborate the Countess's story and strengthen the Arundels' hand in any controversy that might ensue (*Cal S.P. Ven., XVII*, 298). With the Senate's help, Lady Arundel's version of the story was to be given the official stamp of approval in both Venice and London.

The extent to which the English political establishment saw the Countess of Arundel as an international symbol of English-Venetian relations is clear in the number of prominent political figures who acknowledged their gratitude to the Republic for its handling of the affair. As Lando reported, the Earl of Arundel expressed "his great indebtedness to the most serene republic, ... saying that he and all his house would ever look for opportunities to serve you"; the King sent Secretary Calvert to "thank [him] in the king's name for the honour shown to the lady" and to assure Lando that the government "recognized how sincere and steady was the friendship of the republic towards his Majesty" (*Cal. S.P. Ven., XVII*, 328–9). In a later interview with Lando, James himself thanked the Venetian Republic "with every show of affection and regard" and "with offers to reciprocate at every opportunity"; Lando states that Prince Charles, too, thanked him "warmly in similar terms, referring to the obligations of his father" (*Cal. S.P. Ven., XVII*, 340–1). Even Buckingham got involved in the exchange of courtesies: Lando reports that Arundel's rival "passed a very cordial office with me for the honours shown to the countess, offering himself to your Excellencies for every occasion" (*Cal. S.P. Ven., XVII*, 341). Whatever her countrymen's private feelings about a headstrong Englishwoman traveling independently abroad and getting involved in scandals, Lady Arundel had succeeded in transforming herself – at least momentarily – into a symbol of her country whom all the important players at court had to support.

Yet if Lady Arundel had made herself a symbol for the relations between England and Venice, there were still criticisms of her behavior: Chamberlain disapproved of her appearing in "a play never plaide before"; in addition, Lando wrote that while court circles accepted Lady Arundel's version of events, "The populace, however, who do not love the Earl of Arundel and who look askance at the stay of the countess ... have made up their minds that there is something more behind, and after hearing my explanations they stick to this opinion, many saying that the republic is prudent and knows how to dissimulate" (*Cal. S.P. Ven., XVII*, 329). I would suggest that if there was a general suspicion of Lady Arundel, it came less from the fact that she had invented a new kind of theater, as Chamberlain suggests, and more from the fact that her performance evoked problematic theatrical forms and cultural associations that were already familiar in London and ready to be used against her. In particular, she evoked the unsettling figure of the actress, which undermined dominant masculinist conceptions of gender. As Sophie Tomlinson argues, "The threat of the actress in performance lay in the potential for presenting femininity as a vivid and mobile force: the spectacle of the woman actor summoning up a spectre of the female subject" (192). Tomlinson locates the threat of the actress in the specific context of a "feminocentric court culture" that "disrupted the symbolic ordering of gender" and "provided a model for female insubordination in the cultural sphere" (192). I would add that the Italian context further exacerbated the perceived threat of the actress, with the italianate practice of women performing on the professional stage challenging patriarchal ideologies of gender in England.[22]

The ways in which Lady Arundel's Venetian theater pressured English assumptions about class, gender, and national identity would have been familiar from plays presented on the London stage. The Countess would have triggered the same logic of association by which English plays linked women's public performances with social degradation and suspect foreignness. In the popular theater, the mere fact of being on display, subjected to the judgment of public onlookers, threatens aristocratic femininity. In *The Winter's Tale*, for example, Hermione feels tainted by having to stand public trial, even though she is innocent of the charge of adultery:

> For behold me,
> A fellow of the royal bed, which owe
> A moiety of the throne; a great king's daughter,
> The mother to a hopeful prince, here standing
> To prate and talk for life and honour, fore
> Who please to come and hear.
>
> (3.2.35–40)

For Hermione, a public trial compromises her royal status, regardless of her innocence, because it turns her into an object of the common gaze. Similarly, Lady Arundel would have risked compromising her own aristocratic status when she appeared in a courtroom scene, whether or not she was innocent.

---

22 For more on the specific threat of the Italian actress, see Parolin.

Also stoking English hostility to Lady Arundel's performance was its Italian venue, which the English often equated with deceptiveness. A figure like Vittoria in *The White Devil*, for example, actively appropriates theatrical techniques to increase her maneuverability within the corrupt world of Webster's play, yet her theatricality also taints her: it may be justified in the face of her misogynist opponents, but it also leaves the question of her own possible criminality forever unresolved. The reverse of the theatrical woman's deceptiveness was her perceived gullibility, exemplified in Ben Jonson's Lady Wouldbe in *Volpone*. Attempting to perform her own sophistication through her expert knowledge of Venetian ways, Lady Wouldbe is ridiculed not only because she is such a disastrous misreader of Venetian codes but because she has overvalued Venice which, from the play's point of view, represents the pinnacle of worldly corruption. Lady Arundel, too, openly admired Venetian customs. When the Countess returned to England in the summer of 1623, John Chamberlain skeptically commented that she had brought with her "three Italian massaras [stewards] (wherof one is a blackamore) and a Gondola, which I doubt will not so well brooke our river, where there is commonly so much winde" (2:507). In her enthusiasm for things Italian, the Countess of Arundel risked provoking the same kind of scorn as Lady Wouldbe.

Despite her performance skills, then, Lady Arundel could not control all the possible meanings of the theatrical event she orchestrated. The moment of performance always exceeds the predetermined script.[23] As Martin Butler argues, even the court masques, which were designed to collapse the space between form and ideology, left room for multiple interpretations:

> The transcendent closures of the masques were designed to testify to the transcendent power of the King but conversely, any fracture within the masques' aesthetic order must have unsettled that comfortable equivalence. Indeed, as is notorious from reports of eyewitnesses, contemporaries were all too well aware of the likelihood of the idealized images of the texts being less than persuasive (not to say comprehensible) on the night. (29)

The messiness of performance would have been especially apparent in a Venetian Senate Chamber where there was not even an initial fixed script. Even Lady Arundel seemed aware that her performance was not swaying everyone. In her second appearance in the Collegio, she acknowledged that despite her first performance, the rumors against her persisted. Through Wotton, she

---

23   Carol Rutter refers to "that 'excessive' performance text" in arguing that the significance of women in Shakespeare's plays cannot be understood in terms of the text alone but must also always take performance into account: "the body in play bears continuous meaning on stage and always exceeds the playtext it inhabits" (xiii).

reported that even while the senators were clearing her name, "others seek to slander her by reports which have not even yet subsided" (Hardy, 80).

In response to the persistent rumors against her, Lady Arundel turned from performance to the written text, as if implicitly acknowledging the unreliability of performance as a tool for defining personal identity. In her statement to the Doge, she justifies her drive toward written narrative:

> as this false report circulated against me seems to revive daily, with fresh particulars, I have therefore deemed it necessary to obtain from the most excellent the lord ambassador of his majesty the King of Great Britain a narrative, which I here respectfully present to your Serenity, being anxious for it to be seen by my Sovereign's invincible Majesty, and in other quarters, as proof ... of my own innocence. (Hardy, 80–81)

Lady Arundel seems to concede that her situation is worsening, with fresh rumors emerging against her, perhaps provoked by the spectacle of her public appearance in the Collegio. In place of performance, Lady Arundel now offers the authority of the written text: here at last will be the proof that performance could not provide. The Countess's effort to fix textually the meaning of performance echoes the voluminous textual apparatus Ben Jonson provided for the published version of his masques. But the sheer volume of the texts that emerged from Lady Arundel's involvement in the Foscarini affair frustrates any effort to assert a single unequivocal interpretation. Statements were passed from the Countess to the Senate; from Wotton to the Senate; from the Senate to ambassador Lando; from the Senate, through Lando, to English officials; from Lando to the Senate; from King James to the Doge; from the Countess to her husband; from the Earl of Arundel to various correspondents of his own.[24] Each of these statements varies in tone and content, reflecting the specific needs of the writer and producing a slightly different version of events. Lady Arundel may have decided that her Venetian performance needed to be stabilized by an interpretive text, but paradoxically the written texts foreground the construct-edness, and hence the contingency, of any interpretation of her actions. Far from establishing a clear version of events, the textual traces of Lady Arundel's Venetian theater suggest a fierce competition for meaning. As a result, it may not have achieved the goals the Countess had in mind, but it does continue to provide a window into the cultural and political complexity that even an elite

---

24   To the best of my knowledge, no letter survives from Lady Arundel to the Earl on the subject of the Foscarini affair, but the Venetian papers suggest that such a letter existed: "On Friday she sent a full account to her husband, and will perhaps send a special gentleman to his Majesty trying to be avenged on Wotton" (*Cal. S.P. Ven.*, *XVII*, 298).

court lady would have to confront when she sought to turn theatrical tropes and techniques to her advantage.

Through her controversial theatricality, Lady Arundel promoted personal goals such as defending her name, enhancing her status, supporting her husband's position at court, and constructing herself as a cultural go-between who would symbolize English–Venetian relations. Shortly after the Foscarini affair, the Countess was again offering herself up as a cultural mediator of sorts, testifying to her restless desire to work herself into positions of importance. This time, she desired to go to Spain to meet the Infanta, who was thought to be on the verge of marrying Prince Charles. Lady Arundel hoped to accompany the Infanta to England, thus establishing herself, no doubt, as an important Catholic intimate of the Spanish princess. If Lady Arundel used her Venetian theater to prove her suitability for such a mission, she failed. In April 1623, the Venetian ambassador reported that "The Earl of Arundel is not well content. The King refused to allow his wife to go to Spain. There may be divers reasons, but the court ladies, especially those of the marquis [Buckingham], have thrown many hindrances in the way out of jealousy" (*Cal. S.P. Ven.,* *XVII,* 631). A year after the Foscarini affair, court rivalries were still at play, and the Buckinghams were still ahead of the Arundels. The short-term success of Lady Arundel's Venetian theater was thus outweighed by longer-term failures, but the episode is still important as an example of one elite Englishwoman who mined her theatrical experience for the tropes and techniques that would help her promote a desired version of her own identity. From Lady Arundel's case, we can argue that for courtly women as well as men, theatricality was essential to the project of actively negotiating for power and prestige.

Works Cited

Barroll, Leeds. "Inventing the Stuart Masque". Ed. David Bevington and Peter Holbrook. Cambridge: Cambridge University Press, 1998, 121–43.

Bevington, David and Peter Holbrook. "Introduction." *The Politics of the Stuart Court Masque.* Ed. David Bevington and Peter Holbrook. Cambridge: Cambridge University Press, 1998, 1–12.

Brown, Pamela Allen. *Better a Shrew than a Sheep: Women, Drama, and the Culture of Jest in Early Modern England.* Ithaca and London: Cornell University Press, 2003.

Butler, Martin. "Courtly Negotiations." In Bevington and Holbrook, 20–40.

Calendar of State Papers and Manuscripts Relating to English affairs existing in the archives and collections of Venice, and in other libraries of northern Italy. 38 vols. Ed. Rawdon Brown *et al.* London: HMSO, 1864–1947.

Chamberlain, John. The Letters of John Chamberlain. 2 Vols. Ed. Norman E. McLure. Philadelphia: American Philosophical Society, 1939.

Clubb, Louise George. *Italian Drama in Shakespeare's Time*. New Haven and London: Yale University Press, 1989.

Cust, Lionel. "Notes on the Collections Formed by Thomas Arundel, Earl of Arundel and Surrey, K. G." *Burlington Magazine for Connoisseurs* 19 (1911): 278–86.

Dolan, Frances E. " 'Gentlemen I Have One Thing More to Say': Women on Scaffolds in England, 1563–1680." *Modern Philology* (1994): 157–78.

Findlay, Alison. *A Feminist Perspective on Renaissance Drama*. Oxford: Blackwell, 1999.

Gowing, Laura. *Domestic Dangers: Women, Words, and Sex in Early Modern London*. Oxford: Clarendon, 1996.

Hardy, Thomas Duffus. *Report Upon the Documents in the Archives and Public Libraries of Venice*. London, 1866.

Hervey, Mary F. S. *The Life, Correspondence, and Collections of Thomas Howard Earl of Arundel*. 1921; repr. New York: Kraus Reprint Co., 1969.

Howard, Thomas, Earl of Arundel. *Draft Will of Thomas Howard, Earl of Arundel*. Arundel Castle Manuscripts, 1617.

Howarth, David. *Lord Arundel and his Circle*. New Haven: Yale University Press, 1985a.

———. "Lord Arundel as a Patron of Learning and Scholarship, 1610–1640." *Editions du CNRS, Paris, 1985*. (1985b): 139–46.

———. "The Patronage and Collecting of Aletheia, Countess of Arundel, 1606–54." *Journal of the History of Collections* 10.2 (1998): 125–37.

McGill, Kathleen. "Women and Performance: The Development of Improvisation by the Sixteenth-Century Commedia Dell'arte." *Theatre Journal* 43 (1991): 59–69.

McManus, Clare. *Women and the Renaissance Stage: Anna of Denmark and Female Masquing in the Stuart Court 1590–1619*. Manchester: Manchester University Press, 2002.

Novikova, Anastasia. "The Marriage of Signs, or the Signs of Marriage, or the Ideal Marriage of the Arundels." *Object* 2 (1999–2000): 69–88.

Orgel, Stephen. "Introduction." *Ben Jonson: The Complete Masques*, ed. Stephen Orgel. New Haven and London: Yale University Press, 1969 1–39.

———. "Idols of the Gallery: Becoming a Connoisseur in Renaissance England." *Early Modern Visual Culture: Representation, Race, and Empire in Early Modern England*, ed. Peter Erickson and Clark Hulse. Philadelphia: University of Pennsylvania Press, 2000.

Palmer, Thomas. *An Essay of the Meanes How to Make Our Travailes into Forraine Countries the More Profitable and Honourable*. London, 1605.

Parolin, Peter. " 'A Strange Fury Entered My House': Italian Actresses and Female Performance in *Volpone*," *Renaissance Drama*, n.s. XXIX (1998): 107–36.

Prynne, William. *Romes Master-Peece. Or, the Grand Conspiracy of the Pope and his Jesuited Instruments, to extirpate the Protestant Religion*. London, 1644.

Richards, Kenneth, and Laura Richards. *The Commedia dell'Arte: A Documentary History*. Oxford: Blackwell, 1990.

Rosenthal, Margaret F. *The Honest Courtesan: Veronica Franco, Citizen and Writer in Sixteenth-Century Venice*. Chicago and London: University of Chicago Press, 1992.

Rutter, Carol Chillington. *Enter the Body: Women and Representation on Shakespeare's Stage*. London and New York: Routledge, 2001.

Scala, Flaminio. *Scenarios of the* Commedia dell'Arte: *Flaminio Scala's* Il Teatro Delle Favole Rappresentative, trans. Henry F. Salerno. New York: Limelight, 1996.

Shakespeare, William. *The Winter's Tale*. The Norton Shakespeare. Ed. Stephen Greenblatt, et al. New York: Norton, 1997. 2873–2954.

Smith, Logan Pearsall. *The Life and Letters of Sir Henry Wotton*. 2 vols. Oxford: Clarendon Press, 1907.

Summers, Claude J. and Ted-Larry Pebworth. "Introduction." *Representing Women in Renaissance England*. Ed. Claude J. Summers and Ted-Larry Pebworth. Columbia and London: University of Missouri Press, 1997, 1–8.

Tomlinson, Sophie. "She that Plays the King: Henrietta Maria and the Threat of the Actress in Caroline Culture." *The Politics of Tragicomedy: Shakespeare and After*, ed. Gordon McMullen and Jonathan Hope. London: Routledge, 1992, 189–207.

Walker, Edward. "A View of the Life and Actions of Thomas Howard, Earl of Arundel." *Historical Discourses*. London, 1705.

Chapter 11

"Pleaders, Atturneys, Petitioners and the like": Margaret Cavendish and the Dramatic Petition

Julie Crawford

Margaret Cavendish has rarely been considered as a performer. In fact, scholars have made much of the fact that her own plays were never meant to be performed, written, as she herself claimed, for "My brain the Stage" (*Plays* [1662]). Yet this understanding of performance is limited to the public stage, and ignores the disparate arenas of performance used by early modern elites: country houses and coteries, places of political resort and fashionable gatherings, exclusive aristocratic entertainments, the streets of foreign cities, and audiences with the court. A performance, in this broader sense, is a public act intended for a specific audience, a creative and dramatic act, certainly, but one with particular social and political intentions. In this essay I argue that Margaret Cavendish's published drama and related public performances as a noblewoman of considerable reputation manifest an interventionist political sensibility, both in defending and promoting her husband as a political advisor, and in proposing her own political and social views. Much in Cavendish's published work serves as political advice and as a form of petition by which she seeks redress and restitution for her husband's history of loyal service to the monarchy. Yet it is Cavendish's plays, all published in the post-Restoration 1660s, which serve as her most trenchant political critiques. Cavendish explicitly associated drama with noble education and even reprimand, and her plays serve both as indictments of the improperly restored court, and as models for the ideal royalist society she sought to establish. Aristocratic female performance was often a way of attesting to royalist loyalties and resistance in the 1650s – the royal princesses even put on a performance of *A King and No King* in Holland in 1654 (Nicholas 1955, 267)[1] – but it also had a long tradition

---

1 On royalist plays performed during the interregnum see Potter, 83. William Davenant, William Cavendish's former Lieutenant General of the Ordnance (Trease, 111), also held entertainments at Rutland House in the 1650s which

of negotiating for noble privileges *from* royalty. It is this latter aspect, I argue, with which Cavendish is most concerned in her own dramatic work. While her plays offer a range of performances by politically influential aristocratic women, I argue that the plays are meant to exist in dialogue with Cavendish's own political performances – those dramatically public, audience-soliciting self-presentations which she made both in country and court, and, most famously, in London in the spring of 1667. Her audiences were mostly courtly and royal; however, as the challenges to aristocratic privilege changed, so too did Cavendish's perception of her audience.

Cavendish's 1667 London performances are among the best recorded of her public appearances – during April and May of that year she appeared, with considerable dramatic flair, at the theater, at Whitehall, at the Duke of York's, at Hyde Park, and, perhaps most famously, at the Royal Society. Yet they have usually been read according to the judgments of critics such as Samuel Pepys, who noted that Cavendish's behavior was, among other things, most "unordinary," and Mary and John Evelyn, members of the rising classes with their own ambivalent perspectives on the privileges of hereditary aristocracy. Yet I believe that Cavendish's "unordinary" public performances in 1667 were intentional, meant to signal the Cavendishes' sociopolitical desires as well as their politically central aristocratic status (see also Chalmers). Furthermore, the analogues between these London performances and specific scenes in Cavendish's published plays suggest not only that Cavendish meant for her plays to be seen in relationship to her own life, but that she intended them as part of a self-conscious program of advertisement and petition. Cavendish's dramatic presentations of female aristocratic performance are both proscriptive and descriptive: while her plays condemn the social-climbing of non-aristocratic women (and men), they also feature the petitions and political influence of noblewomen and the much-discussed public appearances of famed aristocratic women, alluding often to the specific circumstances and sociopolitical centrality of Cavendish herself. In particular, Cavendish presents codes for female aristocratic performance: a combination of political and rhetorical perspicacity, the public parading and enjoyment of class-specific material privileges and luxuries, and the promotion of one's own notoriety.

---

featured women performers, *The First Day's Entertainment at Rutland* (1656), and *The Siege at Rhodes* (1656) (Randall, 170–71). Cavendish's own sense of the impact of women performers was honed both in her time in Henrietta Maria's court (Hulse, 1996), and by her experience with women actors in Antwerp. In *Sociable Letters* she writes of "two Handsom Women Actors, both Sisters" who performed on the Mountebank's stage in Antwerp: "I took such Delight, to see them Act upon the Stage, as I caused a Room to be hired in the next House to the Stage, and went every day to see them" (206). For more on female mountebanks, see Bella Mirabella's essay in this volume.

While a number of the 1662 plays seem oddly prescient in their representations of publicly sought-after aristocratic women, *A Piece of a Play*, the final play in the 1668 volume, also accurately describes much of the public response to Cavendish's own 1667 performances in London, (re)casting its notorious noblewoman's performance not as misplaced pride or excess but as the appropriate performance, and birthright, of her class. By publishing topically resonant plays outlining the rights and responsibilities of the aristocracy in the early Restoration, including scenes in which noble women petitioners receive audience and redress, Cavendish provides both the codes and the justification for her own behavior. Cavendish's plays, in other words, model the appropriate forms of aristocratic female performance that Cavendish herself exemplifies, as well as the appropriate responses they ought to solicit. Forced to negotiate the politically sensitive matter of petitioning as a royalist woman – petitioning was, after all, the tool of revolutionaries – Cavendish eventually found a way to make her case through female performance and the careful management of its ideological purposes.

The Dramatic Petition

Cavendish saw her plays as appropriately political texts for many reasons, not least of which was the fact that the Cavendish name was associated with drama and with its political uses. William Cavendish had a long history of putting on household entertainments for the Stuart monarchy; during the 1630s he put on two performances for Charles I and Henrietta Maria at his country homes, Welbeck Abbey and Bolsover Castle, and he hosted entertainments for Charles II in exile in Antwerp in 1658, and in his London lodgings shortly after the 1660 Restoration.[2] While these royalist entertainments flattered the king, they were also negotiations for Cavendish's own aristocratic privileges. Household dramas were, as Greg Walker puts it, "moves or stages in a complex negotiation *for* power" (70), including the entrenchment of the entertainer's local power. The Welbeck and Bolsover dramas alluded to William Cavendish's roles as Lord Warden of the Forest of Sherwood and Lord Lieutenant of Nottinghamshire, and served as reminders of the importance of nobility and the great courtier houses to the monarchy (Walker; Hopkins, 27).

---

2   On these entertainments, see Hopkins; Cedric C. Brown, "Courtesies of Place and Arts of Diplomacy in Ben Jonson's Last Two Entertainments for Royalty," *The Seventeenth Century* 9 (1994): 147–71, Nick Rowe, "My Best Patron: William Cavendish and Jonson's Caroline Dramas," *Seventeenth Century* 9.2 (1994): 197–212, James Fitzmaurice, "William Cavendish and Two Entertainments by Ben Jonson," *Ben Jonson Journal* 5 (1998): 63–80.

His Antwerp and London performances served similar purposes; the Antwerp entertainment providing a venue for various aristocrats to simultaneously show their loyalty to and petition the king-in-exile,[3] and the London entertainment reminding the king that Cavendish wanted a place in the newly-restored government. The London drama, known as "The King's Entertainment," both celebrated the return of the monarchy ("by the plessings / of Got, Charles is up, and is up, in spight of aule / the uglie Treasons, and rebellions in the Orlde" [lines 104–6; Hulse 1995, 389–90]), and highlighted the interdependence of royalty and nobility. It featured stylized dances in which Charles II partnered the ladies, Margaret Cavendish among them (lines 312–16), in a performative emblem of royal and aristocratic mutuality, and exclaimed that with the Restoration "there is some comfort now left for Cavaliers & Shentlemen" (lines 149–50). This comfort, however, was not immediately forthcoming; many of Charles I's loyal cavaliers, including William Cavendish, were not rewarded by the Restoration court in the ways they had hoped. When Cavendish was not offered a position in the newly-forming government, the Cavendishes retreated from the court to Welbeck Abbey in the fall of 1660. This was the context from which Margaret Cavendish's own plays, with their own forms of petitioning, were presented to the public eye.

While Cavendish's plays were not household dramas in the same way as her husband's earlier dramas were, they were published when the Cavendishes were living at their country house, and were certainly, like her 1653 texts, meant to "set a worke every *Tongue*" about the Cavendishes' situation (*Poems and Fancies*, A3r). Printed in folio, the most elaborately public and expensive of formats, her plays were also advertised in *The Kingdoms Intelligencer* of 3–10 February 1662, and circulated to major figures in early Restoration London. Furthermore, while the closure of the theaters in 1642 had intensified the politicized status of drama in the 1640s and 1650s (Wiseman, 6), and while plays evincing a nostalgic view of an England with a traditionally hierarchical social order were often a form of aristocratic resistance during the interregnum,

---

3   On the Antwerp Entertainment, see *CSPD 1657–8:* 297. The ball followed the bestowing of the Order of the Garter, and the evening's entertainment was "ushered in by a speech penned by [Cavendish]" and featured a banquet, country dances, and a song performed by Lady Marchioness Moore "dressed in feathers." The epilogue, also written by Newcastle, prophesied Charles II's re-establishment as King of England. The entertainment was attended by most of the important figures of the monarchy-in-exile, and each player and attendee had his or her own set of desires and demands. To take one example, the featured female performer, Lady Alice Moore, was the wife of the Irish Peer Lord Henry Moore of Drogheda, who was at the time of the entertainment simultaneously petitioning Parliament for his property rights lost during the civil wars (the first Lord Moore was a royalist martyr), and trying to maintain the family's influence with the royal court.

such idealization of traditional values was also a form of critique in and of the early Restoration settlement. As Susan Wiseman has argued, the idea of the dramatist as a political commentator owed much to the phenomenon of printed dramatic debate between 1642 and 1660, but it had continuing purchase for Royalists in the early years of the Restoration, especially those who, like the Cavendishes, perceived that status founded on land and titles no longer translated unproblematically into public recognition and privilege (Wiseman, 61–7), and who thus sought to reassert the political necessity of those traditional values by any means possible.

The 1662 *Plays* begin, as do many of her works, by highlighting Cavendish's aristocratic status: they were "Written by the Thrice Noble, Illustrious and Excellent Princess the Lady Marchioness of Newcastle" (in the mid-1650s William sought and received permission from Sir Edward Walker to use the term 'Prince' [Trease, 173]), and addressed to "Noble Readers." This address further clarifies why Cavendish chose plays as a fitting form of noble political critique and advice: plays are instructive "for Honour, and becoming," and it should not be thought "a crime or debasement for the nobler sort to Act Playes," "especially on publick Theatres" (A6). Cavendish, that is, includes public theatres in her claim for drama as the cultural capital of the nobility (Wiseman, 91), as well as for the education *of* that nobility. In one scene in *Youths Glory and Death's Banquet*, for example, the mother of the heroine Lady Sanspareille (a cipher for Cavendish) reprimands her for reciting some verses that she wrote, claiming that her daughter is "transformed … from a sober, young maid, to a Stage-player." The Lady responds by defending "Stages and Publick Theaters" in much the same way that Cavendish does in her introduction: they were first built "for the education of noble youth" as "publick patterns to take example from" and "Scaffolds, whereon vices were publickly executed" (127).[4] Theaters and plays, that is, have pedagogical functions particularly geared towards the nobility. And while they are meant to model exemplary aristocratic living, plays also, as we have seen, present the values and demands of their noble authors and performers, including those of noble women. The above scene from *Youths Glory* illustrates the extent to

---

4   One of the noblewomen in *The Female Academy* (*Plays*, 1662) similarly defends theaters as places where people "may learne what is noble and good, what base and wicked, what ridiculous and misbecoming … what to avoid and what to imitate" (4.22.669). In *The World's Olio* Cavendish writes that "every Scene is like a new master that teaches several arts, not only for the youngest, but oldest men to learn" (10 C1v). "Mode Plays," in contrast, "prove a Nursery of whining Lovers, and not an Academy or School for Wise, Witty, Noble, and well-behaved men" (*Blazing World*, 153).

which Cavendish saw female performance as an integral part of the pedagogical and political functions of such dramatic discourse.

Cavendish's publication of her plays thus drew on her husband's history of noble performance as a means of political negotiation, the newly heightened status of drama as political critique, and a tradition of drama as the ideological training ground for nobility. The plays' concern with the proper behavior of and respect for the nobility, and their particular focus on the performances and political perspicacity of noblewomen, many of whom were modeled on Cavendish herself, sought to provide models for a properly restored social order. While feminist scholars have pointed to the fact that Cavendish's plays are peopled by powerful aristocratic women, they often see these performances as examples of a feminist vision foreshortened by Cavendish's own royalist commitment to hierarchy.[5] Yet the political intentions of her plays were more complex. Featuring numerous scenes of women's petitioning and of women receiving royal audiences, Cavendish's plays are more than celebrations of the empowerment of women; they enact the type of hearing and respect Cavendish sought for her own petitions. These scenes model the ideal political reciprocity between nobility and monarchy that had once been the basis of English government, but was becoming increasingly anachronistic in the 1660s. By highlighting the position of aristocratic women within this dynamic, and by showing the necessity and efficacy of exemplary female performance, Cavendish sought to provide a larger cultural context for her own desires.

Cavendish was deeply critical of the changed customs and laws of post-Civil War England, "where Women become Pleaders, Atturneys, Petitioners and the like, running about with their severall Causes, complaining of their severall grievances, exclaiming against their severall enemies, bragging of their severall favours they receive from the powerful." Our sex, she adds, "doth nothing but justle for the Preheminance of words ... as they do for the Preheminence of place ... thinking to advance themselves hereby" (*A True Relation*, 380). While Cavendish herself had petitioned Parliament during the 1650s, appearing before the Committee for Compounding to seek her share of her husband's estate, she manages this event carefully in her 1656 autobiography, firmly stating that she visited Parliament "as Petitioner" one time only and "received

---

5   While Catherine Gallagher argues that Cavendish's insistence on an aristocratic hierarchical order only allows for recognition of the rights of women to power at the very top of the hierarchy – a position which leads her, ultimately, to aristocratic solipsism – Susan Wiseman points out how the interchangeable meanings of "theater" as public affairs or the stage made transformations possible for the figured female, especially the noble female, and argues that dramatic writing allows Cavendish to renegotiate the place of women in the prestige system (Wiseman, 97, 104).

neither gold nor silver from them, only an absolute refusall" (379).[6] In this record of her unwilling petition, Cavendish even silences her own voice: after Parliament's refusal, she writes, "I whisperingly spoke to my brother to conduct me out of *that ungentlemanly place*, so without speaking to them one word good or bad, I returned to my Lodging." Identifying herself as "ignorant of the Humours, and Dispositions of those persons to whom I was to address my suit," Cavendish highlights not only her gender and aristocratic propriety – her Parliamentarian foes are both "ungentlemanly" and utterly unfamiliar – but her understanding of the performative protocols of obeisance and authority. While "Noble, Vertuous, Discreet and worthy" women (381) may have been forced to petition Parliament during the interregnum, Cavendish has a clear sense of the legitimate audiences and sources of power and of the ways in which such women might address them.[7]

The scenes in Cavendish's plays which feature women petitioners are thus always mediated according to a strict social hierarchy. In one scene in *Loves Adventures*, "poor Souldiers wives" present their petitions for their husbands' lives to "Affectionata" who has become second-in-command to "Lord Singularity," a General who "commands a great Army" (Part II, 12) and a clear figure for William Cavendish, former General of Charles I's northern forces. (Handling petitions was, in fact, one of the governmental tasks given to Cavendish as a member of the House of Lords).[8] In her play, Cavendish both upholds the ultimate authority of the king, and highlights the integrity of the service her husband was responsible for; if their petitions are just, Affectionata tells the women, "my Lord the General will grant your request, and if they be unjust, he will not be unjust in granting them for by intreatie, nor will I intreat

---

6　She received no share of Cavendish's estate because she married him after he "was made a Delinquent," or royalist enemy of Parliament.

7　The language of advancement, trade, and solicitation Cavendish uses to describe the behavior of the majority of petitioners suggests the difference between the "suites" of the nobility and the greedy, and indeed revolutionary, machinations of the middling sort. As Cavendish writes elsewhere, those who "Petition for Reformations of Government, and Complain for the Breach of their Privileges, and Exclaime against their Magistrates, and your Majesties Ministers of State" – all actual complaints made by both male and female petitioners in the 1640s and 1650s – "are to be considered as Dangerous Persons, for their Petitions are Fore-runners of Civil Warrs" (*Orations*, 114–15).

8　Charles I appointed him to the Lord's Committee for Petitions in 1639, and Charles II appointed him to the Committees of Privileges and Petitions in 1660 (the latter, however, was a largely honorary, and thus unpaid, position) (Trease, 85, 181).

therefore" (1.13.51).[9] While it is the General who makes the decisions and receives the appropriate political reward – he is invited by the king to "to attend him in his progress this Summer" – Affectionata, another cipher for Margaret Cavendish, is publicly praised for her political savvy (3.15, 56).

In a similar scene in the aforementioned *Youths Glory*, the Lady Sanspareille is so wise that the "Queen of Attention" comes to hear her speak about government, inverting the order by which Sanspareille, as the subject, ought to "wait at [the Queen's] Court-Gates" (154) in order to be heard. While Cavendish stages the access that she would like to have with the crown, she is careful to balance her political assertions with appropriate subjection. Although the Queen tells her that she is "fit to be a Gouverness ... that can speak so well of Government," Lady Sanspareille responds that "'Tis happier for me to be a Subject to so gracious a Sovereign, than if I were to govern a people my self" (156). A few scenes later in the play, however, a Gentleman reports that Lady Sanspareille "doth intend to plead *in the behalf of poor Suiters*, and hath asked leave of the Queen to be a pleader at the Barr, for all such as suffered wrong as injustices" (3.8.163, emphasis added). While she is a good subject to her Queen, that is, Lady Sanspareille also deploys the tools of petitioning in order to correct the injustices perpetrated on worthy "Suiters"; suitors like the "Noble Worthy and Vertuous women" who had been forced to appear fruitlessly before Parliament in the 1650s. As the play makes clear, the petitioner simultaneously performs hierarchical obedience, displaying her mastery of the art of subjection, and displays the skill, and righteousness, of her own political machinations and desires.

Among the injustices meriting redress in Cavendish's plays are the fates of the families of loyal Cavaliers who were, like Lady Poor Virtue's father, Lord Morality – and like William Cavendish – killed or impoverished "in the defence of his King and Country" (*Lady Contemplation* [1662] 1.2, 184). In another scene, one "Madamoisel Petitioner," ready to give up on a hearing, is ushered into the royal presence by "a noble person, one of the Emperor's Privy Council, who is both generous and just, and hath some power and favour with the Emperor" (*Scenes* not included in *The Presence* [1668], 137). This "noble person," Lord Loyalty, offers to read the petition and to "wait on" the Lady "into the Room before the Council-Chamber" where he will "best hear [her] Cause, and receive [her] Commands" (138). This scene of mediation between a "noble and discreet" woman petitioner and a noble advisor actualizes the role the Cavendishes sought; not only to be heard by the court, but to be the *means of access* into the Council-Chamber itself (William had been a Privy Counselor

---

9   As Cavendish later writes in her biography of William, "he never refuses any Petition, but accepts them; and being informed of the business, will give a just, and as much as lies in him, a favourable answer to the Petitioning Party" [*Life*, 148]).

before the war, and this was the position he repeatedly sought both during the interregnum and in the early years of the Restoration).[10] When the Emperor meets the Lady Petitioner, he listens to her on traditional hierarchical grounds, rooted in the values the Cavendishes both exemplified and sought to maintain: "I knew your Father," he tells her, "he was a worthy Gentleman, and kept a noble House, gave great Entertainment, and I have been made very welcome there" (sc. 23, 140). He was, in other words, an old-style courtier like William Cavendish, whose past services of aristocratic country hospitality and royal entertainment should rightfully win his family rewards in the present.

The decline of the nobility, and of the role of these great courtier houses, is thus represented as a grave political error throughout the 1662 volume of plays. In *A Comedy of the Apocryphal Ladies*, a play whose characters include the "Creating Princess" (who makes a commoner a prince [1.6, 639]), the "Comical Dutchess", who prefers the attendance of "Bourgers Wives" (1.13, 642) over true ladies, and the "Apocriphal Dutchess," whom the "Unfortunate Dutchess", whose rightful position she usurped, hopes will be "hiss[ed] from off the Stage," social mobility and false nobility threaten to knock royalty "from its Throne." Much of the play is absorbed in detailed explanations of honors and titles, and clearly intended to serve as an education about status hierarchy (at one point a Gentleman thanks the heroine Lady True Honour for educating him: "for I was so ignorant, as I knew nothing of Heraldry"). For her part, Lady True Honor simply refuses to acknowledge the false nobles. She "keep[s] up *the Right of [her] place*, because it is the cause and interest of all the Nobility of [her] Country": "if I should give place," she claims, "I should be a Traytor to true Honour, and dignified Persons." It is this "Right of place," and the refusal to "give place" to the wrong persons, which I see as central to Cavendish's negotiations with the court, both in the imagined encounters in her published plays, and in her visits to its places of congregation in London. In performing the very material rites to which she is entitled – "the

---

10 William Cavendish had been made a member of the Privy Council of the exiled monarchy in 1650 (Carte, 376), and proposed as Ambassador to the Dutch states in 1653 (*Nicholas Papers* 2: 11). His political relevance and skills were, however, continually questioned: in June 1650, for example, Edward Hyde wrote to Nicholas that he was "a very lamentable man and as fit to be a gen[era]ll as a B[isho]pp" (Mendelson, 27). Margaret Cavendish was also known for promoting her husband's political career. In 1658 an insider wrote to Secretary Nicholas complaining that Cavendish had been interfering with one of the king's plans: he "(*as his wife has made him*) is industrious to decry the King's estate, being piqued that he did not know of its settlement" (*CSPD 1657–8*: 300, emphasis added). News of Cavendish's actions eventually reached the king, who reprimanded him and blamed his interventionism on malcontents and "his wife, who swears that the affair can not and shall not be effected without her husband" (*CSPD 1657–8*: 311).

Dignity and the Ceremony of Titles" – Cavendish does more than refuse to cede her place to the presumptions and pretensions of the bourgeoisie; she defends, along with her husband, "the cause and interest of all the Nobility of my Country." In her plays, as in her own life, Cavendish is highly invested in the nearly sacred fixity of noble heredity. While she recognizes nobility as a form of performance, and hopes that the false holders of titles will be hissed from the "Stage," Cavendish does not see noble status as a case of everyone doing "what they list." It is a performance that has both its history and its protocols.

The 1662 plays are thus particularly critical of those "Vainglorious" courtiers who did not, and do not, uphold the values of their place (*Wits Cabal*, sc. 32, 279). Rather than "deliver[ing] judicious Counsel" or "purg[ing] a Commonwealth from faction," men who refused to fight for the king during the wars now spend their time on "affected Dresses ... and ... Countenances" (280). They neither keep up country hospitality (from keeping an open house at Christmas to maintaining Orphans and Widows [280]), nor understand the cultural centrality of "a hospitable Gentlemans house in the Country" (5.25, 322). These details, I argue, encode a political critique of the manners and values of the newly restored court – Charles II was famous for promoting former Parliamentarians and for his reliance on what one historian has called "monied interests" (Seaward, 6). But they also indicate the desire to reestablish the old nobility (those who had actually fought factions and wars for their king) and their country demesnes as viable sites of cultural and political influence; to reassert, that is, their "Right of place."

Cavendish thus makes many allusions to the Cavendishes' life as country nobility in her post-Restoration writings, revealing her own knowledge of husbandry, forestry, and the running of a country estate (see, for example, *Orations*, 246, 272). In the preface to the revised 1663 edition of *Philosophical and Physical Opinions*, moreover, she writes that since their return to their "Native Country," she has attempted to employ her "Thoughts and Industry in good Huswifery, knowing [his] Lordship had great Debts after [his] great Losses" (sig. II 2r), and highlights her contribution to the "Repair [of her husband's] ruined Estate." While living at Welbeck the Cavendishes did in fact do much to maintain the honor, wealth, and prestige of their county estate. When the Duke of York traveled through Nottinghamshire in August 1665 on his own summer progresses, for example, the newly-made Duke and Duchess of Newcastle[11] met the members of the party "between Nottingham and Rufford, and attended them to Rufford," both displaying their county and advertising their central role as its leading family (William was again Lord

---

11   On 16 March, 1665 the King turned the Marquess into the Duke of Newcastle-upon-Tyne" and the Cavendishes set off for Clerkenwell, drove in "great state" to Whitehall, and thanked the king (Trease, 193).

Lieutenant) (*CSPD* 1665: 503). The Cavendishes also maintained Welbeck Abbey as a site of elite cultural interest. In September 1668, Thomas Povey wrote to a friend about his travels in the northern counties, expressing excitement about his visit "to see the Queen of Sheba and her more considerable Prince, the Duke of Newcastle and his place, stables, riding-houses, and horses the most extraordinary in Europe" (*CSPD 1667–8*: 602). The title "Queen of Sheba," a term resonant of wisdom and renown, may well be used ironically here, but it does suggest the notoriety that Cavendish had gained and maintained in the English court, and her recognizable, if not universally-lauded, aristocratic bearing. In fact Cavendish's performance as a country lady, its exemplification of the ways in which aristocratic ceremony upheld the dignity of country and crown, was intimately related to her intermittent, and much more dramatic, performances in London.

While the Cavendishes endeavored to restore the values of aristocratic country hospitality and local leadership in the North, these values required regular participation in the political and social life of the capital. As the Cavendishes were well aware, office-holding was key not only to national and local influence but to economic survival (Jones, 83). It was thus in London that they made their most concerted efforts to seek influence in the post-Restoration court. In the spring of 1667, this effort involved a combination of the publication of elaborate texts, Margaret's *Life* of her husband, and William's illustrated book of horsemanship (Chalmers, 327), and pointed appearances in places of note. While the Cavendishes had visited court together a number of times before, the 1667 visit was scripted from its outset to exemplify the ideal behavior of the aristocracy, particularly as pertained to its relationship with the court. In his 1658/9 Letter of Advice to Charles II, William Cavendish stated that the country nobility should come to London at Easter "to the Joy of your Cities, & the Ladyes that have wanted a Courte So long, – & There your Majestie will Entertayne your Selfe with Severall Delights" before making his progresses to the counties (Slaughter, 62). In this fantasy of reciprocity, the county nobility came to court, and then the court came to them. By coming to London at Easter, in accordance with country "Ladyes" desires, Margaret Cavendish was thus in the ideal position to influence royal opinions through the "Severall Delights" of aristocratic performance. Indeed, immediately upon the Cavendishes' arrival in London they were given an audience with the king (Trease, 187; Mendelson, 48–50). The contemporaneous publication of Margaret Cavendish's *The Life of the Thrice Noble, High and Puissant Prince William Cavendish*, a text dedicated to Charles II, was meant to restore William Cavendish's reputation, as well as to give a strict accounting both of his losses in his service to, and of his ongoing commitment and political usefulness to the monarchy. If arriving at Easter and immediately making a public visit to the king was the first step in the Cavendishs' petition, the publication of *The Life* was the second.

The Life defends William Cavendish's merit, reminds the king that "the Army which my Lord raised for the defence and maintenance of the King, and his Rights, was raised most upon his own and his Friends Interest" (191), and complains that "the Lieutenancy of a County is barely a Title of Honour, without Profit" (198). (The Lord Lieutenancy did not bring a salary, and in fact, many unpaid offices in the localities, including Lord Lieutenancies, were granted predominantly to the old cavaliers who were not given prominent places in the Restoration court [Jones, 54; Miller, n.50]). Cavendish's attention to the loyalty and county power base of her husband is buttressed by the notorious calculations of her husband's losses – in property, rent, trees, stock, and lawsuits, and all to the value of almost one million pounds – and by her pointing to the fact that despite these losses, and without "other assistance [such as courtly office-holding] to bear him up," Cavendish "hath since his return paid both for Himself and his Son, all manner of Taxes, Lones, Levies, Assessments, &c. equally with the rest of His Majesties Subjects, according to that Estate that is left him, *which he has been forced to take upon Interest*" (107, emphasis added). Her careful calculations of his estates' economy, including her subtle reminder that the burden of taxation was often borne by the landed nobility, and her equally subtle mention of the interest Cavendish was paying *on his own estates* to the usurious "monied interests" who had been empowered materially by the civil war and commonwealth, attest not only to her own awareness of the Cavendishes' economic situation, but of her own material *usefulness* in their lives and fortunes as county nobility. (In *The Blazing World*, Cavendish posits a scenario in which these losses are remedied, partially through country house hospitality and entertainment. When the "Empress" accompanies the Duchess of Newcastle through Nottinghamshire for a visit to Welbeck, she notices the destroyed woods and buildings and wishes to repair them [109]. The encounter between the Empress and the Cavendishes ends with the Duke entertaining the Empress "with Scenes, Songs, Musick, [and] witty Discourses" – precisely the activities for which both Welbeck and the Duke were famous – and precisely the kinds of entertainments by which Cavendish had endeavored to influence the king politically in the pre-civil war, exilic, and early Restoration eras [111]).

In the real world, however, Charles II was tired of the importunities of returning cavaliers, believing that many of them were politically inept and past their prime (Miller, 164).[12] Furthermore, as John Miller points out, "[i]t made far better financial sense to annoy aged or impoverished royalists and courtiers than the city bankers on whose credit the government depended" (41)

---

12 Cavendish even expresses an awareness of the need for active petitioning: "I have heard my Lord say, That bold soliciting and intruding men, shall gain more by their importunate Petitions, then modest honest men shall get by silence (as being loath

(William Cavendish, in other words, was not the only one paying interest). A pointedly post-Restoration play by the Duchess dealing with such economic problems, *The Sociable Companions* (1668) begins with the disbanding of the army, and the recognition that "when a War is ended, Soldiers are out of Credit." (1.1.7).[13] The "Mass of Wealth," as one character points out, "is in the possession of Usurers, Lawyers, and Physicians" (2.4.41–2). The play's "poor Cavaliers" cannot get "Offices and Employments," and they do not even have access to the wealth of the play's usurer, Get-All, "for they have no Lands to Mortgage, nor Goods to Pawn" (3.1.55). While royalists like William Cavendish lost their estates, others – the new "monied interests" – had become established in property, and therefore in a new power basis which relied less on landed status than on wealth and influence (Seaward, 6; see also Jones, 85–91). At the end of the play, through the clever machinations of cavalier women, the usurer Get-all gives the ruined cavalier Captain Valorous twenty thousand pounds (5.2.92), enacting a fantasy in which monied interests give back to the royalists whose misfortunes made them wealthy.[14]

While the decline of the aristocracy began long before the civil war (see Stone), by the Restoration the rise of new interests – merchant, banking, bureaucratic – had usurped the rights and status of many older cavaliers. It was as much to these new powers as to the royal family that Margaret and William Cavendish presented themselves in their 1667 visit, embodying the old values of land and title in an era increasingly devoted to wealth. Margaret Cavendish's aristocratic performances were thus necessarily geared toward this audience as well as that of the court. While Cavendish idealized a society in which every

---

to offend, or be too troublesome) ... The reason, is, said he, That Great Princes will rather grant sometimes an unreasonable suit, then be tired with frequent Petitions, and hindred from their ordinary Pleasures" (*Life*, 178).

13 The action of the play focuses on three women who have lost their own economic mobility and power – their portions – because of their brothers' wartime loyalty and subsequent loss of estate (1.1.10). In order to maintain themselves according to their quality, the sisters resolve to marry the new men – usurer, lawyer and doctor – enacting the marriage between new professions and the gentry and peers that would characterize the socio-economic landscape of post-Restoration England. The play ends with a remarkable defense of the women's actions: since the Church and State "do allow of buying and selling young Maids to Men to be their Wives, they cannot condemn those Maids that make their bargain to their own advantage, and chuse rather to be bought then sold" (5.3.95).

14 Many of the other plays feature indictments of these new men; fools, often named "Mimick," who want to set themselves up as "Politick Counsel" ("But first, you must give me Lands, secondly, Moneys; thirdly, you must give me a great Office; and lastly, you must make me a great Lord" (*Presence*, 5.2.86).

class "Move[d] in its own Sphere" (*Sociable Letters*, 153), the London she encountered in the spring of 1667 was one of promiscuous mixing: the Restoration may have reestablished the aristocracy's political power, but it was "under new terms of relationship to a state evolving into a great naval, commercial, colonial and industrial power, and to increasing interdependence with the 'middle sort of people'" (Manning, 139). It was the London, in other words, of Samuel Pepys.

"[A] Majesticall presence"

A number of plays in Cavendish's 1662 volume feature famed aristocratic women who are sought out by others; people "flock about the house" to see one woman (*Youth's Glory*, 166) and confer about how to "compass the sight" of another, eventually deciding that a playhouse is the ideal place to find her (*Wits Cabal*, 1.1, 292). They reason further that such women would "rather appear handsomer at a distance than at a near view," for "whole streets of people view Ladies as they passe through it in their Coaches, when perchance not above half a dozen neighbours and acquaintance see them near hand" (304). A detractor wonders why a third woman is "cryed up so," claiming that "she dresses Phantastically, [and] is proud, reserved, coy, disdainful, and self-conceited" (*Natures Three Daughters*, 3.10, 499–500), while her defender, a woman named "Tell-truth," states simply that the famed Lady is "a Majesticall presence" (500). What is fascinating about these scenes is the extent to which they seem prescient, as if Cavendish were writing her own soon-to-be-famous and much-discussed appearances in London: at her house in Clerkenwell; at a playhouse for the performance of a play mistaken as her own; in her coach (often followed by other coaches as well as by seekers on foot); and as a "Phantastically" dressed and "self-conceited" public figure.

Yet what seems prescient in these scenes, I argue, was actually scripted; in her plays, as well as her public appearances, Cavendish self-consciously managed her reputation and appearance in order to foreground her "Right of place" in a society full of imposters and upstarts. All of these aforementioned London appearances, which I am calling performances, were recorded, with a characteristic combination of curiosity and condescension, by the naval bureaucrat Samuel Pepys. While Pepys's observations have become almost axiomatic in summaries of Cavendish's purported narcissism and eccentricity – he comments at length on her dress, notoriety, and self-promotion – I argue instead that Pepys's observations represent key changes in the perception of status, and its performance, in the early Restoration. Pepys's comments thus testify to Cavendish's final form of noble petitioning. By the time Pepys wants to see her play so that he "might better understand her," Cavendish had become a figure of considerable renown, whose very life was seen as something of a performance; as Charles North wrote in the same year, "*The Dutchess Newcastle is all ye pageant now discoursed on*" (cited in Wiseman, 93, emphasis added). According to Pepys, there is "as much expectation of her coming to Court ... as if it were the Queen of Sweden," and "The whole story of this lady is a romance" (163–4, 163). Pepys endeavors to see her on three different occasions: on 11 April, 1667 at Whitehall when she came to court to visit the Queen ("the King having been with her yesterday" [163]), at the playhouse, and at her own London home in Clerkenwell. Only on 26 April, does Pepys actually catch sight of her, "going with her coaches and footmen all in velvet; herself (whom I never before saw) as I have heard her often described (for all the town-talk is nowadays of her extravagancies), with her velvet-cap, her hair about her ears, many black patches ... and a black juste-au-corps" – a fashion, as Sophie Tomlinson points out, recently made popular by Charles II's queen (Pepys, 186–7; Tomlinson, 289). From her own attire to that of her footmen (velvet was historically reserved for noble liveries), Cavendish's presence is suitably "Majestical." On May Day, Pepys and another government official join the fray ("a horrid dust and number of coaches, without pleasure or order"), to try to see her again, but they are unable to, "she being followed and crowded upon by coaches all the way she went, that nobody could come near her; only I could see she was in a large black coach adorned with silver" (196). Like the lady in her play, Cavendish, both widely talked about and sought-after, can only be seen from a distance.

Yet while most Cavendish scholars are only interested in Pepys's observations of Cavendish herself, his people-watching continues in an illuminating vein. Although he fails to get a good view of Cavendish, what Pepys "did see and wonder at" was "Pegg Penn in a new coach, with only her husband's pretty sister with her, both patched very fine, and in much *the finest coach in the park*, and I think that ever I did see, one or other for neatness and richness in gold and *everything that is noble*" (196, emphasis added). "Pegg Penn" was the wife of Pepys's colleague Sir William Penn, a navy bureaucrat and "new man" knighted by Henry Cromwell in 1658. While Pepys seems at first to praise this display of wealth – he notes that the coach was "the finest" in the park – he is also aware of the discrepancies between the fineness of the coach and the status of its owners, noting that "to live in the condition they do at home, and be abroad in this coach, astonishes me" (197). Pepys further observes, not without condemnation, that the Penn coach is better than that which is driven by the king himself (196).

Pepys's self-conscious awareness of the performance of wealth and its relationship to status was, unsurprisingly, one of Cavendish's key concerns. In *Sociable Letters* she condemns Commoners who "strive to Out-brave the Nobles in their Building, Garnishing, Furnishing, Adorning and Flourishing in Gold and Bravery." Even the "Mechanicks in this City," she wrote, "are Suffer'd to have their Coaches, Lacquies, Pages, Waiting-maides, and to wear

Rich and Glorious Garments, Fashioning themselves in all things like the Nobles." The Commons, she continued, should "live according to their Qualities, *not according to their Wealth*" (*Sociable Letters*, 78, emphasis added). In many ways, Pepys seems to concur with Cavendish: while the Penns' gold-embossed coach seems on the surface to exemplify "*everything that is noble*," Pepys is still somewhat invested in the traditional status hierarchy: the wife of a former sea captain (one knighted by a regicide) should not have a grander coach than the king. Although Pepys, himself a member of the new bureaucracy and a descendant of tradesmen and lawyers, ambivalently admires the Penns' coach, he still returns later that day to Clerkenwell "thinking to have met Lady Newcastle before she got home" (197). Pepys, in other words, is one facet of the audience that Cavendish hoped, and, I argue, performed for: one which admires, even follows at a distance, the hereditary nobility. While both Pegg Penn and Cavendish share the same ethos of theatrical self-display, Pepys's discriminations suggest that Cavendish was, to some extent, right: display and pageantry are different for the nobility. Cavendish has, just as she planned in *Poems and Fancies*, set all the tongues to work; like the "cryed up" ladies in her 1662 plays, she is an object of considerable public attention.

Thus rather than providing evidence of her eccentricity, I see Cavendish's public performances of her "Majesticall presence," dressed in the trappings of nobility, and set only in the most trafficked London locations, as precisely the point of her visit. In from their county seat, at the time of year when the nobility are meant to come to court, Margaret Cavendish performs the Cavendishes' noble status and elitism (not everyone, as Pepys learned the hard way, could see her up close), but she also seeks to remind the royal family, and the wider circle of power brokers, of the Cavendishes' proper place. In 1667, William Cavendish's old enemy the Earl of Clarendon was falling out of favor (Seaward, 24; Jones, 17, 160), and he still hoped to be given a position at court, perhaps as the head of the Duke of York's standing army (Seaward, 32). The visit in which Margaret Cavendish, according to Mary Evelyn, went on at length "magnifying her own generous actions, stately buildings, noble fortune, her lord's prodigious losses in the war, his power, valour, wit, learning, and industry" did indeed make Cavendish seem "amazingly vain and ambitious" to Evelyn (cited in Mendelson, 53). Yet such self-promotion was the way in which Cavendish knew how to make her presence, and her political desires, known to the increasingly alien culture of Restoration London, particularly in a social context of increasingly socially-dominant bourgeois women. Evelyn herself recognized Cavendish's visit as a performance, writing that her own "part was not yet to speak, but to admire" (cited in Tomlinson 1998, 384).

"[A]s one of her quality ought to be"

While Cavendish may have imaginatively pre-scripted her notorious visit to London in several of her 1662 plays, the final play in her 1668 volume, *A Piece of a Play*, seems to rewrite that visit according to Cavendish's own values. In this play the entire community is concerned with the question of whether or not "the Lady Phoenix [has] come to Town" (1.1.3, A2r). While it is widely reported "that she is coming to Town in such splendor, as the World never saw the like," those who have not yet seen her seek information (1.2.4 A2v). Much like Pepys himself, one Sir Puppy asserts that while he has not seen her, he has "heard of her" (6 B1v), and "hearing of a wonderful Lady coming to this City," another character "came as speedily as [he] could to this Company to know the truth." While city life, as Cavendish wrote elsewhere, was "Gossiping and Vain" (*Sociable Letters*, 227), this fact could be used to one's own self-promoting advantage. Much like Cavendish, the Lady Phoenix is a subject of gossip, and, also like her model, she is perceived differently by different sociopolitical interests. One gallant, appropriately named Monsieur Ass, reports that while he has not seen Lady Phoenix himself, he is "credibly informed, that she is as proud as Lucifer, she despises her Superiors, and scorns her Inferiors" (1.2.5, sig. B1r). Yet unlike contemporaneous records of her own appearances, Cavendish provides a defense of Lady Phoenix, given by her loyal, and appropriately submissive servant, Dormouse: "[Lady Phoenix] is of a studious nature, in a retired life, ever retiring from much Company, and of a careless humour, not regarding what the World says, or doth; in Company she is of a free Disposition, and an airy Conversation; she is civil to strangers, kind to acquaintances, bountiful to her servants, and charitable to the poor; also, she is humble to those that are respectful, but severe to those that are rude" (7, sig. B2r). Much like Cavendish, Lady Phoenix is described as an appropriately aristocratic country lady, enjoying her retirement from the court, but mindful of the obligations and privileges of her status. When Monsieur Ass insists that she is "the proudest Creature alive," Dormouse delivers the most important line of the play: "She may chance to seem proud to an Ass, and vain to a Buzzard," she says, "but otherwise, she is as one of her quality ought to be."

Lady Phoenix is meant to exist in aristocratic contrast to the "Mode-Accoutrements" (2.1.12) of the social climbers, and her appearances – appropriately distanced from the crowds, and shrouded in luxurious mystery – stand in contrast to the taverns and coffee-houses (those populist dens of indiscriminate mixing) in which the other characters gather to gossip and strategize. Sir Puppy, for one, spends his time in practicing to be a "Mode-gallant" and vying with Sir Bear-man for the attentions of Lady Monkey – "are you for a Play? or Court? or High-Park to day?" (2.2.14). (Cavendish here seems to discredit other forms of theatrical interest in order to further legitimate her own). Both Sir Puppy and Sir Bear-man ultimately offer the

Lady a "Coach and six Horses," and while Bear-man insists that his, "being a Lord's Coach," is a better mode of conveyance, Sir Puppy asserts that "A Gentleman is as good as a Lord." In response Bear-man sends him to "enquire of the Herauld of our Pedigrees" (2.2.15). Although the scene mocks both men, the role of the Herald and of Pedigrees – those recorders of the social order in which Cavendish held such faith – still has resonance as the stop-gap measure for elite privilege in an era in which, as William Cavendish himself feared, "Every Citizens wife will Have six Horses in her Coach," a phenomenon decidedly unfitting for what "is right, & dewe, for their places, & Digneties" (Slaughter, 46).

Traditionally, a gentleman "was one who was certified as armigerous – entitled to bear a coat of arms – by the herald who used to make regular visitations to the counties. Their insistence on authentic gentle birth, and an absolute separation for at least three generations from the degrading pursuit of trade, industry, or usury" had become anachronistic by the Restoration: "a gentleman," as one scholar puts it, "was one who could pass himself off as one" (Jones, 86). While Sir Puppy passes himself off as a gentleman well enough, his tastes betray his true quality; the play he wants to attend with Lady Monkey was written by Monsieur Ass. Followed by Lady Leveritt, a figure of sycophantic emulation, the ladies and their courtly lovers go off to precisely the type of theater Cavendish derided throughout her work: a "Mode-Play," the antithesis of the nobility-educating drama Cavendish promoted (2.2.20). By ending her play – and the 1668 volume – with the vindication of Lady Phoenix, a woman aristocrat who behaves "as one of her quality ought to be," Cavendish flies in the face of those who think status is something emulable, purchaseable, unmoored. True grandeur, her play insists – a play modeled, as I have argued, on Cavendish's own 1667 visit to the capital – rises from the ashes of misfortune with her feathers intact, fully prepared to shine "in such splendor, as the World never saw the like." When Margaret Cavendish arrived at the theater to see her husband's play – which Pepys, for one, believed she had written herself – she arrived in appropriate style: her "intrado" as Charles North wrote sardonically, "was incognito [save for] a triumphale chariot with 12 horses, six more than even the most ambitious Citizen's wife could muster" (cited in Wiseman, 93).

Works Cited

Brown, Cedric C. "Courtesies of Place and Arts of Diplomacy in Ben Jonson's Last Two Entertainments for Royalty." *Seventeenth Century* 9 (1994): 147–71.
Calendar of State Papers, Domestic Series, 1657–8. Ed. Mary Anne Everett Green. [1884]; repr. Vaduz: Kraus Reprint, 1965.

Calendar of the State Papers Relating to Ireland, 1647–60. Ed. Robert Pentland Mahaffy. London: Printed for his Majesty's Stationery Office by Mackie and Co, 1903.

The Calendar of State Papers, Domestic Series, 1664–1665. Ed. Mary Anne Everett Green. London: Longman, Green, Longman, Roberts and Green, 1863.

Calendar of State Papers, Domestic Series, November 1667 to September 1668. Ed. Mary Anne Everett Green. London: Printed for Her Majesty's Stationery Office, by Eyre and Spottiswoode, 1893.

Carte, Thomas. *A Collection of Original Letters and Papers Concerning the Affairs of England, From the Year 1641 to 1660 Found Among the Duke of Ormonde's Papers*, Volume 1. London: John Bettenham, 1739.

Cavendish, Margaret. *Poems and Fancies: Written by the Right Honourable, the Lady Margaret Marchioness Newcastle*. London: Printed by T. R. for J. Martin and J. Allestrye, 1653.

———. *Philosophical Fancies. Written by the Right Honourable, The Lady Newcastle*. London: Printed by Tho. Roycroft, for J. Martin, and J. Allestrye, 1653.

———. *The World's Olio, Written By the Right Honorable, the Lady Margaret Newcastle*. London: Printed for J. Martin and J. Allestrye at the Bell in St. Pauls Church-Yard, 1655.

———. *A True Relation of my Birth, Breeding, and Life*, in *Natures Pictures Drawn By Fancies Pencil*. London: J. Martin and J. Allestrye, 1656.

———. *Orations of Divers Sorts, Accommodated to Divers Places, Written by the thrice Noble, Illustrious and Excellent Princess, the Lady Marchioness of Newcastle*. London, 1662.

———. *Plays Written by the Thrice Noble, Illustrious and Excellent Princess, The Lady Marchioness of Newcastle*. London: Printed by A. Warren, for John Martyn, James Allestry, and Tho. Dicas, at the Bell in Saint Pauls Church Yard, 1662.

———. *Philosophical and Physical Opinions*. London: William Wilson, 1663.

———. *Sociable Letters* [1664]. Ed. James Fitzmaurice. New York and London: Garland, 1997.

———. *Plays, Never before Printed. Written By the Thrice Noble, Illustrious, and Excellent Princesse the Duchess of Newcastle*. London: Printed by A. Maxwell, in the Year 1668.

———. *The Description of a New World, called The Blazing-World. Written By the Thrice Noble, Illustrious, and Excellent Princesse, the Duchess of Newcastle*. London, Printed by A. Maxwell, in the Year 1668.

Chalmers, Hero. "Dismantling the Myth of 'Mad Madge': The Cultural Context of Margaret Cavendish's Authorial Self-presentation." *Women's Writing* 4.3 (1997): 323–40.

Evelyn, John. *Diary and Correspondence of John Evelyn*, ed. William Bray, 4 vols. London: Henry Colburn, 1857.

Fitzmaurice, James. "William Cavendish and Two Entertainments by Ben Jonson." *Ben Jonson Journal* 5 (1998): 63–80.

Hopkins, Lisa. "Play Houses: Drama at Bolsover and Welbeck." *Early Theatre* 2 (1999): 25–44.

Hulse, Lynn. "'The King's Entertainment' by the Duke of Newcastle." *Viator* 26 (1995): 355–405.

————, ed. *The Dramatic Works of William Cavendish*. Oxford: Malone Society Reprints, Vol. 158, 1996.

Jones, J. R. *Country and Court England 1658–1714*. Cambridge, MA: Harvard University Press, 1979.

Manning, Brian. *Aristocrats, Plebians and Revolution in England 1640–1660*. London: Pluto Press, 1996.

Mendelson, Sara. *The Mental World of Stuart Women: Three Studies*. Amherst: University of Massachusetts Press, 1987.

Miller, John. *After the Civil Wars: English Politics and Government in the Reign of Charles II*. London: Longman, 2000.

The Life of the Thrice Noble, High and Puissant Prince William Cavendishe, Duke, Marquess, and Earl of Newcastle ... written by the Thrice Noble, Illustrious and Excellent Princess Margaret, Duchess of Newcastle, his wife. London: A. Maxwell, 1667.

The Nicholas Papers. Correspondence of Sir Edward Nicholas, Secretary of State, Vol. I, 1641–52. Ed. George F. Warner. Printed for the Camden Society, 1887; repr. 1965.

The Nicholas Papers. Correspondence of Sir Edward Nicholas, Secretary of State, Vol II January 1653–June 1655. Ed. George F. Warner. Printed for the Camden Society, 1892; repr. 1965.

Pepys, Samuel. *The Diary of Samuel Pepys*, Vol. 8 (1667). Ed. Robert Latham and William Matthews. Berkeley: University of California Press, 1970; 1983.

Potter, Lois. *Secret Rites and Secret Writing: Royalist Literature, 1641–1660*. Cambridge: Cambridge University Press, 1989.

Randall, Dale B. J. *Winter Fruit: English Drama, 1642–1660*. Lexington, Kentucky: University Press of Kentucky, 1995.

Rowe, Nick. "My Best Patron: William Cavendish and Jonson's Caroline Dramas." *Seventeenth Century* 9.2 (1994): 197–212.

Seaward, Paul. *The Restoration*. London: Macmillan, 1991.

Slaughter, Thomas P. Ed. *Ideology and Politics on the Eve of the Restoration: Newcastle's Advice to Charles II*. Philadelphia: The American Philosophical Society, 1984.

Stone, Lawrence. *The Crisis of the Aristocracy, 1558–1641*. Abridged edn. Oxford: Oxford University Press, 1967.

Tomlinson, Sophie Eliza. "'My Brain the Stage': Margaret Cavendish and the fantasy of female performance." *Readings in Renaissance Women's Drama*. Ed. S. P. Cerasano and Marion Wynne-Davies. New York: Routledge, 1998, 272–92.

Trease, Geoffrey. *Portrait of a Cavalier: William Cavendish, First Duke of Newcastle*. London: Macmillan, 1979.

Walker, Greg. *The Politics of Performance in Early Renaissance Drama*. Cambridge: Cambridge University Press, 1998.

Wiseman, Susan. *Drama and Politics in the English Civil War*. Cambridge: Cambridge University Press, 1998.

PART V
BEYOND THE "ALL-MALE"

Chapter 12

Staging the Absent Woman: The Theatrical Evocation of Elizabeth Tudor in Heywood's *If You Know Not Me, You Know Nobody, Part I*

Jean E. Howard

We now know, partly on the evidence of this book as well as the work of other scholars, that there were many women performers in Elizabethan and Jacobean England. They told jests, jigged, assumed roles in court masques, and performed for one another in plays at secluded country estates.[1] What we don't have is evidence that women performed as actors in London's commercial theater companies prior to the Restoration. Recently, in *Shakespeare Without Women*, Dympna Callaghan has again enjoined scholars not to forget the political implications of this fact (1–25). Evoked at the *representational* level, women were *presentationally* excluded on the early modern professional stage. In this essay I want to return once again to thinking about the paradoxical implications of the phenomenon of the absent-present "woman" of the Elizabethan and Jacobean commercial theater by considering the stage's representation of one woman who was both a powerful historical agent and a talented female player herself: Queen Elizabeth. I will argue that focusing on stage evocations of the historical Elizabeth reveals with unusual clarity something central to the operation of this all-male stage: namely, the irresolvable tension surrounding its exploitation of the absent female body. On the one hand, in the daily and ongoing exclusion of the female actor and playwright, this stage was seemingly free to create whatever representations of woman it desired; on the other hand, by such exclusions it also made itself

---

1   To cite only recent scholarship dealing with a variety of cultural arenas, see Pamela Brown on women's performances in such popular venues as alehouse, fair, and street; Clare McManus on women's performances at court, especially as masquers; and Alison Findlay and Stephanie Hodgson-Wright on women as performers (and often authors) in plays put on at non-commercial venues such as country houses.

conspicuously reliant on the discursive citation of femininity (through dress, cosmetics, wigs and verbal conventions) to evoke women. To the extent that this theater was performatively successful, I will argue, it was necessarily haunted by its own exclusions and confronted with materializations of femininity in many ways as "real" and as unpredictable in their consequences as the empirical bodies of the "women" who sat or stood in the audiences but did not perform as members of the London acting companies. The case of Elizabeth I as prosthetic stage presence will, I hope, help me to unfold some of the implications of such an argument.

My account of how the fantasy of femininity is produced on a stage containing no "real" women is indebted to the work of Judith Butler who, in *Bodies That Matter: On the Discursive Limits of "Sex"* demonstrates that not just gender codes but the sexed body itself is brought into being – her preferred term is materialized – through the citation and reiteration of cultural norms. Matter does not simply pre-exist cultural inscription to form a bedrock of the "real;" rather, it is itself produced over time in relation to regulatory practices and performative rituals. The all-male stage is an important example of a place where femininity is materialized through the repeated citation of cultural codes signifying womanliness, whether those are something as mundane as the long hair of a wig or the fashionable shape of a farthingale, or as "poetic" as the sonneteer's cliches describing the red and white of "true" feminine beauty, probably materialized on stage by a white fucus makeup with red overlay. In this paper I am particularly interested in how the stage femininity of Elizabeth I is constructed, first as she is a princess, and finally as a queen, but my larger point is that all materializations of stage womanhood, whether they veer toward misogyny or toward female affirmation, iterate fantasies of femininity that can belie the artifice of their construction and can have socially unpredictable consequences.

As this book shows, boys performing women on the commercial stage did so in a culture in which audience members would be familiar with female performers in a variety of other contexts. These "real" women may well have helped construct the codes for performing femininity upon which the boy actors drew for their own actions. In the case of Elizabeth Tudor, actors would inevitably have had to work with the elaborate and pervasive conventions that Elizabeth and her supporters had created for representing different aspects of her royal femininity. This is simply a pronounced instance of a general rule: that is, that creating femininity on the all-male stage meant citing and working with discursive constructions of femininity neither originating with nor entirely in the control of the male playwright or the boy actor but capable of making femininity "present" in politically volatile ways even in the "absence" of bodies sexed female.

Let me turn now to some public stage evocations of Elizabeth Tudor. Living monarchs could not, of course, be represented on the London stages. But immediately after Elizabeth's death, Thomas Heywood did what during her lifetime could not have been done: he represented her in the public theater.[2] He did so in two plays, *If You Know Not Me, You Know Nobody, Parts I and II*, both published in 1605.[3] The first, approximately 1,600 lines long, depicts the suffering of the princess during the reign of Mary, including her imprisonment in the Tower of London. It was wildly popular, if printed versions of the play are any indication of the interest it generated. Editions appeared in 1606, 1608, 1610, 1613, 1623, 1632, 1639, as well as in 1605.[4] The second and much longer play has as its focal point the building of the Royal Exchange by Sir Thomas Gresham, and it offers an interestingly complex picture of the commercial life of Elizabethan London.[5] The queen dominates this play less than the first. She appears at the opening of Gresham's Exchange and gives it its formal name, the Royal Exchange; later, she miraculously escapes an assassination attempt on her life; in the final portion of the play she presides over the English fleet's successful conquest of the Spanish Armada. There are two extant versions of the Armada sequence, one approximately 200 lines longer than the other; and it is not altogether clear that this sequence was always intended to be part of the play that focuses on Gresham. In her Malone Society edition, Madeleine

---

2   Of course, the early modern stage regularly staged fictive, mythic, and long-dead queens such as Dido, Cleopatra, and the numerous queens of Shakespeare's history plays. By focusing on Elizabeth, I am using the difficult issue of how to represent a recently dead female monarch to raise larger questions about how femininity in general was performed on the all-male stage. Shakespeare, for example, seemed wary of representing Elizabeth at all and only did so in his late history play, *Henry VIII* or *All Is True*, where she appears as an infant at her christening. I am leaving aside entirely the court masques which not only staged queens, as in Jonson's *Masque of Queens*, but occasionally used royal women such as Queen Anna as performers. These works raise different questions about how femininity was performatively materialized than does the all-male stage, though I would argue that even in the masque femininity was not simply the consequence of a particular sexed body but was a regulated *production*.

3   For a discussion of Heywood's abiding preoccupation with Elizabeth, far beyond these two plays, see Georgianna Ziegler (1980).

4   All references to the play are to the Malone Society edition prepared by Madeleine Doran (1935). For dates of the various seventeenth-century editions see p. vi. The number of editions suggests that the play was popular with readers. Heywood also claims in his prologue to the 8th edition of 1639 that the play had been popular on the stage when it had first been produced, probably in 1604–5; and there was at least one stage revival, probably by Queen Henrietta's Men at the Cockpit in the early 1630s. It is interesting to speculate that this revival was championed by Charles's queen, a known patron of the drama.

5   I examine the commercial ideologies in competition in this text in Henry Turner's *The Culture of Capital* (163–82).

Doran speculates that the Armada scenes might once have been the conclusion of the much shorter *Part I* (xvii).

I am going to concentrate on *Part I* and in the only textual version we have, that is, the short play first printed in 1605 which concludes, not with the conquest of the Armada, but with Elizabeth's assumption of the throne after the death of Mary, an assumption that puts an end to and seems the reward for Elizabeth's prior suffering. I will focus, in particular, on how this play uses the presentational elements of theater to represent and evoke Elizabeth when it cannot rely on the sexed body of the actor as the ground for such a representation, and then will explore what this particular play suggests more generally about the consequences of staging women on the all-male stage. The title of the play, printed on the original title-page as, *If you know not me, You know no bodie*, indirectly raises the issues I wish to address: how does one recognize the dead queen in the living body of a male actor? The dead, after all, no longer have animate bodies, and cannot walk the stage. In the Elizabethan theater, women also had "no bodies," at least not the body natural of their sex. How then was this dead queen given stage embodiment? How did she become unmistakably recognizable to a theater audience? And what is the consequence of this early modern stage evocation of the dead queen for our current thinking about the status of women as players/non-players on the early modern stage?

Elizabeth, of course, is in some ways a very particular subject for stage representation. A powerful historical figure, she had probably been dead only a little more than a year when the play was first performed. Andrew Gurr and Madeleine Doran both assign the play to the Red Bull, where it would first have been staged by Queen Anne's Men (Gurr, 132; Doran, xiv). The part of Elizabeth would therefore presumably have been played by a boy actor in an adult company on an outdoor stage. In this instance, the fact of the boy actor's indeterminate status between boy and man may have resonated interestingly with the theatrical Elizabeth's precarious status as a young princess who might or might not one day be queen. In *Twelfth Night* Malvolio describes to the curious Olivia the appearance of the young messenger (Viola disguised as Cesario): "Not yet old enough for a man, nor young enough for a boy; as a squash is before 'tis a peascod, or a codling when 'tis almost an apple. 'Tis with him in standing water between boy and man" (1.5.139–42).[6] This description fits both the androgynous Viola, convincingly disguised as a young man, and also the boy actor, convincingly impersonating a young woman. While in *If You Know Not Me, You Know Nobody* Elizabeth's gender identity as a princess is not called in question by disguise, it is nonetheless true that Heywood's character is poised in a liminal space between childhood and the adult role that

---

6   All quotations from Shakespeare's plays will be taken from Stephen Greenblatt (Gen. Ed.) *The Norton Shakespeare* (1997), here cited at p.1777.

may come, the role of monarch traditionally reserved for men. For most of the play Elizabeth is young, uncrowned, and in danger. Born in 1533, she would have been in her early twenties during her half-sister Mary's reign. Consequently, both the character of Elizabeth and the actor impersonating her have yet to assume their final social shapes.

In the printed versions of the play the reader would have been given an anticipation of Elizabeth's eventual metamorphosis into the Queen of England through the title-pages that adorned successive printings of the play. In 1605 (and in the four subsequent editions) a quite lovely woodcut shows Elizabeth seated on her throne of state, majestically holding the scepter in one hand, the orb in the other (fig. 12.1). She is festooned with jewels, a crown on her head, a canopy and curtains framing her image. In the sixth and seventh editions of 1623 and 1632 a much cruder woodcut shows a rather featureless Elizabeth standing on a tiled floor against a plain background with two curtains framing the upper corners of the picture. Elizabeth again, however, holds the scepter and orb and wears a crown and an ornate dress, although there are fewer jewels in evidence. In the 1639 edition the title-page undergoes another declension. It contains a much smaller image of Elizabeth, who is shown only from the waist up against a starkly plain background. Crowned, she holds the orb and scepter, and on either side of her head appear the letters E and R for Elizabeth Regina.[7]

Despite the varying quality and ornateness of these woodcuts, they all share one feature: they show an Elizabeth who is a head of state bearing, in every image, the insignia of her office. Appearing on the title-page of the successive editions of the play, these woodcuts would have evoked for readers a powerful memory of the queen who ruled England for forty-five years and who had been frequently depicted with her regalia of office in media as disparate as large-scale oil paintings, title-pages of important books such as the first edition of *The Bishops Bible* in 1568, and in popular texts such as Heywood's play quartos. In some ways, staging a figure who recalled these iconic images might be quite simple: a matter of a red wig, a crown, an ornate gown with face-framing ruff, fake gems, and a property house orb and scepter. This, however, is not the Elizabeth the play depicts, except in the final scene. As I have indicated, up to that point she is not a queen, but a queen in waiting, a princess. The character could not, therefore, be dressed in the crown and robes of state we see in the 1605 woodcut, nor could she carry the orb and scepter before her accession. In short, while the printer of the Quarto texts could use the title-page to prepare the reader to associate the princess of the play with the regal queen, it seems unlikely the stage could do the same, especially not in a play where

---

7   Reproductions of all of these title-pages are included in The Malone Society edition of the play, unpaginated leaves following p.xxxix.

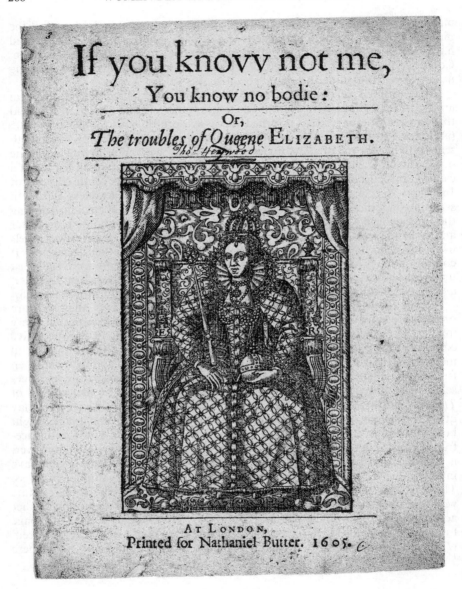

12.1   Title page from Thomas Heywood, *If You Know Not Me, You Know Nobody* **(1605).**

Mary, the ruling monarch, frequently appears and, as early as the second scene, enters in the midst of a procession designed to impress upon the viewer her royal status: *"Enter Tame bearing the purse: Shandoyse the Mace: Howard the Septer; Sussex the Crowne: then the Queene, after her the Cardinall, Sentlow, Gage, and attendants"* (sd. preceding sc. 2, A3v). For 1,500 lines, Mary is the queen, not Elizabeth.

It is only with the play's last 100 lines that Elizabeth, on her way to be crowned, appears on stage surrounded by officers and signifiers of state in a procession echoing and superseding Mary's initial stage entry: *"A Sennet. Enter 4 Trumpetors, after them Sargeant Trumpetor with a Mace, after him Purse-bearer;* Sussex *with the Crown,* Howard *the Scepter,* Constable *with the Cap of mayntenance,* Shandoyse *with the Sword,* Tame *with the Coller and a* George, *foure Gentlemen bearing the Canapy over the* Queene, *two Gentle-women bearing up her trayne, six gentle-men* Pensioners, *the* Queene *takes state"* (sd. preceeding sc. xxiii, G3). Here Elizabeth is wrapped in a ceremony of state that is also a ceremony of the stage. The full theatrical company is probably on the boards at this moment and dressed in whatever impressive court clothes the wardrobe allows, their dignity enhanced by the props they bear and offer, in turn, to the queen as she sits in state. As Peter Stallybrass and Ann Jones have recently argued, material objects (clothes, insignia of office or occupation, armor, spindles, spurs, and writing implements) are integral to the process of constituting subjects during the early modern period (Stallybrass and Jones, passim). Surrounding the new Queen with the material emblems of office, the stage literalizes this process of royal subject construction.

Yet even here questions about staging arise. Historically, on her coronation day Elizabeth wore three different costumes, two inherited from her half-sister Mary, including the expensive cloth of gold gown and mantle of state, the latter trimmed with ermine, which she had also worn the day before in her entry procession through the London streets (Ziegler 2003, 34). A painting in the manner of Hilliard and dated *c*.1600 depicts Elizabeth in golden coronation robes, her golden-reddish hair falling loose over her shoulders.[8] It is tempting to imagine that the stage approximated some version of such a costume,

---

8 For discussion of this painting, see Arnold 1978 and Arnold 1988, 33. Samuel Pepys famously remarked on a 1667 production of the Heywood plays that, while ridiculous, it "shows the true garb of the queens in these days, just as we see Queen Mary and Queen Elizabeth painted" (quoted in Grant in Doran and Freedman, 120). He also commented on the fact that the maid, Clarentia, sang a song in her bare face and nightgown (in Dobson and Watson, 68). Both comments suggest to me how much traditions of stage representation had changed during the course of the seventeenth century. The presence of female actresses allowed for displays of the female body, as in Clarentia's interpolated song, which she delivered wearing a nightgown! Moreover, on the Restoration stage neither Elizabeth nor Mary would

though cloth of gold and ermine were obviously too costly for direct acquisition.[9] Moreover, the issue of Elizabeth wearing articles of Mary's clothing raises questions about how repetition and difference functioned in this final stage procession. To some extent, in assuming royal office, Elizabeth assumes the subject position Mary had just inhabited. The two women were successive embodiments of the undying monarchical body. This seems to be what is signaled by the self-conscious repetition at the end of the play of the earlier procession involving Mary. Elizabeth is now literally surrounded by the emblems of office that surrounded Mary and takes part in the same ceremonies of state.

It is *also* possible that the stage Elizabeth could wear in her coronation procession a gown previously worn by the stage Mary. Inhabiting the garments of one's predecessor was a way of expressing the continuity of rule and the passage of power. For example, in Samuel Daniel's first masque for the Jacobean court in 1604, no new costumes for the masquing ladies were designed since the women, including Queen Anna, wore garments taken from the wardrobe of Queen Elizabeth (McManus 2002, 107–9). Thrift might have dictated this choice, but so, equally, might have the desire to appropriate the dead queen's authority. It is not illogical that Heywood's Queen Elizabeth of the last scene could have worn a dress worn earlier in the play by Queen Mary. Such a choice would have further emphasized the extent to which both women were constructed by practices/clothing/signifiers that existed prior to either's inscription by them.[10]

And yet I myself do not imagine repetition was taken so far, in part because the play is at some pains to juxtapose throughout the virtues of Elizabeth and

---

have had to be sexually constituted solely through their clothes and other material signifiers. Those clothes could therefore simply become, as they are for Pepys, a window into the fashions of a bygone age.

9   Michael Dobson and Nicola Watson (50) use the term "costume drama" to describe Heywood's plays, though they note that only in the last scene does she actually appear wearing robes of state (52). The term "costume drama," however, seems both anachronistic and trivializing. In 1604 Heywood was not evoking a long-past reign through pretty costumes, nor was there a more effective way on the non-naturalistic stage to create socially differentiated characters. All drama in the period, I would argue, was "costume drama," but not in the sense that we have come to associate the term with: the pageant-like evocation by dress of a past historical moment. Rather, dress in all early modern theatrical production was one of the most central technologies for constituting identity, including gender identity.

10 Dobson and Watson (57) speculate that for the second part of Heywood's play the acting company might have been able to get hold of some of Elizabeth's actual clothes for use on the stage. This is an intriguing possibility, but I have been able to find no evidence for it.

the vices of Mary (Grant in Doran and Freeman, 122). Heywood's Elizabeth both is and is not a simulacrum of her older half-sister. Laying claim to her office and the subject position created through that office, Elizabeth nonetheless is different: younger, Protestant, virginal. Were Mary staged as queen with hair up, signifying her married state, and a dark dress, Elizabeth's final appearance in a golden gown with her hair down, signifying her maidenhood, would signal the distance between these two women, even as the paraphernalia surrounding their stage processions would conjoin them. Both stage "women," however, depend on the repeated citation of the codes of queenliness and of different kinds of femininity to materialize the boy actor into a convincing representation of royal womanhood.

But in some ways the final staging of Elizabeth on her way to her coronation is the easy bit for a company to encompass since it relies on a widely shared set of public symbols: that is, the queen is a woman with an orb and a scepter whether or not her ornate dress directly echoes that earlier worn by her half-sister. But what about the Elizabeth of the preceding twenty-two scenes? How could the stage, using the base materials of theatrical production but denied the employment of monarchical regalia, create a stage image of the young Elizabeth that would at once materialize her female gender and distinguish her as a subject of more than common import? Hollywood films have often solved the problem of Elizabeth's pre-queen years by giving her a love life abruptly interrupted by the duties of office.[11] In short, they materialize her femininity by citation of the codes of romance. Heywood does something else: he gives Elizabeth – not a love life – but a position within a Protestant martyrology that I will suggest helps to solve both the representational and presentational problems of staging the young princess. First of all, as I will demonstrate below, in his *Acts and Monuments* John Foxe scripts non-martial forms of heroism that explicitly make a place for female as well as male performers. Following Foxe, then, allows Heywood to create for the princess a particular kind of stage femininity: virginal, virtuous, and yet heroic in her steely adherence to the Protestant faith and in her resistance to the demands of her Catholic half-sister.[12] There are several prototypes for this characterization. She is like patient Griselda, a virtuous woman irrationally tormented by, in her

---

11 Starting with Sarah Bernhardt's 1912 *The Lover of the Queen*, many films dealing with Elizabeth have focused on her private life, and especially on her imagined love relations with such male courtiers as the Earl of Essex (Betteridge in Doran and Freedman, 242–59). The 1998 movie *Elizabeth*, starring Cate Blanchett, is no exception. It depicts a sexual relationship between the Princess Elizabeth and Robert Dudley, Earl of Leicester, a relationship the final renunciation of which is the most painful event of the Queen's life.

12 The fullest discussion of Heywood's debt to Foxe in this play is given by Marsha Robinson.

case, a cruel husband, in Elizabeth's case by Catholic enemies. She is like the "feminine" Christ, meekly enduring the blows and buffets of his foes. But above all, she is like the many Protestant martyrs, women as well as men, who suffered in mid sixteenth-century England under the persecutions of Mary (Robinson 2002, 128–30). And having heroically endured such persecution, she can later be transformed from virginal martyr to virginal queen, from a vulnerable heroine of patient endurance to the iconic monarchical figure familiar from innumerable cultural representations, such as the woodcuts on the successive title-pages of Heywood's own play.

In creating this image of the young Elizabeth, Heywood can only do so by heavy citation of the codes of pious Protestant femininity adumbrated by Foxe and other writers. The entire play is marked by what I call "hypercitation-ality," insistent allusions to the assemblage of stories and myths that had grown up around Elizabeth. But the majority of the actual incidents comprising the plot derive directly from John Foxe's widely disseminated *Acts and Monuments*, and Foxe pointedly includes the young Elizabeth in his pantheon of Protestant martyrs (Martin; Ziegler 1980; Watkins). The first edition of his work appeared in 1563, a scant few years after Elizabeth took the throne, and included a paean to her in which Foxe compared the young ruler to Constantine, the emperor who rescued the Primitive Church from its long period of persecution. This edition also included the famous ornamental capital "C" (for Constantine, here imagined as the Queen's model and prototype) within which Elizabeth sits enthroned with scepter, crown, and orb, a rich canopy over her head, the Pope lying prostrate at her feet, and to her right three grey-bearded figures who may represent Foxe himself, his printer John Day, and Foxe's sponsor, William Cecil (Foxe, sig. Bi; Doran in Doran and Freeman, 174). Elizabeth is thus visually enclosed within the authoritative initial of the Christian Emperor to whom Foxe extensively compares her. Just as God "sent this mild Constantinus, to cease bloud, to staye persecution, to refreshe his people" so He sent Elizabeth to "quenche fier brandes, to asswage rage, to releave innocentes" (sig. B1v).

Making good on his assertion of Elizabeth's own participation in a history of Marian persecution, Foxe includes a lengthy account of Elizabeth's life in the opening pages of "The Sixt tome or Section of the Ecclesiastical history, containing such actes and records as happened in the most florishing reigne of Queene Elizabeth" (1708). It is this section of *The Acts and Monuments* from which derives the bulk of the episodes Heywood puts on the stage in *If You Know Not Me, You Know Nobody*. He shows, for instance, how Mary's men invaded Elizabeth's sick room, demanding that she come at once to London; how she was commanded to go to the Tower; how she resisted landing at Traitors' Gate; how she was questioned by the Bishop of Winchester; how she struggled to have her meals served to her by her own retainers and servants; how a young boy repeatedly insisted on giving her flowers, even on pain of a whipping; how she was removed from the Tower and transferred into the care of Henry Benifield; how she wrote a letter to Mary; how she journeyed to court and met the Queen and was treated kindly by Philip; how she refused to "confess" any crime against Mary; how with the death of Steven Gardiner and Mary, Elizabeth was brought to the throne (Foxe, 1710–16). All of these events and more are drawn directly from Foxe, and early in the play Elizabeth self-consciously defines herself in Foxean terms, saying that "If I miscarry in this enterprise, and aske you why, / A Virgine and a Martyr both I dy" (lines 341–2). The alternative title of Heywood's play, *The troubles of Queene Elizabeth*, repeated on the title-page of each successive edition, simply underscores Foxe's sense of an Elizabeth under siege (even though for most of *Part I* Elizabeth is not yet a queen).

In depicting the young Elizabeth, Foxe thus gives Heywood a template by which to materialize her as a gendered being distinct from other women and exemplary both in her virtue and her virginity. Hers is not a sexualized femininity, and no romance codes govern her depiction. Instead, she is rendered powerful in her steadfast adherence to the Protestant faith in the face of persecution, and this in turn enables her resistance to her half-sister's demand that she confess to crimes against Mary as reigning monarch. The paradigm of Protestant martyrdom thus allows the young Elizabeth to embody heroic though imperiled feminine purity. She is not presented as a female Machiavel, angling for the throne, and yet her endurance in adversity implicitly prepares the way for her later assumption of it. As with all performances of femininity on the all-male stage, this particular materialization of "Elizabeth" depends on the citation of pre-existing cultural codes. The body of the actor, of whatever "sex," is the exploitable medium for this materialization, but not its guarantor of authenticity.

The faithfulness of the play to Foxe's account can provide further clues as to how the actor's effective materialization of "Elizabeth" took shape. It is dependent not only on dense verbal citation of vignettes from Foxe, but also by use of key stage props, the most important being the Bible itself (Robinson, 67–8). Throughout the play Elizabeth is connected with acts of devotional reading. After she has sat down on the cold stones in the rain outside the Tower, she consents to enter provided that her servant Clarentia give her her "booke" (line 607), which she holds as she enters the Tower. This could be a Bible; it could also be a prayer book.[13] A bit later the Constable of the Tower says that he would like to:

---

13 Cranmer's *Book of Common Prayer* had its first edition in 1549; the second edition, with its more radical Protestant alterations to the liturgy, appeared in 1552, several

lay her in a dungeon where her eyes,
Should not have light to read her prayer booke,
So would I danger both her soule and body,
Cause she an alyen is to us catholiques,
Her bed should be all snakes, her rest dispayre,
Torture should make her curse, her faythles prayer.

(lines 718–23)

The darkness of her prison is specifically intended to keep Elizabeth from reading her devotional texts.

The most spectacular scene involving a holy book and the young princess occurs a bit later, however, when Elizabeth, committed now to the care of Beningfield, with his permission writes a letter to Mary. As she is writing, he picks up a book in which he reads the famous lines Elizabeth had supposedly penned in her captivity: "Much suspected by me, nothing prov'd can be" (line 1,036).[14] Examining the book more closely, Beningfield discovers it is "an English bible" (line 1,039). Horrified, he calls for water to clean his hands. Shortly thereafter, when Elizabeth falls asleep and Beningfield leaves the stage, a dumbshow occurs in which Elizabeth's enemies conspire to kill her. Extensive stage directions describe this elaborate episode:

> Enter *Winchester, Constable, Barwick*, and *Fryars:* at the other dore 2. *Angels:* the *Fryar* steps to her, offering to kill her: the *Angels* drives them back. *Exeunt.* The *Angel* opens the Bible, and puts it in her hand as she sleepes, *Exeunt Angels, she wakes.* (sd. following line 1,047)

This is literally a miracle of faith enacted before the eyes of the theater audience. Having trusted in the Lord, the young princess is snatched from the hands of a ravening Friar, protected by the English Bible the angel places in her hands. Here not only Elizabeth's Protestant faith but her very life and also her sexual virginity are imperiled by an intruder who looms over her sleeping form.

In Foxe's 1563 *Acts and Monuments* there are several woodcuts depicting women reading the Bible. A famous one shows Hugh Latimer preaching before King Edward VI (1353). Right in the middle of the picture, seated on steps at the foot of the pulpit where Latimer is holding forth, a woman is intently perusing a large Bible open on her lap (fig. 12.2). On the title-page to the volume, in the lower left quadrant, some women intently listen to a sermon, a

---

years before the events staged in the play. Foxe includes both the incident of Elizabeth sitting on the cold stone before Traitors' Gate and her call for "her booke" (1712).

14   In Foxe's account, she is said to have scratched this message with a diamond on her window while a prisoner at Woodstock.

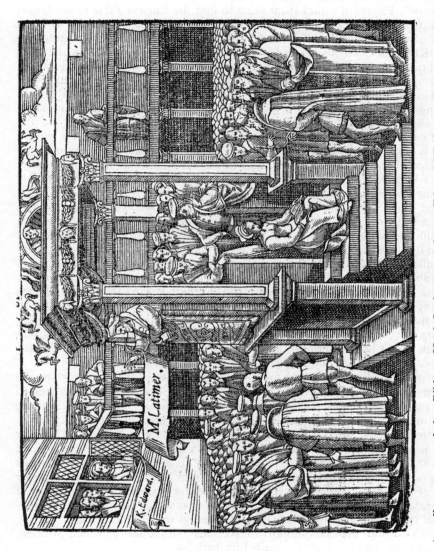

12.2 A godly woman reads her Bible as Hugh Latimer preaches to Edward VI, from John Foxe, *Actes and Monuments* (1563).

Bible prominently open before them. On the right, by contrast, Catholic women hold rosary beads while listening to a priest. The stage moment when Heywood's Elizabeth wakes from sleep to find the English Bible in her hands fits easily within a Protestant tradition associating virtuous women with the reading of the Bible. In "The Godly Woman in Elizabethan Iconography," John King discusses the myriad ways in which Elizabeth, in particular, was associated with the Bible in various cultural productions (pageants, title-pages, woodcuts) throughout her reign. Her commitment to the Word distinguished her sharply from her Catholic half-sister and allowed her to represent herself, holding both Bible and sword, as the defender simultaneously of England's faith and its temporal power.

An early portrait of Elizabeth, painted c.1546, shows the princess with a small book, probably a devotional work, the fingers of her left hand marking the place where she had been reading. Behind her, on a stand, lies what appears to be a large folio Bible. The painting associates the young Elizabeth strongly with the Protestant culture of scriptural reading. Similarly, when Elizabeth first entered London on the day before her coronation, she was greeted by five pageants. In one she was given an English Bible, the word of truth. In a carefully choreographed moment, Elizabeth is said to have taken the book and kissed it, raised it up and then laid it to her breast (Hackett, 43). This moment is recalled in the final thirty lines of Heywood's play. After she is invested with her emblems of office, Elizabeth receives two gifts from the Mayor of London: a purse and a Bible. The play closes with Elizabeth kissing the book and then praising it as "the Jewell that we still love best, / This was our solace when we were distrest, / This booke that hath so long conceald it selfe, / So long shut up, so long hid; now Lords see, / We here unclaspe, for ever it is free" (lines 1,582–6). This might be a description of Elizabeth herself, "the jewel" now released from confinement and set as queen before the eyes of her people.

It would, moreover, be in keeping with Foxe's unmistakable importance to the play's conception to have the Princess of the first twenty-two scenes dressed quite plainly. In the one portrait of Elizabeth as princess, the one in which she holds one book and stands before another, she is dressed elegantly but simply. As Pomeroy says, "all is moderation" (6). Elizabeth wears few jewels, and her dress is far less elaborate than the clothes in which she will later be painted when she assumes the throne. A simply dressed stage Elizabeth would contrast nicely with the pomp surrounding her half-sister Mary, the actual queen for most of the play. Above all, it would allow Elizabeth's eventual assumption of elaborate robes appropriate for a coronation to mark an absolute transformation of her social state from beleaguered princess to ruling monarch.

Foxe's account provides support for the idea of a modestly dressed princess. He says that after her father's death Elizabeth had

... so little delight in glittering gazes of the worlde, in gaye apparell, riche attire, and preciouse jewelles, that in all that tyme shee never loked upon those that her father lefte her, and which other ladies commonly be so fonde upon, but onlye once, and that against her will. And moreover after that, so little gloried in the same, that ther cam neither gold nor stone upon her head, till her sister enforced her to laye of her former sobernes, and bear her company in her glittering gaines: yea and then she so ware it, as every man might see, that her body bare that which her harte mysliked.
(Foxe, 1,710)

I am suggesting, then, that the boy actor may well have played the young Elizabeth in a simple dress, sparingly ornamented; that he may have worn a red-blond wig with the hair unfastened about his/her shoulders; and that his chief props were books: a prayerbook, a Bible. It was by these means, and through the hypercitationality of Heywood's relationship to the Foxean narrative of Elizabeth's early life, that a dead woman with "no bodie" was made into a recognizable "some bodie" on the Jacobean stage through the help of the boy actor.

Steeped as we are in modern conceptions of believability, modern critics still want to ask: could a young boy possibly have portrayed the young Elizabeth convincingly? Would her stage impersonation not, at some level, have been a travesty of majesty, particularly at the moment when he/she ceases to be a vulnerable, half-formed princess and assumes the mantle of rule? I think the answer is "not necessarily," and perhaps particularly not with a figure so iconically conceived as the Elizabeth of this play. We are by now familiar with the arguments that theatrical representation can "desacralize" monarchy by exposing its imitability, the theatrical means of its creation (Kastan, 109–27). But I think a moment such as Elizabeth's coronation procession, highly "theatrical" as it is, has a double potential. One has to take into account both the vagaries of the moment of production (how good are the actors and how effective the props?) and the context of the particular narrative being enacted. When a legitimate monarch such as Richard II is uncrowned, the stage can be highly destabilizing to the sacred nature of kingship, revealing the inherent theatricality and imitability of monarchy. On the other hand, particularly at moments of cultural transition (remember that in 1604 James had very recently assumed the throne), there could also be something profoundly reassuring about the stage's rehearsal of the transformation of a young princess into the iconic queen with whom every member of the theater audience would in some fashion have been familiar. Here the effectiveness of the theater's instruments – a boy actor, an improvised gown of state, an array of bodies holding symbolic properties – in transforming a boy actor into a queen could render intelligible and believable the transformative rituals of state. Elizabeth's entry procession, then, I imagine as potentially a genuine *coup de théâtre*, a thrilling evocation of the political/theatrical moment of transformation in which the low is miraculously raised up, the weak made strong, a girl made monarch. In early modern culture and in early modern theater, the rituals and the implements that accompany this transformation are something other than or more than falsifications of reality; they are, rather, the necessary means of its materialization.

Elizabeth seems to have recognized this truth. By the time of her death, she had become in the popular imagination a tissue of stories, a series of iconic images, as much as anything we might call "an actual woman," and scholars have shown how she participated in making herself so in order to wield power effectively and to influence and sway her subjects (Frye 1993; Hackett; Cole). On a more literal level, Dympna Callaghan has refocused attention on the fact that on the early modern stage *all* women were prosthetic creations (26–48), called into being by white paint, fabric, and prepenned words. Heywood's play is no exception to that rule. Ironically, it is precisely the saturation of this play by iconic stories and images that most powerfully conjures up "the Elizabeth effect," the haunting of the stage by the evocation of a powerful cultural creation. The point may be, to stage the princess Elizabeth, forget life and embrace the oft-told tale, the iterated image, the iconic moment, the overdetermined stage prop, for in them resides the power of the stage to resurrect a dead woman, in her artificial persons as martyr and queen, and thus to create majesty from the base matter of the theater. At such moments the all-male stage both subjected "Elizabeth" to its ideologies and prosthetic technologies and drew on and manipulated images of a powerful femininity that could be put to unpredictable uses by those who witnessed them, men and women alike. As Lisa Gim has shown, seventeenth-century women writers often used Elizabeth's well-known reputation as a writer and reader to authorize their own acts of literary creation (Gim in Frye and Robertson), and Pamela Brown has recently shown how the majesty associated with Elizabeth's famous depiction as the Fairie Queene could be appropriated by a common female trickster and con artist to swindle men out of their money (150–77).

This unpredictability, I would argue, haunts the representation of all of the artificial "women" of the early modern stage. Elizabeth is an exceptional case, and yet her representation only underscores the problematics that haunt each instance of "female" performance on this stage. The materialization of all "women," as with Elizabeth, depends on the citation of familiar codes of femininity; but the consequences of those evocations are, as with Elizabeth's depiction, uncertain. Callaghan is right that the exclusion of women from the public theater reaffirms basic gender hierarchies. Yet she is also right that the mere presence of a body sexed female on that stage provides no guarantee of full and equal participation in cultural production and representation. What is important are the *uses* to which representations are put and female bodies deployed. Every time a boy actor drew on the culture's codes of femininity to create a stage "woman," that actor risked evoking the powerful associations encoded in those discourses and material objects: the often demonized eroticism of the black woman, the verbal dexterity of the denigrated shrew, the spiritual power of the virgin martyr, the political authority of the queen. Though in modern terms there are no "real" black women, shrews, virgin martyrs or queens on this stage, their powerful prosthetic materialization in the words and material elements of stage production constantly evoked what had been excluded, even as it made the qualities associated with those excluded beings available for every kind of timid or reckless, pious or impious appropriation. Representations have ideological implications, but they are not completely in anyone's control. The all-male stage excluded women performers and writers; it could not exclude the unpredictable performance of femininity, nor could it control the interpretation of those representations by cultural players of both sexes.

Works Cited

Arnold, Janet. "The 'Coronation' Portrait of Queen Ellizabeth I." *The Burlington Magazine* 120 (1978): 727–41.
———. *Queen Elizabeth's Wardrobe Unlock'd*. Leeds: W. S. Maney and Sons, 1988.
Betteridge, Thomas. "A Queen for All Seasons: Elizabeth I on Film." In Doran and Freedman, 242–59.
Brown, Pamela Allen. *Better a Shrew than a Sheep: Women, Drama and the Culture of Jest in Early Modern England*. Ithaca and London: Cornell University Press, 2003.
Butler, Judith. *Bodies That Matter: On the Discursive Limits of "Sex."* New York: Routledge, 1993.
Callaghan, Dympna. *Shakespeare Without Women: Representing Gender and Race on the Renaissance Stage*. London: Routledge, 2000.
Cole, Mary Hill. *The Portable Queen: Elizabeth I and the Politics of Ceremony*. Amherst: University of Massachusetts Press, 1999.
Dobson, Michael and Nicola Watson. *England's Elizabeth: An Afterlife in Fame and Fantasy*. Oxford: Oxford University Press, 2002.
Doran, Madeleine, *If You Know Not Me You Know Nobody, Parts I and II*. Ed. Thomas Heywood, The Malone Society Reprints. Oxford: Oxford University Press, 1935.
Doran, Susan. "Virginity, Divinity and Power: The Portraits of Elizabeth I." In Doran and Freeman, 171–99.
——— and Thomas S. Freeman. Eds. *The Myth of Elizabeth*. Palgrave: New York, 2003.
Findlay, Alison and Stephanie Hodgson-Wright, with Gweno Williams. *Women and Dramatic Production 1550–1700*. Harlow, UK: Pearson, 2000.
Foxe, John. *Acts and Monuments*. London, 1563.
Frye, Susan. *Elizabeth I and the Competition for Representation*. New York: Oxford University Press, 1993.
——— and Karen Robertson, eds. *Maids and Mistresses, Cousins and Queens: Women's Alliances in Early Modern England*. New York: Oxford University Press, 1999.

Gim, Lisa. "'Faire *Eliza's* Chaine': Two Female Writers' Literary Links to Queen Elizabeth I." In Frye and Robertson, 183–98.

Grant, Teresa. "Drama Queen: Staging Elizabeth in *If You Know Not Me, You Know Nobody*." In Doran and Freedman, 120–42.

Greenblatt, Stephen and Jean E. Howard, Walter Cohen, and Katherine Eisaman Maus. Eds. *The Norton Shakespeare*. New York: Norton, 1997.

Gurr, Andrew. *The Shakespearian Playing Companies*. Oxford: Clarendon, 1996.

Hackett, Helen. *Virgin Mother, Maiden Queen: Elizabeth I and the Cult of the Virgin Mary*. New York: St. Martin's, 1995.

Howard, Jean. "Competing Ideologies of Commerce in Thomas Heywood's *If You Know Not Me, You Know Nobody, Part II*." In Turner, 163–82.

Kastan, David. "Proud Majesty Made a Subject." *Shakespeare After Theory*. New York: Routledge.

King, John N. "The Godly Woman in Elizabethan Iconography." *Renaissance Quarterly* 38 (1985): 41–84.

Martin, R. G. "The Sources of Heywood's *If You Know Not Me, You Know Nobody, Part I*." *Modern Language Notes* 39 (1924): 220–2.

McManus, Clare. *Women on the Renaissance Stage: Anna of Denmark and Female Masquing in the Stuart Court (1590–1619)*. Manchester: Manchester University Press, 2002.

Pomeroy, Elizabeth. *Reading the Portraits of Queen Elizabeth I*. Hamden, CT: Archon Books, 1989.

Robinson, Marsha S. *Writing the Reformation: Acts and Monuments and the Jacobean History Play*. Burlington, VT: Ashgate, 2002.

Stallybrass, Peter and Ann Rosalind Jones. *Renaissance Clothing and the Materials of Memory*. Cambridge: Cambridge University Press, 2000.

Turner, Henry S. Ed. *The Culture of Capital: Property, Cities, and Knowledge in Early Modern England*. New York: Routledge, 2002.

Watkins, John. *Representing Elizabeth in Stuart England: Literature, History, Sovereignty*. Cambridge: Cambridge University Press, 2002.

Ziegler, Georgianna. "England's Savior: Elizabeth I in the Writings of Thomas Heywood." *Renaissance Papers* (1980): 29–37.

———. Compiler and ed. *Elizabeth I, Then and Now*. (Published in conjunction with the exhibit of that name at the Folger Shakespeare Library, Washington, DC) Seattle: University of Washington Press, 2003.

Chapter 13

Female Impersonation in Early Modern Ballads

Bruce R. Smith

Toward the end of *Othello* comes the only moment in the play when female characters are scripted to be alone on stage together. The scene, some 90 lines in length, is given over in large part to the song that Desdemona sings as Emilia assists her in preparing for bed. What prompts the song is gossip. Lodovico has just left. "A proper man," Desdemona observes. "A very handsome man," Emilia agrees. "I know a lady in Venice would have walked barefoot to Palestine for a touch of his nether lip."[1] The reference to a lady disappointed in love gives Desdemona her cue. (See musical transcription A). The song as printed in the text of the play is interspersed with snippets of conversation between Desdemona and Emilia.

All in all, Act Four, scene three, of *Othello* shapes up as an enactment of women's history. The "song of willow" that Desdemona sings is represented as a creation of women, passed down by women one to another. Desdemona has learned the song from her mother's maid Barbary: "An old thing 'twas," Desdemona says, "but it expressed *her* fortune," as now it expresses Desdemona's (4.3.27–8, emphasis added). An old thing it was, but also an *open* thing, able to accommodate Desdemona's fortune. Barbary may have been disappointed in love, but the plot of her misfortunes is not what the ballad is about. Rather, the substance of the song is sighs, a sycamore tree, green willow, a hand, a bosom, a head, a knee, a stream, moans, salt, tears, stones. The substance of the song is a body and a place, or rather a body *in* a place. The song is not really Barbary's any more than it is Desdemona's. It belongs ultimately to "the poor soul" who sat sighing. When Barbary sang the song, she sang of overhearing someone else's grief – and, in the act of singing, making that grief her own. That is just what Desdemona does when she sings the song, and it is just what a singer does who takes up the song today.

---

1   *Othello* 4.3.34–7, in *Complete Works*, ed. Stanley Wells and Gary Taylor, 847. Further quotations from Shakespeare's plays are taken from this edition and cited in the text.

The poor soul sat sigh-ing by a syc-a-more tree, Sing all a green-wi-low. Her hand on her bos-om, her head on her knee, Sing wil-low, wil-low, wil-low, [wil-low,] Sing all-a green wil-low must be my gar-land.

Musical transcription A.

The attribution to Barbary situates the willow song fictionally among women and perhaps suggests an African origin along the Barbary Coast. The command in the refrain – "Sing all a green willow" – sets up a call-and-response structure that turns the experience of singing and listening into a communal event. Thomas Deloney in *Jack of Newbury* records women workers singing "The Fair Maid of Northumberland" in just this way. Two of them advance the story stanza by stanza while the others join in singing the refrain (Deloney, Sig. F3–G1v). The actual origins of the willow song are more obscure than Desdemona's reference to Barbary. The earliest written record of the refrain "All a green willow" seems to be in a ballad by John Heywood, *c.*1530, that begins, "Alas, by what mene may I make ye to know / The vnkyndnes for kyndnes that to me doth growe?" (BL MS Add. 15,233) – a literate, high-culture production in the idiom of Chaucer's ballads (Heywood, 257–9). Like many of the literary and musical productions favored by Henry VIII's court, the "green willow" refrain was likely taken over from a song that

A Louers complaint being forsaken of his Loue.
To a pleasant new tune.

A Poore soule sat sighing vnder a Sicamore tree,
    O willow, willow, willow,
With his hand on his bosome, his head on his knee,
    O willow, willow, willow,
    O willow, willow, willow,
Sing O the greene willow shall be my garland.

He sighd in his singing, and after each grone,
    Come Willow, &c.
I am dead to all pleasure, my true loue is gone,
    O Willow, &c.
Sing O the greene Willow, &c.

My Loue shee is turned, vntrue she both proue,
    O Willow, &c.
She renders me nothing but hate for my loue,
    O Willow, &c.
Sing O the greene willow, &c.

O pitty me (cried he) yon Louers each one,
    O Willow, &c.
Her heart's hard as Merble, she rues not my mone,
    O Willow, &c.
Sing O the greene Willow, &c.

The cold streames ran by him, his eyes wept apace,
    O Willow, &c.
The salt tears fell from him, which drowned his face,
    O Willow, &c.
Sing O the greene Willow, &c.

The mute birds sat by him, made tame by his mone,
    O Willow, willow, willow, &c.
The salt tears fell from him, which softned the stone,
    O Willow, willow, willow, &c.
Sing O the greene willow shall be my Garland.

Let no body blame me, her scornes I do proue,
    O Willow, &c.
She was borne to be faire, and I die for her loue,
    O Willow, &c.
Sing O the greene Willow, &c.

O that beauty should harbour a heart that's so hard,
    O Willow, &c.
My true loue resisting, without all regard,
    O Willow, &c.
Sing O the greene Willow, &c.

Let Loue no more boast him, in Palace or Bower,
    O Willow, &c.
For women are trothles, and flects in an houre,
    O Willow, &c.
Sing O the greene Willow, &c.

But what helps my complaining in vaine I com-(plaine,
    O Willow, &c.
I must be patient I suffer her scorne and disdaine,
    O Willow, &c.
Sing O the greene Willow, &c.

Come all you forsaken, and fit downe by me,
    O Willow, &c.
He that plaineth of his false loue, mine's falser then (he,
    O Willow, &c.
Sing O the greene Willow, &c.

The Willow wreath weare I since my loue did flit,
    O Willow, willow, willow, &c.
A Girland for Louers forsaken most meete,
    O Willow, willow, willow, &c.
Sing O the greene Willow shall be my Garland.

Printed at London for I.W.

13.1   Ballad, "A Lovers complaint being forsaken of his Love," part one (1615).

already circulated in oral tradition. A mythical greenwood populated by happy huntsmen and frolicking folk was a venue in which Henry and his courtiers liked to recreate themselves (Stevens, 40–57, 154–202). Be that as it may, it is to documents of high culture that we owe our knowledge of the tune to "The Willow Song." The two earliest records are a lute book, dated 1583 and now housed in Trinity College Library, Dublin, that was assembled by Thomas Dallis, who taught music at Cambridge, and a collection of lute songs, c.1630 (now BL MS Add. 15,117), that includes examples by the major English composers of art songs, including Thomas Tallis, William Byrd, Thomas Morley, John Dowland, Michael Cavendish, and Richard Jones (Shakespeare 1886, 277–8; Shakespeare 1997, 216–17; British Museum, 91). Whether or not it originated as a production of high culture, however, the willow song entered popular culture, as witnessed by the printed broadside of "A Lover's Complaint, Being Forsaken of His Love," which repeats sections of Shakespeare's text verbatim (see figs 13.1 and 13.2). Dated to 1615 in the Short Title Catalogue, this broadside, collected by Pepys, may, like others of its type, be a reissue of an older production of which no exemplars have survived. Extant reprints date from 1620, 1628–9, 1630, 1639, and 1640. This evidence suggests that the willow song was situated at the conjunction of high and low culture, of literate and oral. Adam Fox, among others, has demonstrated decisively "the way in which oral, scribal, and printed media fed in and out of each other as part of a dynamic process of reciprocal interaction and mutual infusion" (410). The woodcuts accompanying the 1615 printing suggest that the ballad was likewise situated at the conjunction of male and female. "Forsaken of his love": on part one of the printed broadside a male figure with gesturing arms has taken over the subject position. Part two provides the purchaser with two visual reference points, a man on the left and a woman on the right. For a literate purchaser, used to reading from left to right, the male figure assumes the implicit subject position. Would an illiterate purchaser necessarily follow that left-to-right motion? For a female purchaser, the direction was probably right to left.

It was not just high and low culture, literate and oral that was subject to reciprocal interaction and mutual infusion, I wish to argue, but male and female. Aside from Act Four, scene three, of *Othello*, all other known exemplars of the willow song, including the printed broadside, assume that the singer of the ballad will be male. And yet in early modern culture there was a persistent association of ballads with women. In William Wager's mid-sixteenth-century play *The Longer Thou Livest, the More Fool Thou Art* the fool Moros displays his effeminacy by singing ballads he overheard from "A fond woman to my mother, / As I war wont in her lap to sit" (9).[2] Hotspur,

---

2 I am grateful to Mary Lamb for this reference.

The second part of the forsaken Louer.
To a new tune.

Loue layd by my sorow, begot by disdaine
O Willow, willow, willow,
Against her to cruell, still I complaine:
O Willow, willow, willow,
O Willow, willow, willow,
Sing O the greene Willow shall be my garland.

O Loue so infurious, to wound my poore heart,
O Willow, &c.
to suffer the triumph, and ioy in my smart,
O Willow, &c.
Sing O the greene Willow, &c.

O Willow, Willow, willow, the willow Garland,
O Willow, &c.
A signe of her falsenesse before me doth stand,
O Willow, &c.
Sing O the greene willow, &c.

As here lying painet, it stands in mine eye,
O Willow,
So hang (it friends) ore mee, in graue where I lye:
O Willow, &c.
Sing O the greene Willow, &c.

In graue when I rest me, hang this to the view,
O Willow, &c.
Of all that doe knowe her, to blaze her untrue:
O Willow, &c.
Sing O the greene Willow, &c.

With these wordes ingrauen, as Epitaph meet,
O Willow, &c.
Here lyes one drunk Poyson, for potion most sweet
O Willow, &c.
Sing O the greene Willow, &c.

Though she doth vnkindly hath scorned my loue,
O Willow, &c.
And carelesly smiles at the sorrowes I proue,
O Willow, &c.
Sing O the greene Willow, &c.

I cannot against her, vnkindely exclaime,
O Willow, &c.
Cause once well I loued her, and honourd her name
O Willow, &c.
Sing O the greene Willow, &c.

The name of her sounded so sweete in mine eare,
O Willow, &c.
It coyd my heart lightly the name of my deare,
O Willow, &c.
Sing O the greene Willow, &c.

As then it was my comfort, it now is my griefe;
O Willow, &c.
It now brings me anguish, then brought me reliefe:
O Willow, &c.
Sing O the greene Willow, &c.

Farwell faire fals-harted, plaints end to my breath
O Willow, &c.
Thou dost loath me, I loue thee though cause of my death
O Willow, willow, willow,
O Willow, willow, willow,
Sing O the greene Willow shall be my Garland.

FINIS.

Printed at London for I. W.

13.2   Ballad, "A Lovers complaint being forsaken of his Love," part two (1615).

anxious as ever to prove his manhood, refuses in no uncertain terms the effeminizing blandishments of ballad-makers. When Glyndŵr says that he learned at the English court to sing ditties to the harp, Hotspur declares, "I had rather be a kitten and cry 'mew' / Than one of these same metre ballad-mongers." Not for him the rhythms of "mincing poetry" (3.1.125–6, 130). Shakespeare's Mopsa in *The Winter's Tale* is typical of the country maids who were imagined to be particularly susceptible to ballads. She is especially drawn to the "passing merry ballad" that Autolycus says is to be sung to the tune of "Two Maids Wooing a Man" (4.4.286–7). John Earle in *Microcosmographie* makes fun of itinerant ballad-mongers, whose wares "are chanted from market to market, to a vile tune and a worse throat; whilst the poor country wench melts like her butter to hear them" (66). Once a new ballad has grown stale in town, Richard Brathwait says, the ballad-monger takes them to the country, "till at last they grow so common there too, as every poore milke maid can chant and chirpe it under her cow; which she useth as an harmelesse charme to make her let downe her milk" (B4v). What was it about cows, milk, and butter that made country maids so ripe for ravishment? Contemporary references to ballads, ballad-singers, and ballad-buyers collected by Natascha Würzbach (253–84) and Tessa Watt (12–14) suggest that ballads in fact attracted a wide range of people and were performed in a variety of social circumstances. One suspects that what we are confronting in the association of women with ballads is as much a symptom of cultural anxiety as a demographic fact. "Two Maids Wooing a Man": Mopsa's attraction to that ballad reverses the expected power relationship two times over, turning Mopsa into one of the disorderly women that Joy Wiltenburg finds in a large number of seventeenth-century broadside ballads. Inescapably Shakespeare was drawing on such gender associations when he scripted the ballad-singing in Act Four, scene three, of *Othello*.

Whoever sings the willow song engages in an act of impersonation: the singer takes on the identity of a distant third person, "the poor soul," and endows that distant third person with first-person immediacy. It is this fundamental circumstance of impersonation that makes questions of gender so complicated. In the original production of *Othello*, of course, the singer was male, almost certainly a boy actor. That actor's rendition of the willow song was an instance of female impersonation – and, to judge by one eye-witness, a signally successful one. Henry Jackson's account of the performance of *Othello* at Oxford in 1610 singles out the actor playing Desdemona for special commendation. So captivating was the actor's performance that Jackson preserves the female declension of nouns and adjectives in his Latin description of the performance. Of Shakespeare's whole company Jackson says,

Not only by their speech but by their action they drew tears – But indeed Desdemona, killed by her husband, although she always acted the matter very well, in her death moved us still more greatly: when lying in bed she implored the pity of those watching with her countenance alone. (Tillotson, 494)

Etymologically at least, impersonation is about sound – or rather it is *through* sound. The word *person* in all its guises comes from the Latin word *persona*, or mask. A theatrical mask, to the ancient Romans, was a device that allowed for "through-sounding" (*per + sonare*). The visual features of the mask were fixed; what varied were the sounds that came out through the mouthpiece, which in some cases seems to have been equipped with a megaphone for amplifying the voice behind the mask. Or rather for getting the voice *beyond* the mask. At issue is the relationship between voice and mask. *Im*personation firmly locates the voice *in* the singer's body. The physical body, after all, was the primary sense of the word *person* in early modern English. To talk about impersonation in early modern ballads is, then, to talk about the relationship among three entities: voice, mask, and body.

It is the voice in the body – and the mask that conjoins the two – that I want to attend to here. Understandably, most scholarship on early modern ballads has begun, not with the human body, but with printed broadsides. The surviving sheets, a mere fraction of the millions that once existed, constitute, after all, the primary textual record that we have.[3] Carole Rose Livingston has catalogued all the surviving sixteenth-century sheets and is working on the seventeenth century. Natascha Würzbach has used speech-act theory to demonstrate how *printed* ballads came to life socially as *street* ballads and has assembled a motif index of all the ballads collected from oral tradition by Francis James Child. Joy Wiltenburg and Sandra Clark have directed attention to the ways in which broadside ballads served to negotiate power relationships between women and men in early modern culture. Katharine Craik has studied how broadside printings of criminal confessions inform first-person complaints on the part of women in ballads and in high-culture verse. For the late eighteenth and early nineteenth centuries, when ballads were first systematically collected, Deborah A. Symonds has argued that male and female interests in oral ballads were different. For men, ballads from earlier times were records of heroism in battle, of nationalism in formation. For women, they were memorials of courtship, motherhood, and conflicts with legal authority. I am much indebted to all of this work. My move here is to consider ballads in relationship to the bodies of the people who sang them and heard them. It is a project in historical phenomenology, an attempt to reconstruct the bodily experience of ballads in historically specific terms.

---

3   Watt (11) estimates that as many as three million broadside sheets were in circulation in 1600.

The place of the human body in these transactions can be isolated by considering ballads that have moved in and out of oral tradition over the past four hundred years. Do the versions collected from oral tradition engage the body in different ways from versions that were printed? Do the oral and the printed versions gender the body in different ways? Of the 305 ballads collected from oral tradition by Child at the end of the nineteenth century, at least sixteen were licensed for printing in the Stationers' Register before 1642 or survive in later seventeenth-century broadsides or were copied in manuscript in the eighteenth century (Livingston, 863–4). Space limits me to three examples: "Lord Thomas and Fair Annet" (Child, 73), "The Daemon Lover" (Child, 243), and "Geordie" (Child, 209). What place does the female body assume in these "cross-over" ballads?

Lord Thomas and Fair Annet

Versions of this ballad collected from oral tradition by Cecil J. Sharp in Somerset in 1904 and by Sharp and Maud Karpeles in Nellysford, Virginia, in 1916–18 remain remarkably faithful to the printed broadside "A Tragical Story of Lord Thomas and Fair Ellinor, Together with the Downfall of the *Brown Girl*" (1684–6) that Pepys picked up for his collection in the seventeenth century (see fig. 13.3). The singers heard by Sharp and Karpeles knew the song from oral tradition, not from printed sources. Karpeles testifies that the Appalachian singers in particular were unlikely to know how to read and write. Ballads were part of their inherited culture, part of the rhythm of daily life. "It would often happen," she relates,

> ... that we would hear a voice in the distance and then, following up, we would find, perhaps, a man singing as he hoed his corn-patch, or a girl milking a cow, or a woman nursing her baby. Owing to their isolation, the mountain people had been preserved from commercialized music and the songs they had inherited from their forefathers had been evolved according to the taste of the singers themselves without any extraneous influence. (Sharp and Karpeles, 9)

Here is how Mrs. Pond of Shepton Beauchamp, Somerset, sang the first stanza of "Lord Thomas and Fair Annet" for Sharp in 1904, repeating almost verbatim words that had been printed more than 200 years before – words that Mrs. Pond herself had almost certainly never seen. (See musical transcription B). The 19 stanzas that Sharp collected from Mrs. Pond and other singers in the west of England and the printed broadside's 18 stanzas follow the same story in precisely the same order. Lord Thomas has to choose between two possible brides, "Fair *Ellinor*" and "the *Brown Girl*" (Anonymous 1684–6,

A Tragical Story of LORD THOMAS And Fair Ellinor.

Together with the Downfall of the *Brown Girl*.

To a Pleasant New Tone, called, LORD THOMAS.

LOrd Thomas he was a bold Forrester,
and a Chaser of the Kings Deer,
Fair Ellinor was a fair Woman,
and Lord Thomas he lov'd her dear.

Come Riddle my Riddle, dear Mother, he said,
and riddle us both as one;
Whether I shall Marry with fair Ellinor,
and let the Brown-Girl alone.

The brown Girl she has got Houses & Lands,
and fair Ellinor she has got none,
Therefore I charge you on my blessing,
to bring me the Brown Girl home.

And as it befell on a high holiday,
as many did more beside,
Lord Thomas he went to fair Ellinor,
that should have been his Bride.

But when he came to fair Ellinors Bower,
he knocked there at the Ring:
But who was so ready as fair Ellinor,
to let Lord Thomas in.

What news, what news, L. Thomas he said,
what news hast thou brought unto me,
I am come to bid thee to my Wedding,
and that is bad News to thee.

Oh! God forbid Lord Thomas, she said,
that such a thing should be done;
I thought to have been thy Bride my own self,
or you to have been the Bridegroom.

Come Riddle my Riddle dear Mother, he said,
and Riddle it all in one;
Whether I shall go to Lord Thomas's Wedding,
or Whether I shall tarry at home. (sing.

There's many of your Friends Daughter,
and many of your Foes,
Therefore I charge you on my blessing,
to Lord Thomas his Wedding don't go.

There's many that are my Friends Mother,
if a Thousand more were my foe,
Betide my Life or betide my Death,
to Lord Thomas's his Wedding I'le go.

She cloathed her self in Gallant attire,
and her merry-men all in green,
And as they rid thorough every Town,
they took her to have been a Queen.

But when she came to Lord Thomas his Gate,
she knocked there at the Ring,
But who was so ready as Lord Thomas,
to let fair Ellinor in.

Is this your Bride? fair Ellin, she said,
methinks she looks wonderous brown,
Thou mightst have had as fair a Woman,
as ever trod on the Ground.

Despise her not, fair Ellin, he said,
despise her not now unto me;
For better I love thy little Finger,
than all her whole Body.

This Brown-Bride had a Little pen Knife,
that was both long and sharp,
And betwixt the short ribs and the Long,
prick'd fair Ellinor to the heart.

Oh Christ now save thee, Lord Thomas, he said,
methinks thou look'st wondrous wan,
Thou wast us'd to to look with as fresh a Co-
as ever the Sun shin'd on. (lour.

Oh art thou blind Lord Thomas, she said,
or canst thou not very well see;
Oh dost thou not see my own hearts blood,
runs trickling down my Knee.

Lord Thomas he had a Sword by his side,
as he walkt about the Hall,
He cut off his Brides Head from her shoulders,
and he threw it against the Wall.

He set the Hilt against the Ground,
and the Point against his heart,
There was never three Lovers that ever met,
more sooner they did depart.

This may be Printed,
Ro. L'Estrange.

Printed for J. Clarke, W. Thackeray,
and T. Passenger.

13.3 Ballad, "A Tragical Story of Lord Thomas and Fair Ellinor, Together with the Downfall of the *Brown Girl*" (1684–86).

Musical transcription B.

stanzas 1–2).[4] His mother recommends the brown girl – "The *brown Girl* she has got houses & Lands, / and fair *Ellinor* she has got none" (stanza 3) – and Lord Thomas takes her advice, but not before personally inviting Fair Ellinor to the wedding. For advice on her part Ellinor turns to her own mother, who warns her against attending the wedding. Ellinor goes anyway, insults the rival bride to her face, and provokes three acts of violence:

> The *Brown Bride* had a Little Pen Knife,
> > that was both Long and Sharp,
> But betwixt the Short Ribs and the Long,
> > prick'd Fair *Ellinor* to the heart.
> (stanza 15)

Thereupon Lord Thomas beheads the brown girl, rolls or kicks her head against the wall, and then falls upon his sword.

Among the three versions – the broadside of 1684–6, Mrs. Pond's rendition in Somerset in 1904, and Mrs. Willie Roberts' performance in Virginia in 1916–18 – there may be differences in phrasing (in Mrs. Roberts' version the little pen knife goes in between "the long ribs and the short," not "the Short Ribs and the Long"), stanzas may be dropped (Mrs. Roberts cuts straight to Lord Thomas's question-and-answer with his mother), stanzas may be added (to

---

4   Further quotations are cited by stanza number in the text. Mrs. Pond's version is printed in Vaughan Williams and Lloyd, 63–4; the version collected in Virginia from Mrs. Willie Roberts, in Sharp and Karpeles, 36–7.

balance the journey in which green-clad Ellinor looks like a queen, Mrs. Roberts adds a stanza in which scarlet-clad Lord Thomas comes to Ellinor looking like a king) (Sharp and Kepeles, 36–7). Three things, however, remain constant: (1) the precise order of events, (2) the focus on certain body parts and certain physical gestures, and (3) the telling of the story through impersonation. The pen knife, the sudden thrust, the decapitation, the head rolling on the floor: these things capture the singer's imagination across all three versions. So, too, does the dramatic mode of storytelling. Of the broadside's 19 stanzas, 11 are cast in the first person. The singer of the song becomes a series of forcefully present speakers: Lord Thomas, Lord Thomas's mother, Ellinor, Ellinor's mother. Woodcuts accompanying the 1684–6 broadside provide, on the left, visual reference points for the most important subject positions, those of Lord Thomas and Fair Ellinor. The three woodcuts on the right may simply repeat these two, or they may suggest the narrative situation toward the end of the ballad, in which the brown girl, dressed for her wedding, is flanked by Lord Thomas on the left and the priest on the right. With one exception, when Lord Thomas and Fair Ellinor exchange a two-line question and answer, each protagonist takes on dramatic life in one-stanza units. Only the brown girl remains voiceless, a third-person hand with a knife amid a world of vocal first-person passions. No less remarkable are the bodily details that make up this world of passion: fair skin, brown skin, the green attire donned by Ellinor for the wedding, the thrust through the short ribs and the long, the head that rolls against the wall, the heart pierced by a sword. It is fair to say that the essence of the ballad, maintained across at least 200 years, is a quite specific concatenation of voice, body, and gesture.

The Daemon Lover

The force of impersonation is especially marked in the quite diverse versions of the ballad known variously as "The Daemon Lover," "James Harris," "The House Carpenter," and "A Warning for Married Women." Common to all the versions is a woman who plights her troth to a sailor who must leave on a voyage before the wedding. While he is away (in some versions news comes of his death) the woman is wooed by a house carpenter, marries him, and bears him children. In time, however, the sailor returns and claims his betrothed, offering her riches to abandon her husband and children. There is more than a suggestion that the returned sailor is a ghost or perhaps the devil himself. In most versions, she sails away with him and is drowned. The earliest surviving broadside, "A Warning for Married Women" (1685), purports to tell a true story by specifying the troth-breaker as "*Mrs. Jane Reynolds* (a west-country Woman)" and her promised husband as "James Harris." In keeping with its news-like character, the printed broadside narrates most of the tale in the third person, granting voices to Mistress Reynolds and James Harris only in stanzas 17 through 26 of the total 30, when Harris returns from the sea, claims his bride, and persuades her to leave with him. Even in these stanzas, however, a third-person quality prevails as the speeches are set off with "quoth he" and "quoth she" (see fig. 13.4). The broadside's third-person cast is registered in the woodcuts, which juxtapose a cut of the woman's head with a cut of a ship at sea. James Harris is present only through the metonomy of the ship. In contrast, the oral version collected in Fairfax County, Virginia, in 1914 is cast almost entirely as first-person exchanges, sometimes with "says he" and "said she" attached to speeches but usually without. It is up to the singer to distinguish the dramatic voices. (See musical transcription C). The oral version of "The Daemon Lover" is largely impersonated, while the printed version is largely narrated. Why should that be so? Print is certainly a factor. Oral memory is personal memory; it resides in the body. Print obviates the need for that personal connection (Ong, 31–77). Commercialization is also a consideration. Würzbach has called attention to the double challenge that confronted the singer-sellers of broadsides on the streets (54–9, 236–41). On the one hand, they had to assume the mantle of authority that religious and moral ballads had once conferred on singers, while on the other they had to appeal to a range of target audiences, each of which would have its own standards of what counts as authentic. In these circumstances, third person is a lot safer than first person. Third person comes closest to making one size fit all. It may not be incidental, furthermore, that most commercial ballad-writers were men. The case of "The Daemon Lover" shows even more clearly than "Lord Thomas and Fair Annet" that certain physical fascinations remain constant whether the

Musical transcription C.

A Warning for Married Women.

Being an Example of *Mrs. Jane Reynolds* (a west-country-Woman) born neer *Plimouth* who having plighted her troth to a Seaman, was afterwards, married to a Carpenter, and at last carried away by a Spirit, the manner how shall presently be recited.

To a well-country Tune, called, *The fair Maid of Bristol : Batsman, or, John True.*

THere dwelt a fair Maid in the West,
of worthy Birth and Fame,
Neer unto Plimouth fairly Town
Jane Reynolds was her name.

This Damsel dearly was belov'd,
by many a proper youth;
And what of her is to be said,
in known for very truth:

Among the rest a Seaman brave,
unto her a wooing came,
A comely proper youth he was,
James Harris call'd by Name.

The Maid and Young man was agreed
as time and place did frame,
And to each other secretly,
they made a solemn vow

That they would ever faithful be,
whilst Heaven afforded life,
He was to be her husband kind,
and she his faithful Wife.

All you that faithful Lovers be,
give ear and hearken well,
And what of them became at last,
I will herein I tell.

The Young man he was prest to Sea,
and forc'd was to go,
His sweet-heart must the mirth stay behind
whether he would or no.

And after he was from her gone,
she three years for him stay'd,
Expecting of his coming home,
and kept her self a Maid.

At last news came that he was dead,
within a Foraign Land,
And how that he was buried,
she well did understand.

For whose sweet sake the maiden she,
lamented many a day:
And never was the known at all,
the wanton, to play.

A Carpenter that liv'd hard by,
when he did hear the same,
Like as the other had done before,
to her a wooing came.

But it then that he had gain'd her love,
they married were with speed,
and four years space (being man & wife)
they lovingly agreed.

Three pretty Children in this time,
this loving couple had,
Which made their Fathers heart rejoyce,
and Mother wondrous glad.

But as occasion serv'd on time,
the good man took his way,
Some three days journey from his home,
intending not to stay.

But while he was gone away,
a spirit in the night,
Came to the window of his Wife,
and did her sorely fright.

Which Spirit spake like to a man,
and unto her did say,
Prepare and come away.

James Harris is my name (quoth he)
whom thou didst love so dear,
And I have travel'd for thy sake,
at least this seven year.

And now I am return'd again,
to take thee to my wife,
And thou with me shalt go to Sea,
to end all strife.

O tempt me not sweet James (quoth she)
with thee away to go,
If I should leave my children small,
alas what would they do?

Thy Husband is a Carpenter,
a Carpenter of great fame,
I know not for five hundred pounds,
he would know thy name.

I might have had a King's Daughter,
and she would marry'd me,
But I forsook her Golden Crown,
and for thy love chose thee.

Therefore if thou'lt thy husband forsake,
and thy children three also,
I will forgive thee what is past,
if thou wilt with me go.

What means bad thou to bring me in,
if I should go with thee.

I have seaven Ships upon the Sea,
when they are come to Land,
Both Marriners and Merchandize,
shall be at thy command.

The Ship wherein my love shall sail,
is glorious to behold,
The sails shall be of finest silk,
and the mast of shining gold.

When he had told her these fair tales,
to love him she began,
Because he was in humane shape,
much like unto a man.

And so together away they went,
from off the English Coast,
And since that time the Woman-kind,
was never seen no more.

But when her husband he came home,
and found his Wife was gone,
And left her three Children by the babes,
within the house alone.

He beat his breast, he tore his hair,
the tears fell from his eyes,
And in the open streets he ran,
with heavy doleful cries.

And in this land-distracted case,
he hang'd himself for Woe,
Upon a tree, near to the place,
the truth of all is so.

The children now are fatherless,
and left without a guide,
But yet no doubt the Heavenly powers,
will for them well provide.

Printed for *W. Thackeray,* and *T. Passenger.*

13.4 Ballad, "A Warning for Married Women. Being an Example of *Mrs. Jane Reynolds* (a west-country-Woman . . .", (1685).

ballad is remembered in ink or in muscles: the woman's attachment to her baby or babies and the suspicion that the persuasive sailor is a ghost, a suspicion confirmed by the woman's drowning in the cold sea.

Geordie

Because versions both in print and in oral tradition vary so widely, "Geordie" makes an especially interesting test case with respect to impersonation. Child includes no fewer than 14 versions collected in the eighteenth and nineteenth centuries in Scotland; in England, exemplars were collected around the turn of the twentieth century in Yorkshire, Cambridgeshire, Somerset, Norfolk, Suffolk, Surrey, Sussex, and Dorset, as well as in North America. Here is how the ballad begins in the version Sharp collected from a man named Charles Neville at East Coker, Somerset, in 1908. (One wonders if Charles Neville ever met T. S. Eliot nosing about the village). (See musical transcription D). Despite Neville's gender, the singing "I" in the ballad is not Geordie, but his wife or lover. The event recounted in the ballad is dated by some scholars to 1554, when George Gordon, Earl of Huntly, earned the king's displeasure by showing clemency to a Highland robber (Vaughan Williams and Lloyd, 114). A broadside version of the ballad printed about 1630 makes the hero "a worthy gentleman named George Stoole dwelling sometime on Gateside Moor and sometime at Newcastle in Northumberland" (British Library, Roxburghe Collection 1:186–7). A still later broadside, datable to 1683, makes him

Musical transcription D.

"George of Oxford" (Roxburghe 4:53; Magdalene College, Cambridge, Pepys Collection 2:150).

All these versions present the core narrative situation of a nobly-born man wrongly condemned to death for the theft of some animals (horses in some versions, deer in others) and of a lady who laments his sentence and, in most versions, pleads for his life before a judge. What varies are the subject positions that the singer assumes. In contrast to the first-personhood of the oral version, the "George Stoole" broadside cues the singer to tell the story in third person, shifting on two occasions to assume the voice of "Georgie," first in a letter to his lady and then in a direct address from the scaffold. The listeners are specified in the first stanza (the tune has not survived):

> Come, you lusty northern lads,
>   That are so blithe and bonny,
> Prepare your hearts to be full sad,
>   To hear the end of Georgey.

The refrain, repeated after each stanza, complicates the subject position even more:

> Heigh-ho, heigh-ho, my bonny love,
>   Heigh-ho, heigh-ho, my bonny!
> Heigh-ho, heigh-ho, my owne deare love,
>   And God be with my Georgie!
>   (Anonymous 1630, stanza 1)

Who is the "I" here? The singer? Georgie's lady? Each of the "lusty northern lads" who join the singer in 22 repetitions of the refrain? If so, the lusty northern lads are invited to adopt a female subject position with respect to the ballad's hero. Würzbach calls attention to the way first-person narrators in street ballads can tailor their story to specific audiences, wives for instance, by addressing those listeners at the end (108–10). "George Stoole" complicates the situation by inviting listeners to join their voices in assent, in a gender other than their own.

"George of Oxford" sets up the situation preserved in Charles Neville's oral version: an "I" who walks over London Bridge on a misty morning and overhears the lady lamenting. The lady, specified to be "Lady Gray," sings only one stanza, however. Georgy sings 6 of the ballad's 16 stanzas; the Judge sings one; the rest are cast as third-person narration. Once again, the refrain casts the listeners in an implicitly female subject position (again, the tune has not survived):

> His time is past, his life it will not last,
>   Alack and alas, there is no remedy!

Which makes the heart within me ready to burst in three,
    To think on the death of poor Georgy.
                    (Anonymous 1683, stanza 1)

In the stanzas that Georgie sings, the refrain becomes "*My* life is past, *my* life it will not last," but it remains "his" in all other iterations. Charles Neville's version, like most versions collected in North America, is clearly based on the 1683 broadside, but it is cast almost entirely as dramatic impersonation, almost entirely indeed as dramatic impersonation of the lady. Even details about fighting with broadsword and pistol – words attributed to Georgie in the printed broadside – are attributed to the lady in Charles Neville's version. Or have the roles of lady and singer been collapsed in the final stanza? As we have noted with respect to "The Daemon Lover," it is characteristic that commercial printed ballads take advantage of third-person narration to provide extraneous details, while ballads from oral tradition work their efficient dramatic effects in first person (Livingston, 872–4).

Some Conclusions

What can we say, then, about female impersonation in early modern ballads that move between print and oral tradition? In "Geordie," in "Lord Thomas and Fair Annet," in "The Daemon Lover," as in the willow song, the female body is experienced in terms of parts: hands, knee, bosom, but above all a mouth. It is the voice, specifically the *singing* voice, that constitutes the essence of early modern ballads. Whatever the story may be, implicitly or explicitly, a ballad offers the singer an intense first-personhood (Waage, 731–42). For the duration of the song the singer becomes someone else – or rather, herself *and* someone else. The interplay of subject positions in the willow song – "the poor soul" becomes Barbary, who becomes Desdemona, who becomes "I" – is in fact paradigmatic of all ballads. It is this dynamic of identification that places sung ballads even closer to listeners than dramatic fictions are. In a remarkable essay on "Complex Relations of Simple Forms" Roger D. Abrahams has proposed a continuum of popular forms that stretches from "total interpersonal involvement" at one end (conversational genres would be an example) to "total removal" at the other (crafted objects like folk sculpture and folk painting would be examples). Sung ballads belong toward the middle of this continuum, somewhere in between what Abrahams calls "play genres" (riddling, spectator sports, folk drama) and "fictive genres" (tales, legends, and songs). Mark W. Booth in *The Experience of Songs* describes how this phenomenon of identification and transference tends to obliterate gender distinctions:

In a song where the singer addresses a second person (saying, in all probability, "I love you"), the audience identifies with the speaking voice, and this effect is so compelling as not necessarily to respect even difference of sex: a man who hears a woman sing a declaration of love generally identifies himself, I think, with declarer and not with beloved. This effect is usually true in printed lyric; if it is also true of sung lyric, it is because the identification with a voice is a remarkably strong force, sweeping us past the stage of aesthetic contemplation and even past the fantasy that the words are directed to us. (16–17)

If the song happens to be a narrative, the singer becomes *several* other people: the narrator, Georgie, the Judge, Lady Gray – and the situation with respect to gender becomes more complicated still. When we consider that the listener becomes those people, too, the situation becomes even harder to map.

It is the central fact of the singing voice, I believe, that explains the persistent association of ballads with women in early modern England. Among most educated writers in early modern England, suspicion of music in general ran deep. John Case felt compelled to write an entire book in its defense. Philip Stubbes lets us know in no uncertain terms why such a defense was necessary. Music used for the service of God is to be commended, Stubbes will admit,

> But beeing vsed in publique assemblies and priuate conuenticles, as directories to filthie dauncing, thorow the sweet harmonie & smoothe melodie therof, it estraungeth the mind, stirreth vp filthie lust, *womannisheth the minde*, rauisheth the hart, enflameth concupisence, and bringeth in vncleannes. (sig. O4v, emphasis added)

Stubbes's association of ballads with dancing is telling. The early modern word *ballad* derives, in fact, from the Middle English *balade*, literally "dancing-song," which derives in turn from the Latin *ballare*, to dance. The sixteenth- and seventeenth-century pronunciation of *ballad* as *ballet* makes the connection obvious. In his diatribe against profane music, he makes a connection among music, dancing, and women that points directly to ballads.

Stubbes's fears are grounded not just in ethical principles but in physiological assumptions. "Bawdie songs, filthie ballads and scuruie rymes," as Stubbes calls them (sig. O5), had the power to work such effects because they were thought to alter the body's chemistry. Thomas Wright, a far more sober writer than Stubbes, acknowledges the power of music in "rousing vp choller, afflicting with melancholy, iubilating the heart with pleasure, eleuating the soule with deuotion, alluring to lust, inducing to peace, exciting to compassion, inuiting to magnanimitie" (168). The first three of these effects involve activation of specific humors: choler, black bile, and blood. The listener experiences these surges of specific body fluids as passions. Linda Austern has called attention to the primacy of Galenic physiology in early modern explanations of the power of music and the influence of that physiology on associations of music with effeminacy. Of all forms of music in early modern

298 WOMEN PLAYERS IN ENGLAND 1500–1660

England, ballads seem particularly adept at playing on passions. The result, for the listener, is to enter a state of mind quite distinct from the state of mind one experiences in listening to a play.

English of the twenty-first century conspicuously lacks a word to designate this state of being-in-music. Gary Tomlinson has argued that the effect of music, in all cultures, is to transport the audience into a transcendent state – a state of mind that is, however, constructed differently by different cultures in different historical eras. Tomlinson's own word for that transcendent state is "fascination," and he traces the links of that word to extravagance, unreality, hyperreality, and irrationality in the history of opera, beginning with Jacopo Peri in the 1590s and Monteverdi in the early seventeenth century (4). Is there a term specific to early modern English for this state of passionate attention? Wright gives us a clue, I believe, when, earlier in *The Passions of the Minde in Generall*, he declares,

> indeed the Passions, not vnfitly may be compared to greene spectacles, which make all things resemble the colour of greene; euen so, he that loueth, hateth, or by any other passion is vehemently possessed, iudgeth all things that occur in fauour of that passion, to be good and agreeable with reason. (sig. E2)

Thus the Doctor in *The Two Noble Kinsmen* offers the Jailer a homeopathic cure for his daughter's love madness: "Sing to her such green songs of love as she says Palamon hath sung to her in prison" (4.3.78–9). In her madness she herself has sung in a ballad, "For I'll cut my green coat, a foot above my knee" (3.4.19). Linda Woodbridge in a chapter on "Green Shakespeare" has charted the associations of green with Nature (a feminine noun in Latin) and with the North through Robin Hood lore and ballads like "Chevy Chase" (152–205). I would like to add a connection with coolness and wetness, the essential qualities of a female body in Galenic physiology.

We can witness these connections in depictions of men as melancholy lovers. Take, for example, the woodcut accompanying "The Woeful Complaint and Lamentable Death of a Forsaken Lover" (1625) (see fig. 13.5). A now famous painted image by Isaac Oliver, datable to 1613–14, shows Edward Herbert, First Baron Herbert of Cherbury in the same pose, lying next to a stream amidst intensely green grass and foliage.[5] There are two subject positions in the printed ballad, that of singer/narrator and that of lamenting lover, whom the narrator chances upon amid "a sort of pleasant trees ... a pleasant place with shadows cold." The listener steps within a hollow tree, "because I would his

---

5 This well-known image is reproduced in, among other books, Karen Hearn, ed., *Dynasties: Painting in Tudor and Jacobean England, 1530–1630* (London: Tate Gallery, 1995), 139.

The wofull complaint, and lamentable death of a forsaken Louer.
To a pleasant new tune.

Downe by a forrest where as I did paffe,
  to fee what fpozt abzoad there was,
Walking by a pleafant fpzing,
  the Birds in funday notes did fing.
Long time wandzing here and there,
  to fee what fpozts in forrefts were,
At length I heard one make great mone,
  faying, from me all ioyes are gone.

I gaue goo hæd vnto the fame,
  mufing from whence this Eccho came:
But by no meanes I could deuife,
  from whence this forrowfull found did rife,
But in that place did ftill remaine,
  vntill I heard it once againe.
Then pzefently I heard one fay,
  O death, come take my life away.

I looked downe vpon my right hand,
  a fozt of pleafant trees did ftand:
And vnder them I did behold
  a pleafant place with fhadowes cold.
A fumptuous place was in the fame,
  mufing from whence this Eccho came:
Then in that place I did perceiue,
  a Gentleman both fine and bzaue.

And from that place he did come downe,
  cafting from him a mourning Gowne,
Walking vp and downe the place,
  me thought a propper man he was:

Thus to himfelfe he did lament.
  wifhing to God his dayes were fpent,
His tozments did increafe fo foze,
  his heart was able to beare no moze:

I ftept into a hollow trée,
  becaufe I would his paffion fée :
With folded armes looking to fkies,
  the teares alas ftoo in his eyes:
And careleffe of his life he féem'd,
  pitty he was no moze efféem'd :
Then downe he laid him on the ground:
  no eafe to forrow can be found.

Thus he lamented in wofull cafe,
  feuen long yéeres within few dayes,
faying, while I liue, I muft remaine,
  I find no eafe to helpe my paine:
For fhe that fhould my forrowes remoue,
  fhe doth difdaine to be my Loue,
And hath borne vnce that fhe did beare,
  that I good will to her did beare.

Ye gods aboue come eafe my paine,
  fith heauy griefe doth me conftraine,
For whilft my cozps remaines on earth,
  fhall fhew the caufes of my death.
Euery trée that here doth ftand,
  fhall be engrauen with mine owne hand,
That they long time may witneffe beare,
  Loue was the caufe I died here.

Nature did to her fo much right,
  fcozning to take the helpe of Art :
And in as many vertues bight,
  as euer did imbzace a heart.
Being fo good, fo truly tried,
  O fome foz leffe were deifi'd,
Full of pitty as may be,
  and yet perhaps not fo to me.

When firft I faw her pleafant face,
  me thought a iopfull fight it was :
Her beauty toke my wits away,
  I knew not how one woзd to fay,
A Gentleman toke her to dance,
  fhe gallantly her felfe could pzance,
And kept her ozder in good time,
  I wifh to God fhe had béene mine.

But when I thought fhe had béen mine owne,
  then was fhe fartheft from me growne :
She gaue no eare vnto my cry,
  which makes me here in forrow die.
For fhe was in another mind,
  which to my paines I often find,
O all my hopes I am beguild,
  which makes me walke in woods fo wilde,

13.5 Ballad, "The Woeful Complaint and Lamentable Death of a Forsaken Lover" (1625).

passion see" (Anonymous 1625, stanza 1). A lute accompanies the lover's complaint. The lover's passion becomes the narrator's passion when the narrator repeats what he or she has heard. It becomes the singer's passion whenever a purchaser of the broadside brings the printed words to vocal life. The combination here of visual image and vocal imagination was powerful enough for the ballad to be republished at least five times before 1700.

Let us return to the willow song in *Othello*. The boy actor who played Desdemona was, in effect, enacting the same sort of scene we see in Isaac Oliver's miniature and in "The Woeful Complaint and Lamentable Death of a Forsaken Lover." What the early modern audience imagined themselves to be witnessing in such scenes of female impersonation – so Joseph Roach has argued – is a physiological feat, whereby the player actively induces in himself the passion he wishes to portray. For the boy actor to assume Desdemona's passion, her "green sickness," was to cultivate that female passion – that biochemical condition of coolness and moistness – in his own body (Roach, 41–4). Even the sounds of Desdemona's "song of willow" betray the transformation of reason into passion, of signifiers into phatic sounds, of male into female. In *The Characters of the Passions* (English translation, 1650) Marin Cureau de la Chambre provides an encyclopedic summary of old ways of conceptualizing the passions just at the moment Descartes was giving reason an autonomy *vis à vis* the passions it had never had before in Western thought. Desire can be discerned, La Chambre observes, in "the several inflexions of the voice," in the lifting up in boldness and anger, the falling in fear and languor, the cutting short in grief and astonishment, the drawing out in admiration and joy. The passion of desire:

> causeth the words to go out in a croud; and the darting forth of the Soul causeth a transport of the voice, which is always made by the strongest vowels, which most of all open the mouth, as if she would make a freer passage, that she might issue out the more readily. In effect, we never finde the I nor the U in the ordinary exclamations of Desire, but onely A, O, and E, which she also chargeth with vehement aspirations which shew the force she useth in issuing forth. (sig. T5–T5v)

"Sing [*a*]ll a green will[*o:*]w ... with her head upon her kn[*i:*]": those cadences are as much about [*a*], [*o:*], and [*i:*] as they are about particular words and the things those particular words signify. For a woman to impersonate a man, as the singer is cued to do in all three of the ballads I have studied here, was to activate other humors – blood and choler – but it was still to give oneself up to passion, to put on green spectacles, to abandon reason, to enter a scene of green. Ben Jonson, for one, made several anxious jokes at the expense of "Mary Aumbree," the virago who led English volunteers against the Spanish at Ghent in 1584, or so one of the ballads collected by Thomas Percy claims. In

the course of the ballad the singer gets to make Mary's bravado his or her own
– and to approve that act of impersonation in the one-line refrain:

> Shee cheared her good souldiers that foughten for life,
> with the cominge of Ancyents, with drum & with fife,
> that braue sonding trumpetts with ingines soe free,
> att last thé made mention of Mary Aumbree.
>
> "Before that I doe see the worst of you all
> come in the danger of your enemyes thrall,
> this hand & this sword shall first sett him free;"
> was not this a braue bonye lasse, Mary Aumbree?
>
> (Percy, 2: 136)

Mary Aumbree is the name that comes to mind when noise-sensitive Morose in
Jonson's *Epicene* needs an epithet for loquacious and overbearing Mistress
Otter. Morose dismisses her, her husband, and her retinue with a comparison
to the gender-breaching heroine of the ballad, a catalogue of some of the
loudest noises in London's public spaces, and a fear of the ear-splitting
progeny that such a woman can produce:

> Mrs. MARY AUMBREE, your examples are dangerous. Rogues, Hellhounds, *Stentors*,
> out of my dores, you sonnes of noise and tumult, begot on an ill *May*-day, or when
> the Gally-foist is a-floate to *Westminster*! A trumpetter could not be conceiu'd, but
> then! (Jonson, 5: 226)

At first blush, the singing of the willow song in *Othello* might seem to confirm
gender roles, not confound them, and yet the willow song wrests the audience
into a green state of mind in which violent passions overwhelm gender
differences. "The Willow Song" frames Othello's murder and suicide as just
such an episode as singers and listeners might share in ballads like "Lord
Thomas and Fair Annet" or "The Daemon Lover" or "Geordie" – one in
which the space between the dramatic object and the experiencing subject is
radically foreshortened and the boundary between male and female is liquified.
With their multiple subject positions and their appeals to passion, early
modern ballads call into question the one-to-one identification that has been
assumed in most gender-based criticism of the past twenty years.

Works Cited and Consulted

Abrahams, Roger D. "Complex Relations of Simple Forms." *Genre* 19.2 (1969): 104–
11.

Anonymous. "A lamentable new ditty, made upon the death of a worthy gentleman, named George Stoole, dwelling sometime on Gate-side Moore, and sometime at New-castle in Northumberland." London: H. Gosson [1630].

Anonymous. "The Life and Death of George of Oxford" London: P. Brooksby [1683].

Anonymous. "A Lovers complaint, being forsaken of his Loue." London: I. W. [1615].

Anonymous. "A Tragical Story of Lord Thomas And Fair Ellinor. Together with the Downfall of the *Brown* Girl." London: J. Clarke, W. Thackery, and T. Passage [1684–6].

Anonymous. "A Warning for Married Women. Being an Example of *Mrs. Jane Reynolds* (a west-country-Woman) ...." London: W. Thackery and T. Passenger [1685].

Anonymous. "The Woeful Complaint and Lamentable Death of a Forsaken Lover." London: H. Gosson [1625].

Austern, Linda Phyllis. " 'For, Love's a Good Musician': Performance, Audition, and Erotic Disorders in Early Modern Europe." *Musical Quarterly* 82.3–4 (1998): 614–53.

———. " 'No Women Are Indeed': The Boy Actor as Vocal Seductress in Late Sixteenth- and Early Seventeenth-Century." *Embodied Voices: Representing Female Vocality in Western Culture*. Ed. Leslie C. Dunn and Nancy A. Jones. Cambridge: Cambridge University Press, 1994.

Booth, Mark W. *The Experience of Songs*. New Haven: Yale University Press, 1985.

Brathwait, Richard. *Whimzies: Or, A New Cast of Characters*. London: Ambrose Rithirdon, 1631.

British Museum. Department of Manuscripts. *A Catalogue of Additions to the Manuscripts in the British Museum in the years 1841–1845*. London: The Trustees, 1850.

Case, John [attributed]. *The Praise of Music*. London: Joseph Barnes, 1586.

Chappel, William and J. W. Ebsworth, eds. The Roxburghe Ballads. 9 vols. Hertford: The Ballad Society, 1871–99.

Child, Francis J. *The English and Popular Ballads*. 5 vols. Boston: Houghton Mifflin, 1892–98.

Clark, Sandra. "The Broadside Ballad and the Woman's Voice." *Debating Gender in Early Modern England*. Ed. Cristina Malcolmson and Mihoko Suzuki. New York and Basingstoke: Palgrave Macmillan, 2002, 103–20.

———. "The Economics of Marriage in the Broadside Ballad." *Journal of Popular Culture* 36.1 (2002): 119–33.

Craik, Katharine A. "Shakespeare's *A Lover's Complaint* and Early Modern Criminal Confession." *Shakespeare Quarterly* 53.4 (2002): 437–59.

Davis, Arthur Kyle. Ed. *Traditional Ballads of Virginia*. Charlottesville: University Press of Virginia, 1969.

Deloney, Thomas. *The Pleasant History of Iohn Winchcomb ... called Iack of Newberie*. London: Humphrey Lownes, 1619.

Earle, John. *Microcosmographie*. Ed. Harold Osborne. St. Clair Shores, MI: Scholarly Press, 1977.

Fellowes, Edmund Horace. Ed. *Forty Elizabethan Songs*. Book 2. London: Stainer and Bell, 1925.

Fox, Adam. *Oral and Literate Culture in England 1500–1700*. Oxford: Clarendon, 2000.

Hearn, Karen. Ed. *Dynasties: Painting in Tudor and Jacobean England, 1530–1630*. London: Tate Gallery, 1995.

Heywood, John. *Works and Miscellaneous Short Poems*. Ed. Burton A. Milligan. Urbana: University of Illinois Press, 1956.

Jonson, Ben. *Ben Jonson*. Ed. C. H. Herford and Percy Simpson. Vol. 5. Oxford: Clarendon, 1937.

La Chambre, Marin Cureau de. *The Characters of the Passions*. Trans. R. W. London: Thomas Newcomb for John Holden, 1650.

Livingston, Carole Rose. *British Broadside Ballads of the Sixteenth Century*. Vol. 1: *A Catalogue of the Extant Sheets and an Essay*. New York: Garland, 1991.

Ong, Walter J. *Orality and Literacy: The Technologizing of the Word*. London: Methuen, 1982.

Pepys, Samuel. *The Pepys Ballads*. Ed. Geoffrey Day. 5 vols. Cambridge: D. S. Brewer, 1987.

Percy, Thomas. *Reliques of Ancient English Poetry*. Ed. Henry B. Wheatley. 3 vols. London: George Allen and Unwin, 1885.

Roach, Joseph. *The Player's Passion: Studies in the Science of Acting*. Ann Arbor: University of Michigan Press, 1993.

Shakespeare, William. *Complete Works*. Ed. Stanley Wells and Gary Taylor. Oxford: Clarendon, 1986.

———. *Othello*. Ed. Horace Howard Furness. Variorum Edition. Philadelphia: Lippincott, 1886.

———. *Othello*. Ed. E. A. J. Honigman. Arden Edition. Walton-on-Thames: T. Nelson, 1997.

Sharp, Cecil J. and Maud Karpeles. *Eighty English Folk Songs from the Southern Appalachians*. Cambridge: MIT Press, 1968.

Stevens, John E. *Music and Poetry in the Early Tudor Court*. London: Methuen, 1961.

Strong, Roy. *The Artist and the Garden*. New Haven: Yale University Press, 2000.

Stubbes, Philip. *The Anatomie of Abuses*. London: Richard Jones, 1583.

Symonds, Deborah A. *Weep Not for Me: Women, Ballads, and Infanticide in Early Modern Scotland*. University Park: Pennsylvania State University Press, 1997.

Tillotson, Geoffrey. "*Othello* and *The Alchemist* at Oxford in 1610." *The Times Literary Supplement*, 20 July 1933: 494.

Tomlinson, Gary. *Metaphysical Song: An Essay on Opera*. Princeton: Princeton University Press, 1999.

Vaughan Williams, Ralph and A. L. Lloyd. Eds. *The Penguin Book of English Folk Songs*. London: Penguin, 1959.

Waage, Frederick O. "Social Themes in Urban Broadsides of Renaissance England." *Journal of Popular Culture* 11 (1977): 731–42.

Wager, William. *The Longer Thou Livest, the More Fool Thou Art*. Ed. R. Mark Benbow. Lincoln: University of Nebraska Press, 1967.

Watt, Tessa. *Cheap Print and Popular Piety, 1550–1640*. Cambridge: Cambridge University Press, 1991.

Wiltenburg, Joy. *Disorderly Women and Female Power in the Street Literature of Early Modern England and Germany*. Charlottesville: University of Virginia Press, 1992.

Woodbridge, Linda. *The Scythe of Saturn: Magical Thinking in Shakespeare*. Urbana: University of Illinois Press, 1994.

Wright, Thomas. *The Passions of the Minde in Generall*. London: Valentine Simmes, 1604.

Würzbach, Natascha. *The Rise of the English Street Ballad 1550–1650*. Trans. Gayna Walls. Cambridge: Cambridge University Press, 1990.

Würzbach, Natascha and Simone M. Salz. *Motif Index of the Child Corpus*. Trans. Gayna Walls. Berlin: Walter de Gruyter, 1995.

Chapter 14

Jesting Rights: Women Players in the Manuscript Jestbook of Sir Nicholas Le Strange

Pamela Allen Brown

The British Library's Harleian MS 6395 contains over six hundred anecdotes and jests, page after page of laughter in the dark. The darkness is ours; it takes some imagination to see and hear what the pages might have to say.

Imagine the music room of a great house in western Norfolk in the 1630s, that of Hunstanton, the seat of the powerful L'Estrange family. A consort of amateur viola players saws away at a score by John Jenkins, the resident composer, while guests cluster in the corners to chat.[1] Laughter and gossip make their familiar rounds. Now imagine that there are actually two "scores" sounding together in the room, one musical and one verbal, both based on theme and variation, tempered improvisation and virtuosic repetition. Both are written on the air. In this many-voiced social consort one voice rises and crests for a moment. It belongs to the hostess of Hunstanton, Alice L'Estrange.[2] She finishes up a story her husband has begun about the January–May marriage of a couple they know – topping him with a bit of slander about the bride's rumored bastards by another man. Satisfied, she leans back as she collects the last laugh. Later, in a quieter moment, she reads over her son Nicholas's transcription of one of her jests. Pausing, she corrects a phrase, writing in above it one she thinks works better.[3] She is right. In the odd little jest book

---

1   The celebrated composer John Jenkins was a resident musician at Hunstanton for a decade, moving to a non-royalist household when the family's fortunes declined with the civil war. Sir Nicholas and his brother Roger were avid viola players, and Sir Nicholas spent much time compiling and editing handwritten parts of works by composers their consort played (Love, 29–31; Willetts, 30–43).

2   The two spellings in this essay – L'Estrange and Le Strange – reflect variations by family members in their signatures.

3   All jests in this essay are taken from the Lippincott edition of the Le Strange manuscript, hereafter LS. Items 290 and 291 form a linked pair of gossipy jests told by Sir Nicholas's father and mother about "Mr Abraham Vemat, that married the

compiled by her eldest son Nicholas, she is a lead actor and contributing
author. Both textuality and orality have been put into play by a third power,
the social consort of performance. And in this other consort, some women
excel. Like a playtext or a musical score, the Le Strange manuscript gestures
outward toward a world of "playing" in the broadest sense – an audible, social,
vibrant world that acknowledged some women as laugh-getters, satirists, and
storytellers.

This is projection, of course. But not fantasy. After studying hundreds of
"small merry books," I have found none in print or manuscript so replete with
markers of female performance as Sir Nicholas's *Merry Passages and Jeasts*.
This unusual manuscript compilation is also rich in topical allusions to
religious, political, and inter-familial conflicts of the decades of its creation, the
1630s, 1640s and 1650s. H. F. Lippincott, who prepared the only complete
edition, judges from internal evidence that the book was written over a period
of many years, probably beginning in the 1630s when Sir Nicholas was in his
late twenties, and ending in the mid-1650s, just before his death at 55
(Lippincott, 5). Many members of politically opposed groups were linked via
marriage and kinship to the royalist L'Estrange household, with its powerful
connections to court through the Howards, who controlled Castle Rising. As a
result guests at Hunstanton included Catholics, precisians, pro- and anti-
Laudians, and eventual Cavalier and Roundhead opponents.

Because so many of the jests identify real places and people, and
comparatively few repeat or refit familiar tales from printed jestbooks, the
book is also an unusual chronicle of contemporary manners and social
relations among the gentry, recording who said what about whom during a
gathering or a visit. Harold Love speculates that reading these aloud may have
helped to fill the time during the long pauses for tuning between pieces in
Hunstanton's circle of viola da gamba players, of which Sir Nicholas was part
(31). It seems to me more likely that it was written as a very unusual sort of
diary and *aide-mémoire* between such gatherings – after all, Sir Nicholas played
in the consort and he would have been tuning, too. Others could have read it
and laughed over it while socializing, but then as now there was a stigma
attached to the getting of wit from books, even handwritten ones; recall
Beatrice's miffed reaction to the idea that she got her "good wit" from
jestbooks: "Well, this was Signior Benedick that said so" (*Much Ado About
Nothing* 2.1.130–131).

Lady Peyton." In LS item 16, the key laughline words "done you wrong" are
revised with a corrected phrase, the pithier and funnier "belyed you," written in a
different hand from that of the compiler.

Nearly all of the octavo's 93 pages are written in the same undistinguished transitional italic hand.[4] The manuscript's 611 jests are neatly spaced and tidily written, but otherwise the book is visually unremarkable, even homely. Some pages have small holes that the writer simply detoured around when he enountered them. That is not to say no care was taken with the book; in fact there are revisions throughout. Unassuming as it is, this book has remarkable features: its generic homogeneity, the gender politics of its bawdy humor, and the intricacy of its political gossip. Read straight through, the book takes on a distinct tone of call-and-response (and tit for tat), because many named sources are also characters in other jests, both as laugh-getters and as butts.

Especially interesting is the list that appears between pages 88 and 92. There the methodical Sir Nicholas provides a table in which the number of each jest is paired with a name, often with the relationship of the person first, such as "bro: roger", "sis: eliz", and "my coz: dol gurney," with the most frequent citation being "My mother" and "Ma Mere." Women are credited in the table for 79, or one in seven, of the 611 jests that are attributed. In other words, about 15 percent come from women, most of them relatives of the transcriber. Are the women who told these jests "informants," as an anthropologist might call them, or are they "authors"? Are they creators, or merely transmitters, of common culture?[5] It is my contention that by putting their names to jokes, folklore, and gossip – just as male authors did in popular literature and stage plays – the women function as performers while staking a claim to authorship, albeit of a transient kind.

Of the hundreds of people Sir Nicholas names in his index, the person with the greatest number of stories is his mother, Dame Alice L'Estrange (1575–1656). She gets the credit for 43 jests, the next highest number going to her husband Sir Hamon, with 38. Born in the reign of Elizabeth, Dame Alice lived through the reigns of James and Charles, marrying into the most prominent family in the western part of Norfolk. Her husband, sometime Sheriff of Norfolk and MP from Castle Rising, led the defense of King's Lynn, which was besieged in 1643, capitulating the same year. Both suffered much for their royalist intransigence in a strongly Parliamentarian region, and Alice spent her final years praying for the defeat of the Puritans and the triumph of the royalists and their king. According to historian R. W. Ketton-Cremer, she was an intelligent, outspoken woman who showed great good sense in managing the family's large estate. For four decades she kept an account book, which in

---

4   The last quarter of the book is written in a smaller and neater way by the same hand, leading Lippincott to speculate that Sir Nicholas was making a fair copy at that point, perhaps from a commonplace book or other foul papers (4).

5   For an argument that women were participants in jest culture, not merely transmitters or spectators, see Brown (2003), especially chapter 1.

her later years was filled with "outspoken and indignant comments" about the Roundheads who punished, fined, and harassed them, and who eventually jailed her hot-headed son Roger (Ketton-Cremer, 41, 190, 217–18). She did not live to see the Restoration. Nor did her son Nicholas, who died in 1655, one year before his mother. Roger survived and thrived, and became Licenser and Surveyor of the Press under Charles II – which gave him the standing to warn the king that "not one of forty [libels] ever comes to the Presse, and yet by the helpe of Transcripts, they are well nigh as Publique."[6] If his brother's merry book is any indication of the norms for "harmless" satire transcribed from speech, the censor knew whereof he spoke.

No complete edition of the Le Strange jests was printed until 1974, because of what Lippincott sees as the exaggerated squeamishness of earlier ages and editors. Nicholls, for instance, reprinted about one-third of the jests in 1839, and only a couple of the bawdy ones. Reading through the 93 pages, I begin to understand why. As with some Renaissance recipe books I have read, there are concoctions our age would not want to taste test. Yet it is not only what the jokes say, but who is telling them, that gives pause. How is one to reconcile the familiar icon of the highminded noblewoman ensconced in her stately pile, working Biblical motifs in her embroidery, with the jest Lady Alice relates to her scribbling son?

> An arrant queane in Norwich (that they used to call cold-rost) came once to Sir Philip Woodhouse (who lov'd to heare newes) and told him that she had the heaviest newes to relate that ever he heard: I prythe whats that, says he; O Sir, poore Worsly the Jaylor had such an Hole eaten in his Arse last night with Ratts, that I warrant your worship may turne your Nose in't. (LS item 8)

Shades of Doctor Schreber, the Rat Man! According to Freud's famous theory, the dirty joke was born when a man wanted to sexually excite a female with his story but couldn't because he'd disgust her; so he told another man, with her just out of earshot in the next room. *Jokes and their Relation to the Unconscious* (one of the unfunniest jestbooks ever written) came three centuries after Sir Nicholas, fortunately. *Merry Passages and Jeasts* suggests that respectable women were neither in the next room out of earshot, nor sequestered in private rooms of their own. Le Strange's mother, aunts, and female cousins seem to have enjoyed telling and hearing bawdy – sometimes extremely bawdy – tales, and did not mind having him write their words down. Perhaps they even made some of the corrections that appear in other hands, as in jest 16, credited to "My Mother."[7] The women obliquely sketched by their favorite tales are part

---

6   "Mr. L'Estraing's Proposition Concerning Libells, &c," 11 November 1675. Quoted in Love, 29.
7   See note 3.

of the circle, intrinsic to the fugue of voices and gossip. Eager to occupy the powerful position of laugh-getter, they regularly and memorably claimed what Susan Purdie calls "the mastery of discourse," achieving "discursive potency" through comic means (148). Apparently they held themselves fully capable of the languages of class, of desire, and of satire.

All jest-telling is performance, but many of these jests are encoded with specific directions for delivery. They can be read straight off the page, but to be understood they must be embodied. Take this jest from "My Mother": a tale about "a Northern Lasse" and a gentleman wayfarer. When he asks her for directions along the road, she tells the traveler to "raide me up this way, and raide me doon that way, then raide me to the middle hand" (LS item 9). Now obviously if the teller is to get any sort of reaction out of a listener, she must use both accent and gesture to put this over. While the exact movements aren't indicated, nor the exact connotation of "riding" a woman "to the middle hand," the tale cries out for vigorous gesture and expression. This is a bawdy story, but there is no way of communicating this fully without kinetic mimesis, otherwise known as delivery.

The Northern Lasse is rendered laughable by the teller's quick enactment of stereotypes of class and ethnicity, and indeed this type of jest seemed to appeal to "Ma Mere." Alice L'Estrange often puts on, and puts down, the rude voices of the humbler sort. Half of her 43 stories use the epithet "simple" or "rustic" to cue the socially superior listener that a hick joke is on the way. Setting the generic frame quickly is key to comic performance, a tactic "Ma Mere" deploys constantly. Such top-down jesting is a normative operation of distinction, although in the case of the arrant queane Cold-Rost there is more collusion than satire since her quip occupies the crucial position and earns the laugh. Lady L'Estrange is in this case a piggyback performer, putting her own spin on a lowlier woman's witticism, a situation repeated in other jests told by women.

More than half of the jests told by Dame Alice concern women as subjects or internal narrators. Her own mother and grandmother supplied her with several of these stories, which she in turn passes on to her children and friends. Not the freshness of these jests but their durability and association with past generations seem the point, an association that tends to give Alice "jesting rights" in the written-down tale. Though others may tell it, it is most credible coming from her, who got it from the horse's mouth.

Two jests place Dame Alice's old Grandmother Stubbe in encounters with poorer women. Significantly, one of them touches on the tangled relationships among female literacy, sexuality, and status:

A wench came to my Grandmother Stubbe to seeke a service, and she entertaind her, so after she had been with her 2 or 3 dayes, says she, wench I forgott to aske for the certificate or Testimoniall how you carryed your selfe where you were last: O mistresse sayes she, I have one of those above in my Boxe; and up she runns, and for her testimoniall, brings down a very faire and formall warrant, signifying that she had lately had a Bastard, and was to be passed from Constable to Constable, to such a place. (LS item 358)

No comment is offered on the fate of the wench: illiteracy has condemned her to be passed from mouth to mouth, a nameless wench with no testimonial except a cruel joke. Grandmother Stubbe, employer, joke-teller, and demander of references, can read very well, however, and so her jest also memorializes the gendered hierarchy of literacy in place circa 1550, but still culturally legible circa 1650. In fact a high number of the jests involving women (whether as actors or sources) take as their subject the reading and misreading of texts. While many target ignorant women, a surprising number are directed by women against pretentious men. Several are set in church and satirize preachers, a favorite target for women in the printed jestbooks as well (Brown, 12–14). Alice L'Estrange tells of a preacher losing his place while reading aloud from the Bible, getting flustered when "the congregation laughs in their sleeves," and suddenly bursting out: "I am not such an asse but I can find the right place!" (LS item 460). Another jest about reading has a suitor complimenting a lady in "pure Philip Sidney," but to his bad luck

> she was so well verst in the Author, as tacitely she traced him to the bottom of a leaf, where (his Memorie failing) he brake off abruptly; nay I beseech you Sir, (sayd she) proceede, and turne over the leafe, for me thinks the best part is still Behinde, which unexpected discovery, silenc't him for ever after.[8]

Obviously it was not well to seem too rehearsed, but there were clearly basic scripts for different occasions. Harold Love suggests that gentlemen trying their hand at lampoons, for example, may have felt they were expected to use "the language of the brothel" and "to traduce the great," in this echelon of manuscript culture (189). But it seems unlikely that Sir Nicholas was making a similar effort in his lowest rung of bawdy tales. His table of attributions implies he was trying to replicate speech without intensifying it. (I doubt he had the knack for it: his own jokes are among the dullest in the book, far outclassed by the productions of say, his Aunt Catline, or his cousin Dol Gurney.) To a modern mind there would have been reason to tone down, not heat up, the bawdy language of a female relative. Yet Aunt Catline provides the most sexually explicit jest in the book. It's about "a very simple Ideott" who cuckolds himself with an outrageous wager: he makes a bet that another man can't push his "privy member" through his wife's body and out her back. The loser must forfeit a cheese. Unlike Othello, the Ideott is eager to see his wife "grossly topp'd" while he gapes on, for two reasons: his wife is barren and he

---

8   LS item 484, ascribed to "Mr An[tony] Cooke."

wants the other man to impregnate her, and he is curious to see the "Noveltie" of the act – "for though he had a good Bable of his owne, yet he could never see that doe so much" (LS item 114). I'll let Aunt Catline tell the rest:

> the day was appointed, houre and place agreed on, the Foole to be his own judge, the good woman (like an obedient wife, willing to do anything for the good of her Husband, her selfe, and Posteritie) was very pliant and flexible; The yong fellow falls to his embraces, wimbles stoutly, and cries now looke, now it comes. No, says the Foole, that stood behind his wife watching for the penetration – Then now or never, No nor yet, sayes the Foole – Nor now? (for by this time he had had his end, and was well satiated) No No quoth the Foole, why then I have lost my cheese, sayes [the other fellow]: at which the Foole was very Jocunde, but swore he was never in such a feare in his life, and had not his wife been a notable thick-skinnd wench, he had lost, for he saw it heaving and working at the very Skinne of her Backe. (LS item 114)

So much for the "unrepresentability" of ocular proof, about which so much ink has been spilled. Of course Sidney famously argued that "some things can be said that cannot be showed," but I believe that such a jest was both said and "showed" – that is, *enacted*, as indicated by its script-like and dynamic form which requires (not erases) the unsaid. The gestures accompanying this one were probably quite energetic.

In that more sociable world of truckle beds, with servants and children sleeping in the same rooms as master and mistress, the "act of darkness" was far more evident to the senses than in our nervous culture of locked doors. In the world of jests, "privates" make their appearance in word and deed. One example concerns the more practical side of the *Hic Mulier* debate. In a world in which women did not yet wear undergarments, the discussion over women wearing breeches in the 1620s is here more reminiscent of nineteenth-century "bloomer" debates than the *querelle des femmes*. Cousin Dol Gurney gives us the details:

> The Bury Ladyes that usd [to go] Hawking and Hunting, were once in a great vaine of wearing Breeches; and some of them being at dinner one day at Sir Edward Lewkenors, there was one Mr Zephory, a very precise and a silenc't minister, (who frequented that house much) and discourse being offered of fashions, he fell upon this and declaimed much against it; Rob: Heighem a Joviall blade being there, he undertook to vindicate the Ladyes, and their fashion, as decent and such as might cover their shame: for says he, if an Horse throwes them, or by any mischance they gett a fall, had you not better see them in their Breeches then Naked? [S]ayes the over-zealous man, in detestation of Breeches, O no, by no meanes[!] By my troth Parson, sayes Rob: Heighem, and I commend thee for't, for I am of thy mind too. (LS item 54)

There is also a pair of stories about a "notable bold woman" who spies on a friend at a dinner party as he slyly attempts to urinate in his own boot because he does not want to get up from a crowded table. She grabs his hand and causes him to expose himself to the party and to urinate all over the table, to her "inexpressible delight."[9] As improbable as that scenario sounds to us, such jests function as clues to defunct social practices and bodily regimens. Most early comic tales are rooted in common life, not fantasy or romance, and that is part of what makes them valuable as historical evidence. People actually did put off rising from table to seek out the cold dark jakes, and there is one scurrilous jest in the Le Strange manuscript about King James beshitting himself while hunting, refusing to dismount long enough to relieve himself, causing his royal excrement to leak from his clothes. One among the hunting party convulses the others by scoffing, "My Lerds, see our Salaman, is this the Salaman ye talke on? If ever old Salaman in all his Reyaltie was [arrayed] like ours, Ile be hangd."[10] Keith Thomas sees such scatology as creating a potentially radical laughter at what he calls "'the great primal joke' of the lower body: the constant threat to dignity and formality levied by the rebellious pressure of bodily needs" – thereby demonstrating that an absolute ruler cannot bring all his parts under absolute control (79). Cumulatively all this ridicule can have a corrosive effect on the dignity of kings and nations, as well as dinner guests, and few regimes have toppled without the precedent of covert and overt popular satire to prepare the ground.[11] Many jests describe the shaming laughter of an audience within the narrative, thus mirroring the desired reaction of listeners. Women are full members of these tribunals of wit (or "covens of libel," depending on one's political point of view). No segregation of sexes in this consort of tongues is ever indicated.

I'd like to conclude with the proposition that this process of telling-for-retelling constituted a transferral of "publication rights" to the intended audiences of the jest. It is they, after all, who will (if they choose) spread the news of the humiliation, morphing from spectators to tellers. The meanings of "publication" in the seventeenth century included the speaking of a topic or libel in such a way as to make it public knowledge. The idea that stage performance constitutes a form of publication has been widely accepted in reference to Shakespeare's plays. And, as Marotti and Love have shown, poems by Donne and others which circulated primarily in manuscript became

---

9 LS item 125, ascribed to "My Couzen John Spilman." The leaky guest gets a measure of revenge by giving her a bawdy nickname.
10 LS item 316, ascribed to "Doctor Gamons."
11 See Thomas and Thompson for cogent arguments that popular literary sources, such as the much-reprinted *Banquet of Jests*, can be used to form judgments about the level and kinds of political/religious conflict, not just tension and consent, in the years leading to the Civil War. I am grateful to Tony Thompson for letting me read his paper before publication.

the joint creation of a coterie readership, with authorial intention tangential or superseded by collaborative revision, and the promptings of occasion, politics, and social performance; indeed, some poets' works were published scribally without ever reaching print. In all these cases, textual performance means first of all making a public, calling an audience into being that will collectively create and possess its meaning in the moment and publish its reputation in the future. In the Le Strange jestbook, scores of people listed as sources are also characters in other jests, both as laugh-getter and as butts, so the transformation of listener to teller and author is multiplied many times over. Like a hand-written recipe book, or a marked-up promptbook, his jest-journal gestures toward a world of making, audibility, sociality, materiality, and speech. The hand-written word seems to bear an insistent trace of orality greater than that of print; but Le Strange's unusual manuscript parallels and invokes the printed jest anthology as well. The wit of its transcribed jests depends on a quality of "imprintedness": an exact wording worth transcribing, repeating, and even correcting. Their memorableness inheres in their promise of momentary social triumph. In this these jests are similar to manuscript poetry – meant to circulate, to be spoken, and to be spoken back to, always endlessly revised in the telling.

While studying *Merry Passages and Jeasts* my mind has been filled with voices wished into being through print. I hear Clifford Geertz urging me to get a thicker description of the gentry and their pastimes, and Hélène Cixous's intense challenge, directed to all women, to "break up the 'truth' with laughter" and to "kill the false woman who is preventing the live one from breathing" (258, 250). Norbert Elias breaks in, insisting I trace the banishment of dirty jokes from mixed-gender company after the Restoration, a voice interrupted in turn by Jürgen Habermas arguing that in the all-male coffee-house the so-called "public sphere" had its true birth. As I puzzle over this, I am distracted by the concise directive of Roger Chartier, persuading me that reading silently was the exception, not the norm, in the period, and that most printed texts were meant for shared reading out loud, not for solitary silent perusal. Chartier makes me wonder once again when and why the word "read" finally lost its performative thrust, its status as an imperative – as an invocation to speak to others – and what factors worked to make silence and detachment the preconditions of both politeness and art.

Of course most scholars are avatars of silence. Silence is something I hear encroaching on my own world, from the hushed stacks, from voiceless email, from the grey screen of my laptop, from the isolated hours of scholarship. These, too, are conditions of submission. Is it any wonder that article after article about women in the period, by women of our period, dwells on lack of voice, lack of sound, lack of power? "Silencing" has been our master trope. It is time to retire it and find another. For one thing, it's boring – a kind of boredom few early modern women would have endured.

Works Cited

Brown, Pamela Allen. *Better a Shrew than a Sheep: Women, Drama, and the Culture of Jest in Early Modern England.* Ithaca and London: Cornell University Press, 2003.

Chartier, Roger. "Leisure and Sociability: Reading Aloud in Early Modern Europe." *Urban Life in the Rennaissance.* Ed. Susan Zimmerman and F. E. Weisman. Newark: University of Delaware Press, 1989, 103–120.

Cixous, Hélène. "The Laugh of the Medusa." In *New French Feminisms.* Ed. Elaine Marks and Isabelle de Courtivron. New York: Schocken Books, 1981.

Elias, Norbert. *The Civilizing Process.* Trans. E. Jephcott. Oxford: Blackwell, 1994.

Freud, Sigmund. *Jokes and their Relation to the Unconscious.* Trans. and ed. James Strachey. New York and London: Norton, 1960.

Geertz, Clifford. *The Interpretation of Cultures.* New York: Basic Books, 1973.

Habermas, Jürgen. *The Structural Transformation of the Public Sphere: An Inquiry into the Category of Bourgeois Society.* Cambridge, MA: MIT Press, 1987.

Ketton-Cremer, Robert W. *Norfolk in the Civil War: A Portrait of a Society in Conflict.* Hamden, CT: Archon Books, 1970.

Le Strange, Sir Nicholas. *Merry Passages and Jeasts – A Manuscript Jestbook of Sir Nicholas Le Strange (1603–1655).* Ed. H. F. Lippincott. Elizabethan & Renaissance Studies 29. Salzburg: Institut für Englische Sprache und Literatur, 1974.

[———.] *Merry Passages and Jeasts.* British Library, Harleian MS 6395.

Love, Harold. *The Culture and Commerce of Texts: Scribal Publication in Seventeenth Century England.* Amherst: University of Massachusetts Press, 1993.

Marotti, Arthur. *Manuscript, Print, and the English Renaissance Lyric.* Ithaca: Cornell University Press, 1995.

Nicholls, J. G. "Notices of Sir Nicholas Lestrange, Bart., and His Family Connexions." *Anecdotes and Traditions.* Ed. William Thoms. London: Camden Society, 1839.

Purdie, Susan. *Comedy: The Mastery of Discourse.* Toronto: University of Toronto Press, 1993.

Smith, Bruce R. *The Acoustic World of Early Modern England: Attending to the O-Factor.* Chicago: University of Chicago Press, 1999.

Thomas, Keith. "The Place of Laughter in Tudor Stuart England." *Times Literary Supplement*, 21 January 1977, 77–81.

Thompson, Anthony B. "Jokes and Jests in the Popular Politics of Charles I." Unpublished paper.

Willetts, Pamela. "Sir Nicholas Le Strange and John Jenkins." *Music and Letters* 42 (1961): 30–43.

Afterword

Phyllis Rackin

We've all seen backyard clubhouses adorned with signs proclaiming "no girls allowed." At least in cartoons. I, for one, have never seen an actual clubhouse with such a sign, although I'm sure they must exist, if only in imitation of the cartoons. Popular beliefs about the place – or, rather, the lack of a place – for women in Shakespeare's playhouse remind me of those cartoons. Again and again, we have been assured that the business of playing at the time Shakespeare wrote was an all-male enterprise.

In the popular film *Shakespeare in Love*, as in current popular belief, women are prohibited by law from performing on Shakespeare's stage. Scholars know that this belief is erroneous, but they still assume that the exclusion of women from the London professional stage was based on a longstanding tradition of all-male performance. As the essays collected in this book make clear, however, the all-male companies can better be described as a novelty. These essays remind us that European professional companies included women, and that women regularly performed in a variety of English theatrical venues, ranging from aristocratic masques to local festivals. James Stokes, in fact, has suggested that the all-male companies that performed in London between 1570 and the late 1630s constituted "a cultural aberration." "The 'sudden' appearance of women on the stage in 1660," he argues, "was a recovery as well as an innovation."[1]

Looking "beyond the all-male stage," *Women Players in England, 1500–1660* brings forth an impressive body of evidence that supports Stokes's contention. His own contribution to the collection, along with those of Alison Findlay, Stephanie Hodgson-Wright, and Gweno Williams, documents the widespread participation of English women in the production and performance of guild plays and other local entertainments. Other contributors demonstrate the

---

1   Stokes made this suggestion in an email interview with Pamela Brown, conducted in connection with the seminar, "Women Players in and around Shakespeare" at the 2000 annual meeting of the Shakespeare Association of America, organized by Pamela Brown and Peter Parolin. See also Stokes's earlier essay, "Women and Mimesis in Medieval and Renaissance Somerset (and Beyond)," as well as his essay in this volume.

profound influence that European traditions of professional female performance exerted in England both in aristocratic court circles and also on the public stage. Still others usefully broaden the category of "performance" to include the many English women who could have been seen performing in an abundance of diverse venues, indoors and out, for audiences at every level of the social hierarchy, ranging from the mountebanks staging unauthorized performances to advertise their cures to the Countess of Arundel staging her own defense before the Venetian Senate. The "tradition" of an "all-male stage" that has become so familiar to modern scholars must have looked to the first audiences at the London commercial theaters like an anomalous innovation.

Even during the years when the London-based professional companies excluded women from performing, women were deeply involved in the companies' off-stage activities. As Natasha Korda has demonstrated, if we consider the extensive range of commercial activities that were associated with early modern theatrical production, we will realize that many women took part. They lent money to actors, they owned shares in companies, they provided costumes for performances, and they stood in the entrances to theaters to collect admission fees from playgoers.

The reason the English professional companies excluded women from the stage has never been satisfactorily explained, but Stokes has suggested that it was produced in part by a "poisonous mixture of reform, evangelical extremism, and other factors, both practical and economic."[2] The impact of religious affiliation on women's participation in dramatic performance is persuasively documented in the second essay in this section, where Findlay, Hodgson-Wright, and Williams examine local differences in women's opportunities to perform. But, as Stokes points out, a number of factors would have been involved. Among them may have been a desire among the London professional players to improve their status. The business of playing was new in late sixteenth-century London, and often denounced by moralists. The players may have excluded women from their companies in an effort to insulate themselves from the taints of effeminacy and immorality that were associated with theatrical impersonation. They may also have been motivated by a desire to distinguish their enterprise from less reputable forms of performance, such as the mountebanks described by Bella Mirabella. The exclusion of women made the new professional companies look more like the male students who performed Latin plays at Oxford and Cambridge, and less like the amateurs who performed in local festivals or the disreputable traveling performers, both of which included women as well as men. Restricting their

2   Interview with Pamela Brown, cited in n.1.

companies to male actors also provided a mark of distinction from the European professional companies that did include women.[3]

Although London performances by French and Italian women were vigorously condemned by English moralists, the foreign actresses – the focus of the section entitled "Beyond England" – were clearly popular. As several of the essays in that section demonstrate, the Italian commedia dell'arte, with its celebrated actresses, had a clearly visible influence upon the work of Shakespeare and his fellow dramatists. Confronted with the professional success of the foreign actresses, the English players not only showed their own superiority by excluding women from their companies; they also emulated the most striking attractions of the foreign players, not the least of which were the prominent roles they assigned to women. Witty, independent heroines such as Rosalind and Portia who scripted roles for their own performance recall the actresses of the commedia dell'arte, who displayed their proficiency at on-stage improvisation when they worked from scenarios.[4] In addition to appropriating character types, plot devices, and stage business that had prototypes in the repertory of the commedia dell'arte, the English players also constructed female roles to produce what Rachel Poulsen calls an "actress effect." As Jean Howard points out, the representations of female characters, even when the actors who portrayed them were male, could "iterate fantasies of femininity that ... belie[d] the artifice of their construction" (n.2).

The essays in this collection provide us with evidence that was previously unknown or neglected of the widespread participation of women in the production of every possible kind of show; and in so doing they encourage us to rethink all the assumptions that have previously obscured women's roles in the rich and varied culture of performance that constituted the milieu in which the first English professional theaters were established. For instance, although we know that medieval and Renaissance Englishwomen wrote the scripts for many plays, ranging from liturgical drama to aristocratic and royal entertainments, it is generally assumed that women did not write playscripts for the London professional stage. A large proportion of those scripts, however, have come down to us as anonymous, and it may very well be that some of those plays were actually written in whole or in part by women (commercial playscripts were often the products of multiple authors). Because female authorship is unlikely to have recommended a play, it is entirely

---

3   Cf. Thomas Nashe's 1592 defense of playgoing in *Pierce Penilesse his Supplication to the Divell* (1592), in Chambers, 4: 239: "Our Players," he boasted, "are not as the players beyond the Sea, a sort of squirting baudie Comedians, that have whores and common Curtizens to playe womens partes."
4   See Barasch, Clubb, Brown, the Introduction to this volume, and the essays by Julie D. Campbell and Rachel Poulsen.

possible that some of the many anonymous plays written during the period were written by women, and also possible that some plays sold to the players as the work of the men whose names are now associated with them may actually have been written by women or been the products of collaboration with woman writers. The names of these women and the evidence for their authorship may never be recovered, but a good first step would be to question the traditional assumption that women were never involved in the writing of scripts for the English public theater.

Even without that evidence, and even if women had no part in writing scripts for the English commercial playhouses, the form those playscripts took was inevitably influenced by the widespread culture of female performance and female involvement in theatrical production described in this collection. Moreover, since the players derived the bulk of their income from public performances, their productions were necessarily influenced by the fact that women constituted a sizeable portion of the paying customers in the public playhouses. Players were well aware that they needed to address the interests of female playgoers. The playhouses in Shakespeare's London were not private clubs but public, commercial spaces. The value of a private club derives from its exclusivity – the more people a club keeps out, the more desirable it is to be let in. A commercial enterprise is just the opposite. Its value depends on the number of customers it can attract. With women constituting so many of their potential customers, the players had every reason to cater to women's tastes. Women may not have acted in the earliest public, commercial performances of the plays of Shakespeare and his contemporaries, but they certainly acted *on* them, in a multitude of ways that are only beginning to be discovered.

Works Cited and Consulted

Archer, Ian W. "Shakespeare's London." *A Companion to Shakespeare*. Ed. David Scott Kastan. Oxford: Blackwell, 1999.

Barasch, Frances. "Italian Actresses in Shakespeare's World: Flaminia and Vincenza," *Shakespeare Bulletin* 18.4 (2000): 17–21.

———. "Italian Actresses in Shakespeare's World: Vittoria and Isabella." *Shakespeare Bulletin* 19.3 (2001): 5–9.

Barroll, Leeds. "Inventing the Stuart Masque." *The Politics of the Stuart Court Masque*. Ed. David Bevington and Peter Holbrook. Cambridge: Cambridge University Press, 1998, 121–43.

Bentley, Gerald Eades. *The Profession of Player in Shakespeare's Time 1590–1642*. Princeton: Princeton University Press, 1984.

Brown, Pamela. "The Counterfeit *Innamorata*, or, The Diva Vanishes." *Shakespeare Yearbook* 10 (1999): 402–26.

Cerasano, S. P. and Marion Wynne-Davies. Eds. *Renaissance Drama by Women: Texts and Documents*. London and New York: Routledge, 1996.

————. *Readings in Renaissance Women's Drama: Criticism, History, and Performance 1594–1998*. London and New York: Routledge, 1998.

Chambers, E. K. *The Elizabethan Stage*. Oxford: Clarendon, 1923; rpt. 1951.

Clubb, Louise George. *Italian Drama in Shakespeare's Time*. New Haven: Yale University Press, 1989.

Gowing, Laura. *Domestic Dangers: Women, Words, and Sex in Early Modern London*. Oxford: Clarendon, 1996.

Harbage, Alfred. *Shakespeare's Audience*. New York: Columbia University Press, 1941.

Henderson, Diana E. "The Theater and Domestic Culture." *A New History of Early English Drama*. Ed. John D. Cox and David Scott Kastan. New York: Columbia University Press, 1997, 173–94.

Korda, Natasha. "Household Property/Stage Property: Henslowe as Pawnbroker." *Theatre Journal* 48.2 (1996): 185–95.

Masten, Jeffrey. "Playwriting: Authorship and Collaboration." *A New History of Early English Drama*. Ed. John D. Cox and David Scott Kastan. New York: Columbia University Press, 1997, 357–82.

Orgel, Stephen. *Impersonations: The Performance of Gender in Shakespeare's England*. Cambridge: Cambridge University Press, 1996.

Stallybrass, Peter. "Worn Worlds: Clothes and Identity on the Renaissance Stage." *Subject and Object in Renaissance Culture*. Ed. Margreta de Grazia, Maureen Quilligan, and Peter Stallybrass. Cambridge: Cambridge University Press, 1996.

Stokes, James. "Women and Mimesis in Medieval and Renaissance Somerset (and Beyond)." *Comparative Drama* 7 (Summer 1993): 176–96.

Thaler, Alwin. "Minor Actors and Employees in the Elizabethan Theater." *Modern Philology* 20.1 (August 1922).

Woolf, Virginia. *A Room of One's Own*. New York and London: Harcourt Brace Jovanovich, 1957.

Index

Garavini, Margherita 133
Garnier, Robert 197
  Bradamante 194, 195, 196, 196n.7, 197,
    198, 199, 200, 201, 202, 204, 205,
    206, 207
Garzoni, Tommasso 226
Gascoigne, George
  Supposes 175n.5
Geertz, Clifford 313
Gentilcore, David 96 n.5, 98, 100, 103,
  103 n.10
Gilder, Rosamond 198, 198n.9, 199,
  200n.12, 202n.14, 205
Gim, Lisa 278
Gloucestershire 5, 10, 46, 59–64, 65
Goldberg, Jeremy 50
Gondi, Giovanni Battista 202
Gonzaga, Curzio
  Gl'Inganni 180
Gonzaga, Francesco 129
Gossett, Suzanne 193n.1
Gosson, Stephen 14
Gowing, Laura 8, 230n.20
Green, Mary Anne Everett 199
Greenfield, Peter 64
Guarini, Giambattista
  L'idropica 129
Guild Entertainments 10, 26–34, 41, 47–
  50, 315
Günsberg, Maggie 185
Gurr, Andrew 266

Habermas, Jürgen 313
Hanawalt, Barbara 30
  *The Harangues or Speeches of Several
    Famous Mountebanks in Town and
    Country* 94, 94 n.4
Harbage, Alfred 14, 211
Heck, Thomas 110
Henke, Robert 96, 96n.5, 97, 100, 173n.1,
  197n.8, 201
Henri III 126, 148, 151, 159, 160, 162n.24,
  163, 166, 197, 198
Henri IV 198, 200
Henrietta Maria, Queen 2n.5, 3, 4n.10, 8,
  9n.17, 12, 14, 15, 57, 193, 193n.1, 194,
  195, 199, 202–12, 242n.1, 243, 265n.4

Henry VIII 28, 40, 282, 284
Henslowe, Philip 75, 75n.5, 76, 80, 81
Heywood, John 282
Heywood, Thomas 265, 265n.3, 267,
  269n.8, 271, 271n.12, 272, 276, 277
  *If You Know Not Me, You Know
    Nobody, Part I* 16, 265, 266, 270,
    272, 273
  *If You Know Not Me, You Know
    Nobody, Part II* 265, 270n.10
  Wise Woman of Hogsdon 6
Hibbard, Caroline 203–4n.18, 206, 208
Hic Mulier 6, 84, 85, 311
Hinds, Hilary 57
Hoby, Thomas 156n.17
Hocktide Games 4n.7, 35
Holbrook, Peter 223, 225
Holderness B.A. 73–4
Howard, Jean 9, 16–17, 187, 317
Howard, Thomas, Earl of Arundel 221,
  222, 222n.9, 223, 225n.14, 226,
  226n.15, 226n.16, 228, 230, 233, 236,
  237
Howarth, David 221
Howson, Gerald 79n.9
Humphrey, Chris 48, 54
Hunt, Maurice 154n.14
Hutson, Lorna 186–7
Hyde, Edward, Earl of Clarendon
  249n.10, 256

Ingannati 14, 172, 173, 179–87
Ingram, William 74
Intronati 172, 174, 179, 181, 182
Ireland 5
Italy 5, 13, 14, 90, 91, 96, 98, 100, 109,
  110, 126, 127, 128, 129, 130, 132, 141,
  145, 146, 147n.7, 147n.8, 148, 149,
  151, 154, 155, 156, 157n.19, 158, 159,
  160, 161, 162, 167, 171, 173, 174,
  177n.12, 179, 180, 181, 182, 183,
  184, 185, 186, 188, 193, 194, 197, 198,
  199, 200, 204, 210, 210n.23, 212,
  212n.26, 220, 221, 222, 226, 227, 234,
  235, 317

Jackson, William 211, 211n.25